John Downing
Ali Mohammadi
Annabelle Sreberny-Mohammadi

QUESTIONING THE MEDIA

A Critical Introduction

SAGE PUBLICATIONS
The International Professional Publishers
Newbury Park London New Delhi

58177

For information address:

SAGE Publications, Inc.
2455 Teller Road
Newbury Park, California 91320

SAGE Publications Ltd.
6 Bonhill Street
London EC2A 4PU
United Kingdom

SAGE Publications India Pvt. Ltd.
M-32 Market
Greater Kailash I
New Delhi 110 048 India

Printed in the United States of America

Library of Congress Cataloging-in-Publication Data

Questioning the media : a critical introduction /
edited by John Downing, Ali Mohammadi, Annabelle Sreberny-Mohammadi.
p. cm.
Includes bibliographical references.
ISBN 0-8039-3642-7. — ISBN 0-8039-3643-5 (pbk.)
1. Mass media. I. Downing, John. II. Mohammadi, Ali.
III. Sreberney-Mohammadi, Annabelle.
P91.25.M35 1990 90-32539
302.23--dc20 CIP

EIGHTH PRINTING, 1993

Sage Production Editor: Astrid Virding

Contents

Chronology of Communications Media

This chronology lists the dates of major technological breakthroughs in communications, first media applications, and establishment of major media institutions. Such a list seems to reproduce the "great men" syndrome; for a critique of this, see Chapter 3. Toward the end, the focus is very much on the United States. (Sources for compiling this list include Wilbur Schramm's *The Story of Human Communication* and Frederick Williams's *The Communications Revolution.*)

35000	B.C.	Cro-Magnon period; speculation that language existed
22000		prehistoric cave paintings
4000		Sumerian writing on clay tablets
3000		early Egyptian hieroglyphics
1800		Phoenician alphabet
323		Library of Alexandria built in Egypt
350	A.D.	books replace scrolls
600		book printing in China
676		paper and ink used by Arabs and Persians
1200		paper and ink art in Europe
1453		Gutenberg Bible printed
1535		first press in the Americas set up in Mexico
1555		Della Porta projects light
1639		first printing press in British colonies
1640		*The Whole Book of Psalmes* is first book printed in British colonies
1665		newspapers first published in England
1690		*Publick Occurrences Both Forreign and Domestick* is first American newspaper
1719		Samuel and John Adams publish *Boston Gazette*
1741		*American Magazine* and Ben Franklin's *General Magazine* start
1776		Tom Paine publishes revolutionary pamphlet *Common Sense*
1783		*Pennsylvania Evening Post* is America's first daily newspaper
1790		first federal copyright statute passed by Congress
1791		First Amendment to the Constitution
1817		Harper Brothers establish publishing company

1828	*Freedom's Journal* is first Black newspaper in the United States
1833	*New York Sun* ushers in the penny press
1835	Samuel Morse develops the telegraph
1837	Niepce and Daguerre create the daguerreotype
1848	first news agency/wire service, Associated Press, formed
1851	*New York Times* established
1865	*The Nation* magazine founded
1866	first transatlantic cable completed
1876	Alexander Graham Bell completes telephone
1888	Eastman produces Kodak camera
1892	Edison develops kinetoscope
1895	Guglielmo Marconi develops radio telegraphy
1895	Lumiere brothers develop motion picture camera
1910	first alternative movie produced (*The Pullman Porter,* by African-American William Foster)
1912	*Pravda* begins; restarted 1917
1923	Zworykin demonstrates iconoscope, patents television camera tube
1927	British Broadcasting Corporation founded—model of public service broadcasting authority
1929	Zworykin invents kinescope
1929	Motion Picture Authority formed; Hays Office founded to vet movie content
1931	Workers Film and Photo League established
1933	FM radio demonstrated for RCA executives
1939	paperback books start publishing revolution
1941	FCC authorizes commercial television; WNBT first on the air
1942	first electronic computer in the United States
1943	wire recorders used in World War II by Nazi military
1943	duopoly ruling forces NBC to sell a network; start of ABC
1947	transistor invented; Bell Laboratories established
1947	Hollywood Ten jailed for defying communist witch-hunt
1948	*TV Guide* founded
1949	Pacifica Radio begins broadcasting
1950	CATV developed; cable TV begins, to boost microwave signal
1954	McCarthy hearings on television
1954	first color television sets; color broadcasting begins
1956	Ampex demonstrates videotape recording
1957	Soviets launch first earth satellite, *Sputnik*
1960	Nixon-Kennedy debates televised
1962	*Telstar* television satellite launched by United States
1965	International Telecommunications Satellite Organization (INTELSAT) begins to relay transatlantic communications
1967	Public Broadcasting Act passed by Congress
1968	portable video recorders introduced
1968	MPAA ratings replace Hays Office

1970	Public Broadcasting Service (PBS) established
1975	HBO starts satellite-based pay network
1975	*Wall Street Journal* publishes via satellite
1977	AT&T tests fiber-optic transmission
1977	Qube interactive cable television starts in Ohio
1980	home computer available for less than $500
1981	videodisc systems marketed
1982	cable television grows at varying speeds; 13% of British households have it
1983	FCC allows broadcasters to offer teletext
1985	cellular mobile telephones marketed
1985	PeaceNet established; first alternative national computer network in United States
1986	Deep Dish TV Satellite Network established; first alternative satellite network
1989	first private satellite launched in United States
1989	camcorders used in popular movements in Poland and Hungary
1989	fax used in the Chinese student revolt to communicate internationally
1990s	high-definition television (HDTV)

Acknowledgments

We would like to thank all those who have made this book possible. First and foremost, we thank the authors, who have patiently gone through a series of revisions, aiming for the highest degree of lucidity. Second, we are grateful to Bob White, who early on saw the importance of this project and provided sympathetic critical input at intervals throughout. Third are Ann West, Marie-Louise Penchoen, Astrid Virding, and Judy Selhorst at Sage, who steered it through to publication. Fourth are the students in Mark Schulman's introductory course, "Principles and Practices of Communication," summer 1989, who agreed to use large sections of this book in typescript and to evaluate its usefulness as an introductory text. Their positive responses provided us with a great deal of encouragement through the final stages of preparing a book. Fifth, we thank Liora Schor-Kalish, who tirelessly and perceptively hunted down visual images to complement the written text. Finally, we are grateful to a host of other people, but especially to Andrew Blaner and Kai Chiu of the Academic Computing Center at Hunter College, Al Perez of the Academic Computing Center at Queens College, and Carol Sapienza of the CAS Department, Queens College, who have contributed in different ways toward helping this book into life.

We dedicate this volume to our children and our students.

John Downing
Ali Mohammadi
Annabelle Sreberny-Mohammadi

Preface: A Letter from the Editors to the Beginning Student

This preface provides a way for us to explain the thinking behind this book, the issues and perspectives that are introduced, and why we think a *critical* approach is vital for the study of *communication.*

It thus orients you as to what to expect, how to read and think about the material, the central issues in certain critical approaches, and how you might integrate a critical orientation into your own work and life.

This book presents some new ways of looking at the media, and provides some new tools to help you understand your media environment. So, before you start reading, we want to draw your attention to an especially useful part of this book to which you may often want to refer: the Glossary. All the terms introduced in italics in this preface, and many other, sometimes new, sometimes difficult, terms used throughout the chapters, can be found in the Glossary that appears at the end of this book. There you will find a definition—often many definitions—for each term, and frequently an indication of the chapters in which you can find a lengthier discussion and illustrative examples.

Why Media Studies?

Communications media are everywhere. Video screens, car radios, Walkman-type personal cassette players and televisions, audio and video recorders, compact discs, photographs, newspapers, magazines, newsletters—all play a major part in the way people live in industrially advanced countries. Their role in so many people's lives is why they are often called *mass media.* Behind the media we see and hear are *satellites* hundreds of miles above the earth's surface, ocean *cables* deep beneath the waters of the planet, computers both simple and sophisticated, and increasingly complex telephone systems.

© Jill Posener, The Women's Press, London

In addition to visual images and the human voice, huge volumes of data can now flow immense distances in the twinkling of an eye, such as electronic transfers of funds between banks or scientific and military information gathered from observation satellites. We could describe these media collectively as the world's nervous system.

These media make increasing demands on our time, help to define our patterns of leisure, and play a role in our social lives. These media present us with often overwhelming amounts of information and images, about ourselves and other people. They serve to define what is of political concern, of economic importance, of cultural interest to us. In short, we live in what is often described as a "media culture."

A media culture is the product of an industrialized society, where much of the culture is mass produced in a way quite similar to boots and shoes. While footwear is produced in factories, with supplies such as leather, glue, and eyelets, media culture is produced by large organizations that depend on trained personnel with journalistic skills, technical know-how, and career commitment. With fashion footwear, there are, of course, many different manufacturers and many different styles, and by the time we are adults we have developed tastes, know what suits us and what is appropriate to wear, and are able to discriminate among the great variety of footwear available.

It is much harder to learn to discriminate about media and their contents, although that is clearly a far more important process than deciding about what color shoes to buy. The purpose of this book is to encourage you to ask some basic questions about the media, to criticize their content, and to become more discriminating and critical viewers, listeners, and readers. Of course, people make many kinds of critical comments about the media—for example, that there are too many reruns, or that the formats are repetitive, merely repackaging old themes. People are concerned that programs with "adult" content are scheduled too early in the evening; parents worry about the effects of "antisocial values" and violence on their children. Many are concerned about whether the media reflect and help foster a tolerant multiracial, multiethnic society, while others worry about the lack of real debate about politics and social issues.

And each of these problems raises a host of further questions about how media are organized and controlled, how they maintain and change our culture, how they alter our way of life in numerous ways. Take the images of women in advertising, for example, a topic of considerable concern to many. Women in advertising have been depicted mainly in domestic situations, the "traditional" role of women in American society, or represented sexually, as tools to sell products. The first depiction tends to ignore the millions of women in the workplace at many levels of responsibility and decision making. The second reduces women to objects, sometimes just to legs or torsos to be consumed in the same way that the beer or the clothing or the car is to be consumed. We could ask, What do such images do to the self-esteem of women? How do girls, continually surrounded by such images, think of themselves and their future place in society? What does it mean to have working women represented in programming yet omitted from advertising? What effects do such omnipresent images have on men and how they think of women?

We could further examine the kinds of images of women and the definitions of beauty, slenderness, age, and ethnicity that are shown; the limited range of images suggests a culture that values women only if they conform to a limited range of types and roles, hardly the "open society" that our culture prides itself on being. It is little wonder that women get angry, but what can they do? There are far fewer women than men working as advertising executives, few "alternative" images; no wonder women deface sexist advertising (for example, see the photograph at the opening of this preface). But the increasing use of men in advertising is no great triumph, subjecting male models to indignities similar to those that women have long endured. We also need to step further back to examine the purpose and function of advertising as a whole in our society, and again to ask critical questions about the consumer society we so often take for granted (see Chapter 17, by Douglas Kellner).

Asking questions is perhaps the first step toward developing a critical stance toward the media, and toward society as a whole. It is legitimate to ask whether the media, and our society, are as good as they could be. A critical stance is really nothing new in the United States; a critical tradition is at the root of American life.

A Critical Tradition in the United States

Rebelling against the English autocracy in 1776, the citizens of what was to become the United States were already prepared 200 years ago to defy authority and change a whole system of government. A certain diversity of opinions was tolerated, largely because of the different waves of settlement up to 1776—first Puritans, then refugees from England's civil war, then Quakers, then poor farmers from Scotland and Ireland, not to mention the Dutch. The federal structure of government, inspired in part by the Iroquois Confederacy of six Indian nations, also enshrined the importance of debate, criticism, and openness to new perspectives. Open and participatory communication, therefore, were absolutely necessary if this new society was to survive.

Yet, at the same time, from the very beginning there were limitations, not so readily noticed then, when the struggle against the English took center stage. There were the obvious early limitations to the notion of "the people" in whose name the Constitution was written. The people did not include the Native Americans who occupied the territory before the English settlers. The people did not include Africans, imported as commodities into America to labor on the plantations. Nor did the people really include women; there were no women among the Founding Fathers. Thus, from the start, exclusion and struggles to rectify it have been part of the fabric of American political life, with the numerous amendments to the Constitution reflecting changing circumstances and changing awareness of needs and rights.

Similarly, with public communication, the media, there were powerful ideals established early on—most obviously in the First Amendment—that became embattled ideals as time wore on. The comparative ease of printing a leaflet or pamphlet in the revolutionary period or of maintaining a workers' newspaper was already disappearing by the 1840s. The clamor of numerous voices gave way to the market-oriented newspapers of those select entrepreneurs who could afford to buy the expensive new presses and run a newspaper. While there were brief periods of locally based experimentation with radio and television, both media were very quickly organized into big national networks, and again the potential clamor of many voices was muted.

Censorship and news distortions have also operated, for example, in the limits on the reporting of the various wars the United States has been involved in, from 1812 to the Central American conflicts of the 1980s, even though American lives were at stake and the public had an urgent need for honest reporting. Thus, from the beginning, the noble ideals of the "right to know" and the right to free expression have been embattled ones, pressured by big business and big government, and thus have always been in need of defense. Communication for the people and by the people gave way to media dominated increasingly by the drives for profit and power.

Nonetheless, being critical continues to be a fundamental part of American culture, a healthy feature of American history. It is this tradition that we want to encourage you to call upon and maintain as your own in regard to the media.

Critical Approaches to the Media

Being critical clearly involves posing questions. It means not merely taking information for granted, at face value, but asking how and why the media came to be, why they have the shape and organization that they do, how they work and for whose benefit. Thus thinking about something in a careful, reflective way is the start of a critical orientation. But in regard to the media there are already some well-developed critical frameworks that have names and histories.

Let's take television as an instance. Harold Lasswell, a political scientist and one of the "founding fathers" of the discipline of communications, constructed a basic formula of the process of mediated communication that is quoted in many textbooks: "Who says what to whom through which channel and to what effect?" Clearly this asks some basic questions, and it can be a useful starting point. But in this formulation—a rather typical approach in communications—the communications media are examined in isolation. Other spheres of society, such as the economic, the political, and the cultural, do not get included. Communications is defined as a segregated act, rather than as part and parcel of all social action and all areas of activity. Thus we must expand on Lasswell's list by adding some broader questions. The perspectives that pose many of these broader questions fall under the general label of *critical* perspectives. One of the merits of critical perspectives is that they typically include these other dimensions in their analysis.

Among the most widely used critical perspectives in media studies are *political economy*, *cultural studies*, the *critical theory* of the Frankfurt school, and *feminism*. *Reception theory* and the focus on how *audiences* make sense of the media, analysis of how *myths* develop and circulate in society, and *semiotics*—the analysis of *signs* as units of meaning in a culture—are also represented in this volume. What do these approaches entail, and what makes them "critical"?

Political Economy

From an economic perspective, we might ask questions such as the following: Who owns the media? Do financial assets control access to various media and/or media output? How do people make money through the media? How effective is advertising (Does it persuade us to buy things we otherwise wouldn't?) and who benefits? Such issues are the typical concerns of those people who use the framework of political economy to examine how the media function in society. And, of course, as the media, like many other businesses, become more and more *transnational* in operations, these kinds of questions come to have more of an international flavor. How large a part of media corporate profit stems from exporting programming and advertising? How are media exports priced? Do media help to open up new international markets for both cultural products (such as television shows, magazines, cassettes, and videos) and consumer products (television sets, VCRs, cars, refrigerators, and fashion styles)? This perspective views media in the United States as economic organizations designed to create profit as well as to foster a cultural climate in which profit making is honored. Most of their concerns stem from this orientation.

Karl Marx was one of the earliest critical political economists, although he had little to say specifically about media except for a famous dissection of *censorship*; Herbert Schiller and Dallas Smythe have pioneered North American studies of media and political economy, but it is a perspective more commonly used in Europe, Latin America, and elsewhere. The perspective of political economy is broadly reflected in this reader in the chapters by Herman (Chapter 4), Robinson (Chapter 5), Gandy (Chapter 11), and Hamelink (Chapter 15). Yet, as the name of the orientation suggests, it also refuses to examine the economic dynamics of media separately from their political dynamics.

Media, Politics, and Power

The basic issue underlying political questions is that of power. Critical scholars are all concerned about the relationship between power and communications. Here we should think of the term *political* in both narrow and broad senses. Politics in the narrower sense is the familiar terrain of parties, elections, and the presidency, in all of which the media play an increasingly influential role. The media package not only individual politicians but also policies, yet at the same time, skilled politicians can use the media to enhance their own images and advance their own interests. Critical approaches ask, How much can and do the media affect the democratic process? When they set the *agenda* of political concerns for us to think about, how much are the media influenced by clever political public relations? In their concern for good television images and brief sound segments, are the media constructing political celebrities rather than helping candidates to articulate issues and the public to become informed? In Chapter 5, Cedric Robinson explores the complicated web of relationships between the media and government—both of them elements of the power structure—including the process of packaging the president. But often the electoral process is not sufficient for certain issues to be debated and acted upon adequately. People not only join parties and vote; they also create movements, protest, demonstrate, and agitate. There is a long and rich history of such popular social movements in the United States, and Chapter 12, by John Downing, explores the alternative media that such movements have used.

Ideology and Politics

In broader terms, the "political" also has to do with some basic values and attitudes toward the society we live in. Thus, for example, in the United States we tend to think that "freedom" is a good thing and that this is a country where "freedom" is valued. Closely linked to the notion of "freedom" is that of "individualism," valuing the right of individuals to their own opinions and to "do their own thing." In other countries, different values and different priorities are held. In the Soviet Union there has been a strong stress on the value of "equality," defined economically at least. That idea was perhaps taken to greatest lengths by the "stylistic equality" of the Cultural Revolution in China from 1965 to 1975, when men and women, young and old, professionals and workers, all wore the same blue suits in a very particular attempt to erase social distinctions that are often visible through clothing. By contrast, in his chapter Kellner argues that the U.S. fashion industry deliberately promotes *class* distinction through style. In Japan, by comparison with the United States, the group has been and still is of far greater importance than the individual. For example, people are concerned with the reputations of their families and their factories, and are used to lengthy and wide-ranging consultation processes before any major business decisions are made. Thus the basic political values of different societies, or their underlying *ideologies*, might be quite different.

However, it is also important to be critical, to ask whether the rhetoric about basic values is actually supported by reality. So in the United States, women and minority groups still do not possess the same life possibilities and sense of freedom as do White males, and homelessness and poverty severely limit personal freedom. In the Soviet Union, high-ranking party officials have enjoyed country houses on the Black Sea while city dwellers queue for poor-quality meat, mocking the notion of equality. China during the 1980s rushed full tilt into economic modernization, with an explosion of "style," yet its leadership still resists modernizing the country's political structure, as demonstrated by the June 1989 massacre of dissidents in Tiananmen Square. The Japanese sometimes complain that the group mentality may hinder creativity and ambition. Thus there can often be deep contradictions and value conflicts within systems.

Nonetheless, the dominant social forces in each and every society try to encourage a certain set of values in citizens that fits the particular framework of political and economic structures in which they live. Since these values seem so fundamental, they are often taken for granted; thus it is very hard for people to become aware that these values are not simply the obvious truth, but an *ideology*. It is hard even to get people to think about, let alone be critical of, the values and attitudes they hold. We can recognize this easily for others, when we look at other societies and wonder, "How can these people believe all that?"—but we can be amazingly blind to our own assumptions and values.

The process of socialization, or learning these basic values, particularly as they are reinforced by family, school, religion, the political system, and the media, is often called *hegemony*. Here we can begin to see how the perspective of political economy enables us to make connections between the issue of media ownership and control and the kinds of values, and the diversity (or lack of diversity) of ideas, that the media deliver. Economics affects politics in this broad sense. The sometimes difficult and abstract concepts of ideology and hegemony are explored further in the chapters by O'Connor (Chapter 1) and Kellner (Chapter 17). In Chapter 24, Sari Thomas argues that the media audience is being educated even as it is being entertained, and she explores some of the basic cultural myths about economic life in the United States that are part of the stock of television stories.

Cultural Studies

There are, and have long been, many definitions of *culture*, as Alan O'Connor points out in Chapter 1. An anthropologist would say that culture includes, among many other things, the basic values and attitudes in society, so culture and ideology must have some relationship to each other and to the media. What kinds of values do the media carry, and are they the same from medium to medium, from genre to genre? Do the media carry the same values as other major agencies of socialization, such as schooling and religion? What is the comparative impact of these values on the viewing publics?

If culture includes the various forms of expression that people use—whether through language, the body, music, images—then media act as carriers of some of the cultural material that already exists, but they are also new forms in themselves and they help to create a different culture. *Cultural studies* offer an important perspective on the critical analysis of communication. People who use a cultural studies approach set the mass media within their broad historical and social contexts; they tend to see the area of cultural expression as an arena of competing social and political perspectives, an area where ordinary people can reinterpret and "resist" the dominant values and definitions of reality in society and perhaps create their own culture and meanings. In Chapter 1, O'Connor examines the many different meanings that have been given to the term *culture* and elaborates on many of these critical perspectives.

Critical Theory

One perspective actually bears the term *critical*: critical theory. There was a group of researchers in Frankfurt, West Germany, before World War II, who tried to link Marxist ideas with Freudian ones to develop a better understanding of many dynamics of modern society. These writers included Max Horkheimer, Theodor Adorno, Herbert Marcuse, and Walter Benjamin; much later, Jurgen Habermas also became associated with this perspective. Among the topics they examined was the problem of *mass culture*, which, from their perspective, was a tasteless soup of mass-produced and superficial forms, none of which had lasting artistic or intellectual value. Their perspective was a rather pessimistic one, and they were concerned not only about the loss of artistic insight brought about by mass media, but also and more significantly about the increasing isolation and manipulation of people in modern society through the mass media. Kellner's chapter on advertising (Chapter 17) uses this perspective to discuss the creation of largely artificial needs and desires that supposedly can be satisfied by consumption in a capitalist society.

It is interesting that considerable controversy can be generated when people who hold a rather pessimistic critical theory perspective about the blandness of mass culture argue with people who hold a rather optimistic cultural studies perspective about the creation of meaning in popular culture. Some of that debate can be found by comparing the arguments in Kellner's chapter with those in Chambers's chapter (Chapter 22), or by comparing Gandy's chapter (11) with Ang's (10).

Many Approaches to the Media

Already, from this overview of critical approaches, you can see that the study of communications intersects with many older disciplines. Sociologists, anthropologists, historians, literature scholars, media critics, film specialists, journalists, economists, psychologists, political scientists, legal scholars, telecommunications experts, and linguists can all make important contributions to a better understanding of the interrelations among media, culture, and society. This makes communications a very dynamic field, a place where all these interested specialists can try to communicate with one another across the frontiers of their own disciplines, but it also often makes it difficult for the beginning student, who may wonder which discipline he or she is really studying! It is also not always so easy to get all these specialists to communicate clearly, even with one another.

A news story surfaced as we were putting the finishing touches to this reader in the fall of 1989, namely, that the Japanese Sony Corporation has purchased Columbia Pictures, having already bought the giant CBS Records Division in 1988. Let us use this story to illustrate the variety of approaches that communications scholars might use to explore the event further.

The economist might be interested in the story as yet another sign of the globalization of media ownership, a theme explored in the chapters by Herman (Chapter 4) and McQuail (Chapter 8). The film scholar might be interested in whether the new owners will favor one or another type of movie, let us say megamillion-dollar spectaculars or lower-budget innovative films. The sociologist might be interested in exploring the experience of American cultural producers when employed by a foreign business corporation and in examining the decision-making process used in selecting which movies to make. The cultural studies scholar might be interested in whether the national culture of Japan begins to exert any influence over U.S. culture, or indeed whether a new, hybrid, international film culture evolves. The political scientist might be interested in public debate in Congress and the media about potential Japanese domination of mass communication and corporate investment in the United States, and how far, after half a century, U.S. resentment over the Pearl Harbor attack is still an active ingredient in that debate. The telecommunications specialist might be interested in relating this *software* acquisition to Japan's leadership in communications *hardware* production of all kinds, and its technological and economic implications. The serious journalist might pick up on any of these angles, or evaluate to what extent this story is part of the news agenda and how well various news media covered it.

Ideally, communications scholars should be interested in all these questions and more, although achieving such multiple competencies is not easy. This book tries to reflect the spectrum of concerns and critical approaches current in the field of media studies.

Media and Other People: An International Perspective

Because the media now have such global reach, linking the far corners of the world at a moment's notice, we think an international perspective is vital. Major U.S. media corporations are multinational in scope. American television programs, film, and music flow around the world, often delighting *audiences* but creating concern about national cultural *identity.* These rapidly developing technical communication processes go hand in hand with this century's major changes in the economic, political, and cultural relations among nations and within nations. Communications media both respond to and wield influence over these changes, in ways we can easily see in our everyday lives and in other ways that are not so immediately obvious. Communications media hold many fascinating implications for human relationships and for world development that demand study, reflection, and debate.

It is often through comparison that we learn about ourselves, and study of foreign media systems helps to highlight what is special about the U.S. system and shows how media systems take on the coloring of the economic and political environments in which they function. European media systems have a tradition of *public service,* the Soviet media have experienced more changes than most Westerners realize, and Third World cultures are strongly affected by Western cultural products. An international perspective is vital to understanding ourselves adequately, to comprehending the current dynamics of media systems as a whole, and to understanding others better. Our contributors come not only from the United States but from Britain, Canada, Iran, Ireland, Italy, and the Netherlands, showing that communications analysis is also international in scope and that similar issues and approaches are used in many countries.

These specialist scholars offer a variety of orientations to some of the most lively contemporary thinking about communications media. All of the chapters are original contributions, written especially for this volume, trying to introduce abstract *theories* and complex problems in a manner accessible to the beginning student. The chapters are intended to introduce you to the tasks of analysis, comparison, and, above all, critical thinking. All of these contributions utilize some kind of critical perspective in the way they approach the analysis and understanding of the media.

Criticism as a Positive Activity

There are many different ways of being critical. One obvious way to be a critic is to write your opinions for a newspaper column, in the paid position of television or film critic, for example. What does the critic do? He or she evaluates cultural products from different perspectives, expresses opinions, and develops arguments. The critic can help to steer audiences toward or away from films or books or whatever, so he or she can have considerable influence on cultural trends and even on economic results. The more the critic knows about the genre he or she is analyzing—about its history, the background and aims of its creator, and so on—and the clearer his or her own particular point of view, the more illuminating the commentary.

It is important to move away from the idea of being critical as something bad. "Being critical" often carries the connotation of being purely negative, of being vitriolic, of putting something or someone down, of angry reactions. Sometimes balance appears to be proffered as an alternative—"being in the middle" is the sound, safe position to adopt. We want to suggest that "being critical" is positive and constructive. Criticism is necessary for knowledge to advance, because posing questions and trying to understand the world better and from different viewpoints is what creates the dynamic of science and rational knowledge in the first place. The pages of history are full of critics who were spurned by their societies, often suffering ostracism, exile, or even death, only to be proven correct later on. Socrates faced a public trial for supposedly corrupting Greek youth. Galileo suffered dearly when he dared to question church teachings that held the earth to be the center of the universe. Women heretics like America's Anne Hutchinson, who was banished with her children from the Massachusetts Colony, suffered terribly in daring to question received opinion. Malcolm X was gunned down for his fearless critiques of White racism in the United States, as well as of hypocrisy in the leadership of his religious sect. Criticism may well offend established authority, pose challenges to accepted knowledge, even question cherished values. But in pointing out problems and raising debates, it can also help to spark new solutions, policies, and ethical positions.

All the perspectives presented in this volume differ from what is often called "mainstream" empiricist communications research because they are concerned more with questions, problems, and perspectives than with the mere recital of detailed descriptions of media institutions. Indeed, critical scholars would argue that such descriptive details by themselves are impossible to interpret if they are not placed into some model or theory about how the media and society work. That is why this book does not try to bombard you with a great amount of detailed data. A chronology is supplied (immediately after the table of contents), and of course each chapter contains relevant information. More important, we think, is that each chapter of this book introduces you to a certain way of thinking about the media and offers different frameworks that you might not otherwise hear about until graduate school. We think these questions must be introduced to you early in your academic life, because they will direct you to relevant and stimulating study.

There are many different ways of being critical, and each poses somewhat different questions, considers some issues more important than others, and may even collide with some other critical views. There are numerous areas of disagreement, and one indication of how well you have read and understood this book will be your ability to pinpoint these differences of outlook in critical points of view, such as political economy, cultural studies, and feminism. This book does not wrap up "all you need to think" about the media between its covers, so that all you have to do is swallow it and the process is over. You will be invited to be, even pushed into being, an *active* participant in the process of trying to understand the importance of media today.

Critical researchers are also not content with describing what exists, the status quo of the media, but seek to explain how they came to be, which makes history a key element in understanding the current media map and cultural environment in the United States and globally. We ask how the media function and for whose benefits, and indeed how they might be improved—for women, for minorities, for the poor, for the mass of ordinary people. From the critical standpoint all knowledge assumes some point of view, so that there is no such thing as neutral information. In particular, certain critical points of view about the media have not had the forum for expression we think they deserve, nor have they been introduced into academic programs in the way we feel is necessary. People holding these various critical perspectives would also agree that the kind of information we get about the media is determined by the questions we ask.

Thus, to emphasize the point, in this book we are not proposing *a* critical perspective that we want you to adopt. We don't wish to market a new critical media orthodoxy. We want you to understand the ongoing process of being critical, through learning about some of the major critical perspectives that exist. We also want to give you a sense of excitement and to pique your interest in media studies by showing you how important media are in contemporary society and that many significant and interesting questions about the media remain to be explored.

Knowledge moves through argument. If democracy is vibrant, it is because of the voicing of dissenting opinions, especially the different voices and points of view of groups that have not been heard before and whose perspectives and interests have not been considered. We anticipate that you will have considerable discussions with your teachers and professors stemming from the material presented here, argue among yourselves, even become motivated to write to us. If you finish this book with more questions about the media than you had when you started, we will be more than happy. If you discover the richness of the field and find a further role for yourself as student, analyst, critic, or creative producer, we will be delighted. Being critical means being open to change and new developments. Nothing more positive can be offered you than that. Don't worry, be critical!

Part I Introductory Perspectives: Culture, History, Technology

As you sit reading this volume, you are surrounded by a variety of mass-produced material artifacts, such as furniture, interior design products, consumer electronics, and other cultural objects, like posters, magazines and books, and CDs and tapes. Most of the time we pay these objects little attention, yet we could examine them from a design perspective, ask about their social impacts, and explore their histories, asking how such artifacts came to be developed and investigating the processes of manufacture and the technologies required to bring them into being. Such questions focus on the kinds of applied knowledge that have created the material environment we often think of as so "natural" that we forget it has a history, and a fascinating and complicated history at that.

This entire section places contemporary concerns about communication in broad historical and cultural frameworks. We are not so much concerned that you know certain specific dates of inventions—indeed, it is actually quite unclear which are the relevant dates to know, as Brian Winston explains in Chapter 3. Rather, we are concerned that you think about the kinds of historical processes, events, and changes that play a part in shaping contemporary communications. That is, "history" is much more than dates, names, and places; it is about long-term fundamental developments in technologies, changing forms of media, and new cultural patterns and values.

This section also pays a great deal of attention to language, to the terms that we use in developing models and theories about communication and media, terms such as *technology* and *culture.* It points out that language also changes over time, and that the same word can take on very different meanings when used in different theories. Unlike Humpty Dumpty in *Alice in Wonderland,* who wanted words to mean what *he* wanted them to mean, we want you to become sensitive to language, to the terms that are used in analyzing communications, and to the shifts and nuances of meaning that these terms acquire. Throughout the book we present contending perspectives, arguments that challenge received opinion by questioning the meanings and implications of certain terms. An essential part of "being critical" is thinking about the language used to make arguments and frame theories.

1 Culture and Communication

ALAN O'CONNOR

The following contribution describes and analyzes the very different definitions of culture that theorists have used, and the different implications and concerns of these definitions. The anthropological definition has been broad and inclusive; a narrower interpretation thought of high art, opera, and classical music as embodying taste and "culture"; yet another focus has been the different "cultures" of different nationalities and ethnic groups. Culture also plays a role as social cement, helping to maintain the boundaries and definition of a group, usually a nation-state, and thus is connected to the maintenance of social order and political power. O'Connor explores these various definitions, how they developed, and how they have been used.

You will see how the different definitions of culture imply different roles for the media. The media may be seen as conservative and supporting the existing structures of power in society, the hegemony argument; they may be seen as undermining traditional cultural forms, the Frankfurt school argument; or they may be seen as a democratizing force, creating and spreading contemporary culture to everyone, a cultural studies argument. Don't look for agreement among the various definitions of culture proposed here. Look for the logic of the arguments, and decide for yourself what the implications are of each.

Culture is one of the most complex words in the English language. Often people think that culture means the arts, sometimes termed *high culture*: music, painting, sculpture, and dance. A "cultured" person, by this definition, is a highly educated person who is closely aware of these arts, who goes to the opera, the theater, and the ballet, and who reads poetry and buys paintings.

For anthropologists and others, the concept of culture is not restricted in this way. Culture is everything we do in our everyday lives, from brushing our teeth to putting up a building, and from watching the Olympics on TV to getting married.

Author's Note: I would like to thank John Downing for his help with this chapter.

Still others may think of culture as being almost the same as nation: France and French culture, Japan and Japanese culture, the United States and its culture. Some will think of ethnic cultures within a single society: Native American, African-American, Hispanic-American, Asian-American.

The high culture and anthropology definitions, despite their differences, tend to focus our attention on cultural products or activities, such as music or marriage rituals. The ethnic and national definitions, by contrast, emphasize culture as something that offers a particular perspective on life, a way of understanding the world, of giving it meaning. For example, Native Americans have traditionally held "Mother Earth" in the greatest reverence. That is their cultural perspective. By contrast, most Whites, from the earliest days of settlement in the Americas, have seen nature as something to be exploited for economic purposes, from logging to strip-mining to nuclear fission. Theirs is a different cultural perspective. These two major ways of using the term *culture,* as perspective and as product or activity, do not exhaust the competing definitions of the word.

We may be tempted to set aside these differences and try to find agreement on a single authoritative definition. There is a very good reason not to do this. If people do not agree on the meaning of a word it is often a sign of even more fundamental disagreements. We should investigate those disagreements rather than trying to avoid them. The basic argument of this chapter is that different senses of the word *culture* are often tied to different social and political viewpoints. Thus we cannot just choose a definition and "get on with it." We first must understand the extra baggage that each definition carries with it.

The approach to the question of culture in this chapter is derived from a particular tradition known as *cultural studies.* This interdisciplinary approach was pioneered during the 1960s at the Centre for Contemporary Cultural Studies at the University of Birmingham, England. Universities in the United States have followed the development of this approach and have set up their own units for cultural studies; however, as we shall see at the close of this chapter, the cultural studies approach is actually quite diverse and itself in need of criticism.

The areas to be discussed in this chapter include the following: culture as a human activity that is part and parcel of the endemic conflicts that characterize social life; the use of the term *culture* in some major disputes in the past about how modern society should best be run; popular culture and mass culture; semiology (semiotics); culture and the concept of hegemony (i.e., the political dominance and leadership of certain social classes); the notion of "cultural capital," or culture as a resource; the term *ideology*, which is sometimes used in a way similar to one definition of culture, and sometimes not; and, once again, the cultural studies approach.

Culture as an Active and Conflictual Process

Let us begin by criticizing another common way of thinking about culture. We sometimes think of culture as a *thing*, like an oil painting, or as a *quality*, like a great oil painting. But I would argue that it is better to think of culture principally as an active process, or processes. Who paints? What do they paint? For whom do they paint? Culture is simultaneously an ongoing process and an active process of communication and understanding. The study of culture involves the study of activities and interactions, not just the study of cultural products such as paintings.

So let us choose painting as an example of cultural activity and ask some important questions. Are painters defined, do they define themselves, as "artists"? If they are, we expect them usually to have studios, and from time to time to exhibit their paintings. We expect them to sell their paintings to earn a living, which is an important reason for exhibiting their work. Are they mired in poverty, as so many fine painters seem to have been throughout history? Do they have to wait on tables to get by? Do they know the people who will buy their paintings, as artists used to do, or do they mostly sell them to buyers they have never met before and will never meet again? Do they paint what they want, or—to earn a living—what they know people will buy? Does their need to earn a living take their energy away from more innovative work? How dependent are they on being "in" with the "right" people in the art world's cliques, on positive reviews by art critics? If they have all that in place, does it truly validate their artistic labors? And, very important, how significant for their work are their interactions with other artists and learning from them?

We see at once from these questions that "culture" is only in part the painting itself, the cultural product. Even the prototypical "high culture" artist is engaged with economic realities, with the opinions of wealthy people, with the judgments of strategically situated people in the art world. Even this person is not a solitary genius, but learns from the work of other artists. Culture is an ongoing and interactive process, mired in everyday realities, and certainly not just a spiritual product of the lonely, lofty genius. If we consider the work of the artists who work in the advertising industry, then we can see even more easily how economics, power, and cultural activity interact. Their income and creative activity are guaranteed—so long as their work continues to please their paymasters.

But enthusiasts of high culture will claim at once that artists in advertising are not creative, that they are not "true" artists. In doing so, these critics transform their own judgments on the artistic value of cultural products into the very definition of cultural activity.

How, in turn, should we define modern mural painters, who have set out to create cultural products to be seen, at no charge, by passers-by, and that often contain direct political attacks on the powers that be, such as realtors or the police? How should we define schoolchildren's paintings, or the work of psychiatric patients in art therapy classes? Or graffiti? Or the act of painting the room you live in? In fact, the distinctions between grades of artist become less interesting with each example, and it becomes more and more intriguing to explore the process, the context, and the reception of artistic cultural production. For these latter artists are producing culture for very different audiences, under very different conditions, from those of the prototypical "true" artists. Thus the cultural process is not only ongoing and active, but takes multiple forms even within the seemingly single activity of painting.

I have taken painting as an example because it is so frequently thought of as a cultural activity bringing forth cultural products. Let us examine for a moment a different set of cultural activities and products, namely, clothing and dress. Throughout history, people have made and worn particular clothes to signify particular meanings. A three-piece suit usually means respectability, affluence, status, career. Vividly colored hair often means a "punk" rejection of all four; a baseball cap worn backwards in "hip-hop" culture, the same thing. Doctors wear white coats to signify their medical knowledge; police officers wear uniforms to communicate their official rights of arrest and public control. This last is a very well-understood cultural code. Imagine for a moment its absence, and you will see how important dress culture is in our daily lives.

The following example is a frightening and extreme one, but it also emphasizes the connections between cultural codes and activity, and politics. In Argentina, in a horrific seven-year period between 1976 and 1983, upwards of 25,000 political dissidents vanished forever—imprisoned, terribly tortured, and killed. The secret police who seized them on the street or from their homes in the middle of the night came without uniforms, in unmarked cars without license plates. The absence of uniforms and official signs communicated stealth and mystery, utter freedom from the public's control over their actions, and that the rule of law had been hijacked by people acting like a mob but with the protection of the country's military rulers. What has been called a "culture of fear" was generated, in part by the very absence of signals based on dress and uniform.

We need to be aware, then, not only that culture is an active process that takes multiple forms, but also that the cultural realm often expresses antagonisms, both deep-rooted and more casual. Cultural production is no more harmonious than its context, and where there are major social and political antagonisms—let us say between rich and poor, or between Native Americans and the energy corporations that want to mine on their sacred sites, or the conflicts of racism and sexism—we would expect cultural processes to reflect these in various ways. When people are struggling with each other for power or wealth or survival, the perceptions of reality of one side are likely to be very different from the other's. Chapter 4 of this volume, by Edward Herman, and Chapter 5, by Cedric Robinson, explore this, as do chapters on alternative media in Part III and on racism, feminism, and cultural imperialism and cultural identity in Part V.

Conflicts are then part and parcel of cultural processes, products, and perspectives—not just conflicts of taste about clothes or painting, but deep-seated conflicts. The very history of the word *culture,* as we shall now see, has been mixed up with some quite basic conflicts among social classes.

Culture and Politics in Modern History

Some modern meanings of the word *culture* first emerged in Britain a little before 1800. Until then the word had been used mainly to describe agricultural processes, such as the culture of wheat or corn (rather as the expression "growing a culture" is used in biology today). The word then came to be extended to social processes, as part of an argument about the impact of the newly developing industrial capitalism that was indeed then changing the face of Britain. Some social observers began to worry that industrialization might be wiping out forever the culture they prized. By *culture* they sometimes meant traditional ways of living and sometimes meant the arts.

Conservative observers criticized industrialization because it was destroying an older, aristocratic way of life, based on the land and agricultural production rather than factories, cities, and banks. Radicals were more concerned that the development of industry was exploiting a new class of workers. The conservative argument was designed to defend a fading aristocratic way of life. Those taking the radical argument protested that workers were being forced to work long hours in terrible conditions and to live in overcrowded and unhealthy cities; they also foresaw that with education these new classes would become significant social actors in their own right, no longer just pushed around, but beginning to create new ways of life, new cultural processes.

This dispute is known as the "culture and society" debate. In it, *culture* was grouped together with words such as *art, industry, democracy,* and *class.* In nineteenth-century Britain, a leading exponent of the conservative position was Matthew Arnold. It was a complicated debate to follow at times because the conservative and the radical critiques of industrialization sometimes overlapped, both claiming to offer a harmonious resolution to the abrupt and harsh changes taking place. For conservatives, this harmony would be achieved by turning the clock back; for radicals, by developing more democracy, not less. However, the conservative criticism that industry was destroying a valued way of life, or culture, usually included an attack on democracy. Conservatives were afraid that if the "masses" came to power they would destroy all "culture," all the traditional hierarchical way of life, including its artistic manifestations.

In the second half of the nineteenth century in the United States, the word *culture* took on yet another meaning, being used to honor the dominant classes (DiMaggio & Useem, 1978). Culture was something members of those classes claimed to possess, and that, in turn, they cited to justify their superior authority. Culture signified idealism and intelligence located at the top of society, in its dominant classes; it was supposedly absent from the laboring classes, the farmers and factory workers. Culture replaced earlier religious ideas about the divine right of kings to rule, with more this-worldly ideals drawn from modern literature, philosophy, and the arts, and applied to ruling classes. As Lewis Perry (1984) writes, "The term culture indicated continuing faith in a hierarchy of merit that distinguished the truly 'noble' person from the herd" (p. 264). The word *herd* was being applied to the general population of the United States. The word *culture* thus acquired a new social and political meaning. It helped to justify the rule of dominant classes in a modern social order more credibly than claiming, as kings had done, a God-given mission to dictate to the public. This use of the word *culture* was important in the United States up to the beginning of the 1900s.

From these examples we can learn two things: Meanings of the word *culture,* as mentioned at the beginning of this chapter, often have strong social and political implications; these meanings also change through history.

Popular Culture

Another debate about culture centers on definitions of "popular" culture. The term *popular culture* refers to cultural processes at work among the general public, the people thought to have no "culture," according to the definitions reviewed above. (Properly speaking, *popular culture* means something different from *mass culture,* to be explained below in the section on hegemony.)

Some scholars have tried to defend popular culture against notions of high culture that despise any cultural product other than the classical arts. One very common defense attempts to demonstrate that popular cultural products have at least some of the qualities that are claimed for high culture products. For example, it is argued that Billie Holiday's or John Lennon's song lyrics have some of the same qualities as modern poetry. Or it is argued that a television series can be just as good as a stage play by a respected "literary" author.

The problem with this defense of popular culture is that it still reflects the common claim that culture is a product "above" or "outside" the embracing processes of economic and political life. If popular culture is studied only as a series of products (or, as some scholars would put it, as "texts"), the social and political context of the production is usually not addressed. I would argue that this is a major shortcoming: Text and context should never be divorced; this would be a little like watching a single soap opera episode and expecting to understand the whole saga. Even this parallel oversimplifies the problem, for in the case of cultural products we need to understand the processes of their making, their diffusion, and their reception—the meanings they acquire in the minds of the people exposed to them. Simply ranking a popular cultural product as good or bad barely scratches the surface of the issue.

Another approach to popular culture does not study the products, but the social groups that use them. Herbert J. Gans (1974) argues that it is a mistake to value high culture over popular culture. He goes on to identify not two cultures (high and popular) in the United States, but five, which he names "taste" cultures. Gans argues that these cultures are all equally valid expressions, but of different "taste publics." Although Gans himself considers none of these taste cultures superior to any of the others, he draws attention to the frequent conflicts among their supporters—their "taste publics"—as to their respective merits and validity.

However, Gans's stress on consumers, on taste cultures, is a rather circular argument. He defines a taste culture as a segment of the public that values a particular type of culture. But why does it value that type of culture? That question is not really answered. Does that segment of the public help to produce the particular taste culture? Again, no answer. If it does not help to produce it, who produces the culture for it—and why? Gans draws sociocultural maps, but does not explain them.

Examples of popular culture and its publics would be jazz and the blues. These are the product of several centuries of African musical cultures forged anew through the crucibles of slavery, of legalized segregation after the Civil War, of being pushed to the very margins of survival as migrant workers in northern U.S. cities, and of sustained resistance to institutionalized racism. Jazz and the blues are the most distinctive and vibrant features of musical culture, popular or otherwise, in the United States. Rock music and other forms of widely played music are frequently derivative and often blander versions of these originals.

Saying that there is a taste public for jazz explains nothing of its history, its production, the numerous unacknowledged borrowings from it, the exploitation of its artists by the White music industry, or the contention (to be explored shortly) between "popular" culture and "mass" culture. The truly penetrating argument, in my view, is to cut through the claim that culture and cultural products are above economic and political life and show to the contrary just how they are used to legitimate dominant social and economic structures and also, sometimes, as in the case of popular culture and alternative media, to challenge these powerful structures.

Semiology: A Way of Studying Patterns in Culture

In the early 1960s a new approach began to develop in the study of culture, an approach with much to offer, but also limited in its earliest version by its refusal to consider the question of context. The method is semiology, or the study of sign systems. By *signs* are meant a whole range of things, from film to architecture, from clothes to gestures, all of which have meaning within a society's culture. Semiology, further, examines *underlying patterns* in culture and communication rather than specific content or messages, rather in the same way that a specialist in linguistics might study the grammar and structure of languages without being concerned about specific words and their meanings. Semiology, also sometimes known as semiotics, has been used equally to study high culture and popular culture (see Chapter 23, on film).

For example, one very influential early writer in this tradition of cultural analysis was the Russian Vladimir Propp (1930/1968), who argued that folktales and fairy tales, which number in the thousands, could be reduced to a few basic story lines. Apart from being intriguing, his work is important because it suggests that what is communicated in a folktale is not just the contents, the details. If he and other semioticians are correct, then it is also the form, the underlying structure of the tale, that is attractive and important to the audience. That, at least, is the classical semiological technique of analyzing human culture, to detect the underlying structure.

The basic technique can be used in many different situations. For example, one could try to show that Hollywood's countless western movies all had an underlying structure of bad:good = Indians:cowboys.

Semiology set out to become a science. Its founders thought they were mapping nothing less than the underlying structure of the human mind. It soon became obvious, however, that semiology could not avoid dealing with the specifics of human values and history. It may be true, for example, that all cultures have a fundamental structure of bad/good. But to identify the cowboys with the good and Indians with the bad rests upon a particular value system, namely, White racism. Most people would agree that the pattern in western movies tells us more about a particular history and culture—racial oppression in the United States—than about the fundamental structure of the human mind.

As a result of this kind of criticism, semiology began to revise its goals. It is now often seen as only one tool of analysis that must be supplemented by the study of historical and political issues. Many semioticians have come to acknowledge the importance of placing cultural products in their context (Barthes, 1973; Berger, 1982).

Hegemony: Political Issues in Culture

In the 1940s and 1950s both conservative and radical scholars had a surprisingly similar analysis of mass communication. The "Frankfurt school" was one of the sources of the radical critique, and it is further analyzed in Chapter 17, on advertising. The Spanish writer Ortega y Gasset was one of the most famous of the conservative critics in this vein. Newspapers, radio, popular film, and television were assumed to act in a mechanical way on the public, destroying an existing culture and replacing it with "mass culture," by which was meant a commercial, manipulative pseudoculture.

However, when researchers went to investigate media armed with these concepts, it soon became clear that mass communication did not work in this mechanical way. This model of the media, seeing them almost as a hypodermic syringe injecting beliefs into the public, had to be replaced by a much more complex and careful model of how mass communication actually works. (See Chapter 10 in this volume for further analysis of the mass culture approach.) One such model uses the concept of cultural hegemony. The term *hegemony* is derived from Greek via twentieth-century Italian writer Antonio Gramsci (Forgacs, 1989; Williams, 1977), and signifies in this use a combination of dominance over society and leadership of it by governing classes. This leadership and cultural domination are exerted in tandem with the use of force (through the police, courts, prisons, and, if necessary, the armed forces) in situations that threaten to escape the control of the upper classes. In untroubled periods, however, domination is achieved culturally, not by direct violence.

There are three main aspects to the concept of cultural hegemony. First, it suggests that we should study the arts, mass media, and everyday culture as processes of persuasion in which we are invited to understand the world in certain ways, but not in others (see Chapter 4, this volume, for some examples). Second, it argues that the approved ways of understanding and experiencing the everyday world have important political consequences. Third, it proposes that for cultural hegemony to be successful it must be flexible, responsive to changing conditions, adaptive. The same old ideas, in a situation of change, will usually fail to exert the same hegemony.

Radical scholars of communication who have studied processes of cultural hegemony have tended to concentrate on two examples. The first is the importance of school in shaping people in a certain direction. This is a good example of an everyday hegemonic *process*—that is, what happens at school—rather than a specific product (e.g., a newspaper article). Schooling is indeed a multiple process. Classroom discipline, for instance, may be just as important in the communication process as the subject matter that is being taught. Having a general public that has learned to obey orders through twelve years in school is one part of hegemony. Another part is what typically happens when some students resist schooling, but are told as they do so that they are "choosing" (are they?) to exclude themselves from many types of employment and from further education. They may even be used as object lessons by teachers and parents to other young people to communicate the high costs of nonconformity to the "rules of the game."

Scholars interested in processes of cultural hegemony also study the *active* use of mass communications by youth subcultures. "Subcultures" are usually deviant or minority responses to mainstream cultures, sometimes opposing these, sometimes intensifying them. An example would be ethnic subcultures, such as Italian-Americans. It can be shown that youth subcultures take popular music but use it in their own ways to create their own meanings (see Chapter 22). These meanings may be very different from those intended by the producers of the cultural goods. This is one illustration of culture as an oppositional and subversive process rather than a hegemonic process.

Cultural Capital

Yet another kind of focus on culture and social class is provided by studies in France and in the United States that show that middle-class and professional families use certain kinds of cultural awareness and information to maintain their social and economic position and to attempt to reproduce it for their children. Extra time spent with children by their parents, the development of interests in music and the arts, simply being surrounded by "high culture" in the form of book-lined and compact disc-lined shelves, exposure to adult discussions of art and politics, the use of home computers as active instruments rather than as relatively passive video games—all endow children with "cultural capital," an investment that their parents hope will eventually pay off economically for their children in professional positions or high-ranking administrative jobs—and hence in economic capital. French sociologist Pierre Bourdieu (1984) argues that such a cultural ambiance within the family is far more important than instruction in school. Since valued competencies of the kind described take a long time to acquire, most children of the dominated classes will never catch up.

This manipulation of high culture legitimates the high social status and income of the middle and professional classes (DiMaggio, 1982). Possession of this culture pays off in everything from job interviews to professional contacts and "networking." Members of the lower-middle and working classes may aspire to acquire high culture but find it difficult to achieve. They do not have the background. They do not have the time it takes. The tickets are too expensive, whether to the opera or to the "right" university. The working classes are left with what Bourdieu calls "the choice of the necessary." They tend to feel uneducated and know they are left out. Some of their members may even blame themselves for this, even though they may at the same time be critical of what counts as high culture, its pretentiousness and long-windedness.

Ideology

Another chapter could be written on competing definitions of the word *ideology*, but here I will summarize some of them. One common use of the term is to describe a systematic set of ideas, quite often ones that the writer does not like and considers dangerous to human well-being. For much of the twentieth century, the word has been hurled back and forth between the United States and the Soviet Union, with U.S. commentators describing Marxism as an ideology, and Soviet commentators describing American doctrines of the value of market forces as an ideology. The Americans used to define Marxism as a way of underpinning the power of the Kremlin; the Soviets used to define Western economics as a way of underpinning the power of Wall Street. Much heat, less light. Sometimes the word was also used to suggest a strong emotional and psychological investment in biased ideas, such as the fierce passion of fundamentalist religion, whose followers were usually blind to any reasoned challenge to their views.

One assumption written into these definitions is that ideology needs to be unmasked, stripped away, cleared away like a fog, so that its victims can see the truth, the "facts" as they really are. People were defined as dupes, as sadly brainwashed by Soviet propaganda—or, if you were on the other side of the fence, by capitalist propaganda. There was reality and there was ideology, truth versus lies, persuasion versus propaganda, facts versus mirages, honesty versus deception, freedom fighters versus terrorists. Yet once these simple dualities are pinned down to something as specific as freedom fighters versus terrorists, it becomes rather obvious that human reality is seldom so clear-cut and tidy as ideology versus the "facts." One person's freedom fighter is another person's terrorist.

Some Marxist writers, such as the Frenchman Louis Althusser (1970), also drawing upon Gramsci's work, have tried to give the word ideology a new, much broader sense. Althusser has argued that to see ideology just as a set of ideas is to fall into the trap of seeing these ideas almost as though they had their own arms, legs, brains, and mouths to speak with, and mysteriously traveled around communicating themselves to people. If the social institutions in which ideas are communicated to people—such as schools, churches, family, media, the military, labor unions—are not taken into account, then, according to Althusser, we have to assume that ideology spreads by magic. But if all these social institutions, and still others not mentioned, are active in the process of ideological communication, then ideology is expressed in hundreds and thousands of everyday activities inside those institutions and is influenced by them. It is both as seemingly natural as the air we breathe and as basic as the cement that holds everything in place. And in its numerous manifestations, ideology helps to keep the capitalist system afloat.

Althusser has also gone on to argue that our very sense of our own identity, who we think we are—men, women, baseball fans, patriotic Americans, midwesterners, southerners, New Yorkers, students, professors—is not ours, but is made for us, constructed in the ideological process that saturates modern human society. We feel relatively independent and individual, but in actuality our selves are not of our own making. It is the role of ideology to tell us who we are, what places we should occupy in the scheme of things. This concept of ideology resembles some of the senses of culture as an all-embracing force in society, but stresses that we are vulnerable and rather passive in the face of ideology, more so than we are concerning culture, with its frequently active, creative quality.

I prefer, however, to keep to the narrower sense of the term *ideology* to mean a clearly identifiable set of ideas, without necessarily being prejudiced against those ideas or in favor of them. I prefer to use the word *culture* as a way of acknowledging the very complex factors that lie behind someone's acceptance of an ideology. People can be religious, or patriotic, or scientifically inclined, but most do not give their lives over lock, stock, and barrel to an ideology. The degree to which they subscribe to an ideology can be the result of many factors, from family considerations, to career and promotion, to unreflecting habit, to the standard views expressed around them in the media they use and among their friends, to deep psychological factors of which they are barely aware. The complex set of issues that *culture* covers helps us to understand how and why some people subscribe so strongly to ideologies.

Cultural Studies Revisited

In the original development of the cultural studies perspective at the Centre for Contemporary Cultural Studies in Birmingham University, England, by Stuart Hall (1980) and others, the basic drive was to locate communication processes within their economic, political, and cultural contexts. Drawing on Gramsci, Althusser, Barthes, the Frankfurt school, and still other sources, the Centre developed studies of youth culture, the links between media racism and economic crisis, women's perspectives on culture and media, and many other areas. At its best, the Centre produced a stimulating application of critical theories to empirical research, which until then had generally led separate lives. The keys to the whole project, however, were (a) a respect for popular culture; (b) an acknowledgment that communication cannot be studied effectively outside its cultural, economic, and political matrix; and (c) a commitment to critical perspectives.

I have argued elsewhere that, because the conditions for studying culture from this perspective have been very different in the United States from those in Britain, there has been a danger of presenting only the blandest, most uncontroversial findings and analyses or, if controversial, analyses so mired in technical jargon that they are automatically rendered harmless and inoffensive (O'Connor, in press). What I mean by the conditions being different in the United States is that in the original Birmingham University Centre in England, a very sustained attempt was made to develop research in a collaborative manner, not only opening up the issue to considerable discussion among the researchers and thus combating the professor/research assistant hierarchy, but also—if the research was about ordinary people's cultures, for instance—with a commitment to trying to produce research that would be of some service to the people in question. In turn, at least for some of the work produced, this provided a push to communicate the research in understandable language. In the United States, "cultural studies" have been quickly absorbed for the most part into standard university processes, detached from the public's concerns and used for professional recognition and career advancement.

So I take the position that, to realize its potential, the cultural studies approach must move out of its university ivory towers and both instruct and invigorate itself by working out an ongoing relationship with labor groups and other movements for positive social change. Especially, I argue that cultural studies must be understood as a committed or "educational" activity: Both the researcher and the people who are being studied must learn from the process of doing the research.

Conclusions

In this chapter, we have looked at the different definitions of culture, where some of them came from, and a few of the ways in which culture, economics, and politics interact. We have looked at culture as an active and ongoing process, rather than simply as a series of products. We have introduced terms such as *high culture, popular culture, mass culture, semiology, hegemony*, and *cultural capital*, which in their different ways focus on answers to the questions: What is culture? What is communication? These topics have been only touched upon here, and many other issues have barely been raised at all. The questions below suggest some areas for further exploration.

Further Questions

(1) What is the relation between "popular" culture, seen as cultural processes flowing from the general public, and "mass" culture, seen as the imposition of a bland and superficial culture via advertising, prime-time entertainment, and sensational magazines in supermarket checkout lines? What is the difference between "mass" and "popular"? Do these two categories overlap? What does it mean to hear a sugary version of a fine ballad while shopping in the supermarket? What does it mean to see a historic rock concert on a video in a bar? Are we vulnerable, even helpless, in the face of advertising and prime-time violence? Chapter 17 of this volume addresses this question in relation to advertising. If "culture" is an active process, so too is the audience, as the authors of Chapters 10 and 24 both argue; but what does that mean in our everyday lives?

(2) How great is the impact of American cultural products such as music, film, and TV on other cultures when they are exported around the world? Is it a beneficial impact? Chapter 19, on cultural imperialism and cultural identity, offers further thoughts on these questions.

(3) How viable is it to get involved in producing cultural expression that is an alternative to the mainstream? Is it financially practicable? Is it possible to reach a wide audience and actually make a difference to how people think? Is a wide audience as good as an audience that gives feedback? Is the opportunity for honest feedback a key difference between mainstream and alternative cultural production? In Chapter 12, on alternative media, some of these questions are explored further.

2 Forms of Media as Ways of Knowing

ANNABELLE SREBERNY-MOHAMMADI

A historical sense is vital if we are to understand how contemporary society and our communications media took on the shapes and roles that they have. History does not have to be a dry and narrow catalog of dead men and dusty dates; historical epochs can also be defined by different communications technologies, as in the "age of print" or the "television epoch." Sreberny-Mohammadi presents a very broad historical perspective on the rise of the three major forms of communication—speech, print, and electronic media—and the social and political impacts of these forms. She argues that these forms in and of themselves can affect how many people can be addressed, the persuasive elements that are used, and the kinds of communication and interaction that take place. She argues that the nature of political leadership and social authority were affected by the development of these different forms of communication, and examines their impacts at different moments in human history: oral communication in ancient Greece, print in preindustrial England, and television in the United States.

The focus here is not so much on the development of technology, but on how the technology was adopted and institutionalized and by whom. Sreberny-Mohammadi connects the communications questions to broader sociological and political issues, and shows how different kinds of social groups and different kinds of authority have maintained themselves using these different forms of communication. Thus technology helps to define the kinds of communication that occur, and the communication plays a central role in structuring the culture. All these terms are intimately linked.

In industrialized societies most of us now live in such media-saturated environments that we can hardly imagine a time when such obvious, necessary, and pleasurable parts of our daily life as television, radio, cinema, newspapers, books, and audio and video cassettes did not exist. But we could indeed trace out one strand of the history of human development as a history of the spread of particular forms of communication.

Looking at forms of communication is somewhat different from examining the technologies of communication, which is the focus of Chapter 3. Many theorists would agree with a division of communications history into three main epochs: the earliest period, when orality dominated, the epoch of print, and the advent of electronic media. In each period, those communicating took on different roles. In orality, speaking and listening are the central activities. Print requires writers and readers. Electronic media demand organized production and viewers. Of course, to talk of development does not mean that one form replaces another; clearly, in contemporary industrial societies we may use all three forms of media on a daily basis, even simultaneously.

Let us look at each of these three forms in turn. We shall pay attention to the basic features of each form, no matter in which time period one examines them. But we shall also look at the kinds of societies within which these forms came to dominate and ask about the relationship between the form of media and the form of society. There is not space here to describe the social history of each epoch in great detail. This chapter presents some brief, idealized portraits of societies that correspond to the three major media forms, which means their typical features are highlighted at the expense of the details that do indeed make each historical situation unique. We shall also examine how far each form has provided opportunities for ordinary people to participate in public life, and how far each has been dominated by wealthy and powerful elites to shore up their own positions. Later we will explore the question of whether there is only a single path of communications development, and the implications of studying forms of media.

The Nature of Oral Communication

Oral communication, whether in a historical context or a contemporary one, has a number of formal, or necessary, features. These include the fact that oral communication is face-to-face or public communication in which speaker and audience are copresent (that is, in the same place). Thus the communication is very space bound, since only those actually present will hear the message. It is also highly time bound; since sound dies as it is spoken, speaking is a performance that ends and can be recalled only by those who were present, and we all know how fallible the human memory is. In oral/aural communication the mouth and the ear are the dominant organs and hearing the dominant sense, although all sorts of nonverbal cues—such as clothing styles, facial expressions, and body postures—can also be visually picked up and given meaning by the participants.

Oral communication is one of the oldest and certainly most enduring forms of human communication. The study of oral communication is *rhetoric,* which is also the name for its skillful application, and the roots of the study of rhetoric lie in ancient Greece. By exploring how social and political life were organized in ancient Greece, we can begin to understand why the practice of rhetoric was important, and thus how its study also grew.

Orality: Rhetoric in Ancient Greece

Ancient Greece was made up of city-states, the most important being Athens and Sparta. In comparison to the enormous nation-states of today, these city-states covered very limited territory—Athens was only about 1,000 square miles—and small populations. The active population was even more limited, since political life excluded all women and all men who were not taxpayers, mainly slaves. For the minority, the taxpaying male citizens, the political structure of the city-states provided considerable opportunities for participation, both political and legal. Ordinary people acted as jury members in public trials, but the jury numbered in the hundreds, not just twelve. There were elections of senators to the Assembly, as well appointments of ambassadors to deal with foreign states.

The practice and the study of rhetoric, oral performance, reached its peak in the fourth and fifth centuries B.C. Oral presentation was widely respected, and people admired those who spoke effectively in legal settings, to political bodies, and on ceremonial occasions. The Greek educational system provided instruction in the art of rhetoric and aimed to produce great orators. All education, which currently in the United States is very text(book) based, had to be conducted orally, since not until the fifth century B.C. were there any kinds of textbooks or volumes on business management or agriculture, or any written codes of law (Havelock, 1963, 1986). Education thus took place through the close daily association between adolescent boys and their elders, who served as philosophers, guides, and friends. Most of Greek literature up to Plato was poetic, because poetry's purpose was to preserve tradition through memorization and oral recitation.

Thus for the ancient Greeks, all forms of communication clearly had a purpose and intention. They would have found the contemporary notions of "objective" news coverage quite odd (this concept is indeed critiqued in many places in this volume) since they felt, like Aristotle, who wrote an early and very influential book about the process, that rhetoric is "the effective use of all the available means of persuasion" (Aristotle, 1967). Aristotle identified three main forms of persuasive proof: *logos*, or the use of evidence in rational argument; *ethos*, or the use of personal characteristics to claim credibility and authority; and *pathos*, or the use of emotions, such as hatred, to move people. There were correspondingly three main purposes of persuasive communication: *forensic*, or informative, used mainly in the court of law (hence our forensic science); *deliberative*, or mobilizing, used predominantly in political contexts to try to get people to vote; and *epideictic*, or entertaining or celebratory, used most frequently at funerals of great men, on feast days, and for other national festivities.

Oral cultures developed many different kinds of mnemonic devices, from poetic rhythms and rhymes to repeated formulas like daily prayers, as ways of preserving their cultures. Even today there are many cultures that are still predominantly oral. For example, the Hmong people from S.E. Asia had no written language until some Hmong came to the United States as refugees and became concerned about their cultural heritage. In Western Africa still, the *griot* is an inherited position of great authority, the man who carries the cultural memory of the tribe, and chants out the news to the rhythm of a large drum (Niane, 1965).

The audience for oral communication was and is comparatively homogeneous in comparison to the huge television audiences of today. The audience and the speaker had a certain amount of social contact. The events were collective and meaningful for everyone involved, and provided plenty of opportunity for instant feedback, such as applause and hurrahs, stony silences, or rotten tomatoes. The speaker could adjust his or her language, tone, and even content according to the audience's reception. Of course, these kinds of situations have played important roles in modern political life, as in the stump speeches of politicians and dissidents in nineteenth-century America, and have even provided opportunities for the general public to make their opinions heard. Black Americans' African roots can be traced through their patterns and rhythms of speech, their delight in the "man of words," who was usually the preacher, and in the audience's vocal repetition of and support for the preacher's words. This strong oral tradition also produced preachers who became national political leaders, able to mobilize the trust and affection of congregations across the country for change, most notably the Reverend Martin Luther King, Jr., whose "I Have a Dream" speech helped galvanize the civil rights movement. Even in contemporary society, public speaking at political rallies provides some of the best opportunities for political figures to make their ideas known and for the public to question, argue with, and criticize them in a dynamic, instant-feedback situation.

Thus oral communication bound the community together, maintained a select group of experts with knowledge committed to memory, and endowed old men with authority over the young. It supported a social hierarchy based on gender, age, and the control of collective wisdom. Oral cultures all develop certain formal linguistic structures such as poetry, legends and myths, prayers, and strong theatrical and dance narratives that help in the process of memorizing long and complex stories and human records; many such cultures honor their men of knowledge, such as American Indian shamans, African healers, and Polynesian rememberers. History, according to Fabre (1963), a social historian of language, is the remembered word.

While Socrates *spoke* his ideas, Plato was already *writing*, for by the fifth century B.C. a shift in communication became evident. The use of language shifted from a concentration on the acoustic flow of sounds pleasurable to the ear to visual patterns that demanded the concentration of the eye. If oral communication is universal, the development of writing can perhaps be claimed as one development peculiar to the human species.

The shift to writing depended, of course, on the development of writing systems—alphabets. Let us digress briefly, simply to underline the fact that the history of the development of writing systems is fascinating in and of itself. We can trace the transformations of pictorial systems, hieroglyphics, into more abstract systems, like cuneiform, into phonetic alphabet systems like the Greek, on which ours is based. Other writing systems were based on syllabaries and yet others used ideograms, such as the

Japanese and Chinese use today. Some systems are read from left to right, others from right to left (the Greeks even experimented for a while with a system that ran left to right for one line and then right to left for the next, like plowing a field), while still others read vertically, like the Chinese.[1] It is also important to note that sophisticated calendars, like the Egyptian and Mayan, were developed before writing systems, so quite complex knowledge was possible, but limited.

Not all societies developed alphabets, and some do not to this day possess a written culture, while others developed one only after the arrival of missionaries or anthropologists in the eighteenth and nineteenth centuries. But we do know that in very diverse parts of the world, such as Sumeria, Babylonia, and China, alphabetic systems were independently devised and refined, and a totally different form of communication came to prevail. But let us get back to the invention of writing, and the changes it brought about.

The Nature of Written Communication

Written communication can be divided into two epochs, the epoch of chirographic, written culture (*chirography* meaning *handwriting* in Greek) and that of typographic culture, the era of print. Writing was the first extensive form of information storage. (Lascaux cave paintings and Egyptian hieroglyphics were also ways of presenting information, but they were limited in capacity). What writing provided was a better and more reliable form of record keeping about property ownership, about taxes due, about agricultural cycles and volumes of harvest. The numbers of those who could read or write under chirographic culture was limited, so writing was closely associated with power. Royal power required scribes for accounting and tax collection and for preparing decrees to send across empires. Religious authority used its monks to copy Bibles by hand, creating multiple but authoritative copies, as well as for copying other important texts and for translating. It took considerable time to copy an entire Bible, and books were often embellished with decorative frontispieces and gold leaf, so handwritten volumes commanded a high price. Still, the number of people who could read and write was quite limited.

How do the formal features of writing/print differ from those of oral communication? First, there is a major shift in physiological orientation from the ear to the eye, which becomes the dominant organ. As we have already noted, writing depends on a wholly other form of linguistic development, the development of a symbolic language with written syntax and punctuation. Writing is space oriented because it involves the linear organization of words in lines on a page (no matter in which direction those lines run). It is also space oriented in a very different way, because for the first time a message as a material object could be produced that was transportable far away from its producer. Unlike oral communication, in written communication the writer and the reader do not have to be—and rarely are—copresent, either in space or in time.

What this implies is that because of the separation of the message from the producer and the producer from the audience, the context or situation can no longer be so significant for interpreting the message. It also means that the writer, unlike the speaker, has much less control over the way his or her message is understood or used. (The massive outrage in 1989 among Moslems around the world against Salman Rushdie's fantastical novel *The Satanic Verses*, with Ayatollah Khomeini of the Islamic Republic of Iran putting millions of dollars on Rushdie's head for blasphemous writing, is a tragicomic example of exactly this process.) Writers write for an absent and unknown audience; while an author may have an imaginary audience in mind, there is no guarantee that it is the audience he or she will reach. So print creates decontextualized communication in which, unlike oral communication, the *ethos*, the personal charisma or social role of the speaker, is no longer key to interpreting the text. Certainly you might react differently to an anonymous sonnet when you know it is the last one that Shakespeare wrote; but you can also read Shakespeare on the subway, in your living room, or in a class, and discover different interpretations and inflections.

Written communication also began to allow for flexibility of use; the writing of a text as well as its reading clearly take considerable time, but there are choices available as to when these acts occur, because neither is bound by a particular social event. Writing is also the most individualized form of communication, since almost all writing and almost all reading—both of which require quiet concentration—are done alone. Of course, there are many contexts in different cultures where material is read aloud, particularly where universal literacy does not exist, such as the reading of newspapers in teahouses in the Middle East. But the ideal-typical features of writing promote an extreme individualism, a far cry from the interpersonal nature of oral communication. Writing is essentially linear, logical, and progressive, and thus helped to promote abstract thought, which was very different from the concreteness of oral memory.

The process of book production was limited by another crucial technical factor, the fact that the West did not know how to make paper until the middle of the twelfth century, while the preparation of parchment or vellum was slow and laborious. The Arabs had learned how to make paper after their single and successful military encounter with the Chinese in the eighth century. By the end of that century paper was being produced in Samarkand, now part of the Soviet Union, and in Baghdad, now the capital of Iraq. The advent of paper so lowered the price of books that private and public libraries became common throughout the Islamic world. Perhaps the world's first library was started by Alexander the Great in Alexandria, Egypt, in the first century B.C. From the eighth century, collections were established by the Abbasid Caliph in the House of Wisdom in Baghdad. There international scholars translated—from and into Arabic, Greek, Persian, and Sanskrit—works on mathematics, logic, astronomy, philosophy, and biology; they also wrote commentaries on these works and added original works of their own. In addition, the library housed Korans and book collections on Islamic law and theology; poetry and books of proverbs, fables, and witty anecdotes; and works on genealogy, history, geography, and grammar. Similar collections were built up in Cordoba in Spain, Cairo in Egypt, Shiraz in current Iran, and Bokhara in what is now Uzbekistan, USSR. The library of the Caliph al-Hakam in Cordoba in the tenth century is said to have contained more than 400,000 volumes, with a 44-volume catalog. Many of the Muslim collections were open to the public, to anyone who had the education to benefit from them, so that a general level of scholarship and learning was more widely disseminated through the Islamic world than anywhere in Christian Europe until the early Middle Ages, when the West acquired paper-making techniques from the Arabs via Spain. It is important to note that the history of communications developments is very much a global, cross-cultural history, with techniques learned through conquest, with different civilizations enduring periods of dynamism and decline, and with shifting centers of cultural power.

It was another technical breakthrough in written communication, the development and utilization of the printing press, that brought intellectual and cultural dynamism to northern Europe. The print breakthrough is associated with Gutenberg, who printed the first Bible in 1453 in Mainz in Germany. Although printing techniques were developed much earlier in the Far East, they remained undeveloped. The age of chirography gave way to the age of typography, the age of print. These two are clearly part of one form of communication, writing, but the social and political consequences of the printing press were dramatic enough to demand some attention here.

Printing technique and its products spread rapidly through Europe. Life in sixteenth-century Britain was greatly altered by print. Only about 35,000 books were printed, mainly in Latin, in the whole of Europe by 1500. However, between 1500 and 1640 over 20,000 items in English were printed. These ranged from pamphlets and broadsheets to folios and Bibles. By 1600, nearly half the population in English towns had some minimal literacy. The vernacular spread rapidly, for, certainly outside the universities, people preferred to read in their own languages, rather than in Latin or Greek.

Print immediately had powerful economic effects. It created new jobs: printer, typesetter, proofreader, editor, stationer, publisher, bookseller, librarian, and eventually journalist. Perhaps the most important was the new role of author, someone who could sell his or her words and ideas to a reading public and make a living from royalties paid through this public consumption of cultural products, and who was thus no longer dependent on the patronage of the wealthy. Of course, many in these new positions became "gatekeepers," people who could decide what should and should not be published, who became the new arbiters of public tastes and opinions.

Centers of business and banking welcomed the new technique of printing, for merchants depended upon navigation books and almanacs for safe sea-bound trading, ways of keeping accurate accounts, and reports on prices and sales in foreign markets. The economics of increased cross-cultural contact through trade and travel created demands for current information, so by the early seventeenth century newspapers had begun to develop in northern Europe.

But not all print material was serious or clearly useful. Prose fiction developed as a powerful new form since poetic rhyme was no longer necessary as a mnemonic device, and newspapers serialized novels. One vivid example of the popularity of the new fiction form as well as an indication of the size of the reading public in the 1800s is the story of Charles Dickens being mobbed on his tour of the United States in 1848, much as a contemporary pop star would be today (Postman, 1984).

There were now both more books and more copies of individual books, which helped foster religious debate and schisms, and spread new secular ideologies such as liberalism, nationalism, and, later, socialism. While John Wycliff had been considered a heretic in translating the Bible into English in the 1360s, various editions of English Bibles were the runaway best-sellers of the fifteenth century and began to spread English across the world. While one of the earliest uses of the printing press was to produce papal indulgences, which had a brisk sale, the more long-term effects of print came from the publishing of vernacular Bibles, which heralded the demise of papal control over religious interpretation. Luther's criticisms of the church in 1517 sold all over Europe, and Luther himself said, "Print is the best of God's inventions!" (Lenin argued 400 years later that "film is the most important art"; see Chapter 9, on Soviet media.) So religious authorities lost their monopoly on the production of texts and thus over the control of knowledge and interpretation.

New forms of knowledge and new social authorities began to develop. The new middle class and secular intellectuals began to vie with the aristocracy and the clergy for authority and influence. Secular education helped this process. Universities such as those in Paris, Oxford, and Bologna had been founded much earlier in the thirteenth century, but the growing recognition of the power of the printed word gradually produced social movements for universal education and universal literacy. Literacy rates were high among the Puritan settlers in America, and for a long time they imported a great deal of print material from Britain.

The new intellectuals possessed neither the traditional authority of religious figures nor the political inheritance of royalty and nobility, but claimed their authority through logical argument, critical analysis, and persuasive language, both oral and written, but primarily written. They found an audience in the literate working class and the growing educated middle class, who read and discussed their pamphlets and tracts in what has been called the "public sphere" of bourgeois society—the coffeehouses, pubs, and salons—where free debate could circulate without state control (Habermas, 1979).

Print had strengthened the power of states, which could now more easily inform their populaces of new laws, gather taxes, print stamps with royal faces, and require written oaths of loyalty. Print even served to promote nationalism, because it helped the spread of vernacular languages such as English, French, and German in preference to Latin, thus promoting the spread of national identity and leading to the demise of the multinational empires that had dominated Europe.

At the same time, print created new opportunities for dissident opinion to be heard. For political and religious nonconformists, print allowed the production of pamphlets and broadsheets criticizing the authorities, putting forward alternative ideas, and mobilizing a new "public opinion." (See Chapter 12, on alternative media). Throughout Europe and, indeed, America, revolutionary movements depended on print to disseminate popular demands for political democracy and social justice. In the United States, Tom Paine published pamphlets; in Britain, William Cobbett sold his penny *Chartist* paper; and debate in the salons of Madame de Stael in Paris centered on the now readily available books of Enlightenment thinkers such as Rousseau and Montesquieu. Thus print helped the development of ideological politics, fostered the revolutionary ferment of eighteenth-century Europe, and aided the self-conscious rise of the new middle class, or bourgeoisie, and the new working class of the industrial towns (Gouldner, 1976). Governments tried to limit and quash such political activity by imposing fines, arresting writers, and, in extreme cases, smashing the printing presses.

Thus we can catalog important economic, social, political, and cultural aspects of the impact of print, all of which combined to create a new, dynamic, and conflict-ridden Western industrial society. The third, and last, form we must look at that is a product of that new economic structure is electronic media, most particularly television.

Electronic Media

Although the technological breakthroughs necessary for their development had taken place by the turn of the nineteenth century, electronic media were not developed as public media in the United States until the 1920s, when radio was established, with television spreading rapidly after World War II. The highly televisual society of 1980s America is used as the example here.

Television, of course, recombines the visual and the aural, the eye and the ear. As a new medium, it again created new orientations to both time and space. Up until the development of audio recording and the VCR, electronic media were extremely time bound, from the precise and regular scheduling of programs, to the definition of "prime time," to the length of individual programs, to the pacing within each program. While the reading of a book is totally flexible in terms of time, so that one can sit up all night reading a good book or dip into it over a period of time, finish it, abandon it, return to it, television makes stringent time demands on the audience. While the VCR functions as a kind of storage capacity and allows the audience to "time shift," its widespread use has not caused any visible change in the basic television time schedule, which supports the daily division of work and leisure in highly developed postindustrial societies and reinforces the patterns of family life, gender interests, and subcultural tastes. Indeed, if television schedules are designed to offer up the biggest viewing audiences to advertisers, then there is not much flexibility possible.

Not only are electronic media powerful timekeepers, they also have voracious appetites. Daily, they consume huge amounts of programming, continually demanding new cultural production and keeping audiences in a continuously unfolding present of "and now this." In terms of space, the early large television receiver was given pride of place in the family living room, with the remaining furniture rearranged around it; now televisions have shrunk in size, become multicolored, and have crept into the bedroom, the kitchen, and the subway.

If the ethos of the speaker was of great importance in oral societies, and logical argument became the most important rhetorical factor in print communication, how do we analyze television? Ong (1982) has described both radio and television as forms of "secondary orality," forms that reinforce the power of the ear and listening once more. Television appears to bring back the power of ethos, of the credibility and credentials of media figures like newscasters, whose ability to create trust among the audience is perhaps their biggest asset. Television also seems to undermine the power of logos, the slow development of rational understanding and analysis, in favor of rapid and fragmented bits of information; instead of abstract conceptual language, it provides vivid, particularist images, and instead of intellectuals, it creates celebrities. This was powerfully shown in the presidential races of 1980, 1984, and 1988, where the "photo opportunity" and the "sound bite" worked to undermine any deep discussion of the issues or a critical assessment of political positions. Metonymic images—a helmeted Dukakis in a tank or a photo of a convicted rapist—could be used to stand for huge areas of social policy that should have received careful explanation and analysis.

Electronic media voices have from the beginning been far less plentiful than print voices. Monopolistic tendencies mean the media have enormous control over what the U.S. viewing public will watch, become interested in, and be invited to think about; they can really set the social, cultural, and political agendas of modern society. It is interesting and important to ask who the people are who now potentially wield such control in American life. They are not the philosopher-kings that Plato desired, or the traditional religious and aristocratic authorities of oral culture, or the intellectuals or political activists of print. Rather, they tend to be invisible business moguls with conservative agendas, for whom television provides both profit and influence. Of course, technically, there are avenues for popular participation in electronic media; local community and ethnic broadcasting is established in most big cities, and cable channels have helped. Yet it is also probably correct to say that most "liberal" and "critical" intellectuals, academics, community workers, and so forth are still more attuned to print and putting out pamphlets, newsletters, and journal articles than to talking on the radio or appearing on television. The gatekeepers of television are even stronger than those of print, and the lack of federal support for public television stations in the United States has not allowed those stations to sustain a more invigorating type of television. It is ironic to note that public stations use the largest amounts of imported programming.

If religious figures held greatest authority during the period of oral communication, and vied with secular intellectuals during the epoch of print, the electronic period is the epoch of the Hollywood celebrity and entertainer—for example, Ronald Reagan and Johnny Carson—and the televangelist—such as Jim Bakker and Oral Roberts.

Conclusion

As this chapter itself shows, it is almost impossible to separate the impacts of a medium from the effects of the particular way in which that medium has been institutionalized in a particular society. I have tried to identify some of the necessary formal features of three basic forms of communication—orality, print, and electronic media—but I have also placed these in specific historic contexts to examine the impacts they made and the opportunities they created. History shows that one communications form does not replace another; rather, the new one is added on and often comes to dominate, while the older forms take on different functions. It is important to note also that since the 1960s electronic media have been developed rapidly in Third World societies in very different patterns, and that the stages of media development described here are not necessarily universal. One very different Third World experience is examined by Mohammadi (see Chapter 19).

In the West, at least, these three different forms of communication have tended to privilege different social groups and to provide varied kinds of opportunities for ordinary people to participate. It may be one of the greatest ironies of our modern communication times that we are surrounded by big media that speak to us but that give us comparatively little opportunity to speak back. More media seems to have meant less diversity rather than more.

Further Questions

(1) Monitor the debates about literacy and electronic media in the United States. What are the arguments for and against literacy in the media age? Has the "television age" really turned people away from books?

(2) Keep a daily log of all your media-related activities. With which medium do you spend the most time? For what purposes do you use each medium? Log your media-related expenses: What are you buying? How do you use the cultural products you buy? How does a cultural product differ from other material consumer products?

(3) New technologies challenge the model presented here. The telephone provides us with a process of oral communication at a distance. The modem provides us with a form of written togetherness. Think of other examples that alter the form of communication as defined here.

Note

1. There is also an interesting argument that the development of a phonetic alphabet, with its totally abstract way of depicting sounds using a relatively limited number of letters with enormous possibilities of combination, was the essential basis for the further development of Western abstract thought and analytic and classificatory systems (Logan, 1986).

3 How Are Media Born?

BRIAN WINSTON

Technologies are not neutral. They embody ideas, needs, imagination, possibilities from specific periods and places. They are particular solutions to certain problems, usually not the only possible solutions. The same problem identified in another cultural context might find a quite different solution, as, for example, different architectural styles have developed in different climatic and geographic regions while all satisfy the basic need for shelter.

Yet technologies can often have such profound impacts that we even define historical epochs on the basis of technological distinctions, from the "iron age" to the "industrial age" and even "postindustrial society." Technologies also have a history, or usually a number of histories. Think of the stereo system that may be playing even as you read this. It embodies a history of electricity, of sound recording, of the development of plastics, of the microchip, of interior design and consumer electronics design, even before you begin to talk about your musical tastes, listening habits, cultural spending, and so on. Thus issues about the development of technologies are complex, and very different kinds of explanations have been proposed to account for technological change.

In this chapter Winston focuses on technological change, particularly in the sphere of communications, and the kinds of theories that try to account for such change. He explores the notion of causality, that one phenomenon inevitably follows another, by comparing two broad approaches, technological determinism and cultural determinism. The first is discussed here specifically in reference to media technologies as developing through their own momentum, following an inevitable logic of their own, bringing about other kinds of change. The second approach argues that social and economic factors are the dominant factors in supporting or blocking the utilization of technology, and makes human action the prime mover of change. Using case studies for illustration, Winston investigates the logic of the different approaches and makes a strong case for the cultural perspective.

This chapter addresses two related questions: (a) How does technological change occur in mass communication? (b) What effect, if any, does the

Film Projector, c 1870

technology have on the content, the output, of mass communication? These questions are related in that they both deal with the historical relationship of technology to communication processes.

The first question is clearly historical. There are various accounts available to explain the nature of these changes. In some, technological developments are isolated: The technology is the dominant, *determining* factor in the process. I will be calling such accounts of change *technological determinist.* Other accounts place a greater emphasis on socioeconomic factors. In these accounts, technology is but one of many forces, influenced by and influencing social, economic, and cultural developments. I will be calling accounts of this sort *cultural determinist.*

The second question, about the effects of technology on communication, can also be thought of as historical. The only way a judgment can be made as to the effect of a technology on the content of communications is by comparing the content before and after the technology is introduced. Thus the second question, which seems to address only the issue of effects, is also really addressing the issue of change and, in so doing, is historical.

These two questions are linked in another way. Technological determinist accounts of media history tend to stress the role of media technology in governing the content of communication. Conversely, cultural determinist accounts tend to deny technology this determining role. So the answer to the first question above is likely to condition the answer given to the second.

This chapter presents four successive accounts of the genesis of communications technology. It is not, clearly, a full-blown history of media technology, although you may well find some new information on the subject. It is designed to encourage you to think more carefully about that history, to learn how to evaluate the problems in historical explanations and not just accept them because a scholar has published them.

Technological Determinist Account A

Technological determinism, wrote Raymond Williams (1974),

> is an immensely powerful and now largely orthodox view of the nature of social change. New technologies are discovered by an essentially internal process of research and development, which then sets the conditions of social change and progress. Progress, in particular, is the history of these inventions which "created the modern world." The effects of the technologies, whether direct or indirect, foreseen or unforeseen, are as it were the rest of history. (p. 13)

In its simplest form, this dominant theory explains the "essentially internal process of research and development" as nothing more than the biographies of the scientists and technologists involved, arranged chronologically. This account sees the development and impact of technology as "the progress of great men" (women and people of non-White cultures tend not to figure).

Here, presented as a case study, is a short history of the cinema written as "the progress of great men," based on a classic history of film (Ramsaye, 1926).

Case 1: Cinematic Projection

> One essential element of the cinema is the idea of projection. The line that leads to projection begins with Della Porta, an Italian, who put a lens on the front of the earliest camera—a simple box. An image was produced on a glass screen set in the back wall of the box. Della Porta made this device in 1555. Next, Athanasius Kircher, a German, produced a magic lantern that projected an image onto a screen (1649).
>
> Peter Roget, an Englishman, theorized in 1824 that the retina of the eye retains an image for a fraction of a second after the image is removed or changed. This "persistence of vision" can be used to fool the eye into believing a succession of separate and slightly different images to be actually one moving image. Toys to exploit "persistence of vision" by animating drawings were then "invented" by men like Paris (English, 1824), Plateau (Belgian, early 1830s), and von Stampfer (German, 1832). In 1852, von Uchatius, another German, put an animated strip of drawing (done on glass) into a magic lantern and projected the resulting moving image onto a screen.

A substitute for glass now had to be found. The line leading to this part of the cinematographic apparatus goes back to early experiments with substances that change their color, essentially by darkening, in response to light. More research, like that of Wedgewood (English, 1802), led to the first photograms—images made by laying objects, such as leaves, directly onto materials, like paper or leather, treated with light-sensitive substances. But these images were not "fixed" and would disappear into black if further exposed to the light.

Scientists undertook the discovery of a chemical that would halt the darkening process. In 1837 a Frenchman, Nicephore Niepce, found a way of doing this and, with his partner Daguerre, produced a type of photograph known as the daguerreotype. Meanwhile, an Englishman, Fox-Talbot, invented a photographic process that produced first a negative, made of chemically treated paper oiled to transparency, and then a positive copy.

This, the essence of modern photography, was then refined. A wood pulp extract called cellulose was used instead of paper. Celluloid film finally allowed George Eastman to "invent," in 1888, a camera that anybody could use.

Back to the cinema. It was Edison who took photography and melded it with the developments in animated drawing and magic lanterns to produce the kinetoscope in 1892. There were British, French, and other claimants for the honor of "inventing" the first motion picture device. Two Frenchmen, the Lumiere brothers, gave the first public cinema (their term) show, using a projector to throw a moving image onto a screen, before an audience, arranged as in a live theater, in 1895.

So was the cinema invented.

There are numerous problems with this account. In its eagerness to create "great men," the story becomes highly selective. For instance, Roget's explanation of why we see apparent motion, "persistence of vision," is not really physiologically accurate (Nichols & Liderman, cited in DeLauretis & Heath, 1980, pp. 97ff.), but even very recent histories still begin with Roget and his idea (see, e.g., Beaver, 1983; Mast, 1981).

Real contributions are seen as coming solely from the genius of a single figure, when, in fact, they are the product of collective inventiveness. For instance, it took more than 30 years to go from the development of celluloid, which was originally produced during the U.S. Civil War as a dressing for wounds, to the Kodak. The full story of those years reveals a number of innovations and dead ends. It involves many, many more people than just George Eastman, who successfully marketed a technology to which a lot of hands had contributed.

Edison's role in this process needs to be revised. Edison at Menlo Park was running one of the earliest modern industrial laboratories and pursuing a range of experiments, including investigations into the moving image. His method was to delegate much of the work to his assistants. In the case of the cinema, the work was actually done by a man named Dickson (Hendricks, 1961). Edison knew this full well, but that never prevented him from accepting credit for the "invention" of the kinetoscope.

The poverty, or "thinness," of great-man histories is not based simply on the desire to create heroes. Another crucial factor is the implicit insistence on the primacy of the West. For instance, the camera does not begin with Della Porta but with Arab astronomers at least 300 years earlier. There is even a reference to projected images in China in 121 B.C. It has been suggested that the first magic lantern lecture in Europe was given by a Jesuit who had learned the technique while a missionary in China, and that Kircher had nothing to do with it (Temple, 1986, p. 86). Even without this, it is possible that the camera was in existence in Italy over a century before Della Porta (Winston, 1987, p. 199).

You might also have wondered why, in this account, such emphasis has been placed on nationality. In part, it has to do with national pride. But establishing who did something first has more to it than that. Modern patent rights depend on registering an invention first, and that implies financial advantages.

The failure of the great-man style of technological determinism cannot be corrected simply by writing more comprehensive histories. This sort of history really cannot answer the question of *how* technological change occurs; instead, it simply tells us *when*. The only explanation offered as to *how* is that great men, out of their genius, think of them.

Technological Determinist Account B

There is a more sophisticated version of the technological determinist approach that we need to explore in order to see if these "how/why" questions can be better answered. Here, the changes listed in Case 1 would be treated as a sequence of developments causally related to each other. The "inventors" would be left out, or their parts downplayed. Such a history of the cinema would view its technological development as the inevitable result of scientific progress, part of the never-ending advancement of human knowledge in Western culture. Such an account would suggest that the independent existence of the camera, the lantern, and the lens had to combine to produce the magic lantern. In turn, this development inevitably melded with the development of photography to create cinematography.

The arrival of sound in film provides us with a case study in this more sophisticated mode. This account is based on Ogle (1977).

Case 2: Sound in Film

> Sound recording developed using wax cylinders, discs, and wire before the turn of the twentieth century at the same time as the cinema itself was being perfected. However, these were mechanical recording devices without amplification that would not, therefore, work well in a theatrical environment.
>
> Electronic devices that enabled sound to be amplified evolved out of experiments on the nature of electricity itself, then at the cutting edge of physics. By 1906, a number of independent researchers had produced a tube rather like the electric light bulb then being generally manufactured, but this specialized version could reproduce and amplify electrical signals.
>
> The application of this technology to silent cinema was interrupted by World War I, but experiments continued using various systems. Running film projectors synchronously with phonographs was one. Another, more complicated, converted sound waves, via a microphone linked to a light bulb, into light waves to which the film could be exposed.
>
> The technology was therefore awaiting its moment. That came in 1926, when the industry finally realized that the public would accept sound. Earlier attempts had failed because the technology was not quite developed and because there was inertia about changing over from the commercially successful method of having live music at each screening.
>
> The introduction of sound also made easier the introduction of faster (i.e., more light-sensitive) film stocks. The very bright arc lights used in the silent studios used to hiss. This was acceptable in silent shooting but bothersome if sound was being recorded. Incandescent lights were then introduced because they made no noise, but they were also less powerful, so the industry needed faster stocks. More sensitive film had been available but unused since before World War I.
>
> This new stock was black-and-white but panchromatic—equally sensitive to all colors, unlike the slower orthochromatic stock it replaced. "Ortho" was blind to red, which it therefore photographed as black. The introduction of panchromatic film affected makeup, costume, and set design. It also helped, therefore, to put in place production procedures that would facilitate the next major technical advance—color.

Such an account presents a seamless sequence of technical events, each automatically triggering its successor. Each can be delayed by external factors, such as World War I and industrial inertia. But in the end the technology triumphs.

Yet important clues as to *how* technical change occurs can be gained by thinking of *why* a change occurs at a particular time. This is a more complicated issue than it might seem to be at first sight. Changes do not occur simply when the materials and the scientific knowledge necessary for an advance are at hand. The history of the cinema is a good illustration of this.

The great-man account in Case 1 revealed that there was nothing to prevent Kircher from doing, two centuries earlier, what Ustachius did. Kircher could draw and he had glass. And he had just "invented," or borrowed from the Chinese, the lantern that Ustachius was to use.

Such questions can be extended. Why did Della Porta not place a light where he had put his ground-glass screen? Had he done so, he could have created the magic lantern a century before Kircher. And why did the Arab astronomers not pursue these developments centuries before that? Or the Chinese even earlier?

The great-man style of technological determinism cannot help us to answer such questions. It is equally clear that the sophisticated technological determinism of Case 2 is no better. We do not know from Case 2 why early films did not have sound, since sound-recording techniques and motion picture devices developed simultaneously (Hendricks, 1961, p. 111). And we are no nearer to understanding why the Arabs failed to exploit the camera, why Kircher did not invent the camera, and so on.

A better way we can begin to answer these questions is, however, hinted at in Case 2. There we started to hear about forces other than the technological, such as World War I and attitudes in the film industry. In a technological determinist account these are treated as incidentals, but cultural determinists will take these external factors as significant.

Cultural Determinist Account A

To take a cultural determinist view, it becomes necessary to examine the social context of the technology. This implies an examination of the circumstances into which the technology is introduced and diffused through society. In turn, then, a cultural determinist would need to look at the circumstances preceding the development of a technology. Note that the word *development* is preferred to the word *invention* because invention implies a single moment—but these single moments always obscure long-term developments involving many hands. Thus the cultural determinist will at least be an economic historian.

Let us take an economic history type of account of the introduction of sound in film and see how it compares with the technological determinist account offered in Case 2. Here, in Case 3, the key player becomes a corporation (Warner Brothers), but this key player is not a corporate great man. Rather, the struggle to introduce sound is located within corporate competition (Allen & Gomery, 1985, pp. 105ff.).

Case 3: The Economics of Sound in Film

In the mid-1920s Warner Brothers was a small studio. It obtained from a New York bank, Goldman Sachs, a line of credit to expand its operations and used this money primarily to acquire movie theaters. Warner's biggest rivals were vertically integrated in this way; that is, studios owned chains of theaters and thus had ready markets for their products. Studios that did not own theaters were at a considerable disadvantage in marketing their films.

Warner's also used the money to buy into the new radio industry by acquiring a radio station. This was done because radio was increasingly being used to promote movies. By this acquisition the company gained familiarity with sound-recording techniques.

It was this changing capital infrastructure in the movie industry that constituted the enabling ground for the introduction of sound. Warner, smaller than the five major Hollywood studios, decided after much internal debate to gamble that sound in its newly acquired theaters would give it an edge. The introduction of sound was thus an attempt to improve market share. Acquisition of a chain of theaters alone was not enough to do this; the chain had to attract audiences by offering something different.

It was the potential disruption to their profitable silent film business, reinforced by their experience of failed experiments with sound dating back to the period before 1914, that "caused" Warner's rivals, the Big Five, not to exploit sound. The technology was available, but the commercial desire and need were not.

Warner successfully demonstrated that sound could be popular with audiences by making a series of variety shorts. Fox, another company struggling to catch up with the Big Five, then demonstrated that sound news films could also be popular.

As a result of this challenge, the Big Five agreed to introduce sound film using a common system. The technology they agreed upon, sound on film, was the most complex and expensive, but, because the Big Five had agreed upon it, it was well placed to become the industry standard. It was thus also designed to prevent Fox and Warner, who were using slightly different versions, from continuing to make gains. Warner and Fox fell into line.

The Big Five sound system is the one in use up to the present day.

There are a number of differences between the accounts in Case 3 and Case 2. In Case 3 the development of sound film critically depends on the period before its introduction. In Case 2 this period is seen as a lull, a pause before the inevitable triumph of the technology. In Case 3 it becomes instead a period of struggle of the sort that determines not only the pace at which the technology is introduced, but also its form. It is a struggle waged first within Warner, then between Warner and its rivals, to maximize profits and to have a particular technical solution dominate.

The explanation given in Case 3 is not a substitute for the information in Case 2. It is not that we are writing economic history instead of technological history. Rather, we are attempting to combine the "thinness" of the account in Case 2 by trying to write a "thicker" history, one that describes both. Economic historians, in effect, would add a mass of new information about Warner as a business.

However, economics is a crucial element, but not the end of the matter. Case 3 assumes that the main engines of technical change are the corporation and the market, and that the corporation's motivation will always be to increase the "bottom line." There are two problems with this. One is that technical innovation has not always depended upon the existence of corporations seeking profits. Case 3 is good at explaining sound, but it still does not help us understand why the Arabs, Della Porta, Kircher, and the others did not create the cinema.

Second, much innovation is designed to protect corporations and preserve existing markets, rather than to produce new goods and services for profit. Bell Laboratories is a good case in point. Often considered the most effective industrial innovator in history, Bell Labs was actually established to protect AT&T, the telephone monopoly, from new technologies, specifically radio. By 1878 Bell himself had built a good telephone receiver, but his transmitter was terrible. Edison, by contrast, had patented a superior transmitter, but his receiver was not as effective as Bell's. In this patent standoff, Bell and his business partners hired Emile Berliner to get the infant phone company out of trouble. Berliner, who later built the first device for playing records (the phonograph), did just this. In six weeks' time, he produced a good transmitter without infringing on Edison's patents. Thereafter this pattern of threat averted by patentable innovation was repeated often until, in the radio era, AT&T's research programs were finally organized into Bell Labs.

The result of Bell's research program is that every telecommunications innovation has relied to some extent on Bell patents. This includes radio, television, sound film, fax systems, and space communications. No innovation has occurred in the telecommunications field without Bell both agreeing to it and profiting from it. The expenditures lavished on Bell Labs were not therefore simply to maximize profit. They were designed to suppress the disruptive—to Bell—possibilities of innovation.

Thus we need to go beyond the economic historian's version of cultural determinism to something "thicker" still. Central to my argument is that *all* technological communication innovation can be thought of as a series of events taking place in the realm of technology, but influenced by and reacting to events taking place (a) in the realm of pure science and (b) in society in general. This model has to be rendered even more complex, because society also influences science, which in turn influences the technology. However, for present purposes I will include society's influences on science as part of science itself.

Cultural Determinist Account B

Let us take another case—television—to illustrate this "thicker" cultural determinism.

Case 4: Television

As industrial capitalism, from the end of the eighteenth century onward, began to stimulate scientists' inquiries into more practical and profitable applications, so substances were discovered that responded to light in various ways. The basic chemistry of photography emerged, as Case 1 showed, because it was known that some substances darken when exposed to light. Here we will be concerned with the fact that a group of substances alter their resistance to electric current according to the amount of light that falls on them.

Selenium was noted as such a substance by 1839, but no theoretical understanding of why this occurs was offered and no immediate applications suggested themselves for about 40 years. Then it became possible to theorize a device that would translate an optical image (light waves) into a variable electric current, using selenium as a sensor. This idea was prompted by parallel developments that used the variable resistance of carbon to electricity to construct a device that translated sound waves into a variable electric current—a telephone.

The problem for "seeing by telephone," as it was called, was that it had no practical application except perhaps as a facsimile device. But facsimile devices, which allowed for images to be sent by telegraph, were already in existence and worked better, because with the selenium versions there was no apparent way of creating a hard copy. Nevertheless, a device for turning images into an electrical wave analogue using a selenium sensor was patented in Berlin in 1884. Use of the word *television* as a description of this process dates from 1903.

Various researchers all over the world realized that television could transmit moving pictures. But what use would that be? The live theater had been industrialized in the nineteenth century by the creation of theatrical circuits that brought entertainment to the masses. Film had partially mechanized theater and would eventually largely substitute for it. There was no social need for television at that time.

Nor did any researcher think money could be made by delivering entertainment to the home. The masses, given the long hours they worked and the poor pay they received, had not yet the means to use it. The consumerist economy, about which Kellner writes in Chapter 17 of this volume, was still around the corner.

Thus by the turn of this century television existed as a technical possibility. It was grounded in scientific research but seemingly had no practical application. By 1908 the actual electronic system used to produce TV images had been outlined. The first image was transmitted in 1911 to a cathode ray tube in St. Petersburg, now Leningrad. Major firms were interested, because the technology could potentially be used as an alternative to radio and film, and because of its possible threat to established facsimile systems. Research programs were set up, but they were underfunded. Nevertheless, by 1923 an RCA team, led by Vladimir Zworykin, patented the basic TV camera tube of today.

Further development during the 1920s and 1930s was confused because the major radio industry players were not interested and because other solutions than a purely electronic TV system were also under consideration. These mechanical/electronic systems, which dated back to the 1884 patent, were being explored by a group of researchers largely outside the radio industry.

The confusion persisted because the capital necessary to diffuse TV was then being applied to the movies—by now the talkies—and to radio. The very same firms were interested in all three areas, and judged that TV would be a threat to current business but had interesting future possibilities. Nevertheless, in both Britain and Nazi Germany public television, using a fully electronic system, began in 1936. In Germany it was seen only rarely for theatrical purposes, for the regime continued to focus more on radio, film, and the press to get across its propaganda. In Britain the economic difficulties of the Depression decade prevented its widespread use.

A major factor in the delay in the United States was that RCA so controlled the patents that the Federal Communications Commission was worried about the survival of the other firms that could make TV equipment. It therefore stood in the path of RCA's development of TV from 1936 to 1941. The FCC was trying to prevent the AT&T telephone monopoly from being reproduced by RCA in this area. By 1941 the necessary agreements had been struck, but U.S. entry into the war that year halted further development.

At the end of the war the situation was quite different. The radio industry was looking for a new technology to exploit, having saturated the market with radio sets. In general, the war had greatly expanded the electronic manufacturing capacity of the country, and if that capacity were not to be lost, the public would have to begin to "need" a range of domestic electrical appliances that it had lived without previously. Further, the opportunities for advertising these and other products via TV seemed wide open. The Depression decade seemed to have fixed in policymakers' minds that if consumer demand was flat, no economic growth was possible; and after the many sacrifices of the war, a return to Depression would have been political dynamite.

However, it was not an overnight process. The FCC again suppressed the free development of TV by limiting the number of stations that could be built, even instituting a "freeze" on new construction from 1948 to 1952. There were technical reasons for doing this, including the decision as to which color system was to be used, the power and location of TV masts, and the question of VHF and UHF wavebands. But the reasons were not simply technical.

It is often suggested that TV destroyed Hollywood. The great studios are a thing of the past. But where does most TV production still take place? Hollywood. The FCC freeze also allowed Hollywood to maintain its position as supplier to the new TV industry, for it was during that period that the terms of this trade were worked out.

Case 4 attempts to meld all of the elements used in the other cases—the individual contribution, the triggering effects of increasing knowledge in science, and the application of other technologies, economic forces, political considerations, social policy, and general cultural factors. These various elements can be thought of as relating in the following way.

Imagine the realm of science as a line going from the past to the future:

past ______________________________ future
science

Now imagine a parallel line, which we will call "technology":

____
technology
past ______________________________ future
science

These two lines are connected in the mind of the technologist, the person who has an idea for an application:

____
technology
past ______________/______________ future
science

The idea is triggered by the understanding of science but is expressed "in the metal" as a technological device. History shows the technologist is likely to build a whole series of devices, some slightly, some radically, different from each other. The device we commonly call the "invention" does not differ from the others because it works and they do not. Often the "preinventions" work just as well. What makes the difference is that a point is reached where one of these contrivances is seen to have a real use. After that recognition of the *application* the device is considered an "invention"; before, as a "prototype." I will call the emergence of an application *supervening social necessity.*

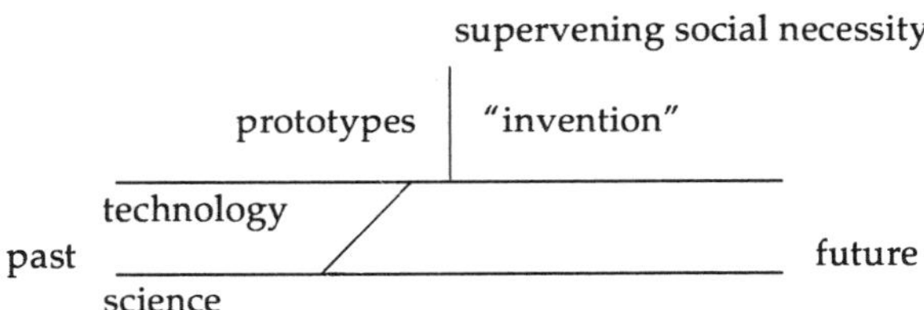

Supervening social necessities are the accelerators pushing the development of media and other technology.

In Case 4 the supervening social necessities that influenced the development of television include the rise of the home, the dominance of the nuclear family, and the political and economic need to maintain full employment after World War II. Because of these, the device finally moved out of the limbo of being an experiment to being a widely diffused consumer product.

Supervening social necessities are at the interface between society and technology. They can exist because of the needs of corporations, as when Kodak introduced Super 8 film because ordinary 8mm film had saturated the market. Or they can become a force because of another technology. Railroad development required instant signaling systems, and so enabled the telegraph to develop. Or, as in Case 4, there can be general social forces that act as supervening social necessities. Telephones emerged in the late 1870s because the modern corporation was emerging and with it the modern office. Not only telephones but elevators, typewriters, and adding machines were all "invented" during this period, although the first typewriter was patented 150 years earlier, the adding machine dated back some 250 years, and the modern hydraulic elevator had been available for over 20 years.

But if there are accelerators, there are also brakes. These work to slow the disruptive impact of new technology. I describe the operation of these brakes as the *"law" of the suppression of radical potential*, using "law" in its standard social science sense to denote a regular and powerful general tendency.

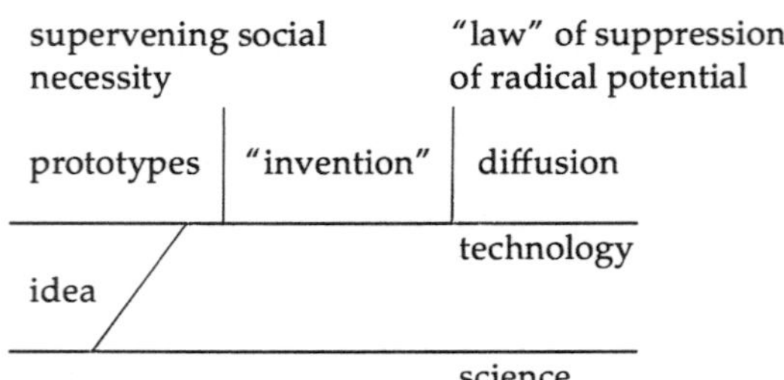

The brakes in Case 4, which caused television to be nearly a century in development, show its radical potential being suppressed, and are thus an instance of this "law." The brakes ensure that a technology's introduction does not disrupt the social or corporate status quo. Thus in the case of TV, the existence of facsimile systems, the rise of radio, the dominance of RCA, and the need not to destroy the film industry all acted to suppress the speed at which the new medium was introduced, to minimize disruption. The result is that all the main film and radio interests of the 1930s are still in business today, and television can be found in practically every house in the nation, sometimes in almost every room.

This concept of supervening social necessities and a "law" of the suppression of radical potential represents one way in which a cultural determinist would seek to understand the nature of change in media technology. I would argue it to be a more effective, more *powerful* way of explaining these matters than any that the technological determinists can produce.

For instance, we can now, using this model, answer our questions about the Arabs and the Chinese. The Arab astronomers who pioneered the camera did so for astronomical reasons, which were their supervening social necessity. Furthermore, their Islamic faith by then forbade the making of realistic images of living beings, so that culturally they would have been prohibited from exploring the camera's image-making potential. That was how the "law" of the suppression of radical potential operated on their research agenda. The Chinese produced these technologies in the context of an imperial system that used them as marks of distinction for the court. The culture made the technologies elite and limited and therefore suppressed their further development. It is these sorts of factors, not scientific knowledge or technological know-how, that condition technological developments.

Effects of Technology on Communication Content

We can now begin to address our second question. All communication modes except face-to-face speech depend on technology. Mass communication requires technologies of a sophisticated kind. The question is whether any such technologies determine what gets communicated.

Answers come in weaker and stronger forms. The weakest form is also the easiest to agree with, namely, that it is obvious that not all technologies can do the same thing. A typewriter cannot convey the same information as a photo. But can we go further?

In his chapter on cultural imperialism, Mohammadi (Chapter 19) reviews a well-known study by Daniel Lerner (1954) that argued, based upon research in the Near East, that when modern media were suddenly injected into a traditional village environment in the Third World, they had the effect of expanding many villagers' horizons and expectations quite dramatically. This is a stronger version of the claim that media technology determines the communication that takes place. Mohammadi notes the highly questionable assumptions also carried with this theory, but we might agree that the theory's basic assertion is plausible, even if we might want to rein it in with further "buts" and "if sos." Similarly, Sreberny-Mohammadi's argument about forms of media in Chapter 2 is an intermediate version of the argument that media technologies must be incorporated into the analysis of media effects. So far there may be room for dispute on individual points, but not on the basic position.

However, the stronger versions are quite frequently to be met with in the generalized pronouncements about media influence in the world today that commentators and editorial writers reproduce from time to time. The most renowned exponent of the strong position was Canadian media theorist Marshall McLuhan, who—even though I am now about to attack his arguments—has the distinction of having first encouraged the general public to think seriously about the impact of media technology on society. He was one of a group of Canadian historians, anthropologists, and literary critics who developed a body of ideas that suggested that in communications, technology was the determining influence. His most frequently quoted aphorism is that "the *medium* is the message" (McLuhan, 1964, chap. 1). He meant by this that media content (the explicit message) explains far less about communication than the communicative impact of the technical medium as such, viewed in terms of its effects on whole societies and cultures over centuries of their development. Actual media output therefore was of comparatively little interest to McLuhan. Here is how he describes the impact of printing press technology:

> Socially, the typographic extension of man brought in nationalism, industrialism, mass markets, and universal literacy and education. For print presented an image of repeatable precision that inspired totally new forms of extending social energies. . . . The same spirit of private enterprise that emboldened authors and artists to cultivate self-expression led other men to create giant corporations, both military and commercial. (p. 157)

The key words here are that "print *presented an image* of repeatable precision that *inspired*." It is a claim not merely that the printing press determined the content of books or pamphlets, but that leading aspects of our communicative culture (literacy, education, self-expression by authors and artists), our institutions (industrialism, giant corporations, mass markets), and our political self-understanding (nationalism) were summoned into being by this media technology. It goes beyond a technical explanation of how media technology developed to provide a media-technological explanation of modern society.

But McLuhan's approach, although grounded in his reading of history, is difficult to sustain on the basis of the historical evidence. All the effects of the printing press he outlines took centuries to manifest themselves. Nationalism, in its modern form, dates from after the American and French revolutions. How then can a device introduced nearly 300 years earlier have "caused" nationalism? Similarly, universal literacy and the rise of great corporations date from the second half of the nineteenth century, some 400 years after the printing press had been introduced into the West.

McLuhan's technological determinism depends upon a very loose idea of historical causality. "Perhaps the most significant of the gifts of typography to man is that of detachment and non-involvement," he asserts (p. 157). This assertion is built upon his prior claim that the printing press gave birth to the individual author and artist. But his position is untenable. In what sense are modern people more communicatively uninvolved and detached than they were in the past, specifically the medieval European past? Certainly our sensitivity to human cruelty toward other people and animals is vastly increased, although we can be just as brutal, and now on an industrial scale, as our ancestors. How could it be shown that before print there were no authors, artists, or ordinary people who thought of themselves as individuals in the way we think of ourselves today?

Furthermore, McLuhan's basic mode of reasoning may have important ideological effects. If technology is an external force, like nature, it cannot easily be subjected to social control. It implies we are helpless in the face of such a force, rather than that we can adapt and use technology for our own freely determined purposes. The chapters on broadcasting in Western Europe (Chapter 8), on Soviet media (Chapter 9), on alternative media (Chapter 12), on the audience (Chapter 10), and on popular music (Chapter 22) are only some of the contributions to this volume that point in quite the opposite direction to McLuhan's position.

One last example: For the technological determinist, the fact that color film does not easily photograph Black skin tones is the result of the technical properties of the dyes used in those films. The cultural determinist will want to explore this matter a little more thoroughly. I would begin with the fact that color film was largely created by White scientists to photograph White skin tones. These products do not simply reproduce nature. Each color film stock the chemists designed contained a different solution to the basic problem of representing—or, better, *re*-presenting—natural colors. Each produces a slightly but noticeably different result.

In doing the creative work involved, the chemists are forced to make choices as to which colors their film will respond to best. For reasons grounded in the fundamental physiology of color perception within the human eye, any one set of choices will result in a film that cannot represent Black skin tones as well as it represents White. Color film stocks in general tend to give Black people a greenish hue. Indeed, the research literature on the development of such stocks reveals that the chemists were primarily interested in getting so-called White (i.e., Caucasian) skin tones as acceptable as possible. They simply did not concern themselves with how Black people would be photographed (Winston, 1985, pp. 195ff.). In this way we see once again that it is the social context, not the technology, that determines the content of communication forms.

Conclusions

At the outset, we noted that the answers given to the question as to how media technologies develop will in turn condition the answers given to the parallel question of what impact technology has on the content of communication. The technological determinist, who wants to see the technology as all-powerful, operating as though in a historical vacuum, will tend to see the influence of media technology on content as overwhelming. The cultural determinist, who wants to place the technology firmly in its social context, will also want to see that context as the primary factor determining both media technology and media content.

Technological determinism tends to present us as being comparatively impotent, as malleable consumers, unthinking and unprotesting, in the face of media technology power. The cultural determinist view, by contrast, is empowering. By drawing attention to the ways in which society constantly conditions technological developments, this view gives us the power to evaluate media technologies and to understand that we are not in the grip of forces totally beyond our control.

These implications also show us why theories in general are important. Theories can help or hinder us in coming to an understanding of the world. Without that understanding we cannot act. Thus theory is critical to action.

Further Questions

(1) Can the pattern described above—of supervening social necessities and of the suppression of radical potential (Winston, 1986)—be applied to the history of any mass medium (e.g., radio)?

(2) How do media technologies affect one another? What has been the impact of the compact disc on recorded music? Has television changed as a result of the VCR?

Part II Media, Power, and Control

In this section, you are introduced to the key linkages between communications media and power, both political and economic. More than any other factor, power determines what happens; it is a central issue for anyone interested in understanding human society, whether through power in relationships in the family, in the classroom, in the economy, or in international relations. However, how power actually works, what the ingredients are in a power relationship, are very hotly debated. Defining power precisely is not straightforward.

However, we can make some basic statements. Governments have power to make laws and policies. The armed forces, the judicial system, and the police have power to enforce laws, just or unjust. Major social movements, such as the U.S. civil rights movement of the 1950s and 1960s or the ecological movement, also have power—the power to press for change. Big corporations have power, too: to hire and fire workers, sometimes thousands at a time; to close plants and move elsewhere; to decide what to produce, and how, and what prices to charge; and power in government, like the muscle of defense contractors in their multibillion-dollar dealings with the Pentagon.

The study of how these centers of power in government and the economy interact with one another is often called *political economy*. One important approach to the critical study of communications focuses on the political economy of the media: their relation to the state and to the domination of the economy by giant corporations. (The *state* as used here does not refer to one of the states of the Union; see the Glossary.)

Some basic questions are as follows: Are the media free and independent to present views, news, and entertainment just as they want? Are they free to be diverse from each other, not just in format, but in the expression of opinion? Are journalists and cultural workers in the media industries empowered to write and screen what they themselves feel they should?

While no one would expect unlimited freedom for every media employee, a basic assumption of many U.S. citizens is that "our" media are indeed free, diverse, and abundantly opinionated. This freedom is guaranteed by the First Amendment to the Constitution, by the absence of government control over media, and by the fact the media are owned by many different firms, not just one business. U.S. media are proudly claimed to be the best in the world, holding up a torch of liberty to less fortunate countries.

Two chapters in this section address the use of media power and control in non-U.S. contexts: Chapter 8, on Western European media, and Chapter 9, on Soviet media. We should note that it is a sign of the rapidly changing times we live in that even the labels we use here for political divisions—Eastern Europe and Western Europe—are coming under challenge at the beginning of the 1990s.

4 Media in the U.S. Political Economy

EDWARD HERMAN

Edward Herman begins this section by arguing—against those who would celebrate the freedom of U.S. media—that there are no fewer than five "filters" through which media content has to pass before it can be presented in mainstream U.S. media. These filters "fix the boundaries of media discourse and the definition of what is newsworthy."

In his emphasis on the fifth filter, "anticommunism," Herman underlines a theme stressed elsewhere in this volume. One of the uncertainties at the outset of the 1990s was how far this powerfully entrenched ideology was capable of survival in the face of sharp changes in the Soviet Union and Eastern Europe in 1989 and 1990. Its continuing strength, however, should not be underestimated.

Herman goes on to argue that the U.S. media are used for propaganda campaigns. This is something that many Americans think is characteristic of Soviet-style media, but not of "ours." The very word propaganda sounds alien to the American way of life—but is it? Is not advertising economic propaganda? (For a discussion of advertising, see Chapter 17.) Herman's essay challenges us to reconsider exactly what we mean by propaganda, and prods us to be very careful before unthinkingly claiming that U.S. media are independent and politically diverse.

Three Alternative Perspectives

It is widely agreed among media analysts that the mass media play an important role in the political economy of the United States, managing the flow of entertainment, news, and political opinion. But there is sharp disagreement on the nature and character of media influence and on the degree to which they are an independent force or merely reflect and transmit the views of other important power interests in the country.

For example, there is a neoconservative school that points its finger at the centralization of the media in a top tier of "East Coast Establishment" newspapers and television networks, and also at the elevated status of

Wall Street, New York

star journalists and TV interviewers—their high salaries, their alleged power, liberal background, and bias. In this view, the very high status of the media stars and their ability to command large audiences gives the "liberal culture" considerable freedom of action in the mass media. Its representatives are therefore said to be able to push views hostile to business and the government's foreign policy, and at odds with the majority attitudes of the working class and "middle America" (Lichter, Rothman, & Lichter, 1986).

Representatives of the liberal/"gatekeeper" and propaganda analyses (discussed below) deny both that the stars can do as they like and that the mass media have any kind of bias against the status quo. They stress three types of evidence against the neoconservative view: the checks built into the way media operate; how unlikely it is that institutions so firmly embedded in the corporate government world could display systematic anti-establishment bias; and the evidence of actual media output. Both consider the neoconservatives to be speaking for just one wing of opinion inside the national power structure, attacking representatives of the liberal wing of elite opinion as though its members were dangerous enemies of the American way of life.

The most prominent analyses in the United States of how the media came to be as they are come from liberal newsroom and "gatekeeper" studies, as exemplified by the works of Leon Sigal (1973), Edward J. Epstein (1973), Gaye Tuchman (1978), Herbert Gans (1979), and Todd

Gitlin (1983). While there are differences among them, they all focus on journalists and media organizations rather than on the system at large or government and major advertisers. These latter are only brought into the picture as sources, pressure groups, regulators, or commercial clients. "Gatekeeper" researchers interview media personnel and watch them working to see how they decide on output, with little emphasis on examining and comparing actual outputs and their results. They stress how practical organizational needs shape news media choices directly or indirectly. Let us explore this view a little further.

News organizations seek sources of authoritative and credible news on a regular basis. These requirements are interconnected: If a highly placed person makes some statement, this is newsworthy in itself. The more authoritative and credible the source, the easier it is to accept statements without checking, and the less expensive is news making. Hence the paradox that even if untrue, such statements may be broadcast without commentary, as "objective" news.

The most highly placed news source is, of course, the government. An oft-cited statistic by Leon Sigal, based on the examination of 2,850 stories in the *New York Times* and *Washington Post*, shows that 46% originated with U.S. federal government officials or agencies and 78% with government officials in general, domestic or foreign. Second only to the government as a news source is business, which also showers the media with a vast array of press releases from individual firms, trade associations, and public relations offshoots.

It is also the case that internal media rules and professional codes help powerful board members or media owners not to have to intervene all the time in editorial decisions. For the most part, journalists reproduce the standard choices of the powerful by a process of self-censorship (see Schulman, Chapter 7, this volume). Those on the lower rungs of the news ladder need to be alert to the news values at the top in order to produce acceptable copy.

Newsroom gatekeeper studies have added a great deal to the understanding of media processes. Nevertheless, they focus too heavily on organizational criteria of choice, often illustrated by struggles within the media as told by media personnel. They suffer from a lack of theory and measurement of actual media output. As a result they tend to exaggerate the potential media professionals have for dissent and "space," and to neglect how the usual news choices reinforce the status quo.

A third way of looking at the workings of the mass media stresses their role as part of the national power structure. This approach, which will be examined below, shares a number of features with gatekeeper analyses, but pulls the threads together into an integrated whole, and gives more attention to the real interplay between the media and their sources, and to the purposes and effects of news choices and propaganda campaigns. I will call it the *propaganda* model.

The Political-Economic Filters of Mass Media Messages

The basic proposition of this chapter is as follows. In a system of concentrated wealth and power, the inequality in command of resources inevitably affects access to, and the performance of, a private media system. Money and power will penetrate the media by direct control or indirect influence, and will filter out the news thought unfit for most of us to consider. We may trace out this filtering process through the following:

(1) the size, concentrated ownership, owner wealth, and profit orientation of the dominant mass media firms
(2) advertising as the primary income source of the mass media
(3) the dependence of the media on information provided by government, business, and "experts" funded and approved by these primary sources
(4) "flak" as a means of disciplining the media
(5) "anticommunism" as a national secular religion and ideological control mechanism

These elements interact with and reinforce one another. They fix the boundaries of media discourse and the definition of what is newsworthy, and they explain the origins and operations of propaganda campaigns.

Size and Ownership of the Mass Media: The First Filter

By 1850, improvements in technology and the drive to communicate with a mass audience that could be "sold" to advertisers had developed newspaper technology to a level that made entry into the business very difficult without substantial financial resources. Thus the first filter—the very large investment needed to own a major newspaper or other mass medium—was already in force over a century ago, and has become increasingly effective since. In 1987 there were some 1,500 daily newspapers, 11,000 magazines, 10,000 radio and 1,500 TV stations, 2,400 book publishers, and 7 movie studios in the United States—some 25,000 media entities in all. But most of the news dispensers among this set were small and depended on the national media and wire services for all but very local news. Many more were part of multimedia chains.

In 1983, Ben Bagdikian reported that by the beginning of the 1980s most U.S. mass media—newspapers, magazines, radio, television, books, and movies—were controlled by 50 corporations (pp. 4-5). Four years later, in his 1987 revision of *The Media Monopoly*, Bagdikian observed that 29 corporations now accounted for the same majority fraction as the 50 largest had controlled shortly before (p. xvi). These giants are also diversified into other fields, including insurance, banking, advertising, frozen foods, tobacco, weapons production, and nuclear energy.

The dominant media companies are large profit-seeking corporations, owned and controlled by very wealthy boards and individuals. Many are run completely as money-making concerns, and for the others as well there are powerful pressures from stockholders, directors, and bankers to focus on the bottom line. These pressures intensified over the 1980s as media stocks became stock market favorites and actual or prospective owners of media properties were able to generate great wealth from increased audience size and advertising revenues (e.g., Rupert Murdoch, Time-Warner, and many others). This encouraged the entry of speculators and takeovers, and increased the pressure and temptation to focus more intensively on profitability.

These trends accelerated when the rules were loosened limiting media monopolies, cross-ownership of media in the same area of the country, the number of TV and radio stations the networks could own, and media control by nonmedia companies (e.g., ABC, CBS, NBC). The Federal Communications Commission also abandoned many of its restrictions—which were not very strict anyway—on broadcast commercials, TV violence, and the "Fairness Doctrine" (which supported equal broadcasting time for opposing views), opening the door to purely money-making dictates over the use of the airwaves. (See Chapter 14, this volume.)

Those who control the media giants come into close relation with the corporate community through joint membership on boards of directors and business relations with commercial and investment bankers. These are their sources of credit, who help with banking services and advise both on opportunities to buy media firms and on takeover threats from other firms. Banks and similar "institutional" investors are also large owners of media stock. These holdings, individually and collectively, do not convey control on a daily basis, but if managers fail to pursue actions that favor shareholder returns, institutional investors will be inclined to sell the stock (depressing its price) or to listen sympathetically to outsiders contemplating takeovers. These investors constitute a force that helps to integrate media companies into market strategies and away from responsibility to the democratic process.

The large media companies have also diversified beyond the media field, and nonmedia companies have established a strong presence in the mass media. The most important cases of the latter are GE (General Electric) owning RCA (Radio Corporation of America), which owns the NBC network, and Westinghouse, which owns major TV broadcasting stations, a cable network, and a radio station network. GE and Westinghouse are both huge, diversified, multinational companies heavily involved in the controversial areas of weapons production and nuclear power.

Another structural relationship of importance is the media companies' dependence on and ties with government. Apart from the issues raised in Chapters 5, 6, and 14 of this book, the major media also depend on the government for more general policy support. All business firms are interested in taxes, interest rates, labor policies, and the level of enforcement of the antitrust (antibusiness monopoly) laws. Thus during the 1980s the systematic reduction of business taxes, weakening of labor unions, and relaxation of antitrust law enforcement benefited media corporations as well as other members of the business community. GE and Westinghouse depend on the government to subsidize their expensive research and development of nuclear power and defense. The *Reader's Digest, Time, Newsweek,* and movie and TV syndication sellers also depend on diplomatic support for their rights to penetrate foreign cultures with U.S. commercial and cultural messages. The media giants, advertising agencies, and great multinational corporations have a close interest in a favorable climate of investment in the Third World, and their relationships with the government in these policies are intimate.

The Advertising License to Do Business: The Second Filter

Newspapers obtain about 75% of their revenues from advertisers, general-circulation magazines about 50%, and broadcasters almost 100%. Before advertising became prominent, the price of a newspaper had to cover the costs of doing business. With the growth of advertising, papers that attracted ads could sell well below production costs. Papers without advertising faced a serious dilemma: to raise their prices or to have less surplus to invest in making the paper more salable (features, attractive format, promotion). An advertising-based media system will tend to drive out of existence or into marginality the media companies that depend on selling price alone. With advertising, the free market does not yield a neutral system in which the consumers decide which media will suit them best. The *advertisers'* choices heavily influence media prosperity—and survival (Barnouw, 1978).

Since the introduction of press advertising, working-class and radical papers have constantly been at a serious disadvantage, as their readers have tended to be of modest means, a factor that has always reduced advertiser interest in media they patronized. Working-class and radical media also suffer from more overt political discrimination by advertisers, as many firms refuse to patronize media they perceive as damaging to their interests.

Advertisers also select among specific broadcasts on the basis of criteria that are culturally and politically conservative. Advertisers on national television are for the most part very large corporations, such as Philip Morris, Procter & Gamble, General Motors, Sears, and RJR Nabisco. These advertisers will rarely sponsor programs that seriously criticize sensitive corporate activities, such as ecological degradation, the workings of the military-industrial complex, or corporate support of and benefits from Third World tyrannies. As advertising spots increase in price, the broadcasters lose even more money on programs if the advertisers shun them. For instance, ABC Television's once-in-a-blue-moon feature on the impact of nuclear war on the United States, *The Day After* (1983), had almost all advertisers canceling their options on spots during or around the program. So as the broadcasters come under (a) more pressure to behave as profit makers and (b) less pressure from the FCC to operate a public service, there is a strong tendency for them to eliminate programming that has significant public affairs content.

Sourcing Mass Media News: The Third Filter

The mass media are drawn into an intimate relationship with the power structure, national and local, because of cost factors and mutual interests. Cost savings dictate that the media concentrate their reporters where significant news often occurs, where important rumors and leaks abound, and where regular press conferences are held. The White House, Pentagon, and State Department in Washington, D.C., and, on a local basis, city hall and the police department, are the subject of regular news "beats" for reporters. Business corporations and trade groups are also regular suppliers of stories deemed newsworthy. These organizations turn out a large volume of material that meets the demands of news organizations for reliable, scheduled input.

Government and corporate sources also have the credibility associated with their status. Partly to maintain the image of objectivity, but also to protect themselves from criticisms of bias and the increasingly serious threat of libel suits, the media need news that can be portrayed as accurate. Information from sources that may be presumed credible also reduces investigative expense, whereas material from sources that are not seemingly credible, or that will elicit criticism and threats, requires careful and costly checking. Thus when President Reagan asserted in March 1986 that the Nicaraguan government was heavily involved in drug smuggling, this was immediately published without checking. (It was a false statement.)

On the other hand, a steady stream of claims by imprisoned drug traders and even by U.S. intelligence and Drug Enforcement Administration personnel that the U.S.-backed Nicaraguan Contras were smuggling drugs into the United States, with official connivance (Cockburn, 1988), was treated much more cautiously, was held to require stringent checking, and got little media coverage (even though, in this case, the claims were true).

The information operations of the powerful government and corporate bureaucracies that constitute primary news sources are vast and skillful. They have special and unequal access to the media. Because they supply news, have continuous contact with the reporter on the beat, and can freeze reporters out of news stories if they are uncooperative, the powerful can use personal relationships, threats, and rewards to influence and coerce media personnel. Perhaps more important, powerful sources regularly take advantage of reporters' routines and need for copy to "manage" the media, to manipulate them into following the agenda of one vector or another in the power structure. Part of this management process consists of showering the media with stories that serve to reinforce a particular framework by which to interpret events.

The relation between power and sourcing extends beyond providing continuing "news" to molding the supply of "experts." Official sources could be threatened by highly respectable alternative sources that offered dissident views with obvious knowledge. Energetic attempts are made to reduce this problem by "co-opting the experts" (that is, finding like-minded specialists, paying them as consultants, funding their research, and organizing think tanks that will hire them and help to publish their findings.) During the 1970s and early 1980s a string of institutions was created and old ones were reactivated in order to propagandize the corporate viewpoint. Among the most important of these institutions were the Heritage Foundation, the American Enterprise Institute, and the Georgetown Center for Strategic and International Studies. Many hundreds of intellectuals were brought to these institutions, and their work was funded and disseminated to the media in a sophisticated program that can reasonably be defined as a propaganda effort.

Flak and the Enforcers: The Fourth Filter

Flak here refers to negative responses to media statements or programs. It may take the form of letters to the media, telegrams, phone calls, petitions, lawsuits, speeches and bills before Congress, or other modes of complaint, threat, and punitive action. It may be organized centrally or locally, or it may consist of the entirely independent actions of individuals. For example, individuals may call in or write to protest the showing of a movie they regard as sacrilegious or subversive; or the gun lobby may mobilize its members to complain about a program pointing up the hazards of private gun ownership.

If flak is produced on a large scale, it can be both uncomfortable and costly to the media. Positions have to be defended within the organization and without, sometimes before legislatures and possibly even in court. Advertisers may withdraw patronage. TV advertising is mainly of consumer goods that are readily subject to organized boycott. During the McCarthy years in the early 1950s (see below and Chapter 12, on alternative media), many advertisers and broadcasters were coerced into silence and blacklisting of employees by organized and determined Red hunters' threats to organize consumer boycotts. Advertisers are still concerned about possibly offending constituencies that might produce flak, and demand for "suitable" programming is a continuing feature of the media environment.

The ability to produce flak, especially costly and threatening flak, is related to power. The 1967 CBS documentary *The Selling of the Pentagon*, which focused on armed services and military contractor propaganda designed to scare the public into believing that more weapons are always needed, aroused the ire of very substantial interests, and the negative feedback was great, even including congressional hearings.

Serious flak increased in close parallel with business's increased resentment of media criticism of its activities, and the corporate offensive of the 1970s and 1980s. Along with its other political investments of those years, the corporate community sponsored the growth of institutions like the American Legal Foundation, Capital Legal Foundation, Accuracy in Media (AIM), the Center for Media and Public Affairs, and the Media Institute. These may be regarded as institutions organized for the specific purpose of producing flak. The function of AIM, for example, is to harass the media and put pressure on them to follow the corporate agenda and a hard-line rightist foreign policy. It conditions the media to expect trouble and cost increases for violating conservative standards.

Anticommunism as a Control Mechanism: The Fifth Filter

The final filter is the ideology of anticommunism. The threat of social rather than business ownership has always been the specter haunting property owners, as it threatens the very root of their class position and superior status. The Soviet (1917), Chinese (1949), and Cuban (1959) revolutions were all traumas to U.S. elites. The ongoing conflicts and well-publicized abuses of communist states have contributed to elevating opposition to communism to a first principle of U.S. ideology and politics. This ideology helps mobilize the populace against an enemy, and because the concept of "communism" is fuzzy, it can be used against anybody advocating policies threatening property interests or supportive of accommodation with communist states, or any kind of radicalism. Being labeled "communist" has almost always unnerved the U.S. Left and labor movement and served to slow down radical opposition movements.

Liberals, often accused of being procommunist or insufficiently anti-communist, are kept continually on the defensive in a nation where anticommunism is like a dominant unifying religion. This generally causes liberals to behave very much like conservatives. In the cases of the U.S. subversion of Guatemala, 1947-54, and the military attacks on Nicaragua, 1981-87, allegations of communist links and a communist threat caused many liberals to support CIA intervention, while others lapsed into silence, paralyzed by fear of being tarred with charges of disloyalty to the national religion. In the 1950s and 1960s, the FBI under J. Edgar Hoover defined support for African-American civil rights as "communist," and even though this did not stop the movement, almost all felt compelled to take the charge seriously.

The anticommunist control mechanism penetrates the system to exercise a profound influence on the mass media. In normal times as well as in periods of "Red scares" (see below), issues tend to be framed in terms of a two-sided world of communist and anticommunist powers, with gains and losses allocated to one side or the other, and rooting for "our side" considered entirely legitimate news practice.

Propaganda Campaigns and the Mass Media

The five filters discussed above narrow the range of news that passes through the gates, and even more sharply limit what can become "big news," that is, sustained news campaigns rather than occasional dissident reports ("little news"). By definition, news from leading establishment sources meets one major filter requirement and is readily used by the mass media. Dissident voices, opposition to U.S. policies from poorly funded individuals and groups, domestic and foreign, are at a disadvantage as credible sources. They do not seem "serious" in terms of the way reality is perceived by the gatekeepers or other powerful parties who influence the filtering process.

The mass media and government can therefore make an event "newsworthy" merely by giving it their sustained attention. By the same token, they can make another perfectly newsworthy event a nonhappening for the bulk of the population. The government and mass media can also make a story that serves their needs into a major propaganda campaign.

Major propaganda campaigns are not spontaneous. They tend to be well timed to provide the ideological mobilization sought by important domestic power groups. The Red scare of 1919-1920 took place at a time when labor organization was very active across the country, and when big business was alarmed at the challenge to its power in the factories. Many thousands of radicals of all sorts of views were arrested, violently hauled from their homes; many were imprisoned, and a number were deported (Kennedy, 1980, pp. 278-279, 288-292). It was claimed that they were plotting to overthrow the government.

A second example of a propaganda campaign is that of Senator Joseph McCarthy and the Red scare associated with his name ("McCarthyism") in the late 1940s and early 1950s (Caute, 1978). Once again, the nation was said to be under dire threat of collapse from communist subversion, including 205 supposed Soviet agents in the State Department. This campaign served well to weaken the New Deal reform coalition that had formed under the Roosevelt presidency in 1933-1945, and replaced it with a Cold War/arms race/business/labor control policy alignment.

A third example is the alleged Bulgarian/KGB involvement in the 1981 shooting of Pope John Paul II. This factually flimsy claim was transformed into a major international propaganda campaign (Herman & Brodhead, 1986). It was a period of heightened tension between the Soviet Union and the United States—and its allies, including Italy—over the placement of advanced nuclear missiles in Western Europe. Antinuclear movements were becoming extremely active in both Western Europe and the United States, and the "news" of a sinister, callous plot to assassinate the most important leader of world Christendom was a potent way to revivify the communist specter.

News stories in this framework are selected on a highly politicized basis. In 1984, a respected and militant supporter of Polish Solidarity, Father Popieluszko, was kidnapped in Warsaw, beaten, and murdered by a cell of the Polish secret police. This ugly event was highlighted in U.S. media: The *New York Times* ran 78 articles and 3 editorials; *Time* and *Newsweek*, combined, ran 16 articles; and CBS News broadcast 46 news items.

Yet the murders, sometimes even more hideous, of 100 clergy, nuns, and other religious workers by agents of U.S. client regimes in Latin America over the period 1964-80 attracted far less media coverage. Only 57 *New York Times* articles (no editorials), 10 *Time* and *Newsweek* articles, and 37

CBS News items were allocated to their fates, indicating that "unworthy" victims in a friendly state were valued at less than one-hundredth of "worthy" victims in a communist state, as measured by media attention.

These split standards have great ideological significance. Continued emphasis on the real and alleged misdeeds of the enemy serves to convince people to feel seriously threatened by stop-at-nothing enemies and so of the need for new weapons, even though their research and development have usually been under way for years already. The playing down and rationalization of "own side" repression in friendly client states, such as Indonesia, Zaire, and Guatemala allow us in the United States to hold on to our self-image as citizens of a beneficent and humane government, in contrast with the image of enemy countries, whose governments assassinate leaders and repress democratic movements.

The elite and the mass media, however, are not a solid monolith on all issues. Where the powerful are in disagreement with each other, the agents of power will reflect a certain diversity of tactical judgments on how to attain their shared overall aims. They will still exclude views and facts that challenge the aims.

Even when there is no internal elite dissent, there is still some slippage in the mass media, and information that tends to undermine the official line can be found, though rarely on the front page. This is one of the strengths of the U.S. system. The volume of inconvenient facts can expand, as it did during the Vietnam War in the period from 1963 to 1975, in response to the growth of a critical constituency. Even in this exceptional case, however, it was very rare for news and comment to find its way into the mass media unless it was inside the framework of established dogma (postulating benevolent U.S. aims, the United States responding to communist aggression and terror).

Apologists for U.S. policy in Southeast Asia at that time still point to "communist atrocities," periodic "pessimism" of media pundits over the war's winnability, and the debates over tactics as showing that the media were "adversarial" and even "lost" the war (Braestrup, 1977). The seeming "reasonableness" of the media process, with inconvenient facts allowed sparingly and within the official framework of assumptions, with fundamental dissent excluded altogether from "big news," and with small-scale alternative media harassed but not wiped out altogether, makes for a propaganda system far more credible and effective in putting over a patriotic agenda than one with official censorship.

Conclusions

The political economy of the U.S. mass media is dominated by communication gatekeepers who are not media professionals so much as large profit-making organizations with close ties to government and business. This network of the powerful provides news and entertainment filtered to meet elite demands and to avoid offending materials. The filtering process is imperfect, however. While agreeing on basic premises, the elite frequently disagree on tactics, and beyond this, normal news-making processes do not screen out all inconvenient facts and stories. It is extremely rare, however, for such dissonant items to graduate to act as a *framework* that questions generally accepted principles, or to be part of "big news." This presentation of dissident themes only episodically, within official frameworks, and implemented by free-market forces without state censorship enhances the credibility of the dominant ideology and perspectives.

Further Questions

(1) Who owns the controlling interest of the top U.S., British, French, Canadian, and Mexican media companies (TV networks, newspaper chains, national newsmagazines, large metropolitan dailies)? Are they individuals or corporations? What are their business, government, and social connections?

(2) How can people who legally own a magazine or network control or influence its content if they do not manage it on a day-to-day basis and if interference in news decisions is considered bad practice? Can they influence the work of a reporter on their staff who covers Central America or South Africa or the Middle East? Or who covers poverty in the United States? Or the Pentagon?

(3) Were the media adversarial during the Vietnam War? Study this question taking account of different periods of the war and the differences between criticisms of tactics and basic assumptions. Compare Peter Braestrup (1977) with Daniel Hallin (1986) and Herman and Chomsky (1988, chap. 5, Appendix 3). Were the media adversarial during the 1989 Panama invasion where, it appears, several thousand people died? (See NACLA, *Report on the Americas*, forthcoming.)

5 Mass Media and the U.S. Presidency

CEDRIC J. ROBINSON

In this chapter, Cedric Robinson investigates a key dimension of the media and political power in the United States, namely, how media relate to the presidency, the nation's highest political office. Ever since Franklin Roosevelt used radio in the 1930s to broadcast his famous "fireside chats" to the nation, the media and the presidency have been intimately connected. From 1960 on, the relationship became more and more problematic. In that year, the narrow presidential victory of Kennedy over then Vice President Nixon was widely attributed to Kennedy's superior television image, for Nixon had done better when his message was carried by radio. When Nixon finally attained the White House in 1968, he did so after the first of the minutely crafted media campaigns that seem now to be taken as inevitable in a presidential election.

Robinson discusses some of the key moments in the media-presidency relationship since, but takes the trouble to place this recent history in the longer perspective of the development of the U.S. presidency from the turn of the century. By doing this, he is able to direct our attention away from what might be called "petty" explanations of the cautious respect with which the media normally handle presidents—that is, in terms of how telegenic presidents are, or how successfully they get along with journalists—and focuses rather on both media and presidency as institutions of the same power structure.

It is important that you realize why Robinson and some of the other contributors to this volume focus so closely and critically on the period 1980-88, the years of the Reagan administration. There are two issues at stake here. One is that the study of media cannot be undertaken seriously without recognizing that their role can change from time to time, sometimes quite sharply. The Reagan years were one such period, although, as Robinson points out, the change did not emerge out of the blue. Media are not unchanging institutions about which one can learn permanently true "facts."

The second issue is that the contributors are not motivated in their critiques by loyalties to the Republican party's rival party. Their critiques are based on their independent analysis of the 1980s as a turning point for U.S. media, one that led in some very disquieting directions.

The presidency is the single most important subject reported by U.S. news media. The White House, together with a select group of agencies of the federal government, is routinely the focus of two-thirds of the news reported on the nightly news programs of the three major television networks, and news of Washington occupies 50% of airtime (Hertsgaard, 1988, p. 6). It is also the case that officials of the U.S. government serve as the primary sources for a third of the news stories appearing on the front pages of America's leading newspapers (Gans, 1979, pp. 15ff.). Not surprisingly, then, network news, newsmagazines, and newspapers are rather uniform in both story content and news emphasis (Brown, Bybee, Wearden, & Straughan, 1987; Foote & Steele, 1986; Riffe, Ellis, Rogers, Van Ommeren, & Woodman, 1986). It is just such news that constitutes an important part of the information environment for public opinion.

The dominance of the presidency prompts a number of questions about the relationship between the White House and news production. The most important is whether media coverage of the executive branch arises out of independent journalistic inquiry or from government manipulation of news production. In short, are the media functioning as free and, when need be, critical instruments of democratic debate, or are they largely means of official manipulation of public opinion?

Traditionally the first, "adversarial," interpretation of the media was upheld by professors of journalism as well as by professional journalists themselves. But more recently, critics—journalists and researchers—have taken more seriously the second, "hegemonic," view (Altschull, 1986; Halberstam, 1979; Parenti, 1986). To understand these alternative perspectives we should treat them not just as conflicting points on a continuum of debate but also as the products of particular historical and political events. Let us begin by looking at that background, which is essential if we are to understand the real nature of the U.S. presidency this century, rather than a rosy myth of the presidency. Once we understand the presidency itself better, we can assess its relation to the media more clearly.

"The American Century" and the Presidency

The strong presidency so frequently evoked by the Reagan and Bush administrations has its roots not in any vague tradition of U.S. leadership of the free and democratic nations, but in the colonies seized by the American state from the end of the nineteenth century (Drinnon, 1980; Williams, 1980, pp. 136ff.). Under the presidential leadership of McKinley, Roosevelt, Taft, and Wilson, the U.S. undertook military adventures and interventions with regularity between 1898 and 1920. These episodes are not generally focused on in high school or college classes on U.S. history, but that they occurred is not in dispute. Their frequency is astonishing, as the following listing makes clear:

> In 1898, the U.S. sent troops to Nicaragua and China; in 1899, to Nicaragua, Samoa, and the Philippines; in 1900, again to China; in 1901, to Colombia; in 1902, again to Colombia; in 1903, to Honduras, the Dominican Republic, Panama (where they remained from 1903 to 1914), and Syria (now Lebanon); in 1904, to Korea and Morocco; in 1906, to Cuba (until 1909); in 1907, to Honduras; in 1910, to Nicaragua; in 1911, to Honduras and China; in 1912, to Honduras, Panama, Cuba, China, Turkey, and Nicaragua (1912-25); in 1913, to Mexico; in 1914, to Haiti, the Dominican Republic, and Mexico (1914-17); in 1915, to Haiti (occupied until 1934); in 1916, to the Dominican Republic (until 1924); in 1917, to Cuba (until 1933); in 1918, to Mexico and the Soviet Union; and in 1919, to Honduras.

These were not isolated episodes, but a continuous part of presidential decision making in support of the global quest of U.S. business for commerce and empire. To understand the U.S. presidency, knowledge of these actions is central.

This list does not cover all such actions. In 1898, spurred on by the hysterical nationalism of the yellow press led by William Randolph Hearst and Joseph Pulitzer, the Spanish-American War secured American control over sugar-producing Cuba and Puerto Rico, the labor-rich Philippines, and strategically located Guam. Hawaii was seized at the same time. This bounty would prove of great benefit to American businesses, not the least of which were the varied interests of National City Bank (a Rockefeller concern).

In 1900, this war—and its companion press—also produced the first imperial president, Theodore Roosevelt. Two years earlier it had been Roosevelt, as assistant secretary of the Navy, who had initiated the Philippines war by ordering the Pacific Squadron to Manila. Later, during Roosevelt's administration, in anticipation of the construction of the Panama Canal, a secessionist rebellion in what was then a northern province of Colombia was manufactured by the United States (four months before the fact the exact date for the revolution was published in the *New York World*—Pulitzer's paper). It was thus that Colombia lost a valuable part of its territory and the country of Panama was created.[1]

The press scarcely missed a beat in supplying its readers with supposed justifications for these invasions. In domestic newspapers, nationalist resistance on the part of Filipinos, Haitians, Cubans, and others was characterized as savagery and banditry; American military repression of them, however, was costumed as "pacification." The seizure of their resources by American corporations and banks was claimed as amends for native misdeeds (i.e., rebellion) or as acceptable because the natives were not exploiting them commercially themselves. But General Smedley Darlington Butler, the Marine commander of many of these missions, put the objective more starkly:

> I spent most of my time being a high-class muscle man for Big Business, for Wall Street and for the bankers. . . . Thus I helped make Haiti and Cuba a decent place for the National City Bank to collect revenues in. . . . I helped purify Nicaragua for the international banking house of Brown Brothers in 1909-1912. I brought light to the Dominican Republic for American sugar interests in 1916. I helped make Honduras "right" for American fruit companies in 1903. (cited in Pearce, 1982, p. 20)

As a consequence of similar observations, General Butler, for two whole decades one of the most celebrated military figures in the press, suddenly became a "nonperson" to American journalism and practically vanished from the press. The major media were rather consistent in their support of these foreign policies.

The presidency also developed in relation to domestic events in the period 1890-1920 (Zinn, 1980, chaps. 12-15), a period of mammoth industrial expansion fueled by vast labor immigration. At home, presidents, business, and the mainstream press assigned clear priority to commercial interests over social needs, a policy that was soon contested by the public. Large sectors of the American people—Blacks, women, socialists, labor, and the new immigrants—pressed for democratic reforms: desegregation and civil rights, votes for women, trade union rights, and anti-imperialism. An adversarial press was largely confined to alternative media such as magazines, foreign-language newspapers, and books (Jack London, Theodore Dreiser, Frank Norris, Upton Sinclair, Sinclair Lewis, F. Scott Fitzgerald, John Steinbeck, and Ernest Hemingway), all with limited readership.

During the 1920s and 1930s this growing political and economic instability escalated. The era was marked by bitter and often violent labor strikes, political marches, race riots and other civil disorders, lynchings of Blacks and immigrants, government corruption scandals, and, not least, the Great Depression. The growing disparities of income between the rich and the poor—between 1922 and 1929, one-tenth of 1% of the families at the top received as much income as 42% of the families in the nation (Zinn, 1980, p. 373)—gave new urgency to democratic demands.

Nevertheless, ordinary Americans had diminishing impact on the presidency and the selection of candidates for that office. The political system did not adapt to be more responsive. Instead, factions among the wealthy fought over control of the presidency and of the two major political parties, often making elections a mockery of democratic expression. Power continued to gravitate toward the center.

On the domestic front, the mainstream American press achieved an unenviable record of news distortion and the suppression of information about business and political elites. Examples are many. News of the Teapot Dome scandal (fraudulent leasing of naval oil reserves) was suppressed for nearly two years. In 1925, under pressure from none other than newspaper *publishers*, the Congress passed legislation forbidding the publication of income tax figures. In the 1920s the gathering Depression and bank instability went unreported until the Great Crash of 1929. The magnitude of unemployment, layoffs, and farm and housing evictions was concealed until after the height of the Depression. In 1933, the *press* denounced the findings of the Senate Banking and Currency Committee that the J. P. Morgan banking interests "had given away valuable stock options to political, financial, journalistic and social leaders." In 1934, the *press* denounced the charges by General Butler that Morgan agents had conspired to organize a fascistic coup against President Franklin Roosevelt (Archer, 1973).

More than any other factor, World War II pulled the nation out of the Depression through massive industrial rearmament under government financing. The United States became the dominant economic and military power in the capitalist world-system. With this global prominence came policy responsibilities and obligations, political resources and opportunities that further contributed to centralizing the federal power structure away from Congress to the executive branch (the White House, the State Department, the Justice Department, the Defense Department, and so on). As defending the "national interest" had come to be defined as maintaining U.S. imperial power, so checks on executive action shrank in both foreign and domestic spheres. By the time of Eisenhower's presidency in the early 1950s, whole areas of national policy—nuclear policy (see Chapter 6, this volume), the CIA overthrow of the Iranian government (1953) and the Guatemalan government (1954)—were outside the sphere of public debate or beyond congressional scrutiny and accountability.

In other words, in the eighteenth and nineteenth centuries the U.S. presidency enjoyed an international image as a progressive institution, as a democratic alternative to hereditary monarchy and despotic rule. As the twentieth century gathered momentum, that tradition of the presidency was actually eroding rapidly under the pressures of U.S. development as a world power. The mainstream media were much more likely to be approving than critical of this world role. In practice, from very early on, this meant supporting presidential actions, especially overseas, and not being "adversarial" in foreign policy. Enthusiasm for "bipartisan" foreign policy in Congress underpinned this concentration of power.

The most frequent public defense of this centralization of decision making has been managerial: The Constitution's separation of powers besets the presidency with "structural rigidities" or, as the Committee on the Constitutional System complained in 1988, it produces "confrontation, indecision and deadlock" (Moore, 1988, pp. 56-57). In other words, the Constitution's "checks and balances" are a practical nuisance in the eyes of supporters of the contemporary presidency.

In considering the relation of the media to the presidency, therefore, this twentieth-century accumulation of power in the executive branch and the reasons for it must all be kept firmly in mind. To assess how adversarial the media are means to judge their performance not in the abstract but in relation to this centralization and its basic causes. Are the media a part of this process, or do they set themselves apart from it? And if the latter, how and how much?

Commercial Modes of News Production

The commercial development of mass communications is itself an important source of change in U.S. politics. So too is the continuing malign influence of Cold War perspectives in restricting news judgments (see Chapter 4, this volume).

Presidents, as the ideological symbols of American power, the personification of the government, and the center of bureaucratic activity, have been the most natural focal point for journalists (Paletz & Entman, 1981, pp. 55ff.). Television has had the greatest influence of all media on the power of the presidency. As David Halberstam (1979) has observed, "The rising power of communications . . . loaded the institutional balance vastly toward the executive branch" (p. 693). It was precisely this supportive relationship between the presidency and mass media that was in evidence during much of the Vietnam War and the more recent American interventions in Grenada, Nicaragua, and the Middle East (Herman & Chomsky, 1988; Hertsgaard, 1988).

Television journalism has also contributed to the impoverishment of public debate. Television, with its 40-second scraps of news and its dependency on visual images, tends to diminish informative or investigative journalism to illustrated bite-size fast food. Thus in national elections catchy campaign slogans, percentage wobbles in opinion polls, and the minutely crafted images of candidates have displaced democracy, which requires an interrogation of party philosophy, in-depth discussions of policy priorities, and analyses of the social impact of economic policies. The government effort devoted to the manipulation of public opinion and information has supplanted the democratic principle of an educated citizenry.

Furthermore, as Herman (Chapter 4) and Demac and Downing (Chapter 6) note, from the late 1940s onward the Cold War and McCarthyism established new limits, still rather effective to this day, on mainstream media debate—ideological limits. The elimination at that time from the American political spectrum of every view to the left of center in the name of "anticommunism" (see Chapter 4) produced a major shift in the American political vocabulary: Centrists became liberals, conservatives became moderates, reactionaries became conservatives—and the Left became voiceless radicals (Jezer, 1982). This displacement of the center of political debate toward the conservative end of the spectrum still largely holds sway.

These ideological restrictions provided the conditions for a new relationship between the news media and the government and other official sources of news. According to one theory of news, "government and other 'official' news sources [became] co-participants with the media in the creation of standard news themes" (Bennett, Gressett, & Haltom, 1985, pp. 50-51). This raised major problems for the standard professional claim of journalists, that they report the news objectively. Normally they interpret this as giving balanced space to different perspectives. In response to the government-endorsed Cold War ideology, however, most mainstream media defined left-of-center perspectives—for example, in favor of civil rights and labor union freedoms, against invasions of other countries—as communist, hostile to freedom, disloyal to one's fellow citizens, and at best softheaded. Yet unless the government is also to be defined as objective, then media professionals certainly cannot pretend to be objective if they allow the government to make their news judgments for them. Bennett et al. (1985) maintain:

> In place of an operational definition of objectivity, mass media journalism . . . substituted the popular myth that the pronouncements of government officials and institutional elites somehow represent the reality in which the majority of people live. (pp. 50-51)

Yet for a century and more, effective challenges have been mounted and important criticisms voiced about the everyday reality of this majority, mostly from one quarter: the left of center. In understanding the media and the presidency, then, we have to extend our historical vision. We need to acknowledge the long-term impact of omitting these perspectives from the mainstream media's list of views and policy options to be taken seriously. We also need to recognize the role of centralized power and the presidency in encouraging the mass communication of Cold War ideology over so many decades, and thus in encouraging this narrowing of acceptable political debate.

It is only from the vantage point of this history that we can begin to understand two of the crucial episodes in the more recent history of media coverage of the presidency, namely, the attempts by Presidents Johnson and Nixon to pursue the Southeast Asian war up to 1975 without the congressional oversight the Constitution requires, and the Watergate scandal that ultimately forced President Nixon to resign from office two years into his second term.

The Vietnam War, Watergate, and the Media

Though the news media are widely credited (or blamed) for ending American involvement in Vietnam, a more accurate construction would place greater emphasis on their role in encouraging public support for the war. For six years, from 1962 to 1967, with few exceptions the news media portrayed the war in terms faithful to "the framework of interpretation formulated by the state authorities" (Herman & Chomsky, 1988, p. 200). In painstaking detail, Hersh (1983), Halberstam (1979), Hallin (1989), and Herman and Chomsky (1988) have demolished the farcical claim of an independent American press during the Vietnam War. Through its duration, those who opposed the war remained "at the bottom of the media's hierarchy of legitimate political actors" (Hallin, 1989, p. 192). Thus, even in the final years of American military involvement, the press followed the Nixon administration into the empty slogans (Herman & Chomsky, 1988, pp. 193-206) of "pacification" (creating hamlets secure from guerrilla presence), "Vietnamization" (turning the fighting over to the unenthusiastic South Vietnamese army), and "peace with honor" (no humiliation for the United States).

The Watergate scandal had been the final and traumatic turning point for the Nixon administration. Watergate took its name from an apartment complex in Washington, D.C., where the Democratic party had its national head office. During the period leading up to the 1972 presidential election, burglars were caught trying to raid the office. After a considerable period of media silence, it gradually began to trickle out in some media that the burglars had been sent by leading officials in the Nixon presidential cabinet. After sustained denials, some officials confessed their involvement, and the order was traced directly to President Nixon. Faced with an impeachment vote, he resigned in 1974. Most mainstream media were quiet on the subject until the final stages of the scandal. Rooted in Nixon's and Henry Kissinger's conduct of their Vietnam policy, the program of illegal wiretapping and domestic spying had led to the destruction of Nixon's presidency:

> It had come full circle. Nixon and Kissinger had designed a policy for Southeast Asia of secret threats and secret military activities. To protect those secrets they had resorted to illegalities. And then, years later, those illegalities had become a public issue just at a time when the administration was finally on the verge of achieving a stalemate in Vietnam. (Hersh, 1983, p. 637)

The trauma of Watergate and its parent, Vietnam, was not confined to those who had served Nixon and later served Reagan. It also took its toll on the media. Lessons learned in that crisis not only prepared Reagan's communication strategists for the task of news manipulation but also conditioned the media for subservience.

The conventions of news production conspired against the emergence of an adversarial press during the Watergate scandal. Summarizing their analysis of the performance of the news media, Paletz and Entman (1979) observe:

> They began by neglecting the scandals, calling them a caper. Then, when events were thrust into prominence by investigations and hearings, the bulk of the press cooperated with Nixon's strategy of laying the blame on his associates—thereby preserving the legitimacy of the president and the presidency. Then, as evidence of Nixon's guilt became overt, dramatic, and threatening, the media contributed to his downfall. But they then helped to resolve public disquiet without pursuing the underlying lessons of the corruption. (p. 158)

The "Adversarial" Press and the Reagan Presidency

The period 1973-1980 was one of considerable disarray among the country's economic and political policymakers. It had begun with the civil rights movement, the opposition to the Vietnam War, and the Watergate crisis, and had been extended into activist consumer, women's, and environmental movements. The Reagan presidency, Bagdikian (1987) argues, was the response of corporate power:

> Corporate leaders counterattacked. . . . They raised large quantities of money to elect a government majority sympathetic to big business. They created a countrywide network of foundations and intellectual institutes to promote corporatism as a national philosophy. They achieved the repeal of

> laws and regulations that had been in place for decades. But they turned their most vituperative attacks upon the mass media. (p. 211)

As we have seen, these attacks coincided with a massive reorganization of media corporations. So when Ronald Reagan assumed the presidency in 1981, he was received by a compliant Washington press corps. For the most part during the next several years, following the lead of these correspondents, the national press would either ignore or misinterpret evidence of the public's lack of support for the president just as earlier it had ignored his campaign misrepresentations (Barber, 1987).

Within the Reagan administration itself, news managers like James Baker, Michael Deaver, David Gergen, Larry Speakes, and Richard Darman were assembled in order to "package" the news.[2] Their job, as Hertsgaard (1988) documents, was deception, even down to the smallest detail:

> The extensive public relations apparatus assembled within the Reagan White House did most of its work out of sight—in private White House meetings each morning to set the "line of the day" that would later be fed to the press; in regular phone calls to the television networks intended to influence coverage of Reagan on the evening news; in quiet executive orders imposing extraordinary new government secrecy measures, including granting the FBI and CIA permission to infiltrate the press. (pp. 5-6)

Disingenuously, Larry Speakes kept a sign on his desk that read: "You don't tell us how to stage the news, we won't tell you how to cover it" (Hertsgaard, 1988, pp. 26-27).

It was from their experiences of news production during Vietnam and Watergate that many in President Reagan's media team developed their confidence in "damage control" (acting quickly to isolate embarrassing news), the "line of the day," and "spin" (telling the truth, but with a particular edge or angle) as devices for the effective manipulation of news production.

Some analysts have suggested alternative explanations for the failure of the press to give an accurate accounting to public opinion: Reagan's "genial relations . . . with the Washington political and media establishment" (in contrast to Carter's); Reagan's "large" electoral victory; Reagan's success with Congress; his "highly affluent and efficient right wing" support; or "an enormous subconscious desire in Washington for the president to succeed after a string of failed presidencies" (King & Schudson, 1987, p. 39).

Far more important than these factors, however, are the consequences of corporate ownership and control of the news media, the increasingly routine dependency of journalists on government officials for information, and the subsequent reluctance among media executives and managers to perform the role of an adversarial press. It was politics and organization, rather than psychological constraints, that provided Reagan's communication managers the leverage and opportunities to manufacture the image of the "Great Communicator" in the national media.

This was most effective in the Iran-Contra scandal of 1986 and the years following (Hertsgaard, 1988, chaps. 13-15). It transpired that Reagan—who had defined Iran as a "terrorist state," and had committed himself never to deal with terrorists—had not blocked his aides' sale of weapons to the Iranian government. Nor had he interfered with the profits on the sale being used to support the "Contras," a mercenary force supported and directed by the CIA as part of the Reagan administration quest to overthrow the Nicaraguan government by violence. This arms supply was illegal, since the United States was not at war with Nicaragua, and arms deliveries had been voted down by Congress.

Despite considerable media comment, the media's considerable resources were never deployed to follow the story through to the end. It can only be speculated that none of the powers that be, including top media owners and executives, wanted a second, even more explosive, Watergate within twelve years of the first. The heat never got as far as Reagan or his vice president, George Bush.

Conclusions

The claim to the existence of free, independent, and impartial media in the United States has come under increasing scrutiny and criticism. In large measure, the reason for this is the dismal and indifferent performance of the media themselves. And nowhere have they been more pathetic than in their reporting of the presidency. Given the spectacular technical advances in news production, it is ironic that the news media appear less competent today than ever before.

The character of American journalism has been traced to several causes, ranging from an organizational reliance on elite and official news sources ("objectivity" and "balance," in journalistic parlance) to the mass media's voracious appetite for a high volume of news matter. At root, however, is the continuing concentration of corporate ownership and control of news media organizations and the resultant subordination of news production to the interests of corporate capital. Equally, the electoral interests of presidential aspirants and the executive concerns of presidents make them hostage to the resources and interests of corporate capital. It is not too surprising, then, that the presidency, in seeking to fulfill these commitments, has set out to achieve substantial influence in the production of news.

Further Questions

(1) Consider whether the cultural hegemony of the news media is eroding. One piece of evidence for this might be the decline in popular support for sitting presidents; another, the persistently lower turnouts for presidential elections. What might be the bases of that erosion? Perhaps what Ellen Wood (1988) has termed the "devaluation of democracy" (p. 14)—in other words, its reduction to the fanfare and procedures of elections rather than the extension of real power to the majority—is a factor?

(2) Is it imaginable that increasing division between rich and poor in the United States and the nation's declining global power will converge with these other trends to produce social forces that will in turn compel the creation of a more responsible media? Or social forces that will lead to even less responsible media?

Note

1. Work on this chapter was completed before the 1989 U.S. invasion of Panama. Some commentators have suggested that "narcoterrorism" is replacing the Cold War as a rationale for U.S. foreign intervention.

2. James Baker was Reagan's chief of staff (1981-1985) and secretary of the treasury (1985-1988) and Bush's 1988 campaign director; in 1989 he was appointed secretary of state. Deaver was Reagan's deputy chief of staff, 1981-1985. He subsequently joined the serried ranks of Reagan administration officials indicted in court, in his case accused of earning money shortly after leaving office by using his government connections to represent another government to the United States. Gergen was White House director of communications (1981-1984), later senior editor at *U.S. News & World Report*. Speakes was Reagan's press secretary (1981-1986), then briefly chief press spokesman at Merrill Lynch until forced to resign due to his public admission that he had concocted some of Reagan's official public statements without consultation with the president. Darman was Reagan's low-profile, high-influence presidential assistant (1981-1989), who monitored the entire paper flow in and out of Reagan's office. In 1989 Bush put him in charge of the extremely powerful Office of Management and Budget.

6 The Tug-of-War over the First Amendment

DONNA A. DEMAC
JOHN DOWNING

The First Amendment to the U.S. Constitution is for many media specialists the jewel in the crown of the U.S. media system. Demac and Downing examine its actual impact, along with laws such as the Freedom of Information Act and relevant presidential orders. They proceed to review the continual challenges to these protections of free speech and the right to know, particularly from government itself, by the FBI and the CIA, with their passion for secrecy and surveillance. Far from open information being an established fact, the battle for it is one that is constantly being fought and refought in the United States.

The history of the nuclear industry, both military and civilian, is an example the authors cite at some length in illustrating the practical problems of realizing free speech and information rights in the United States. From its very beginning, nuclear policy of all kinds has been shrouded in secrecy and public relations doublespeak ("nukespeak," as it has been termed). Through this focus, Demac and Downing emphasize that these freedoms are not just abstract liberal ideas, but go to the heart of our lives. Military confrontations with the Soviet Union and permanent nuclear poisoning of the environment are not abstract issues. They affect our future and that of our children and grandchildren. As has often been said, what we do not know can kill us. It is of little use celebrating democracy as a label to attach to the United States if it does not work properly in such crucial areas as these.

> Congress shall make no law respecting an establishment of religion, or prohibiting the free exercise thereof; or abridging the freedom of speech, or of the press; or the right of the people peaceably to assemble, and to petition the Government for a redress of grievances. (First Amendment to the U.S. Constitution, 1791)

Almost 200 years ago, when these words were first voted into the U.S. Constitution, they were an extraordinary advance in political rights. Only in revolutionary France were the citizens of another country already possessors of such guarantees by the year 1791. Yet, only 7 years later, Congress passed the Sedition Act, which permitted prison sentences and heavy fines for anyone criticizing the president or the government. It was aimed at suppressing the Republicans. A wave of resistance from newspaper editors and publishers, despite prison sentences, eventually led to its repeal in 1800.

The First Amendment is often trumpeted as an impregnable guarantee. However, the story of the Sedition Act suggests that the First Amendment actually resembles a battleground on which freedom of speech (of the press and the right to follow one's religious beliefs or lack of them) must continually be fought for in the face of attempts by the state to punish those with dissident views.

In the pages that follow, we will argue in favor of this interpretation, basing our argument on more detailed presentations elsewhere (Demac, 1985, 1988; Downing, 1986). The issue is not one for historians or lawyers only, however; if the "tug-of-war" view is correct, then we need always to be vigilant against attempts to reduce our rights to free speech and freedom of the press. If the opposing view is correct, no effort is needed on our part; the First Amendment will be automatically respected.

Those who think the First Amendment needs no defending need to give close attention to the role of the courts. U.S. law works a great deal from "precedent." This means that if, in a particular case, existing law is interpreted by the court more widely or more narrowly than had been done before, the new judgment can be used to argue in favor of other extensions or restrictions to the law. If, for example, pornographic magazines are banned, many people would not worry about freedom of speech, and some people would think pornography was an abuse of free speech anyway. But legally, it is impossible to ban pornography without opening the door to the banning of other communications. For instance, if a pornographic magazine can be censored, then why not a sexually explicit novel by D. H. Lawrence, or pamphlets that explain clearly about contraception or AIDS?

So being relaxed about First Amendment protection of our right to free speech and information is more complicated than one might think. The danger does not arise only in a dramatic situation, such as if Congress were to consider abolishing the First Amendment. It typically arises in small ways, in areas where we are inclined to trust the good sense and decency of those in authority. Below, for example, we will examine the use of the doctrine of "national security" as it has been used to justify government secrecy and strict controls on access to classified and unclassified information. No one wishes their nation to be insecure, but under the banner of national security, exactly what needs to be classified as secret? And who decides?

Threats to freedom are typically small and gradual, but they accumulate. In countries such as Germany, Italy, Spain, and Portugal, all of which have had fascist governments within the past 50 years, the laws restricting freedom were put in place only a piece at a time, never all at once. The relaxed view needs to take this into account. Indeed, in our view, we all need to recognize that we have many tendencies toward censorship and self-censorship in any society, which can be allowed to expand or can be fought. The contributions in this book by Herman, Robinson, Schulman, Corea, Gruneau and Hackett, and Sreberny-Mohammadi on international news *all* raise issues that show the practical complexities of the issue.

One key matter should never be lost sight of: Without free speech and information, democracy cannot function. People unjustly in prison cannot begin to communicate their cases. Governments that can keep their plans secret do not need to care what the people think. Public debate over alternative national policies could be suppressed; antiwar movements or campaigns for racial justice and environmental safety could be outlawed if there were no right to voice questions.

We will now examine other laws and presidential decrees that directly affect freedom of speech and information. We will then note the importance of the courts in enforcing laws (or not). Finally, we will examine some major instances of U.S. institutions that have sought, and seek, to restrict public information in defiance of the spirit of the First Amendment.

Information Legislation and Orders in the United States

The Freedom of Information Act

Up to 1966, when the original version of the Freedom of Information Act (FOIA) was passed, federal officials could decide arbitrarily whether or not to release government information. The FOIA for the first time imposed an affirmative duty on federal agencies to make available information about their operations. The FOIA was strengthened in 1974 because of a series of revelations about government misbehavior, ranging from the Watergate affair (see Chapter 5) to covert CIA and FBI harassment and break-ins against domestic political activists, and to assassination attempts against foreign leaders.

How does it work? Agencies are supposed to respond to FOIA requests within ten working days, and to appeals against refusal of information within twenty. These appeals may be taken to federal courts. In practice, the CIA often takes up to two years to respond. In its strengthened form, the FOIA declares firmly in favor of disclosure—but there are nine exemptions in the act, including classified documents and confidential business information. Others have been added every year; in 1985, for instance, the CIA's operational records were added. The tug-of-war continues, including at the state level, where each state has some version of such legislation.

Also in practice, the attitude of each presidential administration directly affects the operation of FOIA. In 1982 the Reagan administration gave government agencies permission to classify information retroactively. It also eliminated an earlier requirement to balance the government's concern with secrecy against the public's right to information, so that "When in doubt, classify!" became the guiding principle of government. On top of this, the fees for FOIA use have continued to rise, and refusals have frequently been based upon an official's subjective interpretation of why the request was being made.

On the credit side, the federal FOIA has enabled writers to document intense FBI harassment of Dr. Martin Luther King, Jr., safety problems at nuclear power plants, and sloppy federal enforcement of environmental and civil rights laws. One of the ironies of its operation, however, is that its most intensive users are corporations seeking to uncover information on their competitors.

The Sunshine Act

Passed in 1976, the Sunshine Act declared that "the public is entitled to the fullest practicable information regarding the decision-making processes of the Federal Government." It required that the public be allowed into the meetings of some 60 federal agencies. So far, so good—a clear application of the First Amendment. But a number of agencies fought back, especially the Nuclear Regulatory Commission, by redefining what a meeting was, by having its commissioners vote over the phone, or by "finding" wide-ranging uses of specific exemptions in the law.

Whistle-Blower Laws

The First Amendment has never applied to the workplace. Employees' rights to free speech and information there have been subject to complete control by management, without any legal redress. Since the mid-1970s, however, the federal government has passed a dozen laws to protect employees who go public with information about improper or dangerous behavior by their employers, if this information serves the public interest.

The dangers of nuclear and other forms of pollution are obvious cases in point. Nonetheless, both government and corporations often take strong action against whistle-blowers. As one writer has observed:

> In the Soviet Union, whistleblowers are sent directly to criminal psychiatric wards. In this country, we drive our whistleblowers to the borders of insanity and sometimes over the edge by humiliating them, taking their jobs, demoting them, or forcing them to do non-work; slander and character assassination are frequently used. (Ball, 1984, p. 307)

One such instance of such treatment was the case of Roger Boisjoly of Morton Thiokol, who warned his employers that the space shuttle *Challenger* might explode if launched under cold conditions. Interviewed on TV, he said he had meant to act in the company's best interest. However, he was ostracized in the company, and he resigned. Another was the mysterious road death of Karen Silkwood, the antinuclear campaigner whose story was dramatized in the film *Silkwood*, with Meryl Streep portraying the lead. It is important to remember that the law may at times be a very blunt and clumsy instrument to defend the freedom of speech and information in the workplace.

The Paperwork Reduction Act

Passed in 1980 with the ostensible purpose of reducing the volume of bureaucratic paper flow, the Paperwork Reduction Act was promptly used to curtail public access to government information. Under the guidance of the powerful Office of Management and Budget, government agencies used the act to transfer management of key information programs to the private sector. By 1985, one-fourth of all government publications had been dropped. In some cases, information was made available only on computer tapes, which put its utilization out of the financial and technical reach of the vast majority of citizens.

Among the government publications stopped as a result of the act were *Health Care Financial Trends, Analysis of Child Abuse and Neglect Research*, the *Civil Rights Directory*, and the *Conservation Yearbook*. Pamphlets on high blood pressure and prenatal care were cut, as was a series of booklets on daily living skills for the mentally retarded. Information about health, safety at work, and education was sharply reduced. No study was ever done to assess whether or not cutting a particular publication would be damaging to the public interest. The application of the Paperwork Reduction Act tellingly illustrated how misleading the titles of laws can be, and how easily their objectives can be distorted by the agencies that implement them.

The Federal Depository Library Act

Passed in 1902 and administered by the Government Printing Office, the Federal Depository Library Act provides government publications free of charge to about 1,400 libraries, on condition that they in turn provide access to the public. It is one of the most practical ways of ensuring that citizens can obtain important information, and puts flesh on the bones of the First Amendment.

Yet here again, the forces discouraging the flow of information have been active, especially since the 1980s. The Reagan administration initiated a policy of leaving private agencies to supply information previously made available by the government. In other words, market forces were expected to respond to single out which forms of information were in demand, as measured by who would pay for them. Not only did private agencies not take up the slack, as the free-market doctrine asserted they surely would, but in the few cases where they did move into the information domain, libraries now had to pay for the information.

Presidential Orders

A major shift occurred with the arrival of the Reagan administration in 1981. Hertsgaard (1988) has suggested that the Reagan team and its influential backers were determined to recoup the ground lost in the 1970s for government and corporate freedom of maneuver, as a result of the Watergate scandal and the ensuing demand for open information. Indeed, the promised "Reagan Revolution," rolling back social programs developed since the 1940s and hugely expanding military spending, made public information access potentially a source of greater opposition to the changes.

Certainly new restrictions on information flow were put into effect almost immediately, with wide-ranging consequences. Government employees were required to sign "nondisclosure" contracts binding them for life, in other words, preventing them from publicizing any negative experience of government service. Some 300,000 had signed these contracts by 1988. A considerable amount of unclassified information became defined as "sensitive," thus barring widespread access to it. A number of scientists working on government contracts were prevented from publishing their results or communicating them at professional conventions, to the point at which distinguished university presidents and others warned of the dangers for productive scientific exchange of information.

As regards restrictions on freedom of speech, the FBI and the CIA—the latter supposedly a foreign affairs agency—were allowed to conduct surveillance of political opposition groups. The Sanctuary movement—a largely religious movement dedicated to enabling Salvadoran refugees to escape from their government's terrorism and avoid deportation back to El Salvador at the hands of the Immigration Service—was infiltrated and spied upon, had its phones tapped and its offices raided. This was confirmed by a former FBI agent who had been involved in the agency's program, and by 1,000 pages of FBI files released by an FOIA court case.

Thus the Reagan years marked a low point in the history of freedom of information and speech, masked though they were by the president's television charm and national popularity. At the time of this writing, there are no signs that their successor administration under President Bush has any intention whatsoever of reversing policy in this respect. Bush's earlier tenure as CIA director and as Reagan's vice president give little cause for optimism.

Taking all the laws discussed above into account, including the attempts to get around those that encouraged freedom of information, as well as the relevant presidential orders of the 1980s, the case for the "tug-of-war" position looks strongly confirmed rather than disproved. The declaration of rights in the First Amendment is only as good as the existence of specific laws supporting those rights and court decisions enforcing the laws. Also, let it be clearly recognized, these processes are only as good as the existence of an informed public prepared to insist vociferously upon those rights. In the 1980s, the victor in the tug-of-war was not the public. Many associated Reagan's casual attitude toward facts with a hands-off administration, until the Iran-Contra affair (see Chapter 5) showed his administration was operating behind a veil of secrecy and censorship.

The Importance of the Courts

Above, we made reference to court enforcement of the laws and the Constitution. It is important to recall that both the Constitution and the country's laws depend entirely upon being enforced in practice. Ringing declarations of principle are powerless on their own. Let us examine two instances in order to illustrate this point as it applies to freedom of speech and information.

In the early 1960s the movement for African-American civil rights was spreading through the South—too slowly for those without civil rights, too quickly for the Whites who were opposed to them. A number of state governments tried to stop the national media from reporting the brutal handling of peaceful protest. The mechanism they sought to use was the libel law, arguing that the news media were damaging state officials' public reputations by their reporting on events and policies. The U.S.

Supreme Court, adjudicating the initially successful case of Police Commissioner Sullivan in Montgomery, Alabama, against the *New York Times*, overturned his lawyers' argument. It required future plaintiffs to demonstrate "a reckless disregard for the truth" on the part of the media they were suing for libel. The national and international impact of press and TV coverage of the demonstrations was able to be sustained, and was vital in pushing the federal government to support civil rights more actively.

In 1988, 24 years later, the Supreme Court evinced a sharply different attitude toward freedom of speech. Three St. Louis high school students had appealed the fact that their school principal had cut two articles from the school magazine they edited. The topics were teen pregnancy and the impact of divorce on children. The Supreme Court, though not unanimously, argued that educators have the right to censor material in school-sponsored publications if it is out of line with "legitimate pedagogical concerns."

Perhaps high school publications do not seem very significant, but this is exactly the point at which the issue raised at the outset of this chapter begins to be important—namely, the question of precedent and its use in the legal system. Why should high school students not be encouraged to think about teen pregnancy and the impact of divorce on families? What kind of education is being offered that can rule these subjects out?

These were the points raised about the case by a dissenting Supreme Court justice, and in turn they underline another important issue in this matter. The composition of the Supreme Court makes a huge difference to the interpretation of the laws and the Constitution, and one of the legacies of the Reagan years has been the packing of the Court with politically conservative members. There is a myth that the Court stands above politics, yet both of President Reagan's appointees, and President Roosevelt's unsuccessful attempt in the 1930s to expand the number of Supreme Court justices to sway a hitherto hostile conservative Court in favor of his New Deal policies, explode the myth. A whole layer of lower-level justices was also appointed during the Reagan years, so that it is certain that court judgments on information issues, not to mention many others, will be sharply influenced by these men and women well into the twenty-first century.

Subversion of Information Freedom: Some Examples

In this section, we propose to introduce some major cases in which the free speech and information principles of the First Amendment have been flouted. Other contributions to this volume, such as Robinson's on the presidency and the media (Chapter 5), Herman's on the propaganda model (Chapter 4), and Downing's on alternative media (Chapter 12), cite further instances, especially the period of McCarthyism in the 1950s and the Iran-Contra conspiracy of the 1980s. The two examples to be investigated are secrecy about nuclear issues and the use of arguments centering on "national security" to justify government secrecy. Both issues have been quite closely related in practice.

Nuclear Secrets

From the very outset, nuclear weaponry was shrouded in the deepest secrecy (Hilgartner, Bell, & O'Connor, 1983; Morone & Woodhouse, 1989). President Roosevelt set up the Manhattan Project, which developed the atomic bomb, without notifying Congress, despite the fact that it employed tens of thousands of people and involved the construction of whole towns whose existence was kept off maps. It might be thought that wartime conditions justified this secrecy, but after the war, in 1946, the Atomic Energy Act classified as secret all material related to the design, manufacture, or utilization of atomic weapons, the production of special nuclear material, and the use of special nuclear material in the production of energy. This last restriction was very important, because it set the tone for nuclear power plants, nuclear waste disposal, the transport of nuclear waste, and safety standards at nuclear power plants, up to the time of this writing.

The same 1946 act created a special category of classified information, technically referred to as "restricted data," but more usually referred to as "born classified." Any information, idea, or concept in this category is automatically classified from the moment someone thinks it, unless it is specifically declassified by the Department of Energy. By contrast, other government information withheld on grounds of national security requires a specific decision to classify that information. Hilgartner et al. (1983, pp. 63-64) cite the case of a journalist who wrote to his congressional representative and raised a series of questions about the costs of expanding production at the Savannah River and Hanford nuclear plants. His letter was forwarded to the Department of Energy by his representative—and promptly declared classified. (Both plants were later proven to have flouted safety regulations repeatedly, and to be responsible for nuclear contamination on a scale yet to be assessed fully.)

One of the strangest but most revealing episodes in the saga of nuclear secrecy occurred in 1979. A small monthly magazine, *The Progressive*, was set to publish an article that the government claimed contained the formula for making a hydrogen bomb. The information was all derived from public sources, and of course it is much less plausible that someone could obtain the massive infrastructure to make an H-bomb than that he or she could learn how to do it in principle. Nonetheless, in the course of the government's campaign to stop the article's being published, a series of actions or propositions were advanced in court, each of which raises major questions about First Amendment rights to the freedom of information (Hilgartner et al., 1983, pp. 66-71).

First, a federal court imposed prior restraint, banning the magazine from publishing the article, and classifying it. The magazine's editors had to work very hard to find scientists with sufficient security clearance to be allowed to read it who would also be prepared to testify that its information was entirely and easily derived from the public domain. The scientists' affidavits, gathered by the editors, were themselves promptly classified by the government. The editors' lawyers had to obtain security clearance to be allowed to represent them.

Second, in the trial the government put forward the argument that it was legitimate to classify materials retroactively. Which materials? They included an article in an eighth-grade encyclopedia and the journalist's copy of his college physics text, because he had underlined parts of it. The Justice Department also argued that arguments over whether these books contained secrets were also secret, and therefore the hearing could be held only be in secret.

Third, when the case went to appeal, some fascinating responses made themselves evident. A researcher for the editors working at the Los Alamos library went out to lunch, only to find on his return that an unclassified document he had been consulting was missing, its card had vanished from the library card catalog, and that the librarian denied all knowledge of the matter. Shortly afterward the entire library was closed "for inventory and review." It was later moved entirely into a classified category.

Fourth, during the appeal the government argued that technical information was exempt from First Amendment coverage on the grounds that science has nothing to do with political debate, and that the courts were not sufficiently informed to make judgments on technical matters.

The government then withdrew its case mid-appeal, because the material had by now been published by several other media in order to solidify the case against censorship. At the same time, no reform of the classification system was introduced. This saga indicates, perhaps more than anything else, that the secretive mind-set that many people in the West attribute exclusively to Soviet bureaucracy and its clones is alive and well in the United States of America, at least in the nuclear policy area—which is hardly a trivial area for public concern.

The National Security Argument

Above we have noted that while no one wishes the nation to be imperiled, this desire cannot reasonably be used to justify giving power to a small group of people to decide more or less in secret what the majority can be trusted to know. The terror of nuclear annihilation and the legitimate desire for national security are easily used by some against the public interest. The wider the security net, the less the powers that be need to be accountable to us, for it becomes easy for them to claim that we cannot be allowed to review the evidence for their actions. "Trust me!" they say.

This trustful attitude is also worryingly common among journalists. As information professionals, they might be expected to cast a cautious eye on such claims. In practice, however, this is not so (see Chapter 7 for more discussion of this issue).

The national security argument became very solidly established in the 1980s under the Reagan administration. A 1982 classification order listed the following government information as eligible for classification:

> (1) military plans, weapons or operations; (2) the vulnerabilities or capabilities of systems, installations, projects or plans relating to the national security; (3) foreign government information; (4) intelligence activities (including special activities, or intelligence sources or methods); (5) foreign relations or foreign activities of the United States; (6) scientific, technological or economic matters relating to the national security; (7) United States government programs for safeguarding nuclear materials or facilities; (8) cryptology [i.e., secret code construction or breaking]; (9) a confidential source; or (10) other categories of information that are related to the national security and that require protection against unauthorized disclosure as determined by the President or agency heads or other officials who have been delegated original classification authority by the President. (Executive Order 12356)

The statement is worth reading slowly, both for its catchall vague clauses (notably the last one), which could justify practically any classifying action, and for its seemingly more reasonable and understandable clauses. An example of the latter is the programs to safeguard nuclear materials and facilities (item 7). No one wants them to be vulnerable. Yet the very secrecy in which nuclear matters had been shrouded was precisely the factor that enabled so many of these facilities to operate unsafely, as a 1989 FBI investigation demonstrated. A closer consideration of items 1 and 2 also raises questions about how far the public could be excluded from information about costly and ineffective weapons systems.

In other words, our national security and well-being demand we know more, not less. Decisions must be broadly arrived at; they cannot be the private province of some appointed officials whose technical information might or might not be sufficient, never mind their capacity to reason in ways that represent the majority of the public. Some writers have coined the term "national security state" to refer to the intensive and growing concentration of secrecy at the apex of government in the name of the public's security.

Conclusions

We have seen that freedom of information and of speech are principles enshrined at the highest level of the Constitution, but that in practice the issues are part of a continuous tug-of-war. In turn, the actual decisions that have to be made about information—such as decisions concerning national security or nuclear safety—are often clouded over by the claim that government experts know best what we should or should not be allowed to know. No one needs to argue that each and every item of information should be automatically and instantly made public. There is, however, a very large area between that extreme position and the claims put forward by the U.S. government during the 1980s—the precedent for which in many ways was the 1946 Atomic Energy Act, which invented the concept of "born classified"—that huge discretion over secrecy and publication should be handed without further ado to what Hilgartner et al. (1983) describe as the "classification priesthood."

Further Questions

(1) A further issue concerns the censorship of books to be used in schools and to be available in public libraries. At intervals throughout this century, fundamentalist religious groups have tried to get certain books banned from school use, and others removed from library shelves. The same groups have striven to make sure that only the biblical version of human origins—the Adam and Eve legend—should be taught in schools, or, if not that version alone, then with equal time to scientific accounts. Texts that did not do so have actually been excluded from classrooms in a number of schools and school districts. Teachers could not adopt them. In other communities, certain books have been banned from public libraries; the favorite, it seems, is the J. D. Salinger novel *Catcher in the Rye.* Does this indicate that censorship is not simply a government or corporate vice, but that there are powerful forces in society in general that are unhappy with the general application of the First Amendment? Does the existence of such forces represent the same danger as government censorship?

(2) How do we estimate the threat to the well-being of the U.S. population from leaks to competitor countries such as Japan or West Germany, or to the other superpower? Are there alternatives to classifying everything in sight? What happens to scientific exchange and progress inside this country, and internationally, if scientists working on government contracts are subjected to heavy restrictions on communicating their research?

(3) What is the likelihood the federal government will make sure that electronically stored unclassified information is made easily accessible to the public? Soon, this will be the only form in which most government information will be available, and at present computer tapes are the typical mode of storage. These are beyond most people's technical and financial means to access. Ensuring access to the new technology for storing and disseminating information is a vital part of strengthening First Amendment freedoms in the information age.

7 Control Mechanisms Inside the Media

MARK SCHULMAN

There is one key question that many critical media analysts leave out. What are the mechanisms by which journalists and other media employees are kept seemingly loyal to their editors, senior executives, publishers, and corporate boards? It is one thing to point to the ever-growing concentration of corporate power over U.S. media, but unless these executives are to write the news and direct the sitcoms themselves, how are they able to ensure a compliant staff? What are the intervening stages by which media employees are kept on track?

Mark Schulman explores the daily world of the media worker, and traces out how the levers of power operate in that setting. He concludes that a mix of factors is at work to keep media employees in line, ranging from their own comfort with the status quo to their desire for career advancement to the normal workplace requirement to follow orders. These organizational factors work differently for different employees, but they have also often operated to assist in excluding women and people of color from positions of responsibility in the media. Even when women or minority-origin journalists are hired, they frequently find that the pressures to fit in prevent them from bringing their own experiences to bear in their work. Nonetheless, many have stayed to push for change piece by piece, sometimes at considerable psychological cost. The question of self-censorship by journalists, which is at the heart of Schulman's argument, is a wide-ranging one on this level as well as on a more general level.

Every day, everywhere in the world, a comparatively few media workers (it's hard to estimate for the entire globe, but let's guess at half a million people) make decisions about which stories will emerge to inform and to entertain the rest of us (now approaching 4 billion people). To many media workers, this is a natural process, an example of professional and creative principles at work. Such professionals claim merely to be reflecting events, but their representation of the significant aspects of our contemporary lives define the lenses through which the world is to be viewed.

CBS Headquarters, New York

Rarely does a news journalist or broadcaster transcend the limits directly or indirectly imposed by the media organizations for which he or she works. So the question to be addressed here—simple to state, but complex to explain—is, How exactly do journalists know what to do? How do they know where to begin and where to stop, what to include and what to omit, what to foreground and what to mention in passing, and, perhaps most important of all, what the appropriate wording and images are? It is the aim of this chapter to delineate the mechanisms by which media workers know their limits and through which media systems exert control over how the media product is compiled by their work force.

There are two central contending paradigms, or basic frameworks for analysis, for answering the questions posed above. One is called the *structuralist-functionalist* social science of mainstream communication studies, while the second uses a *critical or social class-based* foundation for analysis, influenced by Marxism.

The structural-functional approach fits within the research tradition called "liberal-pluralist," which tends broadly to accept societies such as Western European nations and the United States as "the best of all the rest." The assumption is that, whatever the problems and contradictions, Western industrial capitalism and its political and cultural structures are where we start and where we wish the rest of the world to end up. In journalistic studies, this approach posits the "free press," which operates without interference from the state, as the model to emulate. The commercially dominated, profit-oriented media enterprises are taken for granted as the way things ought to be organized. Their flaws are recognized, of course, but they are accepted as better than any alternative. This provides a framework that I identify by the metaphor of the *gatekeeper.*

A critical approach questions these assumptions and does not accept a certain model as "natural" or "given." Concerns about the broader relations between media and social classes in society, and about the values that media carry, suggest this viewpoint can be identified by the metaphor of the *ideologue.*

When these two approaches are used to address specific questions about media workers in their organizations and the mechanisms of control, two parallel lists of issues to consider beckon our attention. They divide up the issues approximately as follows:

liberal-pluralist	*critical/class-based*
gatekeeping	(self) censorship
ethical considerations	ideological considerations
professionalism as opportunity	professionalism as control
technological possibilities	technological constraints
colleagues seeking the truth	workers aiming to please

The critical tools of study in the right-hand column organize around a perspective we could call the *production of culture.* The liberal tools of study in the left column coalesce in a media organizational attitude that might be labeled *socially responsible profitability.* Assessing the validity of the two perspectives allows us to come to some conclusions about our object of study and, even more important, to agree about what questions merit further attention.

Let us turn to the world of the media worker in mainstream U.S. media organizations. Such organizations share some basic characteristics—they are almost always commercial enterprises, large organizations, comprehensive in scope of activity—bureaucratic hierarchies. While our focus is the commercial news media in the United States, state-run media systems in other industrialized countries and public broadcasting in the United States share some of the same features, and other media settings such as Hollywood film studios and general circulation magazines could be analyzed in the same way.

Gatekeeping Versus Self-Censorship

The image of a gatekeeper, the professional media worker opening and closing the portal that lets information through the fence between events and their report, is central to the liberal-pluralist account of how control works. In this view, the journalist uses the "professional judgment" that he or she has developed to decide what is newsworthy. Developing professional judgment is a process of gradual socialization, of formal and informal education and training in the appropriate roles of the professional journalist.

Often the process begins with undergraduate or graduate training in journalism. In the classroom context, the aspiring journalist learns the acceptable modes of inquiry, content, and style. While several decades ago this aspect of gatekeeping was irrelevant—there were few journalism programs—in the 1990s there will be tens of thousands of majors in well over 300 journalism and communication programs in the United States. Like premed and prelaw majors in undergraduate programs, "pre-journalism" students undergo a fairly rigorous socialization in their college years.

Once they enter the hierarchical structure of the newsroom, eager to apply their newly received training to their jobs, journalists discover that the gatekeeper function is directly proportional to the amount of power and responsibility the individual has written into his or her job description. In the newsroom hierarchy, a cub reporter is a neophyte at the gate. A beat reporter keeps the gate somewhat more professionally than a cub reporter. A seasoned veteran is better at gatekeeping than a beat person; a city editor better than a reporter; an editor-in-chief better than an editor; and a publisher best of all.

Day-to-day work in this hierarchy tends to displace the sense of responsibility from lower-level workers up through the hierarchy. Just as anyone at the bottom of an organizational totem pole can shrug his or her shoulders and say, "I don't make the rules—I just follow them," the media worker can claim one of the benefits of hierarchy: diversion of criticism from the individual to higher-ups.

Within media organizations, the liberal-pluralist viewpoint says, socialization continues where school-based training leaves off, through apprenticeships and on-the-job training, what in more modern vernacular is called "mentoring" and "networking." This is the essence of the gatekeeper metaphor, which is fundamental to this viewpoint's description of how control operates—to the benefit of the "free press" model of media organization.

Censorship is the central concept, as opposed to gatekeeping, in the critical/class-based view. The form of censorship, however, is rarely of the variety that comes down hard, with punishment and embarrassment, on those lower in the hierarchy. Instead, these media workers engage in self-censorship. The careful self-censor does not need a figurative beating for frequently transgressing the perspectives of those in charge. The control is more subtle: The worker knows, inside and when it counts, what the boss wants his or her work to look like. What occurs is the inhibition of any reportorial and editorial (even cultural) urges to push outside the established boundaries. Rewards—money, fame, authority, autonomy—are proffered to those who self-censor most effectively. Most of the time it works, and the gate swings shut not on the basis of professional standards, but whenever events might pass through with interpretations upsetting to the status quo.

And if self-censorship does not work? "The claws are ready for use hiding behind soft paws" (Mortensen & Svendson, 1980, p. 175). A journalist may lose prestige, power, security of position, and, ultimately, his or her job. Former Federal Communications Commissioner Nicholas Johnson describes this process in concrete terms:

> The story is told of a reporter who first comes up with an investigative story idea, writes it up and submits it to the editor and is told the story is not going to run. He wonders why, but the next time he is cautious enough to check with the editor first. He is told by the editor that it would be better not to write that story. The third time he thinks of an investigative story idea but doesn't bother the editor with it because he knows it's silly. The fourth time he doesn't even think of the idea anymore. (quoted in Bernstein, 1988)

Thus a journalist becomes an ideologue of his or her own volition; hence this is the central metaphor of the critical perspective. As an ideologue, an individual adopts, unexamined, the credo of those in power, and comes to accept it—to believe it—as natural, timeless, and universal.

Ideological Considerations Versus Ethical Considerations

Ideological considerations, according to the critical view, dominate the way media workers think. There are many definitions of ideology (some others are explored in Chapter 1); the description by Richard Ohmann (1987) satisfies our purposes:

> Ideology is the whole of ideas of a group of people with common interests—a nation, a party, a government, a social or economic class, an occupational group, an industry, etc. The most common tactic of ideology is to show how the interests of the group are "really" the same as the interests of the whole society or of humanity in general. (p. 107)

Those who own the media share certain common concerns with owners of other industries in the transnational world economic order. Of course, in many cases, they are actually the same people across industries, both within the United States, as Herman shows in Chapter 4, and internationally, as Hamelink argues in Chapter 15. The media they own push their ideological considerations, the "mainstream ideology" of the current status quo. Because media workers who make a living from these bosses see the mainstream ideology as permanent and fixed, they are often unaware that their perspective could be controversial; that people of color, for example, in the United States condemn the established media. So inbred are the perspectives of those in charge—almost always White, usually male, certainly with high incomes—within the media organizations that charges of racism often seem wrongheaded to the identified perpetrators. When the American Broadcasting Company's sports team missed the finish of the 1987 New York Marathon, many viewers charged that this unprecedented event was a racist incident, since the winner was an African—and, they alleged, ABC could not deal with a front-runner who was not a White man in what had always been a "White race." ABC, as you might expect, blamed the camera operators for "bad news judgment."

Most journalists identify strongly and comfortably with mainstream values. During the strike of printers and other production workers at the *Washington Post* in the mid-1970s, one famous veteran reporter explained why the editorial workers would not support the strike. It was simple, he said to me with a sneer when I joined the picket line: We eat lunch at the same restaurants as Henry Kissinger, and thus identify with those kind of people. We may work in the same building, he added, but the journalists work in offices; the printers work in a factory.

From the liberal-pluralist view, "news judgments" such as the one ABC cites in the Marathon coverage are simply an example of ethical considerations, not ideology. The decision making, in this view, is influenced by the ethical standards each journalist brings to the situation, not his or her mind-set. Since some journalists have "sound ethics" and a few have "unsound ethics," the socially responsible way to approach the problem is to concentrate on training ethically sound journalists.

Professionalism as Opportunity or Control?

An ethical journalist who is also well trained and talented, according to the liberal-pluralist view, is a professional. Since the professional media worker enjoys a field of opportunity and success, what media worker would not choose to be joyful, successful, professional?

The critical analyst says things are more complicated than that. The process whereby a particular occupational category becomes a "profession" is in itself a questionable notion, especially for communications workers. Media occupations have no strictly enforced codes of ethics, nor do they exist within a structure of licensing. Thus journalists are *not* bound by the professional strictures that, in theory, bind doctors or lawyers. An occupation, in distinction from a profession, has little commonality of standards. One well-known mass communication textbook puts it this way:

> You become a journalist when you declare that you are one, and you remain a journalist as long as you keep declaring that you are one. It is hard to think of another occupation of comparable importance to society that exercises so little formal control over itself—no entrance requirement, no explicit code of ethics, no system for weeding out the incompetents and the scoundrels. (quoted in Goldstein, 1985, p. 157)

Of course, my point in this chapter is to argue that the *informal* controls serve quite well enough. So this may not be a useful distinction in figuring out the way organizations control media workers through more subtle forms than ethical codes and entrance requirements. Within the media, also, organizational constraints are not intended to encourage creativity and standards of excellence as fundamental aspects of the occupational creed, a necessary theoretical characteristic of professionalism in other fields, even if it is not always followed in practice. Instead, institutional practices in the media constrain a worker's imaginative impulses by exerting controls that encourage conformity.

In everyday practice, the media "professional" is bound by such constructs as deadline pressures, adaptation to environmental forces beyond an individual's control (such as the capacity and speed of the presses in print or the technical characteristics of video in broadcasting), and the limitations on artistry in favor of conventional, "efficient," and "accessible" procedures. These and other occupational realities make professionalism a mechanism for controlling the worker's production, channeling limited creativity into the safe and the mundane, not the risky and experimental.

Opportunity, says the critical perspective, is not the reward of the professional, as the liberal perspective asserts. It is the illusion through which people who believe their occupations are creative make themselves stay well within the prescribed boundaries.

Workers or Colleagues?

To the liberal, the journalist is a colleague in the enterprise with all his or her coworkers, and all the members of the media organization are seeking truth. Being objective in reporting, presenting both sides, and avoiding bias are all subcategories of the overarching category of truth seeking. There is an almost religious quest, with the canons of journalism guiding the truth seekers.

But to the critical observer, the "all for one, one for all," "we're all truth seekers here" stance mystifies the organizational realities. The tenet of objectivity, defined in the liberal dictionary as the result of standing as an unbiased observer outside the events being transformed into news, is false, according to the critical view. In fact, interpretation *always* changes the report to one more or less subjective.

To offer "both sides," another liberal approach to assuring truth, is to forget that there are often more than two sides on any issue. Issues that cannot conveniently fit into the package of liberal versus conservative in political journalism, for example, defy a "both sides" approach, as do complex social phenomena such as the women's movement, or convoluted medical/societal debates such as the long-term controversy on smoking and health, or the economic and political dynamics of the developing world, which is too often portrayed as simply the "us versus them" battleground of "democracy versus communism."

How can bias be avoided, the critical observer also asks, when the structure by its very nature excludes the viewpoints of those without access to the sources of decisions and conclusions? Above all, in this critical view, truth is not an absolute, as it is in the liberal-pluralist ideology. Instead of a single truth, there is a shared cultural vision within which different interpretations of the world are still possible. Workers are not colleagues in the great search for truth; they are players in a drama of conflict, contention, and struggle among unequals. This disequilibrium is a product of varying degrees of capability to manipulate the levels of power. Media consumers and media producers who are not aligned with and attuned to media owners have nowhere near equal ability to create their definition of news and their version of truth. When those toward the bottom of the hierarchy agree to join those at the top in "seeking truth," they are, even if they do not realize it, aiming to please their superiors.

As with the issue of ideology versus ethics, the aim to please is an urge to be rewarded within an inegalitarian power structure, not an agreement that everybody is in it together, living out their sound ethics to uncover the good. More often than not, to the critical/class-based analyst, the goal to which media workers must uncomfortably accommodate is to cover up the bad. The unconscious limits of the journalistic occupations tie the workers within them to values and attitudes that have little to do with truth, balance, creativity, or art.

The liberal-pluralist perspective recognizes limitations imposed by the nature of the audience, technological capabilities, ethical standards, available talent, and so on. But within those limits, adherents of this perspective assert, the U.S. media are doing a hell of a job, and are among the best in the world. This claim should be evaluated in the light of critiques developed elsewhere in the book.

The Claws in the Soft Paws

Although it is rarely necessary for the powers that be to act against their media workers, what does happen when self-censorship and other constraints do not keep media workers in line? Journalism provides some interesting examples.

Journalists and other media workers do get fired, but it is often impossible to link their dismissal to specific questions of control from above. Decisions to terminate workers can be attributed to business efficiency, a "tough but necessary action" in the context of networks closing bureaus and reducing staffs to accomplish the "lean and mean" news operation they desire for the 1990s. Sometimes the decision is framed as a matter of quality or talent, often based on ratings and the tricky question of what sells. Especially in broadcasting, a personality is there one day and gone the next; media workers have an aphorism that recognizes this reality: You're only as good as your last show.

But often business efficiency and talent mask the ideological reasons for dismissal of workers. On occasion, employers drop the mask and reveal their brute powers to suppress ideas beyond the boundaries of the permissible. The case of A. Kent MacDougall reveals the wrath of editors at journalists who cross the line. MacDougall (1975) writes about his experience:

> In December 1971, after informing managing editor Frederick Taylor that I had decided to resign from the *Wall Street Journal*, I returned to my desk in the newsroom, rolled a half-sheet in the typewriter and dashed off a message. . . . It read:
>
> . . . ON JANUARY 7, AFTER 10 YEARS AND 3 MONTHS OF DJ (DOW JONES) PEONAGE, I WILL BE FREE AT LAST, FREE AT LAST, GREAT GAWD ALMIGHTY, FREE AT LAST.
>
> RGDS
> MACDOUGALL, NY
>
> [Taylor] stood over me shaking with rage . . . wheeled and marched angrily back to his office.
>
> Now I had to be fired. Late that Friday afternoon, Taylor summoned me to his office and summarily announced that . . . he didn't want me on the premises another day. I was now being given the same bum's rush that

> previous managing editors had accorded to at least three other reporters after they had the audacity to resign. (p. 271)

MacDougall wrote that account in 1972. Fourteen years later, in an article in the independent Marxist journal *Monthly Review,* he revealed that he had written (under a pen name for leftist publications) many articles advocating socialist ideals while at the *Journal* and other mainstream papers (MacDougall, 1988a, 1988b). MacDougall claimed to have "subverted" the *Journal* as well as the *Los Angeles Times,* where he also worked, and to have "helped popularize radical ideas," citing the "very narrow ideological spectrum in the American news media" (cited in Taylor, 1989). Taylor, for his part, was quoted as saying that "if he had known about those articles at the time, MacDougall would have been fired" (Shaw, 1989).

So we see that the steel claw does rake the career of progressive journalists who challenge mainstream ideology. It has happened in France, where Maurice Siegel, then director general of Europe Number One, "France's most popular independent radio station . . . heard in six countries in Western Europe . . . was fired for essentially political reasons" in 1975 (Englund, 1975). But it has happened in the United States more times than you might think, in a way that is different from the French syndrome. In Greensburg, Pennsylvania, for example, in 1973,

> [reporter] Jude Dippold . . . was fired. A simple staff restructuring had eliminated his job, according to *Tribune-Review* officialdom. . . . Within hours of the dismissal, ten of the paper's editorial employees, some of them long-term staff veterans, had resigned their own jobs in protest. And within two weeks, the *Tribune-Review*'s managing editor of twelve years had been fired and his replacement had quit.
>
> The staffers are still stunned by the bloodletting. Their recollections of the events that lead to Dippold's firing reflect far less bitterness than incredulity. A newspaper they had always regarded as a garden of freedom, one in which their own news judgments could blossom, had been systematically defoliated by the policies of the publisher. (Carroll, 1974)

Other examples could be cited, such as Sydney Schanberg's losing his *New York Times* column and Ed Asner's difficulties with television networks, but these are sufficient to make the point. From reporters to directors, if you do not accept the ideological limits, you may get the sack.

So are there any alternatives for media workers who wish to push back the limits imposed on them by the control mechanisms under which they labor? There are contradictory trends at work within journalism. For the most part, recent trends are toward more superficial news coverage in print and broadcasting, a discouraging tendency. Yet, at the same time, some newspapers are increasing their serious coverage, and polls indicate that the public desires greater seriousness in both print and broadcast news. For the media worker, there are new organizations, such as Fairness and Accuracy in Reporting (FAIR) and the Union for Democratic Communications (UDC), that aim to foster debate on precisely the issues raised in this chapter.

People of color, women, gay men and lesbians, and anyone with critical or different perspectives may find themselves at odds not only with their superiors but also with their more conservative peers in various media settings. The new, critical journalists can push and prod to assert their demands and their voices. They can ally with the progressive elements of their audiences and with their unions or professional associations to sandwich those in charge between worker and customer. Both as media practitioners and as media consumers we can question authority by challenging the attitudes, approaches, and conditions we are asked to accept.

Further Questions

(1) It is suggested that the further up a hierarchy one goes, the more of a company person one becomes. What are the implications of this for media "stars" and media content?

(2) Look in detail at how media covers "trouble in the media" such as strikes, resignations, and new appointments. Is there a lot of coverage, and what approaches are presented?

Other Resources

- The Cinema Guild (1697 Broadway, New York, NY 10019) distributes videotapes on journalism and mass communication. These include *Making the News Fit,* on U.S. media coverage of El Salvador; *If It Bleeds, It Leads,* which analyzes spot news coverage; and *Six O'Clock and All's Well,* a dissection of contemporary broadcast journalism.
- Media Network (208 W. 13th St., New York, NY 10013) publishes resource guides on a variety of subjects that lead to alternative interpretations to mainstream coverage, and maintains a data base of alternative media sources.
- Paper Tiger Television (339 Lafayette St., New York, NY 10003) has produced an excellent series of documentaries in which media critics such as Herbert Schiller and Ben Bagdikian analyze print publications; a catalogue of other critical materials on the media is also available.

- Pacifica Radio (Program Distribution, 5316 Venice Blvd, Los Angeles, CA 90019) makes available audiotapes on various topics, including media issues, which are listed in a comprehensive annotated catalogue.

Among contemporary narrative films available on video that address topics of journalists and their work are *Absence of Malice, Medium Cool, A Cry in the Dark, Network, Broadcast News,* and *Under Fire.* Though not about journalists, the film *A Question of Silence* is a stunning portrayal of the relationship of professionals, in this case psychiatrists, to their clients, with resonances to media workers and their audiences worth considering.

8 Western Europe: "Mixed Model" Under Threat?

DENIS MCQUAIL

Western European nations have a long tradition of organizing broadcasting as a legal monopoly via a public corporation. To the American reader who knows only the U.S. free enterprise broadcasting system, where even the minority public channels are heavily sponsored by corporate advertising, such a situation may sound potentially fraught with danger. Who will be able to prevent the government from broadcasting only what it wants people to know?

It is true that, notably in France, governments have tried to control broadcasting on sensitive issues, and that during the fascist periods in Germany (1933-1945), Italy (1921-1944), and Spain (1939-1976), rigid government control was in force, but the general pattern of state-sponsored broadcasting has been nowhere near as subservient to governments as the American reader might suppose.

Indeed, as McQuail points out, in many of these countries there has been a strong commitment among broadcasters to what is called "public service" broadcasting. Broadcasting has been defined not as a market commodity to be sold and traded, but as a common valued resource that a democratic government should organize for the collective welfare of its citizens to ensure they are properly informed and educated, as well as entertained and amused. Hence a public corporation at partial arms' length from the government has seemed the most viable way to provide this service.

Gradually since World War II, and with more momentum during the 1980s, these public broadcasting systems have encountered competition from newer, privately owned commercial networks almost everywhere in Western Europe. The effects have been mixed, and they are the subject of many disputes. However, the argument that publicly controlled networks of this kind automatically produce government propaganda is rarely heard in the disputes.

If for no other reason than that you should be aware that it is perfectly possible to organize media systems in various ways, McQuail's account of the traditional broadcasting model in Western Europe and how it is changing is an important one for you to study. Like the final chapter in this section, he also presents you with a sense of the importance of different media "philosophies" in shaping media organization and output. The free-market model is dominant in the United

Europe: West and East. From Contemporary World Atlas © 1990 by Rand McNally & Company, R. L. 90-S-45.

States, but that does not automatically make it normal for the rest of the world. Are there not advantages to be considered in the "public service" philosophy?

These philosophies are sometimes termed "normative theories" because they proclaim "norms" for the media that should be followed. There are several others besides the public service and free market positions, such as the development philosophy (see a problematic version discussed by Mohammadi, Chapter 19), the Soviet philosophy (see Downing, Chapter 9), and the democratic participation philosophy (see Downing, Chapter 12).

The decrease in state regulation and the sharp rise of corporate power over the media that McQuail documents were even more marked in the United States during the 1980s. Demac's chapter on new communication technologies (Chapter 14) also provides a review of these policy developments this side of the Atlantic.

The Old Order

There was a time when one could speak of broadcasting in Western Europe as having a similar pattern across most countries, with many features common to the different national systems. This model may be considered to represent the "old order," which held sway until the early 1980s. With some necessary oversimplification, this old order had the features described below.

(1) Public service. There was a strong component of public service in the media goals. The main elements of cultural policy were that diverse tastes, interests, and subcultures in the nation should be represented, along with different regions and minority languages. Public service philosophy also discriminated in favor of cultural and informative programming and special services for children and young people.

(2) Public accountability. This was achieved mainly through regulatory bodies and parliaments that had ultimate control over most funding. The normal method of financing broadcasting in Europe was by an annual license fee set by governments from time to time and collected from each household by the post office or a similar agency.

(3) Monopoly. Broadcasting was a monopoly or almost so. One public body, such as the British Broadcasting Corporation, was licensed to broadcast by the government. Monopoly privilege was usually based on the argument that only a few channels were available, a pretext that concealed a determination not to let this potent communications medium slip out of government control. However, public broadcasting monopolies had a good deal of independence in overall editorial policy and day-to-day decisions, despite ultimate accountability to government and the general public. Yet government monopoly did not involve the close control of all media output that typified the Soviet Union from 1930 to 1985 (see Chapter 9).

(4) Politicization versus neutralization. Broadcasting was usually either highly politicized or politically neutralized. It occupied a politically sensitive position and responded to the typical concerns of the elite of the political system. The forms of politicization or neutralization varied a good deal across Europe, depending on the local political culture and conventions. At one end, political parties and groups colonized broadcasting in proportion to their voting strength—though parties of the left had to fight to be given proportional access. At the other end, the general aim was to keep parties at a distance and minimize the direct involvement of politicians in broadcasting. The former pattern was more typical of continental Europe, the latter of Britain and Scandinavia. A variation could be found in Italy and France, where conservative parties in government ran broadcasting more or less as their own property until other parties gradually achieved proportional access (from 1968 in Italy, from 1981 in France).

(5) National scope. European broadcasting has generally had a national character. This has been shown by the legal requirement to serve the

entire territory, the expectation that the national language and culture would be protected, the location of broadcasting headquarters in the capital, and the task of representing the country in international cultural events. There were cases that deviated from this national model, for instance: Germany, where provincial governments organize broadcasting; Holland, with its inclusion of religious and labor organizations in broadcasting; and Belgium, with its division into French and Flemish communities.

(6) Noncommercialism. While there are many examples during the old order of significant funding from commercial sources—especially through charges for spot advertising—the balance of revenue in hardly any European country came from advertising. There was a widespread policy that broadcasting should not be dominated by the search for profit, but by the priorities of professional broadcasters and audiences. Where income from advertising was allowed, it was under strict conditions, designed to shield program making from the need to make money. This gave management and broadcasters considerable scope and created "space" in the system that could be used for cultural or social purposes that were not necessarily profitable.

The Mixed Model

It is clear from this account why the typical European broadcasting system could be called a "mixed model": It had mixed sources of revenue, with advertising as well as license income from audiences, and it had mixed goals, some determined by governments and politicians, some by professionals, some by various interest groups, and some even by the audience, which could exert indirect political pressure.

This system rested on diverse supports within each society. The main interests that sustained it were (a) the political elite, who were able to achieve access or neutralization, and still retained the right to intervene on particular issues, either in public or behind the scenes, and did not have to worry about broadcast challenges that they could not control; (b) the cultural elite (whether of the right, favoring traditional values, or of the left, disliking commercialism); (c) the public postal and telecommunications authorities (PTT), who generally also enjoyed a privileged position in supplying the hardware and controlling technical standards; (d) the press, who were protected from unsettling competition for advertising revenues; and (e) the audience, who over the years in most countries seems to have been more appreciative than critical of a service that, although limited, was reasonably high in quality and low in cost and fulfilled its expectations of a public service.

Before looking at the changes that affected the old order in the 1980s, we must remember that this is a simplified model. There was much intercountry variation under the old order (Kleinsteuber, Siune, & McQuail, 1986). This diversity is an important benefit of non-commercialism, since the logic of commerce is to standardize structures as well as profit-making goals. Most Western European broadcasting systems fit within three main groups of nations: four small Nordic countries—Denmark, Sweden, Norway, Finland; the big five—Britain, Germany, France, Italy, Spain; and several small countries left over (e.g., Holland, Belgium, Austria, Switzerland). The Nordic countries generally conformed very closely to the model of the old order and were strongly noncommercial. Of the big countries, Britain and France were quite close to the model, as was Germany, apart from its federal structure. Italy deviated from the model from 1976, when private, commercial broadcasting at the local level proliferated outside the system of public control. Spain was both heavily dominated by the state and heavily dependent on commercial revenue—a different type of mixture. Generally, each small country created some variant of the model to suit its particular circumstances.

The Model Destabilized

This mixed model came under considerable strains and pressures in the 1980s. These appeared to destabilize it, to present the old order as an anachronism, and to raise doubts about its survival (Dyson & Humphreys, 1986; Euromedia Research Group, 1986). It is vital to understand the reason behind the changes if we are to be able to predict the longer-term development of broadcasting in Europe. The most fundamental reason for change appears to be the changing technologies of distribution (De Bens & Knoche, 1987). The widely accepted justification for monopoly rested on arguments about the scarcity of broadcasting channels and resources and thus the need for close regulation. With cable and satellite able to distribute messages over much larger areas at relatively lower costs, promising an abundance that print media already enjoyed, the old argument for monopoly crumbled. New technologies offered greater freedom to send and receive, and a much greater potential for choice.

These technological changes coincided in Europe with another kind of change, in the political climate. These policy changes are complicated, and varied somewhat from nation to nation, but essentialy they included the following: (a) a trend toward limiting taxpayer support and greater reliance on market forces; (b) a widespread belief that the new communication and information technologies would underpin future economic growth and thus should be stimulated; (c) the ripple effects of U.S. deregulation; (d) the acceleration of plans to create a more integrated Europe, politically and socially as well as economically, which implied a convergence of broadcasting systems (European Economic Community, 1984); and last, but not least, (e) renewed pressure from old and new commercial operators, including individuals such as Rupert Murdoch and Sylvio Berlusconi and corporations like Hachette SA and Bertelsman AG, to open up European broadcasting to commercial competition.

Media Mogul 1: Rupert Murdoch[1]

Rupert Murdoch has been called the "Magellan of the Information Age" (Bagdikian, 1989), since he comes splashing down on one continent after another. He inherited an Australian newspaper, the *News*, in Adelaide from his father in 1954. In 1960, at the age of 29, he began to buy out papers in Sydney, Melbourne, and Brisbane, and established the first continental newspaper, the *Australian*, in 1964. In 1969 he embarked on acquiring newspapers elsewhere, purchasing the British *News of the World* and the *Sun*; in 1977 the latter became the biggest-selling newspaper in the English-speaking world, with a circulation of 4 million, combining sexy pin-ups on page 3 with souped-up dramatic headlines. Murdoch acquired the establishment London *Times* and *Sunday Times* and used them to support Margaret Thatcher into power, as he used the *New York Post* (which he resold in 1988) to support the Reagan administration. In the United States, the Federal Communications Commission permitted him to do what no other broadcaster had been allowed to do: He acquired a television station in a city where he also owned a daily newspaper and was allowed to keep both of them. The launching of Fox television as a fourth network has constituted a major change in American television. Combined, Murdoch thus owns and controls two-thirds of newspaper circulation in Australia, almost half of New Zealand's press, and about a third of the British press, as well as a number of American newspapers. He also has considerable stakes in book and magazine publishing companies in Britain, while his *TV Guide* enjoys a circulation of 17 million in the United States. He owns the 20th Century-Fox movie studio and Sky Channel in Europe, making him one of the century's biggest media moguls.

Media Mogul 2: Reinhard Mohn and Bertelsman AG

Reinhard Mohn is part of a long-established publishing family, and presides over one of the largest media corporations in the world. In 1988 Bertelsman AG had 42,000 employees in 25 countries on four continents, with revenues of over $6.5 billion and net profits of $230 million. The company has reached the limit of print market share permitted by West Germany's Federal Cartel Office, including the popular West German magazine *Stern*, and recently outbid two governmental public systems for the new TV satellite channel that will cover Germany. It also owns U.S. publishing firms Doubleday, Bantam, and Dell, the Literary Guild book club, and RCA and Arista record companies. The family owns 89% of company stock, yet none of Mohn's sons is an heir to the fortune, control of which will go to a charitable foundation.

Media Moguls 3, 4, and 5: Henry Luce and Harry and Jack Warner

The Time-Warner merger in 1988 created the largest media corporation in the world, with a total value of $18 billion (far more than a number of Third World countries combined) and a work force of 335,460. This merged company has subsidiaries in Australia, Asia, Europe, and Latin America. The company now includes Warner Brothers film studios, publishing ventures (such as Warner paperbacks; Scott Foresman; Little, Brown; Time-Life Books; and the Book-of-the-Month Club); record companies (such as WCI), and American cable television companies (such as Home Box Office and Cinemax). It is the largest magazine publisher in the United States, with *Time, Life, Sports Illustrated, Fortune, People,* and others, with a worldwide readership estimated at 120 million.

Some of these pressures are clearly related or mutually reinforcing. Governments like to relax regulation and encourage expansion and innovation that they don't have to pay for, since financiers and media barons produce the investment money. The "Europeanization" of broadcasting policy supported the logic of commercial development as a way of fighting off the increased competition in both hardware and software markets from the United States and Japan.

So far we have said nothing about the "consumer," the audience for broadcasting, in whose interest and at whose expense the old order was supposedly run. It is hard to know how to assess the consumer's position, because so many self-interested parties claim to represent the consumer's point of view. The most obvious argument is that the public in general welcomes changes in the direction of more choice and variety in radio and television programming. The success of the VCR in many countries indicates this. But the evidence of strong demand for more television channels is not very clear, and it would be wrong to suggest that this revolution in European broadcasting was the result of unstoppable consumer demand for new suppliers or pent-up dissatisfaction with the old order.

Assessing the Changes

This section will summarize the degree and kinds of changes that have occurred in the various national broadcasting systems of Western Europe. Italy was the trailblazer; from 1976, private local broadcasting was permitted and there was a mushrooming of private, commercial, and unregulated, mainly local, television and radio stations. These have now been institutionalized into a set of advertising-supported commercial channels, heavily dominated by the media magnate Berlusconi, which compete with RAI's state television, which draws on public income as well as advertising. The system has settled into a mixed form not dissimilar to the British system, even if the content of Italian television, through lack of regulation, is very different. Changes in Italy had little to do with new technologies, and more to do with the stifling dominance of the conservative party (Christian Democrats) for decades.

Britain has had a closely regulated system, divided more or less equally between the BBC, funded solely by a household broadcast license fee, and Independent Television, which is supported by advertising revenue. This system has changed little, despite the Thatcher government's efforts to encourage commercial cable and satellite television, although long-term plans do aim to phase out public funding. Cable, which was licensed in the mid 1980s, was to have created change but has not proved very popular; less than 15% of British households had cable by 1989. Murdoch's direct-broadcast satellite service, Sky Television, launched in February 1989, cost $120 million in its first five months and now aims to reach just over a million homes within a year, a much more conservative estimate than the 2.5 million originally projected. Its main competitor, British Satellite Broadcasting (BSB), is scheduled to operate from spring 1990.

The German government similarly encouraged private competition via cable and satellite against the main public television channels. While this has been more successful than in Britain, still the extent of cable is limited, with less than 20% of houses reached by the end of 1989.

France adopted the most radical changes during the 1980s, including the sale of one state-run channel and the licensing of three or four new local or satellite-distributed channels, funded by subscription and advertising. The public sector remains quite strong, however, and despite the extensive publicity given new technologies, these have not really created significant change in the system, although the content of television offered has changed.

The countries with the strongest traditions of "public service" broadcasting have been those that are smallest, most concerned with protecting their national language and culture, and most socialist or collectivist in their policies. This is particularly true of Scandinavia and the Netherlands. Scandinavian broadcasting has been least destabilized by technological and commercial pressures, although there are signs of acceptance of satellite and cable reception of foreign commercial channels, and Denmark has added a new advertising-financed channel to its one public service television channel. The Netherlands has retained its unique system of allocating broadcast time to key social groups such as religious and labor organizations, but has relaxed its monopoly controls over time and methods of financing. As of October 1989 a new, purely commercial, channel has succeeded in gaining entry into the extensive Dutch cable system and will be fully legalized in 1990. For other small countries, such as Belgium, Ireland, and Finland, adaptation has meant more commercialism, more television, and less restrictive public controls.

Thus throughout Europe the changes in broadcasting have involved an increased supply of television on new or expanded channels, although the scope is less universal than under the old order. The consumer has acquired more choice, especially where cable is developed. There is more commercialism, which means more orientation to consumer demand, more funding directly from advertising or the consumer, more emphasis on the profit motive and business efficiency, and consequently less consideration of the cultural aspects of broadcasting. In the main, governments have sponsored these changes and helped to diffuse new technologies.

Commercialization and Transnationalization

Broadcasting has also become more transnational, as media conglomerates such as those of Murdoch and Berlusconi begin to cover Europe, and a new kind of broadcaster has sprung up: the purely commercial entrepreneur with multimedia, multinational ambitions. Two dominant trends now influence the direction of European broadcasting policy, those of commercialization and transnationalization.

Commercialization refers to a process by which broadcasting comes increasingly to rely on revenue from advertising, sponsorship, or subscription and to change accordingly: tending toward cutthroat competition, adopting profit maximization as a goal, seeking the largest possible audiences, neglecting unprofitable high-cost programming for minorities. Thus central goals of public broadcasting are undermined, as is the value of noncommercialism itself.

Transnationalization (Sepstrup, 1989) refers to the increasing transborder flow of services and programs and the increased exposure of audiences to imported culture. This is fueled partly by consumer demand, but mainly by the need to fill the proliferating channels from a limited supply of European programs. While this is may be a threat to national cultural identity, it is also inevitable in the new, more integrated, Europe, for which the slogan "television without frontiers" has been coined (European Economic Community, 1984). The threat of transnationalization has actually stimulated local commercialization, on the grounds that the domestic market might as well benefit from what appear to be inevitable changes; it has also provoked some efforts to protect local and European audiovisual production via subsidies and quotas (European Institute for the Media, 1988), rather similar to Third World cultural strategies (see Chapter 19).

The New Entrepreneurs

There have been a variety of entrepreneurial strategies for penetrating European broadcasting. The first model was to hire satellite transponder space to beam cheap bought-in material to cable systems in other countries in return for international advertising revenue. Rupert Murdoch's Sky Channel was the first such, based in Britain but aiming for the Continent. This example was closely followed by Super Channel, which broadcast commercial British programming. Massive pan-European projects have developed in Luxembourg, always an island of commercialism in European broadcasting, such as the abortive Coronet plan and currently the multichannel Astra satellite, which concentrates on medium-power direct (to household) broadcasting.

A different commercial model has developed on the Continent, especially by media magnates with extensive empires such as Berlusconi of Italy and Bertelsman of Germany. Their aim has been to penetrate particular markets with advertising-supported content in the national language—especially Italian, German, and French. This model has been more successful than the pan-European ventures, and is being followed up by assaults on the remaining bastions of public service in Scandinavia and the Netherlands. All of these ventures are ambitious and unashamedly commercial, exploiting loopholes in existing law and spending and losing considerable venture capital in the hope of future profit.

More limited commercial models include subscription cable, which offers specialized content like film or sporting events, and interactive cable and videotext services. The European Broadcasting Union (EBU) supported an attempt to mount a pan-European, advertising- and subsidy-supported public service television channel under the name Europa TV; this foundered for want of sufficient backing, advertising revenue, and audience after 18 months on the air during 1986 and 1987.

Clearly, then, the 1980s for European broadcasting have been a time of change, experiment, and adaptation. There has been a shift from broadcasting being a national matter of control over finance, content, and standards, largely exercised by political parties, governments, and powerful monopolies, to the current state, where there are new players in the game, new rules, and new stakes. The main new players are the media entrepreneurs in the business of production, marketing, distribution, and advertising with national and transnational ambitions. There are also the transnational agencies concerned with technical and hardware standards, legal issues, and European-level policymaking. The new rules are more permissive, but also more complex and confusing. The stakes are no longer limited to the traditional supply of culture and public information services, but include potentially huge profits and significant future markets for telecommunications infrastructure and domestic appliances.

The New Politics of Broadcasting

It is not clear that the new order is any less politicized than the old, but the politics are different. First, the response to or engineering of change has generally been a matter of policy. Britain, Germany, and France quite deliberately set out to make their systems more commercial and to encourage the expansion of new technologies in this way. In many cases, socialist parties have been supportive of or reluctant to oppose change because they too recognize the possible economic benefits. Thus more or less conscious political decisions have been made to let commerce pay for risky innovation.

Second, European-level politics and the economic goals of the European Community as well as the more cultural goals of the broader Council of Europe have exerted strong influences on national broadcasting policy, especially in harmonizing and liberalizing regulations for commercialism and promoting the health of European media industries (European Institute for the Media, 1988). Third, politics has turned toward widespread reregulation, drafting new rules for new commercial operators and new remits for public broadcasting and telecommunications. Media policy is now an important part of the political agenda across Europe.

Over the decade, the European debate has shifted from cultural and political issues to economic and industrial ones. There has been a shift in emphasis away from "public service" and the needs of citizens to the supposed interests of consumers and entrepreneurs. Media politics are no longer a solely national matter, but transnational influences are recognized, and there is a more developed sense of the interdependence of various media, especially when cross-media ownership has become such a powerful commercial reality.

The Limits of Change

The legitimacy of the old order of European broadcasting is thus severely challenged and there is a change of climate, policy, and institutional arrangements. At the end of a dramatic decade, how much has actually changed on the ground and in the air? First, monopoly arrangements have been largely dismantled to allow for independent competition for viewers. Second, there is a good deal more television and more choice available to European viewers than in 1980, even if they have not always taken advantage of this. Third, there is somewhat more freedom of content as a result of less strict control and more time on the airways. Fourth, with the exception of video, the "new media" have not reached mass markets, despite considerable sponsorship, especially of interactive media. Fifth, the new means of distribution that are supposed to erode the frontiers of Europe are still barely exploited. Cable has so far made real headway only in a few small countries such as Belgium and Holland; it is growing quite well in Germany and Sweden, but very little or not at all in France, and it has been a great flop in Britain. The alternative, low-cost direct-broadcast satellite transmission, is being tried out very expensively by some large commercial operators with very poor initial results. There seems to be a rejection of grandiose transnational efforts in favor of exploiting separate national markets for commercial television using cable or satellite.

Finally, despite all the changes and the debates, the very same public broadcasting organizations that were visible in 1980 are still, by and large, in place. Only one public channel—TF1 in France—has been privatized by selling it off. For the most part, public broadcasters have been quite adept at dealing with the increased competition, supported by their fairly secure revenue base. They have often entered the audience market aggressively, trying to attract and keep large audiences through scheduling more popular programming at peak times, a practice that has been criticized as "backdoor commercialization." Yet while noncommercialism has been eroded, many other public service goals remain.

The barriers of language and the preference for a domestic product explain audience resistance to change. Changes in leisure time and lifestyle have also made television less of an all-consuming preoccupation than in its heyday, and, so far, many of the changes have not offered much novelty or greater quality, only more of the same.

Conclusions

Politically sponsored and technologically driven change have not been powerful enough to destroy the old system, but they have modified it and left it vulnerable to future shifts of fortune. It is not easy to predict the future of public broadcasting, although the changes of the 1980s offer some lessons. The most important factor is political willingness to continue to sponsor and regulate broadcasting, whether for cultural, political, or economic reasons. If the will remains, then elements of the older European model will remain. Since politicians do not like to lose what they control, given the political sensitivity and utility of broadcasting, it is unlikely that broadcasting will be abandoned to the free market.

The "Europeanization" of media politics, which had brought a certain commercial "liberalization," still carries expectations of national performance and responsibility. There is still considerable nationalism in European countries, which can be used to mobilize public opinion against foreign intervention, whether in the form of "Europe" (i.e., the central bureaucracy of the European community is based in Brussels) or transnational media operators, with their foreign content and designs on the home market.

The technological environment is probably more uncertain than the political environment, yet new technologies alone are nothing without the institutional framework and public support to implement them. We are likely to see a decade of further testing of the viability and appeal of new broadcasting technologies, particularly DBS, but we may still end up with a more open, more diverse, more commercial, more populist, and more loosely regulated version of the old order. There are anxieties, particularly about the preservation of some space outside the market for other voices in society to communicate. The biggest danger lies in further surrender to the commercial imperative and in the loss of the inter- and intracountry diversity that has kept alive alternate possibilities to the monotony offered by capitalism and its market logic.

Further Questions

(1) Compare the television schedules of European television channels with American schedules. Are there differences in the amount of news programming, entertainment, original drama, and so on over one week?

(2) The issue of "cultural identity" has been raised in Europe and in the Third World (see Chapter 19). Explore the arguments made and the different solutions adopted. For whom is this a bigger issue, and why?

(3) What are the benefits and the dangers of a media future dominated by such enormous transnational cultural producers?

Note

1. This account is drawn from Bagdikian (1989).

9 Soviet Media Before and After Glasnost'

JOHN DOWNING

Many people in the United States think very confidently that they understand the Soviet media system. For them it is quite simply the readiest illustration of a top-heavy government media monopoly that can produce only boring propaganda. It is the example that—by its contrasts—defines conveniently and perfectly the virtues of the U.S. system.

So entrenched is this view that someone who suggests Soviet media are not quite so straightforward as this is liable to be defined as an apologist for them; the strong anticommunist strain in U.S. culture about which Herman writes (see Chapter 4) seems never too far from the surface. This chapter sets out to describe how Soviet media have changed in character during the decades since the 1917 Bolshevik revolution. The analysis challenges the easy assumption that Soviet media have been fixed, frozen in a pattern begun in 1917 and continuing to this day, or at least until the glasnost' era that began in earnest in 1985. Downing also notes how alternative underground media (samizdat') have operated in Soviet society, and how the Soviets have used new communications technologies. There is certainly power and control through media in the Soviet Union—but the actual mechanisms have often been more complex than glib Western critiques have claimed. The point is not to excuse Soviet media, but to understand them.

It is important to recall that Soviet media were originally conceived according to yet another normative theory, namely, that media existed for the purpose of developing political awareness and commitment to work for a just and fair society, a socialist philosophy. One of the tragedies of the twentieth century is the process by which those ideals became perverted into their opposite under the Stalin regime and at the hands of most of his successors at the helm of the Soviet state.

For our immediate purposes, however, we may note that the socialist normative theory of the media in its original form was designed to avoid the tilt of free-market media toward the capitalist class, and to give voice to ordinary working men and women in their desire for a better world. It was thought that the most effective role of socialist media was either to help organize revolutionary activists, in the case of the Marxist party newspaper, or to mobilize the general public, in the case of other more mass-based media. There was never any wish or expectation that these media would depend upon advertising revenues, although for a while after 1917 some of them accepted advertisements. Politics were always the priority.

To some degree, the development philosophy of media is a cousin to this original perspective. The needs of nations in the Southern Hemisphere for effective communication about infant hygiene, literacy, nutrition, and agricultural techniques make media potentially valuable sources of information, perhaps marking the difference between life and death. If they fulfill this role, who could object? Yet just as socialist media became instruments of untrammeled state power, so too may "development" media. Who aside from the state has the right to define what is socialist media policy, or what is development media policy? That is a crucial question to consider—and yet the original objectives cannot simply be junked because there are no easy answers.

A Brief History

The Soviet Union has an enormous diversity of media in many different languages. Russian is the main one, but there are more than a hundred languages spoken, from Ukrainian (43 million speakers) to tiny language communities of a few thousand. The Soviet literacy rate (95-99%, depending on the region) is considerably higher than the U.S. literacy rate (variously estimated but certainly lower than 90%), with the result that more citizens can use print media in the Soviet Union than in the United States.

To understand some of the basic features of Soviet media (Kagarlitsky, 1988; Remington, 1988) it is necessary to go back to the period before the 1917 revolution, when the founders of Soviet Communism were revolutionaries living mostly in hiding, banned not only in Russia but from many other countries as well. They were planning the overthrow of a heavily militarized, powerful government run by the hereditary rulers of the Russian Empire, the czars. There is almost a parallel with South African apartheid. In both, the majority had no vote and no leverage, and often lived and worked in appalling conditions, spied upon by the secret police and informers. Democrats abhorred the Russian political system then as they do the apartheid regime today. As in South Africa, there were those who dreamed not just of replacing the present regime with one only marginally better, but of creating a dynamic new society where farmer and worker, thinker and government official would unite to break down division and privilege forever.

In this situation, despite occasional let-ups for a year or so, selling an opposition newspaper openly was to invite police raids on the press, the seizure of lists of activists, and their arrest and imprisonment. To the

Bolsheviks, therefore, only a secretive, tightly disciplined organization had any chance of survival.[1] The party newspaper, circulating clandestinely, was the voice of the Bolshevik leadership, and if the latter had voted to establish a particular policy, the paper would publish it and develop it—but not question it. We must, argued Lenin, be no less disciplined than our opponents—indeed, we must be more so. It was out of this situation, then, that the Bolsheviks developed what became the hallmark of their media system, the tight relationship between the Communist party and the media (although for a political party to run a newspaper directly was much more common then than now).

The other component of the Soviet media system was the Bolsheviks' view that media existed to mobilize the public in a revolutionary direction. Before the revolution, this meant they focused on the ills of czarism and capitalism, and what might be done to overthrow them. During the war, to a society of starving soldiers, workers, and farmers, they called for "bread, peace, and land!" After the revolution, the media focused on defending the revolution, especially during the desperate years of the civil war, 1918-20, and on the vision of creating a new type of human being appropriate for the new Communist era. Clearly, this was a radically different set of objectives to those typical of Western media, a socialist normative media theory rather than a free-market philosophy.

Once the Bolsheviks had seized power in 1917, they were faced within a few months with the civil war, which at its height stretched over three fronts totaling 5,000 miles. Their opponents were armed by fourteen Western nations, but their own resources had to come from inside the country, itself devastated after the 1914-1918 world war.

To begin with, most of the other political parties were allowed to publish their papers, even when they spoke out against the Bolshevik government's policies. However, not long into the fray non-Bolshevik media were suppressed. Other nations at war have taken similar actions against the media and free expression—but after the civil war was over, the full range of previous media was never restored. Similarly, with disastrous implications for the future of open expression, the Communist party banned organized "factions" within its ranks. This meant that with the Communist party by then the only legal political organization, people were denied the right to set up groups inside it that could push for varying policies and keep debate alive.

Despite this, from 1917 to the late 1920s there was an extraordinary blossoming of inventiveness and imagination in certain Soviet media, especially in film, poster art, theater, poetry, literature, and the arts in general (Gleason, Kenez, & Stites, 1985). Some of the most advanced artistic work in Europe was taking place in the Soviet Union during those years. It reflected, especially after the civil war was won, the existence of active public debate, though this declined toward the end of the 1920s and began to revive again only from 1985, with the Gorbachev era (apart from 1956-1964, while Khrushchev was premier).

It was during the 1920s that Stalin and his apparatus were gradually establishing their extensive control over Soviet society. It would not be until 1938 that this control could be defined as total, but in the process of establishing it, the space for debate—and therefore for open media—shrank to vanishing point. Then the expression of alternative views, even painting in disapproved styles (e.g., abstract art), became not just unpopular but downright dangerous.

Miserably, this straitjacketing process took place in the name of socialist development, not of the dictatorship that it actually was. Lenin, who in 1924 had been embalmed physically as well as politically, was cited to sanctify each new turn of policy, rather in the way some people will quote little gobbets from religious texts to justify whatever they wish to do. It was an ironic as well as a tragic development, given that Lenin had spent his entire political career in heated debate with one or another political adversary, and had quite often been outvoted in the Bolshevik party, even after the revolution.

The resulting Soviet media were indeed leaden, doctrinaire, given to effusive praise of Stalin and his favorites, and totally silent about the crushing grip of the secret police over the nation. The purpose of this brief history, however, is partly to point out how this description fits media in the Stalin era, but that it takes no account of variations before or since.

Stalin died in 1953, and media changes began to be evident from about 1956. The premiership of Khrushchev in 1956-1964 saw the publication of some novels quite sharply critical of the Stalin era, such as Solzhenitsyn's famous *One Day in the Life of Ivan Denisovich.* Remember, novels that dealt with the terrible atrocities of the Stalin era were not pulp spectaculars to be bought for distraction in a shopping mall, but stories of suffering and political repression that were penetrating public debate for the first time. Their impact was enormous.

Certain publications, such as *Izvestiya* (*The News*), the main government newspaper—*Pravda* (*Truth*) is the main Communist party organ—and the literary magazine *Novy Mir* (*New World*) enjoyed Khrushchev's special patronage, and acted as his mouthpieces in the struggles he had with Stalin's old guard. This period is often referred to as the "thaw." After Khrushchev was ousted in 1964, there was a landmark trial the following year of two writers named Sinyavsky and Daniel, who received long jail terms for writing critically of the regime. This heralded the end of Khrushchev's relaxation of controls. In particular, dissent in Czechoslovakia and Poland in 1968 panicked the leadership into a systematic clampdown from 1969 onward, when many critical writers began to be sent to jail or psychiatric wards.

At the close of this chapter the most recent act in this drama will be discussed, the glasnost' period that began formally in 1985, for which samizdat' acted as a slow fuse.

Samizdat': The Soviet Underground Media

No one had expected to be able to publish dissonant material before Khrushchev, and so many publications were "for the drawer," as the expression went—a typescript that was completed by the author in the hope that one day things would change and it could be published. Following the clampdown, however, an alternative public sphere developed underground: the unofficial circulation of typescript books, articles, and plays (multiplied by using sheets of carbon paper and sometimes barely legible as a result). The convention was that if you got to read one, you agreed to type more copies for further distribution. This was "self-publishing" (which is what the word *samizdat'* means) outside the censorship restrictions of the government.

The penalties for doing this were severe, though they no longer meant execution, which might easily have followed in the Stalin era. Technically, making up to nine copies was legal, but in practice this protected no one from arrest or jail. Not only writing was circulated in this way, but also audiocassettes of songs (called *magnitizdat'*), which sometimes directly, sometimes indirectly, challenged the inherited political order. Some of the most famous writers and singers circulated their work in this way (G. S. Smith, 1984). Other people had books published by Soviet émigré presses in Paris and elsewhere, and then smuggled back in. The advent of the videocassette recorder, predictably, took this process an interesting stage further.

Thus the creative development of alternative media, which other chapters in this book also discuss, has been an important feature of the Soviet media situation too, even though the circulation of samizdat' works was relatively small (Medvedev, 1984). Thus Soviet media, themselves alternative media before the revolution, eventually sparked alternative media of their own. Kagarlitsky (1988) emphasizes how samizdat' was part of the long Russian tradition of dissident intellectual communication, but how it retained a potency within that culture that dissident views rarely achieve in the West. Condee and Padunov (1989) provide an absorbing account of how developments in the semiofficial theater began to pave the way for glasnost' before it was officially declared in being.

The other major everyday response to a media system that failed to give information on certain major issues, or that wrapped it up in official platitudes, was the elevation of rumor, word-of-mouth communication, to greater significance than is usual in a more open media situation. The telling of political jokes against the regime also became a major art form. Both phenomena are well known from many different countries as grass-roots responses to an overly controlled media system.

The Structure of Soviet Media Until Glasnost'

After this brief historical survey, let us now look at the inherited structure of Soviet media, which obtained until the end of the 1980s. Although in the era of Glasnost' very significant changes began to be seen, this inherited system was likely to bear influence for some time to come.

Organization

Before we can proceed to describe the various features of Soviet media, the basic relation of the Communist party to government and media has to be understood. The Communist party in a Soviet-style society is not comparable to a conventional political party in the West. In the United States, for example, although both major parties have their devotees, the party organizations are primarily machines for getting presidential candidates, congressional representatives, governors, and mayors elected. The Communist Party of the Soviet Union (CPSU), by contrast, has been the unique political party of the land, officially containing within its ranks the cream of the Soviet working class, farmers, and thinkers. In practice, joining it has often been a necessary career move for promotion to high office, rather than an act of political commitment.

This body has considered itself uniquely qualified to act as the leading institution in the nation's life, to propose policy to government that it is then government's responsibility to legislate. It has acted as an omnipresent spur to compliance with CPSU priorities through the network of Party cells organized in virtually every factory, every farm, every office, every media institution, every school in the land. From a few years after the revolution, the CPSU developed a list (the *nomenklatura*) of appropriate individuals for high office in the Party or the state, rather like a directory of the Soviet power structure. Its ability to use this list, to handpick whom it approves and to exclude those it disapproves, is perhaps the single greatest mechanism of its power.

Thus official media are all directly under the control of the government, with a Party cell inside them, or under the Party's immediate control, like *Pravda.* Radio and television are government run, with the State Committee for Radio and Television (*Gosteleradio*) formally in charge of their operation. All the hundred thousand or more journalists are licensed through the Union of Journalists.

Until the Gorbachev era, there were three further bodies concerned with exercising control over the media. One was the Chief Board for the Preservation of State Secrets in the Press, known as *Glavlit,* which was the official censorship body, exercising both pre- and postpublication censorship. The second was more important, namely, the Propaganda Department of the CPSU Central Committee, whose task was to set out the fundamental guidelines that editors were to observe. The third was the State Security Committee (KGB), whose role enabled greater flexibility and promptness in dealing with problems than either of the other two. It could simply send its operatives to the editorial offices, or call in editorial staff to account for their actions. From 1985 onward, all these agencies began to have less and less to do in the media sphere.

These, then, were the "gatekeepers" of the Soviet media system. The main mode by which control was exerted, however, was that journalists censored themselves. Self-censorship is, as we saw in Chapter 7, a very widespread phenomenon. Its ultimate form, perhaps, is to be seen in the person who opts not to become a journalist at all, because of the hopelessness of acting as one in such a situation. Such responses were well known in Soviet society before 1985. Journalism was not a respected profession. From 1985, it became much more so.

Technology

Under this heading needs to be mentioned the use of new technologies for media transmission. The expansion of television in the Soviet Union, to which great attention has been given ever since the early 1960s, has been made possible through the use of satellites (Downing, 1985). The costs of extending television service to the whole country by building booster relay stations would have been stupendous. For this reason, the development of satellite transmissions has been of the greatest importance. Now military conscripts in far-flung regions and sailors on icebreaker ships in the Arctic are no longer cut off from national TV. *Pravda* is now printed via satellite facsimile simultaneously across the country's 11 time zones.

Other new communications technologies have been slower to take off. Cable television is in the process of experimental development in Moscow City. Personal telephones are very rare by comparison with the United States. Personal computers are very seldom in individual hands, with printers and modems hardly ever to be found outside official institutions. Photocopying machines are licensed by the state; individuals cannot own them, and access to them is strictly controlled.

Typical Media Contents

I have deliberately phrased the subhead this way to remind the American reader of his or her probable prejudices. We are so conditioned to think of Soviet society as a gray, uniform monolith that it is easy to slip into assuming that all their media will be "typical." Yet with a vast range of weekly and monthly magazines covering sports, science, literature of all kinds from the intense to the trivial, international current affairs, history, wild life, architecture, fashion, and hobbies, this assumption is unwarranted. Admittedly, girlie magazines, fanzines, violent and lurid comic strips, and trade magazines on fast food and endless other money-making projects are not on sale, so some variety to which Americans are accustomed is missing, for what that variety is worth. The quality of the paper is less glossy than that of many U.S. publications, although this is not true of many books.

In 1989 there were about 8,000 daily newspapers in the Soviet Union, amounting to about 170 million copies a year, and another nearly 8,000 weeklies. Of the 4 leading national dailies, *Pravda* had a circulation of more than 10 million, the Communist Youth paper *Komsomolskaya Pravda* was close to that figure, *Izvestiya* had 8 million, and *Trud* (*Labor*), the labor union paper, had 14 million, making it the largest-circulation newspaper in the world. Compare these figures to the United States, where neither of the two top-selling newspapers sells more than 2 million (the *Wall Street Journal* and the *New York Daily News*), and the difference is plain. The *Wall Street Journal* and *USA Today* are the nearest to being widely read national dailies in the United States. Another difference, however, is that most Soviet newspapers have only four to six pages and the most minimal advertisements.

The Soviet Union has four program channels for television and four for radio, which probably seems very few to Americans. Only in the western, most highly populated, part of the country can all four TV channels be received, and even then only in certain regions. The first TV channel broadcasts from about 8 a.m. to midnight, and transmits the most important materials, including news and current affairs and the leading evening news program, *Vremya* (*Time*). The second channel, *Programma 2*, carries more entertainment and local material, and has in recent years been more innovative. The third is an educational channel, through which people can take courses for credit. The fourth offers plays, feature films, and variety shows. The second and fourth channels broadcast only in the evenings. Programs are broadcast in color, although most television sets are still black-and-white. The picture quality (on a good TV set) can be better than in the United States, because a higher-resolution system is used. Until very recently, advertisements played no economic role in Soviet media, which are financed directly by the government, offset to a greater or lesser degree by sales.

Film

Movies have always been an important aspect of Soviet mass communication. Lenin defined the cinema as "the most important art" because of its dramatic potential and its wide distribution capacity. Some Soviet directors, notably Sergei Eisenstein, have been among the leading names in world cinema. As well as documentaries of all kinds, the Soviet Union produces about 240 feature films a year. The majority come from the big studios in Leningrad and Moscow, but each of the fifteen republics that make up the Soviet Union has its own studio. Interestingly, some of the smaller republics, such as Georgia in the south, have managed to produce more original films than the leading centers. The contents of feature films fall into the following categories: contemporary, historical and about the revolution, World War II, historical/biographical, adaptations from literature, adventure, comedy, and musical.

Films about the "Great Patriotic War" (World War II) have been made constantly since 1945. They reflect the horrifying wound dealt to Soviet society by the Nazi invasion, with a resulting 20 million dead. (The Americans, British, and allied nations lost less than 2 million.) This is a wound of which older Soviet citizens are inevitably highly conscious, for few families failed to lose members. But it is also a wound that the regime utilized skillfully for decades to heighten public anxiety about the West's militarism, and so to help unify people around itself. (The Cold War paid off politically for the regimes of both superpowers.) The result is that World War II films have been as frequent in the Soviet Union as western adventure movies used to be in the United States, or as police series are today. All kept alive major cultural myths for their respective societies, although younger Soviet audiences began to react against endless Great Patriotic War epics.

Production Values

The types of shots, editing cuts, and camera angles in Soviet film and television have often been different from those common in U.S. visual media. Although in the very early period some now-familiar devices were actually pioneered in the Soviet Union—the split screen, for instance—the legacy of the Stalin era has weighed heavily upon visual media as upon other areas of social life. The tradition of what was called "socialist realism" in art, which under Stalin was the only artistic style permitted, has left its mark. The typical socialist realist painting showed the good guys looking strong and positive and smiling, and the bad guys looking the opposite, not unlike the white-hatted and black-hatted cowboys in many American westerns.

The suspenseful, fast-cutting, quick-paced style of most U.S. films and TV movies is only gradually registering its presence on Soviet screens. At the same time, the use of young women's sexual allure as a major component of filmmaking only began to surface in the late 1980s. By the end of the 1980s, some Soviet TV programs were beginning to reflect the fast pace of TV formats in the West.

Audiences

Since the late 1960s, it has become much more common in the Soviet Union to poll opinions, including audience and readership surveys. The result is that much more is now known about Soviet preferences and habits in using media (Mickiewicz, 1981). Since television now reaches practically the entire population, film has done so for a long time, and print media are also universally available, it is interesting to note which media offerings are popular.

Circulation figures in themselves do not necessarily tell the whole story: Party newspapers are required reading if you are in the CPSU. Here there is an amusing comparison with the habit of many New York City subway users on their way to work, who read the *Daily News* or the *New York Post* on the subway, and then walk into work carrying the *New York Times* or the *Wall Street Journal.* However, surveys have indicated that the Soviet audience has a strong appetite for international news. Movies and musical variety shows appeal most of all. Sports programs and nature documentaries are very popular. By contrast, programs about industry, poetry readings, and news analysis are well down the list of preferences. Adventure, comedy, musical, and World War II movies top movie audiences' preference ratings.

Media use figures show that in the country people watch much more TV than in the towns, presumably because of the lack of other leisure amenities. As in the United States, older people watch more TV. Women in urban areas watch less than men, due to the "second shift" pattern, where they work for a wage and also do most of the household chores, like standing in line, food shopping. Political activists use newspapers and magazines much more intensively than any other segment of the population, for the print media they read are tied in with their activism.

Readers' Letters

No description of Soviet media would be complete without noting the importance of this institution. At *Pravda* alone there are 45 full-time staff members to handle readers' letters, and the volume is estimated at twice the number received by U.S. newspapers. The process of selection for publication is shrouded in some mystery, but some surprisingly frank accounts of everyday problems and miseries are regularly printed. Those who write in are overwhelmingly older people, and many more industrial workers or farmers write than professionals or intellectuals. The tradition is, however, that every letter is to be answered, at least in some fashion.

Clearly, these letters function as both a safety valve for the public and an early warning system to the Soviet authorities. However, contrary to many Americans' belief that public criticism is totally banned in the Soviet Union, these letters have always been widely used. There are certain conventions in force, so that what is criticized is apparently a problem in one factory or in one city agency, not a systemic problem. Nonetheless, readers are likely to feel some resonance with their own experiences, and thus the institution is an important way of airing common social grievances. Sometimes reporters will be sent on special assignment to investigate these letters, and a major feature article will appear on the subject.

In the initial years of the Gorbachev era, the use of the letters page became even more widespread. When, however, the new Congress of Deputies was set up in 1988, letter writers began to divert their communications to deputies rather than sending them to the press.

The Experience of Glasnost' and Some Conclusions

Steering a course through common misconceptions about Soviet media is not always easy. Some of the misconceptions are so gross that once students discover them they sometimes lurch to the assumption that Soviet media display a general superiority to Western media. There is no need to seesaw in this fashion. The beginning of wisdom is to recognize that although the Soviet Union has a particular history, one very different from that of the United States, it is all the same a normal society in which a vast range of everyday activities are fulfilled, from working for a living to using the transport system to spending time exposed to media.

It is also a society that, like many others, has undergone social, economic, and political change. Today, the Soviet population is highly urbanized, and more highly educated than ever. These developments are part of the groundswell that produced the Gorbachev era. The word *glasnost'*, which has become the symbol of Gorbachev's intended new approach, has a direct bearing on the media. Its basic meaning signifies publicity, the public sphere, and is derived from a word for *voice.* In the new context it has come to denote the drive to voice endemic problems and embarrassing issues out in the open, instead of concealing them or cloaking them in jargon, which had previously been the typical method of dealing with them.

How far glasnost' will reach is the subject of keen debate both inside and outside the Soviet Union. The 1986 Chernobyl nuclear plant disaster would probably have been hushed up, as was a similar disaster in the Chelyabinsk area in the 1950s, if it had not been for the new policy. The fact that some Western media might have reported Chernobyl instantly, rather than 48 hours later, should not blind us to the sharp change in media policy that was evident from that point on (Mickiewicz, 1988, pp. 60-68). A different example is the treatment of the Soviet invasion of Afghanistan in 1979, which began by being automatically endorsed by the media, but then came to be more and more vigorously criticized once Gorbachev announced a policy review on the subject (Downing, 1988d).

One very evident feature of glasnost' in the later 1980s was the open exploration of hitherto hidden and shameful pages of Soviet history, especially the huge network of slave-labor camps in the 1930s and 1940s and Stalin's massive liquidation of potential opponents, Communist and non-Communist alike. Much of this was known in outline in the West, but had never been published in Soviet media. On the other hand, some changes—such as "rehabilitating" major architects of the revolution whom Stalin had had tortured, executed, and systematically denounced as traitors—concerned a history now long past, and thus were no longer genuinely controversial. The media future in the Soviet Union is fascinating, but still somewhat opaque.

There are many other issues deserving of consideration that have not even been touched upon in this chapter. For instance, the system of public meetings to convey and debate government and party policies in the workplace is a key aspect of public communication in the Soviet Union (Remington, 1988, chaps. 2-3). The role of the Telegraphic Agency of the Soviet Union (TASS) is very important, as the major news agency for national and international reporting, with authority over other media far greater than news agencies such as Associated Press, but also as the source that supplies the Soviet leadership with detailed, up-to-the-minute briefings that are not published in the media.

Of interest on the international front is the development of foreign television broadcasts via satellite, mostly to allied nations, using the Intersputnik satellite organization and the program exchange body in Prague, the Organization of International Radio and Television. These bodies are approximate Eastern equivalents of Intelsat and the European Broadcasting Union, although smaller in scope (Downing, 1989). Of equal interest is the impact of Voice of America, the BBC, and other foreign broadcasters inside the Soviet Union (Shanor, 1985). Finally, the recent political upsurges in Eastern Europe and the 1989 switch to non-Communist governments there, and their media repercussions, are all likely to exert a considerable impact on Soviet media.

In general, the study of the Soviet media system is interesting not only in itself, and in the light of changes under way in the late 1980s, but also for the contrasts it affords with the U.S. media system, the Western European systems summarized by McQuail in Chapter 8, and still other modes of organizing media, notably democratic and participatory alternative media.

Further Questions

(1) Do all forms of state try to control the media? How far do major media ever go to oppose this assault on their activity?

(2) What importance do a country's history, politics, and culture have in shaping its media system?

(3) What is the significance of self-censorship among journalists in any media system?

(4) Do U.S. media, too, albeit without officially so acknowledging it as do Soviet media, serve as political mobilizers? (See Chapters 4 and 5.)

Note

1. At the turn of the century, Communists were called Social Democrats, a term that has now come to be used to describe socialists who accept parliamentary democracy as the only major road to socialism. The Russian Social Democrats split in 1903 in a hotly contested party congress into majority and minority factions, the majority being termed (in Russian) *Bolsheviki.* This was Lenin's group.

Part III Audiences and Users

The nature of the media audience is currently one of the most controversial areas of media analysis. It raises some fundamental questions about our models of human action, or why we think people act the way they do and believe what they do, and our models of media power, or the way we think that the media exercise power in society. While each of us thinks *we* choose media content and react "simply" as individuals, early media analysts used to describe us as the "mass" audience, rather uniform in our responses, passive, and manipulated by media content. Gradually, however, media analysts and professionals alike have come to see the audience as diverse, segmented by social backgrounds, cultural tastes, and patterns of consumption. However, the extent of this diversity is questioned by Thomas in her chapter on the educational functions of entertainment in Part V of this book. It is also challenged by the commercial dynamic of U.S. media, which themselves "package" audiences for advertizers and hence "package" specialized content for target audiences. As Gandy argues, the monitoring of audiences is becoming more refined and pervasive. How far, and in what ways, people can resist these attempts to structure our media use and consumption habits, and find new and resistive meanings is of crucial social significance. The logic of this "active" and resistive audience idea is for people to become involved in the actual production of media texts. This frequently happens in processes of social change, as Downing explores in his chapter. More people producing more and diverse media would, of course, be a great change in and of itself.

10 The Nature of the Audience

IEN ANG

Ang, by contrast with Gandy in Chapter 11, focuses on explaining how audiences make sense of television, and the kinds of meanings and pleasures they derive from media in their everyday lives. Such an approach tends to downplay the "power" of the media to create universally understood messages, and examines instead how people make meanings. Ang reviews various theoretical models of the audience, including the notion of a "mass audience," and the original opposition view to it, the "uses and gratifications" approach. She shows, among other things, how new theories develop and how criticism of one approach becomes the basis for a different perspective. Ang also stresses how diverse audiences have diverse reactions, so that women do not use the media in the same way as men (a point elaborated by Rakow in Chapter 16). Similarly, members of racial, ethnic, and other minority groups might view certain news content or entertainment programming from a critical standpoint that is different from that of members of the dominant culture (a point elaborated by Corea in Chapter 18). Ang's emphasis, therefore, is on "active" and "diverse" audiences.

Our everyday lives are permeated by the mass media. At home, you may casually watch television together with your family, or listen to a record you have just bought. Driving to school in your car, you may have the car radio on, while you pass dozens of huge billboards along the road that are there to be seen but that you hardly notice. Or you wear your Walkman on your head, listening to some music while waiting for the subway. During lunch hour, you may be reading today's newspaper or exchanging the latest gossip about the love lives of the stars with your friends. Meanwhile, your VCR is taping your favorite soap opera so that you can watch it after school. On the weekend, you may go to a movie or go dancing to the latest dance hits. Alternatively, you may have decided to stay at home, reading an engrossing science fiction novel or browsing

---

Author's Note: I would like to thank James Lull for comments on an earlier draft of this chapter.

through a stack of magazines. In all these activities, you are part of the media audience. Or, to put it more precisely, you are a member of many different media audiences at once. How can we make sense of this fact? What does it mean for us to live as audience members for the mass media?

These are interesting and important questions, but strangely enough communication scholars have not come up with too many satisfactory answers so far. Our knowledge about the nature of media audiences is thus rather limited. This is because the most influential conceptions of the audience are incapable of doing justice to the heterogeneous ways in which, as the summary above suggests, the media are used and take on meanings for people. In the next section, two of these dominant conceptions will be described: the audience as "mass" and the audience as "market." In the past few decades, however, more and more communication scholars have realized the limitations of these conceptions and have attempted to develop new perspectives on media audiences. In a subsequent section, some of the more recent perspectives on media audiences will be explored. In these perspectives, theory and research are designed precisely to get a more nuanced picture of the specific social and cultural meanings of media use and reception for people in different contexts. The chapter will end with some concluding remarks.

Classic Conceptions: The Audience as "Mass" and "Market"

The term *mass audience* is easily associated with the media because the media are generally assumed to involve processes of mass communication. The concept of "mass" was especially influential in the first half of this century. At that time, media such as film and radio made their entrance and rapidly gained a popularity that was unprecedented. These media attracted millions of people, a startling development that concerned many cultural observers and critics. They saw these popular media as important constituents of what they called a "mass society," and perceived their audiences as "masses" who absorb "mass culture."

Sociologist Herbert Blumer (1950) described the "mass" as follows:

> *First,* its membership may come from all walks of life, and from all distinguishable social strata; it may include people of different class position, of different vocation, of different cultural attainment, and of different wealth. One can recognize this in the case of the mass of people who follow a murder trial. *Secondly,* the mass is an anonymous group, or more exactly is composed of anonymous individuals. *Third,* there exists little interaction or exchange of

> experience between members of the mass. They are usually physically separated from one another, and, being anonymous, do not have the opportunity to mill as do members of the crowd. *Fourth*, the mass is very loosely organized and is not able to act with the concertedness or unity of a crowd.

The conception of media audiences as masses, then, emphasizes their large size and their being composed of isolated and unknown individuals. Although this conception was presented as a purely descriptive way of perceiving audiences, it is surrounded by many additional, evaluative, meanings that are usually very negative. Since the model held that community and religious organizations no longer helped people understand the world, the mass was often seen as individualized, essentially passive, and easily manipulated. It is therefore not surprising that a lot of early fears about the powers of the media were fed by the idea of the mass. Some early theorists were concerned that the media—especially very popular media such as movies, radio, and later television—were acting like "hypodermic needles," injecting messages directly into the veins of their completely defenseless viewers and listeners. More generally, the mass audience was often looked down upon as being composed of people with low taste and intelligence.

An early example of the condescending image of media audiences that was derived from the conception of mass is the following description of the "typical" radio listener. It comes from Roy Durstine, a very prominent 1930s advertising agency executive:

> The typical listening audience for a radio program is a tired, bored, middle-aged man and woman whose lives are empty and who have exhausted their sources of outside amusement when they have taken a quick look at an evening paper. . . . Radio provides a vast source of delight and entertainment for the barren lives of the millions. (quoted in Stamps, 1979)

It should be added that similar views can still be heard, but nowadays more often in relation to television than in relation to radio. It is now the television audience that is still occasionally perceived as a huge mass of more or less passive, faceless viewers, as the name "couch potato" suggests.

In sum, the concept of the mass can be criticized because it does not give us any understanding of the world of media audiences themselves. After all, do we see ourselves as passive, easily manipulated, and anonymous while we are watching television? As British cultural analyst Raymond Williams (1961) has put it, there are in fact no masses, but "only ways of seeing people as masses" (p. 289). And those ways of seeing tend to be elitist and moralistic.

Another influential way of perceiving media audiences comes from the commercial context in which media industries operate. In this, audiences are seen as potential "consumers" of media material, as "market." Furthermore, they are seen as potential consumers for the products offered for sale in advertising, which forms the financial source for the production of media material (see Chapter 11). However, because market researchers are generally concerned merely with quantitative and "objective" information about numbers of viewers, listeners, readers, and so on, they do not give us insight into the more qualitative and more "subjective" aspects of media consumption. Thus looking at ratings and similar figures does not give us any sense of what the experience of television viewing, music listening, or book reading means to people. As Todd Gitlin (1983), a critical communications scholar, has remarked about the meaning of ratings: "The numbers only sample sets tuned in, not necessarily shows watched, let alone grasped, remembered, loved, learned from, deeply anticipated, or mildly tolerated" (p. 54). And media sociologist Denis McQuail (1987) has put it this way: "The market view is inevitably the view 'from the media.' We never conceive of ourselves as belonging to markets, rather we are placed in market categories or identified as part of a target group by others" (p. 221).

Changing Perspectives

Although the concepts of mass and market have very different origins, they also share some assumptions about the nature of media audiences, of which two are most important. First, they tend to ignore the fact that media audiences consist of human beings who do not merely respond to media output more or less passively, but who are actively involved, both emotionally and intellectually, with particular forms of media material. Second, they do not take account of the fact that we do not consume media material as isolated and solitary individuals, but in particular social settings and cultural frameworks.

Some communication scholars have long challenged the dominant concepts of mass and market. They have attempted to develop alternative perspectives on media audiences, in which the study of the meaning of media consumption *as a social and cultural activity* is emphasized. The earliest attempts to do this were undertaken by researchers of the "uses and gratifications" tradition. Their starting point was that the media are functional for people, that using media gratifies certain needs and wants. Another group of researchers interested in audience activity are those who study media reception. These researchers are concerned with the ways in which people interpret and make sense of media texts. Finally, a recent trend within academic audience research is growing awareness of the necessity to understand how mass media fit into the context of everyday life.

Uses and Gratifications

Uses and gratifications researchers assume that media audiences are active in their choices of media material. From this perspective, the use of media is a highly selective and motivated activity, and not just a mindless pastime. In general, people use the media because they expect that doing so will give them some gratifications—hence the name of this research tradition. These gratifications are assumed to be related to the satisfaction of social and psychological needs experienced by the individual (Blumler & Katz, 1974; Rosengren, Palmgreen, & Wenner, 1985).

In a typical empirical study within this tradition, audience members are asked to fill out a long questionnaire about why they watch a certain television program or pick out any other kind of media material. Over the years, responses gathered from these studies have shown a rather regular pattern. It turns out that the reasons repeatedly mentioned by people can be divided into the following categories (McQuail, 1987, p. 73):

- *information:* finding out about society and the world, seeking advice on practical matters, satisfying curiosity and interest, learning
- *personal identity:* finding reinforcement for personal values, finding models for behavior, identifying with valued others, gaining insight into oneself
- *integration and social interaction:* gaining insight into circumstances of others, gaining a sense of belonging, finding a basis for conversation, helping to carry out social roles
- *entertainment:* being diverted from problems, relaxation, getting cultural and aesthetic pleasure and enjoyment, filling time, emotional release, sexual arousal

Most people will be able to recognize themselves in many of the items mentioned; it has been the merit of uses and gratifications researchers to have provided sufficient empirical evidence for all of them. That is, people turn to the media and make use of them for a variety of reasons, not just one. Yet there are also problems with this approach. Only some of the most important criticisms will be summed up here (Elliot, 1974).

First of all, the approach is individualistic: It takes into account only *individual* uses of the media and the psychological gratifications derived from them. The fact that people get in touch with media in particular *social* contexts tends to be ignored. As a result, the approach does not take into consideration that some uses of the media are not related to the pursuit of gratifications at all. For example, some media use may be forced upon people rather than freely chosen. For instance, think about parents who have to endure the sound of loud rock music because their teenage kids have turned the volume up. As another example: Feminists will resent sexist billboards.

A second problem has to do with the lack of attention within the approach to the *content* of media output. In other words, uses and gratifications researchers attempt to find out *why* people use media, but forget to analyze exactly *what* people get out of a TV show, a book, or a pop song. What are overlooked here are the *meanings* people give to media culture.

Finally, there is a political problem, which stems from the general starting point of the uses and gratifications approach. By emphasizing the fact that using the media is always *functional* to people—that is, that uses are always related to gratifications—the approach may implicitly offer a justification for the existing ways in which the mass media are organized. If people always find some satisfaction in their media use, it could be argued that they must also be perfectly content with the material that is made available by the media. Thus we could all too easily conclude that because the media give us what we want, there is no reason whatsoever to change them. But this reasoning takes into account only what is actually available, and ignores the possibility that alternative kinds of media output (e.g., more documentaries or penetrating news reporting on television, or more programing for Blacks, gays, or other cultural and ethnic minorities) might be even more gratifying for many people.

Reception Analysis

Another group of researchers has taken up the task that was left aside by the uses and gratifications approach: They have started to examine how audiences construct meanings out of media offerings, generally called "texts." This kind of research can be assembled under the heading of reception analysis.

The starting point here is the assumption that the meaning of media texts is not something fixed, or inherent, within the text. Rather, media texts acquire meaning only at the moment of reception, that is, when they are read, viewed, listened to, or whatever. In other words, audiences are seen as *producers* of meaning, not just consumers of media content: They *decode* or *interpret* media texts in ways that are related to their social and cultural circumstances and to the way in which they subjectively experience those circumstances.

From this perspective, reception researchers have begun to study the different ways in which diverse audience groups interpret the same media text. Their interest is directed not to the individual ways in which people make sense of such a text, but to social meanings, that is, meanings that are culturally shared. Some reception researchers have used the term "interpretive communities" to denote groups of people who make common interpretations of a text (Radway, 1987). We could also speak about "subcultures" (Hebdige, 1979) consisting of people who share a preference for a particular type of media material (e.g., soap opera lovers or heavy metal fans). Such communities or subcultures do not have to be physically united in one location, but can be geographically dispersed and can consist of many different kinds of people who do not know each other, but are symbolically connected by their shared interest in a media product. In general, what reception researchers aim to uncover is how people in their own social and historical contexts make sense of all kinds of media texts in ways that are meaningful, suitable, and accessible to them.

For example, it is interesting to see how a massively popular TV show such as *Dallas* has been received and interpreted by different groups and peoples throughout the world. For most Americans, the fact that Dallas is the center of the Texas oil industry must be quite familiar knowledge. However, many people who live in Europe or in Third World countries and who watch *Dallas* may not even be sure where Texas is. As a result, it is very likely that their interpretations of the story will be different from those of Americans. Several researchers, including Tamar Liebes and Elihu Katz from Israel, have found that non-Americans are more ready to see in *Dallas* a "realistic" representation of the United States than are Americans themselves, who are more inclined to emphasize the showy aspects of the glamorous soap opera (Liebes & Katz, 1986). Thus one viewer in another study from Holland gave this comment about the Ewings of *Dallas*: "Actually they are all a bit stupid. And oversensational. Affected and genuinely American—money-appearance-relationship maniacs-family and nation, etc!" (Ang, 1985, p. 108). In short, although *Dallas* is an almost globally popular program, that does not mean that it is interpreted and made sense of in identical ways. *Dallas* is a different program in the United States than in Europe, and still different again in Nigeria or Japan.

However, this still does not mean that all Americans will make the same interpretations of *Dallas* or any other show. After all, there are many groups, communities, and subcultures within the United States too, and, according to reception researchers, each will "negotiate" a text in ways that make sense within its social and cultural situation. For example, adolescent girl fans of Madonna (whose songs, films, performances, magazine interviews, and so on can be regarded as a set of texts) will interpret her in ways entirely different from those of male, middle-class readers of *Playboy*. The girls may adore and imitate her for her image of independence. As one girl fan has said: "She's sexy but she doesn't need men. . . . She's kind of there all by herself" (Fiske, 1987). The *Playboy* readers, however, may stress her sexual attractiveness to men in their reception (Fiske, 1987).

Unlike uses and gratifications researchers, reception researchers do not usually use the standard questionnaire as a method of investigation. Instead, they use more small-scale, qualitative methods such as group interviews and in-depth individual interviews, in which they try to unravel the interpretations made of certain media content by a small group of viewers or readers. Thus they generally do not construct a complete set of categories such as the list of gratifications mentioned above. This is because they think that reception and the production of meaning cannot be isolated from the specific contexts in which they take place, and can be understood only meaningfully. Thus Radway (1987) has examined the ways in which a group of avid readers interpret romance novels; Hobson (1982) and Seiter, Borchers, Kreutzner, and Warth (1989) have investigated how working-class women in England and the United States make sense of their favorite soap operas; and Peterson (1987) has studied the diverse meanings a group of college students give to Cyndi Lauper's pop song "Girls Just Want to Have Fun" (feminist approaches are explored further in Chapter 16).

The perspective of reception analysis is not without its limitations also. In their emphasis on interpretation and production of textual meaning, reception researchers still tend to isolate the text-audience relationship from the larger context in which the media are consumed by people. That context is everyday life, and it is to this important consideration that we turn now.

The Media in Everyday Life

Uses and gratifications researchers have attempted to answer the question of *why* people make use of media offerings. Reception researchers are interested in *what* people see in the media—which meanings they get out of them. The question being left out in both approaches, however, is the deceptively simple one of *how* people live with the media. In other words, how are the media integrated into our everyday lives?

One audience researcher who has begun to tackle this question is David Morley (1986), from England. He remarks that when we examine what it means for people to watch television, it may be more important to look at the domestic context of family life in which people use television than to find out which interpretations people make of any particular type of programming. He is thus interested in the role of watching television in what he calls "the politics of the living room." The overall aim of his research is to show that "watching television" cannot be assumed to be a one-dimensional activity that has equivalent meaning or significance at all times for all who perform it.

To illustrate this point, consider a woman saying the following: "Early in the evening we watch very little TV. Only when my husband is in a real rage. He comes home, hardly says anything, and switches on the TV." According to Herman Bausinger (1984), a researcher from West Germany, in this case turning on the TV set doesn't signify "I would like to watch this," but rather, "I would like to hear and see nothing." Bausinger also sums up some general points that we need to keep in mind when we want to understand the place of the media in everyday life. Here are the most important ones:

- To make a meaningful study of the use of the media, it is necessary to take all the different media into consideration, and examine the "media ensemble" that everyone deals with today. Audiences integrate the contents of radio, TV, and newspapers.
- As a rule, the media are not used completely or with full concentration. We read parts of sports reviews, skim through magazines, and zap from channel to channel when we don't like what's on TV.
- The media are an integral part of the routines and rituals of everyday life. Thus media use cannot be isolated, because it is constantly interrelated with other activities such as talking or doing housework. In other words, "mass" communication and "interpersonal" communication cannot be separated.
- Media use is not an isolated, individual process, but a collective process. Even when reading the newspaper one is often not truly alone, but interacting with family, friends, or colleagues.

In his study of the place of television viewing in family life, Morley (1986) interviewed 18 working-class families in London. Among the most interesting results of his study are the gender differences he found in viewing preferences and styles. For example, men prefer to watch factual programs (news and sports), while women prefer fiction (soap operas and other drama series). Furthermore, men more than women favor watching programs attentively ("in order not to miss anything"), while women tend to combine their viewing with other activities, such as knitting, talking, and doing household chores. Indeed, many women feel that just watching television without doing anything else would be a waste of time. As one woman says: "You've got things to do, you know, and you can't keep watching television. You think, 'Oh my God, I should have done this or that.' "

Another general conclusion drawn by Morley is the fact that when the family is together, men are usually in control of the selection of programs. As Morley remarks: "Masculine power is evident in a number of the families as the ultimate determinant on occasions of conflict over viewing choices." He quotes one man as saying: "We discuss what we all want to watch and the biggest wins. That's me. I'm the biggest." Symbolic for the power exerted by the man in the house is his control over remote control devices, both of the TV set and of the VCR. One daughter says: "Dad keeps both the automatic controls—one on each side of the chair." This does not mean that women do not get the chance to watch their favorite programs, but more often than not they have to do it when they are alone, when other members of the family are "out of the way."

Of course, such gender-related patterns of viewing do not occur in all families. The situation may be different in families of different class and ethnic backgrounds, in single-parent or two-career families, and so on. Still, that these are predominant patterns in the United States is confirmed by several American researchers (Lindlof, Shatzer, & Wilkinson, 1988; Lull, 1982).

It is important to note that these patterns are not based on differences between women and men or on a natural authority possessed by men. Rather, they are the effects of the particular social roles that men and women occupy within the American home. For men, the home is primarily defined as a place to rest from a hard day's work. Therefore, they tend to consider watching television as something they have naturally earned. Women, however, are usually the ones who are responsible for the well-being and care of family members, and for running the household—even though today most women work outside the home as well. As a result, women's television viewing is often interrupted by a continuing sense of domestic responsibility, and they often give up their own preferences in the service of others.

Research such as Morley's is beginning to map the intricate social circumstances in which patterns of media consumption are organized in people's day-to-day routines. Those relationships are shot through not only with pleasure and gratifications, but also with power and conflict. But much remains unknown about the place of the media in our everyday lives. Most of the research done so far is limited to television, perhaps because it is the most widely used medium. Furthermore, it would be interesting to look not only at male-female relationships in terms of patterns of media consumption, but also at the relationships between children and parents, among siblings, among friends and colleagues, and so on—both at home and outside it.

Even more than in reception analysis, the study of media in everyday life depends on methods that are capable of capturing the fine-grained details in which the media are part of our routine activities. It is for this reason that "ethnographic" approaches of studying media audiences have recently gained interest among communication scholars. In such approaches, researchers attempt to come to a culturally sensitive understanding of the complex subjective worlds of media audiences, by using a variety of methods of investigation such as in-depth interviewing and spending time with their subjects in participant observation.

Conclusions

Media audiences are not "masses"—anonymous and passive aggregates of people without identity. Nor are they merely "markets"—the target groups of the media industries. Media audiences are active in the ways in which they use, interpret, and take pleasure in media products. Furthermore, the media have come to play a central role in the shaping and arrangement of our everyday lives and social relationships. Why and how people engage with different media are issues that remain to be explored further.

Further Questions

(1) How do we account for the vast differences in taste and preference among media audiences, and how do we understand the power of the media if people actively engage with media in their own ways?

(2) How might our patterns of media consumption be influenced by the growing importance of new technologies such as video and the computer?

(3) Which content areas in the present structure of the media could, from the perspective of media audiences, be improved?

11 Tracking the Audience

OSCAR H. GANDY, JR.

In studying media audiences, Gandy adopts the critical approach of political economy. He analyzes the close relationship between the media industries and the consumption promoted by advertisers, and how the audience is created as a "product" and fashioned by marketing aimed at specific segments of the audience, such as women, children, or high-earning young professionals. He links this perspective to that of the "audience as labor," which analyzes the "work" audiences have to do to comply with the insistent commercial massaging of the media. In general, he shows how managed and monitored media audiences are in the United States. This kind of approach tends to support a "dominant media" perspective that sees the audience primarily as objects of a strategy based in the economic dynamic of privately owned media systems.

Crises of Control in the Information Age

Computers, and the telecommunications networks that carry information between them, are said to be the harbingers of the latest industrial revolution. Computers have changed the way we work, play, understand, and relate to the environment around us (see Chapter 13). As devices to store, process, and exchange information, computers greatly amplify and extend the power of those who control their use. It is essential to understand that the growing importance of computer-based information systems does not rest in the technology itself, but in the continually changing interactions among technologies, the economic and social conditions that characterize their primary uses, and the cultural practices—including the systems of laws, regulations, and regulatory institutions—that govern us. In this chapter, some of these complex interactions will be examined through an exploration of the role of computers and telecommunications networks in the audience assessment process.

The use of computers and the intellectual technology of management planning and marketing research are all part of a process of rationalization. Here the term *rationalization* refers to the pursuit of efficiency in the production, distribution, and sale of goods and services. Rationalization

Panopticon-Shaped Prison, Britain

can also be applied to the business of government through its role in the collection and redistribution of wealth, or in the performance of its police function. Rationalization is an information-dependent process, requiring more and more workers who are producing information and analysis, or utilizing information technology to store and transmit this information. Thus, for some analysts, the transformation of industrial economies into "information economies" is primarily a reflection of the increased need to rationalize complex, interdependent systems, rather than a decision to produce information instead of some other material goods.

Surveillance and rationalization also imply an increase in the ability of capitalists to exercise control over individuals in their roles as employees, consumers, and citizens. Their control is increased to the extent that the initiative, independence, and autonomy of the individual is reduced or transferred to other people. Surveillance provides the information necessary for greater control.

The kind of control that surveillance provides is not absolute. Social control under democratic social organization can be as subtle as the distinction between discipline and punishment. Discipline in individuals and society is maintained by virtue of a continual threat of punishment. Discipline also involves people's accepting for themselves the belief that the behaviors maintained by the threat of punishment are in fact correct, rational, or moral behaviors. Once accepted, or internalized, those beliefs and values provide the basis for self-control, the most efficient form of discipline.

An early nineteenth-century design for a prison was named the panopticon. This prison was designed in an octopus shape so as to provide the guards at the center with a continuous and unobstructed view of all the prisoners. Prisoners would never know for sure who was watching, or if they were actually being watched, at any particular moment. This design for a prison was thought to be particularly efficient because it also allowed the guards to isolate prisoners and to locate them in special wings or areas on the basis of their past behavior, their degree of rehabilitation, or their particular tendencies and habits. Many critical communications scholars see the panopticon as a useful metaphor. They see contemporary society as developing into a panoptic system, with similar forms of isolation, grouping, and surveillance, organized for the purposes of discipline and control. Such perspectives may be also applied to the study of audiences.

Rationalization in the information economy involves increased, almost continuous, surveillance of individuals in all those areas of existence that have been or are being brought under the control of capitalist logic. That is, surveillance is necessary to rationalize, or to make human behavior more efficient and profitable in all conceivable activities. More generally, we can recognize tendencies toward increased surveillance of individuals for the purposes of rationalizing their behavior in the spheres of employment, consumer behavior, and citizenship. The analysis of audiences has relevance for each and every one of these spheres. This chapter's discussion begins with an exploration of two new alternative ways of understanding audiences: as products and as labor.

Perspectives on Audiences

Audiences as Products

Although it is not a universal or even the dominant view within traditional discussions of mass media, many critical observers see audiences as the products of an industrial or manufacturing process. The notion of audience as product provides a particularly insightful perspective from which to understand mass media in general and advertiser-supported media in particular. The focus in this discussion will be on commercial television as the premier advertising mass medium.

There is no direct economic relationship between the broadcaster and the audience in the United States. Commercial broadcasters "produce audiences" or, more precisely, blocks of time during which it is possible to communicate with audiences, which they then sell to advertisers. The market that exists is between broadcasters and advertisers or their agents. When we talk of "selling time," the reference is to the unit of time, the "spot" during which the advertiser is free to make a pitch to the audience the broadcaster has promised to produce and deliver. The rates that the broadcaster is able to charge these advertisers depend upon the size and income level of the audience. The broadcaster realizes profits when the costs of producing the audience are substantially less than the advertising fees they are able to charge for access.

Not all audiences, even audiences of equal size, are of equal value to advertisers in general, or to advertisers of particular products. Part of an audience's value is associated with the amount of its spendable income and its propensity to spend that income for particular goods and services. Advertisers of expensive, "big-ticket" items are unwilling to pay very much at all for an audience that is unemployed, retired, or, for some other reason, falls into the low-income category. Thus the broadcaster, or any other producer of audiences for sale at a profit, is sensitive to the demand for particular audience attributes.

The size and quality of the audience produced is also the result of the technologies and raw materials used in its production. Just as one might produce a variety of cakes with different combinations of flour, sugar, and spices, the same is true of the audience product. Because of different tastes for violence, "action," sexual explicitness, comedy, and music, different combinations of these qualities in programs will attract different audiences.

If we also consider the potential audience member as an input into the eventual "product," the availability of some of those inputs will vary across times of day and across days of the week. Now that so many more women work outside of the home, the proportion of women available to be sold as audience members during the day is smaller. Still fewer men are available for "sale" during those hours. Thus the scarcity of males makes it costly to attempt their production as audience members during weekday hours. Socially active teenagers also tend not to be available on Saturday evenings, and a review of the television schedule will reveal that network programmers have generally taken that fact into account.

As with other products, the cost of input is governed by the nature of competitive demands. "Audience producers" are essentially in competition with one another for the attention of potential audience members. However, some analysts would suggest that there has been an unspoken agreement among the major competitors (the networks) that their mutual interests are best served if each programmer specializes in the production of a specific audience type during a particular day part. This "counterprogramming" strategy would operate to divide the audience members up without blurring objectives between the dominant audience producers.

Such specialization is more clearly the case with radio, where programming style is fairly uniform across the program schedule, and stations can be easily classed into types on the basis of their formats and the audiences they traditionally produce. This specialization, which is also increasingly characteristic of cable networks, is referred to as the *magazine model* or *narrowcasting*. Over the years, especially since the emergence of television as the principal mass medium, general-interest magazines have likewise given way to targeted advertising vehicles that treat a quite narrow range of topics and appeal to specialized audience interests.

It is this view of audience as product that explains why popular programs may be dropped from the broadcast schedule: Not just any audience will do. If the program fails to produce or "attract" an audience with a realizable market value exceeding the cost of producing it, it will not be renewed. Thus programs that might have respectable ratings in terms of audience size are dropped from the schedule because the audiences produced are not valued by the advertisers. For example, in those markets where Black people make up a large share of the primary audience base, high local ratings have not generated corresponding support. This is attributable to low estimates of Black people's purchasing power as well as to conventional racist assumptions.

This perspective also makes clear the tendency of networks to keep programs in their schedules that generate smaller-than-average audiences, if these particular audiences have attributes that are in great demand. This is the character of programs such as the yuppie-centered series *thirtysomething*, which has been identified as "cable proof." That is, the upscale audiences that have been increasingly turning away from the networks to view premium cable fare have been returning to the networks to view this and similar shows. Because of this, networks have been assured that higher-than-normal fees would be paid for these audiences because of their relative value as consumers.

Audiences as Labor

To think of the audience as labor takes a bit more work. Communication theorist Dallas Smythe (1981) is credited with early attempts to specify the nature of the work that audiences do. Smythe introduced this concept in the context of a critique of capitalism that suggested that under advanced capitalism, we have less leisure time than was once assumed. Time away from work is the time in which workers must regenerate their energies in order to return to the factories and offices the next day.

Unfortunately, Smythe argues, when workers sit down to relax, to watch a little television, this viewing is not entirely recreation but is, in part, exploitative labor. Television viewers work as audiences.

Audience work, in Smythe's initial formulation, is the work of watching commercials, making sense of them, and ultimately behaving as consumers appropriate to their social position. The payment for this work is the pleasure, stimulation, or entertainment the individual derives from consuming the material that appears between the commercial messages.

More recently, Sut Jhally and Bill Livant (1986) have sharpened Smythe's analysis and attempted to extend the metaphor further. Their task was to describe how broadcasters captured the profits produced by these audience workers, and how they utilized improved technology to increase the rate of exploitation of this labor. In their analysis, audiences are made to work harder by being made to view more individual commercials for each minute of entertainment. Thus we have seen the one-minute commercial give way to 30-, 15-, and 10-second spots, which increases the amounts programmers can charge for the same minutes of audience access. This increase in productivity does increase broadcasters' profits.

Another way audience workers may made to work more efficiently is by exposing them to only those messages for which they are best suited by virtue of life-style, income, or other measures of consumer potential. Thus the messages will be more closely tied to the tastes, preferences, experiences, and resources of the audiences working for a particular broadcaster at a particular point in time. Audience research, within this model, is similar to the kind of management research that seeks to inform employers how to select the best workers for their factories or organizations—in audience research, the best consumers are chosen.

Many examples of this effort to improve the productivity of the audience worker can be found in those advertiser-dependent media not subject to strict government or industry regulation. Popular magazines, such as those for hobbyists interested in photography, are filled with commercials. It is impossible to turn a page without meeting an ad, brushing aside an insert, or picking up a reader response card that has fallen to the floor. And, as we might expect, the ads are clearly linked to the editorial focus of the periodical, offering cameras, film, or processing services. Cable television programs are frequently advertisements disguised as documentaries. These "program-length commercials" seek to increase the efficiency of the audience work force by recognizing and working around the tendency of some laborers to goof off, sleep, talk to each other, read the paper, "zap" the commercials, "graze" between programs, or even leave the room during a clearly identifiable commercial.

Audience Measurement as Surveillance: New Developments

Audience measurement is surveillance. It is performed for the same reasons as surveillance of workers in factories or in the secretarial pool. In the pursuit of expanded profits, the surveillance of audiences seeks to fine-tune the main mechanisms of "audience production." Gary Marx (1988) identifies several attributes of the new surveillance environment that have clear reflections in the technology and practice of audience assessment. It is clear, for example, that the new surveillance technologies transcend time, distance, darkness, and other physical barriers. Audiences are measured electronically and continuously. Records of audience behavior can be stored electronically and transmitted instantaneously to remote sites upon request. Audience viewing behaviors can be combined easily with other information about individuals or groups. Increasingly, audience assessment technology is becoming automatic, "passive" (with no action, such as filling out a viewing diary, needed), and relatively unobtrusive. People are less and less aware that their behavior as audiences is being measured. Indeed, as Marx (1988) reminds us, the new surveillance is frequently involuntary—there are no simple ways to avoid being counted.

The growth in surveillance accelerates because the process is increasingly technology intensive, that is, dependent more upon machines, essentially computers, that operate more efficiently than humans and are capable of monitoring multiple sites at the same time. The declining costs of surveillance mean that more and more firms in the audience business will consider its use to be essential. The new surveillance is both more intensive and more extensive. It measures more attributes and behaviors of more people across more aspects of their lives.

Increasingly, the surveillance of audiences resembles police surveillance of suspected criminals. It has become interventive and preventive, rather than reactive and investigative. Specials and made-for-television movies are audience "stings," pretested to see if audiences will be attracted (usually by new variants on old themes). Fringe time periods and fringe programmers test limits of public acceptability, to see how many and what kinds of people will be tempted by unusual or more "adult" content. Such a role in pushing the limits of mainstream tastes has been played by Rupert Murdoch and the Fox network in reaching new depths in violence and sexual explicitness.

Rather than pursuing particular individuals or suspects, the new audience surveillance approaches focus on categories, groups, or "types" of individuals. Just as "terrorist" or "drug smuggler" profiles are used by security specialists to select those travelers who will be subject to more intensive searches, similar profiles are used to target messages to audiences likely to respond, or to avoid those for whom particular messages or programs will have little appeal. For instance, "two-car pet owners" may be a possible targeted group.

Peoplemeters

Peoplemeters are merely the latest in a continuing string of improvements in the technology of broadcast audience measurement. This search for increasing accuracy and precision in "audience ratings" has been described in fine detail by Hugh Beville, Jr. (1985). From the beginnings of the industry in 1928, when market researchers relied upon costly personal interviews to determine how many American households actually owned radios, to the development of passive infrared detectors that take note of which household members are in front of the television set, the goal has been the same—rationalization. Technical developments in statistical sampling, which increase the accuracy of estimates of audience behavior, have been pursued with dedication. Similar efforts have been directed at increasing the scope of the data gathered from those sampled.

Personal recall of television programs watched has always been seen as unreliable. Ratings specialists and their clients have recognized that diaries tend to be completed from memory, often on the day before they are to be returned, rather than being filled in on an hourly or daily basis. In addition, most diaries tend to be filled in by one member of the household who serves as the unreliable recorder of family viewing. Telephone coincidentals, where a sample of respondents are asked to identify what program were they viewing when the phone rang, had long been the method used for quality control of the diary method. However, their use was severely restricted in practice by the cost of employing telephone interviewers, people's objections to intrusion, and associated problems of administration.

Automatic, passive devices have improved significantly from the time of the Nielsen audiometer, first installed in test markets in 1935. This primitive device involved a mechanical stylus inscribing a waxed-paper tape in response to the location of the broadcast tuning dial. In a creative portent of contemporary audience measurement, the early A. C. Nielsen market research services included gathering data about what kinds of consumer goods households had in their pantries at the times when their agents went to collect the audiometer tapes. While these meters were eventually improved to the extent that they could be read automatically and continuously from Nielsen's remote data-processing center, meters were still limited by the fact that they measured only the use of the household set at a time when advertisers were interested in more detailed demographics and personal viewing patterns.

The peoplemeters, introduced into the United States by AGB Research in 1982, represented a significant improvement in individual audience assessment. While still plagued with problems of sampling and concerns about the validity of estimates of viewing by youngsters who rapidly tired of "tapping in" to note the beginning and end of their viewing periods, by 1987 the technology was firmly established. Improvements in peoplemeters can be expected in the direction of greater "passivity." Heat sources (body temperature), heartbeats, and body size (adults or children) can be registered, and passive set-top devices can record when known individuals (i.e., members of the household) enter or leave the viewing environment and whether or not their eyes are open. The presence of guests is likely to be queried with an on-screen display, and encoding devices will allow households to record relevant demographic data about guests for the duration of their stay.

Addressability

The peoplemeters in use, or on the drawing board, even those that now measure exposure to commercials and provide ratings for commercials, rather than programs, do not, however, provide the most valued information about audience exposure—whether audiences are paying attention to, and being influenced by, the commercial message (see Chapter 10).

Addressability refers to the ability of advanced telecommunications systems to direct a message stream to a particular device (e.g., a TV set or a mainframe computer) with a digitally encoded address. *Verifiability* refers to the ability of advanced systems to note the status of tuners, decoders, and response devices to "verify" the status of information systems, to note whether or not messages have been received, and at what time. *Segmentation* and *targeting* refer to the classification of audiences into groups on the basis of information provided in response to questions or on the basis of past performance as consumers or viewers. The qualities of addressability and verifiability make it much easier to segment audiences into different types. These segmented audiences may then subsequently be targeted to receive specialized messages previously determined to be highly effective in reaching similar segments. Addressability allows targeted messages to be sent to particular segments.

Thus, in test-market communities, individuals are recruited to be part of programs with informative titles like Behaviorscan or ScanAmerica. In return for small payments and the opportunity to participate in pools for larger prizes, families agree to provide detailed personal, social, and demographic information about themselves. They also agree to utilize a special identification card when they make purchases at selected stores in the community. The UPC (universal product code/bar code) scanners in the checkout counters link the consumer purchases with the viewing behavior of the particular household. In some other systems, family members are paid to run an electronic scanner along the UPC stripes of all purchases the family makes. It thus becomes possible to establish the correlation between the commercials a family is exposed to and the purchases they make.

Where more advanced dual-cable, or addressable, systems allow different commercials to be sent to different households, it is possible to achieve true laboratory control over the presentation of this commercial stimulus, and even to select the editorial environment in which it will be viewed. Thus marketers will be able to determine whether ads for cookies that emphasize the crunch work better with youngsters than with adults. More than that, such systems provide information to advertisers about whether youngsters who like comedy shows prefer crunchiness more than youngsters who like action adventure.

The goals of social management through these home networking systems have been described in careful detail by Kevin G. Wilson (1988). Advanced telecommunications systems will present more and more information to individuals in their homes through high-capacity cables. As the nation's cable systems are updated to provide more sophisticated systems capable of digital addressability of programs and messages (see Demac's discussion of ISDN in Chapter 14), it will be more common for individuals to be charged directly for the material they receive. Some projections call for "pay-per-view" TV in 20 million households by 1991, and 40 million by 1996. It is the blending of commercial and pay-per-view, or cost-per-unit/page/screen systems, that will delink advertising from generalized-appeal TV ads and will spread its reach to the entire realm of individual and family information processing. Reading, viewing, listening, banking, communication, and shopping activities will increasingly display the same quality of commercial transactions. As such, those transactions will provide the surveillance information necessary for the efficient operation of capitalism, as its reach is extended into all aspects of daily life.

Tracking the Audience Wherever It Can Be Found

Tracking audiences is not limited to the volunteers who participate in paid research programs. A great many of us are part of experiments and market tests that are conducted without the courtesy of requesting our informed consent. Magazines and discount coupons are frequently utilized in the effort to link editorial content to commercial appeals. Advances in printing and binding have made it possible for marketers to insert coupons in magazines that are code marked with the identification of the household or address to which it was sent. Thus when an individual decides to use one of these coupons to purchase an item, the advertiser soon knows not only what kind of person responded to which kind of appeal, but to which store, with which prices or advertising pressure, the consumer responded. Such coupon marking also allows market researchers to determine how many miles people are willing to drive from their homes in pursuit of an apparent bargain.

Even general-interest magazines are being produced in specialized regional, neighborhood, or ZIP code-specific editions. The coming years will see magazines that are subscriber specific in terms of the advertisements they contain. Because of advances in ZIP code analysis, led by the Claritas Corporation, magazines have become highly competitive vehicles for targeted appeals, and the lists of their subscribers represent valuable data resources that may be sold at varying costs per thousand to advertisers who want them.

Indeed, there is a large and growing industry in consumer lists. Each week, a newsletter serving the direct marketing "industry" describes new lists that have just come on the market, with prices ranging from $40-$90 per thousand names for one-time-only commercial use. There are lists of magazine subscribers that might provide information about individuals' hobbies and recreational interests, their political orientation, their level of education or sophistication, or even their degree of ethnic identification. Other lists are easily developed from computerized records of sales and other transactions. Even calls to 800 numbers for information contribute to the growth of marketable lists. Commercially available telephone services automatically provide firms with the name, address, and phone number of the inquiring party. All of these lists provide the possibility for developing rather comprehensive profiles of individuals.

Advances in computer software have lowered the costs involved in simultaneous comparison of two or more lists. This procedure is called *matching*, and it has been used extensively by government agencies at the federal and state levels to identify individuals who, for one reason or another, would be considered ineligible for some public service. Thus matches of lists of bank accounts with requests for welfare or public assistance might turn up a "good hit" if an individual appears on both lists. For marketing purposes, a good hit might involve a person turning up on a list of buyers of quality chocolates who is also on the list of participants in weight-control programs. Individuals so identified might become the prime targets for discount coupons for some new designer chocolates that will be inserted in their next issue of *Time* or *People.*

The Realm of Social Consequences

Why should we be concerned about this movement toward greater control or management of the behavior of audiences? Clearly it depends upon your expectations of a democratic society. From a critical perspective, one that recognizes the contradictions and conflicts between the logic of capitalism and the values of freedom and equality that are part of the democratic ideal, it becomes important to identify the consequences that flow from the uncontrolled and unchallenged extension of that logic to greater and greater areas of our daily lives.

One critique of the application of computer-based systems to the rationalization of audience production is that this technology deskills and devalues the contribution of labor. Where formerly skilled workers are unemployed and newly hired workers are reduced to button pushers, there is no pride in or attachment to the product of their labor. There is irony and danger in these developments. The irony is that one of the merits of a capitalist economy is supposed to be its encouragement of risk taking by capitalists. Yet the developments discussed above demonstrate an intense preoccupation with *reducing* risk for advertisers and their business clients—even, if possible, to cancel risk altogether. It is the same logic that has led to clone products on TV and that could reduce our skills as consumers, packaging our likes and dislikes until we begin to lose the talent to make our own choices among goods and services, to use our own imagination to plan our daily consumption. And what future is there for low-income consumers when all these ads are targeted to the supposed needs of the wealthy?

Privacy and the Control of Personal Information

Perhaps the greatest threat these computer-based systems for audience assessment represent is their potential to worsen the balance of power between individuals and bureaucratic organizations. Personal information streams out of the lives of individuals much like blood out of an open wound, and it collects in pools in the computers of corporations and government bureaucracies. Public access to similar data about the firms and organizations that increasingly structure our options and opportunities is more costly to obtain and impossible to access.

Personal privacy, as it is currently conceived, is concerned with the individual's right to control the collection, distribution, and use of information about him- or herself. The courts and legislatures have come to define the limits of that right in terms of what society agrees is a "reasonable expectation" of privacy. To the extent that we accept the rationale of market efficiency, and that sophisticated marketing is progress, most business and government uses of personal information can be justified in those terms. Rather than considering the overall implications of a loss of individual power and control, protective legislation focuses on restricting a specific information practice that has been identified as an abuse. Thus, rather than an absolute limit on the collection or use of personal information, we have a flexible limit that contracts each time some abuse becomes routinized by bureaucratic practice. The social security number has, through routine use, become the universal identifier capable of linking virtually all records of our interaction with the commercial system. Its collection has become so commonplace that the courts will likely assert before too long that there is no longer any reasonable expectation of privacy with regard to it.

There is a fairly widespread concern that our personal privacy rights have come under attack. People know that government and corporate bureaucracies can and do collect and share information about them in ways that they are powerless to control and that will not return to benefit them. Surveys suggest that there is a glimmer of understanding about the nature and use of profiles based on the compilation of personal details. But resistance is almost nonexistent, and what little there is may be seen as passive and defeatist. Marketing and public opinion researchers are reporting more refusals and survey terminations than at any time in the past. A few individuals refuse to apply for services or opportunities because they would rather not provide the information such applications would require. A nearly invisible minority simply refuses to enter the system of records, giving up the convenience of credit cards and acquiring goods and services under assumed names or aliases. To escape the information net means to become a nonperson. One maintains privacy through the loss of all else.

Information Grazing and Zapping

A good many of those who still view broadcast programs have videotaped them, are screening them at times other than their actual broadcast, and, more important from the advertiser's standpoint, are fast-forwarding through—or "zapping"—the commercials with their remote control units. This workers' revolt is taking place in the homes of high-income, technologically advanced families, who are also highly valued by advertisers. Many others switch frequently among channels ("grazing"), which means neither advertisers nor broadcasters can rely on their being exposed to the commercials. These practices are signs of dissatisfaction on a wide scale, but it is atomized, not yet a rebellion with a voice and articulated demands. What the prospects are for an increase in organized opposition is a major question to be considered.

Further Questions

(1) How do you relate individuals' attempts at control through grazing and zapping with the degree to which audiences may be "active"?

(2) How can we organize to protect our privacy from information surveillance?

(3) What kinds of consumer education movements exist, and how important are they or could they be in developing public awareness?

12 Alternative Media and the Boston Tea Party

JOHN DOWNING

In this chapter, Downing pursues the notion of the "active audience" to its logical conclusion, analyzing a number of moments in U.S. history when people moved beyond being an audience to developing their own communications and putting various kinds of small media to popular use. He cites historical examples, like Tom Paine's pamphleteering during the American Revolution, as well as current processes, like peace activists building a network of contacts using personal computer technology. Here the "active audience" is connected to "alternative media" to become a real or potential political force for change in society. Downing shows how media are the products of but also help to mobilize social movements, a point elaborated by Mohammadi in Chapter 19, and thus injects an optimistic note about the potential for popular participation in communications against the top-down commercial messages of the big media.

Thinking about the audience means thinking about who we are in relation to the media, to our culture, and to our society; among the questions raised in this book, this is one of the most important.

The label of *alternative media* can be applied to a host of different cultural activities. Clearly, they must be alternative to the mainstream media such as the big broadcasting and cable companies or newspapers of record, such as the *Washington Post* or the *Wall Street Journal.* But that still leaves a great deal of space for variety. Within the United States alone there is a gigantic mass of small-scale publications for particular audiences. These range from the specialized bulletins of different branches of industry that circulate to select executives and have subscription rates of $1,500 per year and up, to little parochial newsletters that cost pennies or are entirely subsidized. In between there are endless specialist magazines for cycling, cooking, cat, and computer enthusiasts, to name but a few. Ethnic media that cater to the many different groups in the United States are yet another important category of alternative media. In this chapter, however, the term *alternative media* is reserved for certain categories not so far mentioned: politically dissident media that offer radical alternatives to mainstream debate.[1]

It must be said immediately that the political mainstream in the United States is a rather thin stream compared to political debate in many other countries. Politicians get very heated, and debate can be quite rowdy and rude, but in terms of real issues the mainstream politics in the United States, essentially between Democrats and Republicans, is like a media circus in a pork barrel. The issue is pork—what goodies can come the way of our congressional district, our sector of the economy?—and the circus is television performance aided by megabuck campaign funds. Real public issues—homelessness, poverty, racism, AIDS, ecology, military support for despotic foreign governments—are mostly on the margins of mainstream political debate. So "alternative" is quite an extensive zone for serious political debate in the United States. Nonetheless, a frequent reaction to small-scale radical media is, What good are they? How can they possibly make a dent? Who reads them or watches them? How many even know they exist?

That is where this chapter's title reference to the Boston Tea Party comes in. For some years now, a replica of the original sailing ship that brought the tea cargo to Boston has been moored in Boston harbor as a floating museum. The replica actually made the Atlantic crossing, yet it is such a minute vessel compared to the size of ships today, it looks so flimsy, that it is hard to believe it could survive the Atlantic Ocean. Yet from such a tiny vessel were tipped the tea chests in the American revolt against British tyranny. That action, minuscule as it was, captured the imagination of the rebels and played a vital part in galvanizing resistance to the British crown. Not everyone became a rebel; George Washington had to draft people to fight. All the same, size alone was no index of the impact of the Boston Tea Party. And that is the beginning of wisdom in thinking about radical alternative media.

Another consideration is important. In Chapters 10 and 11, we have been examining the work that audiences do in reinterpreting the TV programs they watch, or in absorbing commercials. The notion of the "active" audience is an important one, to get away from the rather contemptuous attitude that says the audience is passive, inert, the model of the couch potato. But active audiences are but one step away from being media creators and producers themselves. In the earliest days of radio broadcasting in Germany in the 1920s, the great dramatist Bertolt Brecht (1983) wrote:

> Radio should be converted from a distribution system to a communication system. Radio could be the most wonderful public communication system imaginable, a gigantic system of channels—could be, that is, if it were capable not only of transmitting but of receiving, of making the listener not only hear but also speak, not of isolating him but of connecting him. This means that radio would have to give up being a purveyor and organize the listener as purveyor. (pp. 169-172)

What Brecht said sums up the essence of the alternative media idea, namely, the creation of *horizontal* linkages for the public's own communication networks, to assist in its empowerment. Such linkages contrast sharply with the *vertical* communication flows of the mainstream media, owned by giant corporations, and basically sharing an entertainment-oriented, mainstream angle of vision on the issues that concern ordinary people. In a democratic society, such media are not nearly democratic enough. To be precise, their communication flows are not simply vertical, but top-down, from them to us. The only flow in the opposite direction that is genuinely ours, not just part of one of the commercial audience surveys Gandy discusses in Chapter 11, occurs when we write them letters—hardly an evenly balanced communication interaction.

Let us now move to an outline of the history of radical alternative media in the United States, to give a sense of the quite significant roles they have played in the country's history—despite their absence from many journalism histories.

Alternative Media in the United States, 1760-1990

In Chapter 2, Sreberny-Mohammadi noted how the use of the vernacular in books and pamphlets encouraged the ferment of ideas and rebellious political movements in Europe at the time of the Reformation. By the time of the American War of Independence, literacy had increased further in the Colonies, with the result that many flyers, pamphlets, newspapers, and books circulated as part of the buildup to the armed struggle, and during it, to support the campaign. Prominent among such revolutionary writers was Tom Paine, whose pamphlet *Common Sense* (1776) went through numerous printings and was very widely read. Here is an excerpt:

> This is supposing the present race of kings in the world to have had an honorable origin: whereas it is more than probable, that, could we take off the dark covering of antiquity and trace them to their first rise, we should

> find the first of them nothing better than the principal ruffian of some restless gang, whose savage manners or pre-eminence in subtility obtained him the title of chief among the plunderers; and who by increasing in power and extending his depredations, overawed the quiet and defenceless to purchase their safety by frequent contributions. . . . But it is not so much the absurdity as the evil of hereditary succession which concerns mankind. . . . Men who look upon themselves as born to reign, and others to obey, soon grow insolent. Selected from the rest of mankind, their minds are early poisoned by importance. . . . But where, say some, is the King of America? I'll tell you, friend, he reigns above, and doth not make havoc of mankind like the Royal Brute of Great Britain. (in Conway, 1967, pp. 80-81, 99)

Paine later went on to publish in favor of the 1789 French Revolution. Along with Paine were no less than Samuel and John Adams, who worked for the weekly *Boston Gazette* from the 1760s onward. And there were many, many more.

In the nineteenth century a labor press began to develop, representing the growing body of workers that was beginning to build the industrial might of the United States. Concentrated in the 1830s and 1840s in cities such as Philadelphia, New York, and Boston, these working-class newspapers strove to bring about changes in the wages and conditions in American factories. The first ethnic press also began about this time, with the Black newspaper *Freedom's Journal* starting in New York in 1827, the *Cherokee Phoenix* in the South in 1828, and the Chinese-language *Golden Hills News* in San Francisco in the 1850s.

Perhaps the most striking example of alternative media in the first two-thirds of the century was the abolitionist press, which urged the ending of slavery in the United States. Of the many campaigners, preeminent was Frederick Douglass, himself born into slavery, largely self-educated, and then, as a freedman, a tireless campaigner and writer against the barbarity of racism and enslavement. This is an excerpt from one of his articles, originally printed in his newspaper, *North Star*:

> I have been made to feel keenly that I am in an enemy's land—surrounded on all sides by hardships, difficulties and dangers—that on the side of the oppressor there is power, and that there are few to take up the cause of my deeply injured and down-trodden people. These things grieve, but do not appal me. Not an inch will I retreat—not one jot of zeal will I abate—not one word will I retract; and, in the strength of God, while the red current of life flows through my veins, I will continue to labor for the downfall of slavery and the freedom of my race. I am denounced as an offender. I am not ignorant of my offences. I plead guilty to the worst of those laid to my charge. Amplified as they have been, enormous as they are alleged to be, I do not shrink from looking them full in the face, and glorying in having committed

> them. My crime is, that I have assumed to be a man, entitled to all the rights, privileges and dignity, which belong to human nature—that color is no crime, and that all men are brothers. I have acted on this presumption. (in Foner, 1950, p. 126)

As the century moved on, women too began to organize, in support of their right to vote, and they too began to publish newspapers and pamphlets. Among the newspapers were *Lily* and *Revolution*, edited, respectively, by Amelia Bloomer and by Elizabeth Cady Stanton and Susan B. Anthony. *Lily* lasted ten years, *Revolution* four, but both contributed to the slow groundswell in women's consciousness and organization. Equally important, as Rakow shows in Chapter 16 of this volume, was the growth in the numbers of women writing novels and short stories that contributed to the expression of women's perspectives and sensibilities.

With the tremendous upsurge of labor immigration from the 1880s on, much of it from southern and eastern Europe, the American labor movement took on a new character. Until then, the political perspectives of American workers had largely been confined to demands for a better deal at work. The new arrivals brought with them wider perspectives on social and political change, derived from socialist, Marxist, and anarchist philosophies that sought to understand society as a whole. Such perspectives tried to point out the interconnections between exploitation in the workplace and slum housing, between industrial accidents and poor health care, between factory discipline and the police force.

Many publications reflected this new flowering of political debate, such as the Socialist party's Kansas-printed but nationally distributed *Appeal to Reason*, which ran from 1895 to 1917, and at its high watermark in 1912 sold three-quarters of a million copies. Less widely circulated, but still influential, was *Mother Earth*, a magazine published by the anarchist and feminist Emma Goldman, whose parents had fled from Russia in the 1880s to escape anti-Semitic persecution, and who herself became a byword for militant campaigns for peace, birth control rights for women, prisoners' rights, and many other movements. Here is a sample of the spirited writing she produced:

> The State is commonly regarded as the highest form of organization. But is it in reality a true organization? Is it not rather a sample of the kind of arbitrary institution, cunningly imposed upon the masses?
>
> Industry, too, is called an organization; yet nothing is farther from the truth. Industry is the ceaseless piracy of the rich against the poor.
>
> We are asked to believe that the Army is an organization, but a close investigation will show that it is nothing else than a cruel instrument of blind force.

> The Public School! The colleges and other institutions of learning, are they not models of organization, offering the people fine opportunities for instruction? Far from it. The school, more than any other institution, is a veritable barrack, where the human mind is drilled and manipulated into submission to various social and moral spooks, and thus fitted to continue our system of exploitation and oppression.
>
> Organization, as we [anarchists] understand it, however, is a different thing. It is based, primarily, on freedom. It is a natural and voluntary grouping of energies to secure results beneficial to humanity. (Goldman, 1969, p. 35)

Another very lively socialist newspaper in the early twentieth century was *The Masses*, edited by Max Eastman, who later switched his social and political views almost totally and ended up editing the cozy, conservative monthly, *Reader's Digest*. *The Masses*, however, was irreverent, imaginative, and unorthodox.

Until the 1930s, African-Americans had been alone in developing film as an alternative medium (Nesteby, 1982, chaps. 5-6). In the 1930s Depression decade, however, the joblessness and poverty familiar to many African-Americans suddenly became a reality to White America as well. Between a quarter and a third of all Americans were thrown out of work, and until U.S. entry into World War II in 1941 at last fired up the industrial machine, there seemed no hope of economic or social improvement for millions upon millions of families.

Hollywood films mostly sought to entertain, to give people something to take their minds off the situation, but small groups of alternative filmmakers set out to provide something more constructive. They wanted to use film to communicate as vividly as possible the true scale of the economic disaster, and the efforts of people across the country to fight back against the callous imposition of poverty and hunger. They also wanted their films to be discussed locally after they were shown—quite unlike the Hollywood theatrical system, where audience members go their separate ways as soon as the credits roll. In other words, they wanted to foster an active audience that could use the film to discuss the practical options open to unemployed workers to fight for justice and social change. Units such as the Workers' Film and Photo League, and later Nykino (Alexander, 1981), joined the marches of the unemployed. From inside demonstrations they would film the police clubbing the marchers, rather than keep to the safe and implicitly biased position behind the police lines that most news camera operators preferred (and still prefer).

After the war there was an explosion of militant labor activism in the 15-month strike wave of 1945 and 1946. This resurgence was also fueled by the political optimism generated from having won the war, having crushed fascism in Europe and Japan, having said farewell to the Depression, and having both Americans and Soviets working together to defeat the Nazis.

Almost immediately, however, the first Cold War between the United States and the Soviet Union began, generally dated from March 1946 (the second Cold War was in 1980-1986, in the early part of the Reagan presidency). Following the Communist-led revolution in China in 1949 and the Korean War of 1950-1953, during which Korea was partitioned between a Communist North and a pro-West South, the political leadership in the United States moved from strongly anticommunist to hysterically anticommunist. China was widely declared to have been "lost," and when it joined in the Korean War on the other side, the military repeatedly urged Presidents Truman and Eisenhower to use nuclear bombs against it.

In this tense and overheated climate emerged a senator from Wisconsin, Joseph McCarthy, who would spearhead a four-year reign of fear inside the United States, causing teachers, film directors, screenwriters, State Department officials, labor activists, and a host of others to be dismissed from their work and to be effectively unemployable—often simply on the *accusation* of being traitors to their country, that is, communists or "fellow travelers." The definitions were pretty loose. To be, or to have been, active in working for Black civil rights; to have known some communists during the Depression decade and to refuse to name them to the FBI; to be an ad production director who employed a suspected "red" actor in a TV commercial; to be a labor union activist; to be a university instructor who tried to analyze the reality of China, rather than simply condemning it—any of these could get an individual into deep trouble.

Alternative media during McCarthyism faced enormous problems. The response of many political dissidents was to keep their heads down and hope the storm would pass. Let us consider two cases of media that fought back. One was the weekly newspaper the *National Guardian* (from 1967, the *Guardian*). The other was KPFA, a listener-supported radio station in Berkeley, California, which eventually led to the foundation of four other similar stations in Los Angeles, New York, Houston, and Washington, D.C. (the Pacifica stations). These cases are interesting; they illustrate the special importance of alternative media in periods of political suppression, and they have continued in existence for more than 40 years—and KPFA is the first major example of alternative radio in the United States.

The *Guardian* is edited in New York City. It has nearly always taken a very independent line both in relation to the U.S. government and in relation to revolutions abroad. Whereas newspapers belonging to political sects would always trot out the sect's current "line," the *Guardian* generally retained a distance from all ready-made political positions. In the 1950s when Yugoslavia was pursuing an independent path, aligned with neither Moscow nor Washington, the newspaper supported it. In periods when mainstream media reporting of ongoing political struggles in Latin America and Africa was sketchy, to say the least, the *Guardian* would include reports from people on the front lines. In the civil rights struggles in the South in the late 1950s and early 1960s, the paper was passed from hand to hand at marches and rallies as practically the only source that would cover the situation fully and honestly. It was read not just by big-city political activists, but by citizens scattered the length and breadth of the country, in remote villages and towns. It never achieved the circulation of, say, *Appeal to Reason*, but in the frightened days of McCarthyism, it was one of the few media beacons of sanity and fearlessness.

KPFA was founded to be a public forum for a variety of views, but with special emphasis on pacifist perspectives, some Quakers having been active in setting it up. During McCarthyism, the continued existence of a radio station in which a full spectrum of views could be expressed was a major achievement. In the early years, the political spectrum included Caspar Weinberger, who would eventually (as President Reagan's defense secretary) force through the largest military budgets in U.S. history, communist activist Dorothy Healy, and people of all persuasions.

The achievement was fragile, however. Both the *Guardian* and KPFA received their share of unwelcome attention from the government during McCarthyism and afterward. It seems strange that small-scale media of this ilk should attract repeated attempts to squelch them, but as the account of Soviet underground (*samizdat'*) media indicates in Chapter 9, size alone does not indicate significance. Even if some observers are inclined skeptically to dismiss alternative media as of no account, neither the U.S. nor the Soviet government has agreed.

The ways in which the government tried to shut them down, without taking the provocative step of officially censoring them, were various. In the case of the *Guardian*, pressure was put on news vendors not to put it on sale or they would face FBI inquiries themselves. Subscribers in some parts of the country received visits from local FBI agents, asking them whether they approved of what they were reading—which could in turn lead to their encountering all kinds of problems from antileftist zealots in their local communities. Every time the *Guardian* presses were about to print the paper, the staff meticulously checked for foreign objects that would wreck the machinery. From time to time such sabotage was avoided. Cedric Belfrage, one of the paper's three founders (along with James Aronson and John MacManus), was imprisoned and deported, albeit on no criminal charge. This was possible because of his British citizenship, although he had lived in the United States for 20 years and had an American family.

In the case of KPFA, there were repeated threats to have its license to broadcast suspended by the Federal Communications Commission, and it was also once subjected to review by the Senate Internal Security Subcommittee. Not only was this unnerving and dispiriting, but, in the FCC cases, it meant spending a considerable amount of extremely scarce funds on hiring lawyers to represent the station. Other tactics used to close down alternative media have included IRS tax audits (which mean engaging the costly services of accountants for audits that might drag on for a year or more) and government pressure on landlords not to renew leases on premises occupied by alternative media projects. These methods fall well short of the savage repression practiced in some countries, but they are completely disloyal to the spirit of the First Amendment.

The four major political movements of the 1960s—the continuing civil rights movement, the student movement against the Vietnam War, the movements of ethnic and racial protest in the inner cities, and the revived women's movement—proved to be highly fertile ground for new alternative media. KPFA was deeply involved in the pitched confrontations between students and police in the Berkeley free speech movement of 1964, and the *National Guardian* very early on identified the Vietnam War as an unjust and barbarous crusade, long before mainstream media began to criticize it. Many other media projects, mostly print—such as *Rat, Seed,* and *Liberation News Service,*—sprang up and played a key part in the movements, and later folded. Some continued, such as *Report on the Americas,* from the North American Congress on Latin America, and *Akwesasne Notes,* a Native American publication based in the Mohawk nation. During the 1960s, 16-millimeter film began to be used again, following the precedent of the 1930s, and a number of documentaries were produced on the Black struggle and the antiwar movement. One, made in 1974 and titled *Hearts and Minds,* exposed the real character of the Vietnam War as opposed to its TV news presentation, and went on to win an Academy Award.

Indeed, one of the most absorbing alternative media sagas of that period was the alternative media explosion inside the armed forces, examples being the *Bond,* published by the American Servicemen's Union, and *Ally.* Try as they would to stamp these publications out, the Army top brass faced such powerful interest among GIs in these underground papers that arrests for distributing them dropped away. The generals feared further alienating their unwilling troops by creating martyrs to censorship. An example of writing that appeared in the *Bond* follows:

> I was an apathetic person without any strong views on subjects dealing with peace, war, oppression, rights, etc., until I was sent to Vietnam in January of

> '69. While "serving" my country in that crime of illegal involvement, I saw the people of Vietnam degraded, cursed and humiliated almost daily. I saw the way North Vietnamese prisoners were treated by our "wholesome" American soldiers. . . . Most of all I talked with the people of Vietnam and heard what THEY wanted and how they felt about U.S. involvement.
>
> I came back a changed person, no longer apathetic, sickened by the war and what it was doing.
>
> At the present time I am on the editorial staff of a recently started underground newspaper and I am very interested in starting a chapter of the American Serviceman's Union here. (in Aronson, 1972, p. 214)

Current Initiatives

To bring the story more or less up to the present, the discussion now moves to some more contemporary alternative media projects that have used electronic technologies for their work. The two selected are PeaceNet and Deep Dish TV Satellite Network.

PeaceNet, based in Berkeley, California, since 1985, uses the power of the computer and the modem (see Chapter 13) in order to link up various peace activists with others across the United States, within Western European countries, and in some other countries, such as Kenya and Costa Rica. For a relatively small monthly fee, users can hook into continuing messages and debates and current information about a whole variety of issues including peace and disarmament strictly defined, environmental issues, Native American struggles, Central America and Southern Africa support groups, and many other matters. The isolation often experienced by small groups working on particular issues in this vast country can be quite quickly broken down by this means, and up-to-the-minute information can be made available much more readily than by newspapers or mail. Indeed, groups working with each other across substantial distances can send documents to each other much more cheaply and quickly than they could by mail. Given the tiny budgets of many alternative projects, this is a major consideration.

Deep Dish TV Satellite Network first transmitted in New York in 1986. Using satellite communication technology and hooking up with 300 public-access channels on cable stations across the United States, it offered 10 one-hour programs a week for 10 weeks in that year, and in 1988 expanded to 20 weeks. Its objective is to make community TV programming, estimated by Deep Dish at over 16,000 hours produced each year, more widely available, so that all the effort and creativity involved are not limited to a single cable channel. The programs transmitted have been compilations of locally produced TV, on many issues:

Latino images, young people, aging, homelessness, AIDS. The types of issues that mainstream media deal with so rarely and poorly, with their vertical communication flows, are substituted in the Deep Dish project by people—old, young, Latino, the homeless, workers, gays—speaking for themselves and producing media coverage about their own concerns.

In other words, the tradition of Sam and John Adams, of Tom Paine and Frederick Douglass, of Emma Goldman and countless others like them, continues. It is a tradition alive and well in most countries of the world, in one form or another, although there is no space to review those experiences here. What we must now do is to stand back for a moment from this information about alternative media, and assess what can be said about alternative media impact in general.

Conclusions: The Alternative Forum of Political Movements

There is little doubt that alternative media flourish most vigorously in the wastelands left by mainstream media. When the latter, because of the biases of their owners, editors, and, often, journalists, choose not to represent important slices of social and political reality, then the public becomes increasingly hungry for honest and comprehensive information about those issues. When the mainstream media misrepresent social and political realities, then, again, alternative media come into their own. They provide an alternative public forum—sometimes referred to as the "public sphere" or "public realm"—to the official forum and the official story (Downing, 1988a). They meet a heartfelt need for both information and the opportunity to share experiences and strategies, mistakes and successes.

These media have a much harder road to walk when they appear to be voices crying in a wilderness, when only a dedicated minority seems to listen, like the *Guardian* and KPFA in the McCarthy years. Without a vigorous political movement to feed into their columns or wavebands, and to be fed and stimulated in turn by what they produce, it takes tremendous commitment to sustain the effort and the creativity needed. In crisis situations, a poorly photocopied typed sheet of paper will be seized upon and shared by many people because its contents are in demand. In more normal situations, questions of presentation, style, format, wit, imagination, and—not least—finance require sustained attention.

There is a vital interaction between political movements and media (see Chapter 19): Without their own media, political movements are stymied. Communication from above, the vertical communication criticized earlier on, will fill the gap left open. The powers that be will have a free run. Equally, however, whether or not political movements come to maturity has a great deal to do with the prior existence of opinion centers, media that have begun to arouse people's awareness of the scope and source of the problems they face on a daily basis.

Further Questions

(1) What is the relation between ethnic media and alternative media? What is the significance of the facts that the history of African-American media is mostly one of challenge to the status quo and the history of Latino media (admittedly often owned by Anglos) is mostly one of compliance (Downing, 1989, in press)?

(2) What are the practicalities of alternative media? These can vary from the most immediate, namely, how to meet the bills and organize distribution, to the tougher still, namely, how democratic the organization of the newspaper or video production team should be. If media are to promote democracy, should not their own organization be democratic? And if this is agreed, then what kind of democracy works best in the media (Downing, 1984)?

(3) What is the comparative international experience of alternative media? This can be very illuminating in regard to many such questions, as also in regard to the relations between such media and political movements. Political cinema in the Third World (Downing, 1987), clandestine radio stations and guerrilla movements, samizdat' works in Eastern Europe, and the audiocassettes in the Iranian revolution discussed by Mohammadi in Chapter 19 are only some of the international examples that repay careful study.

Note

1. Some people would include extreme rightist alternative media, such as the computer "bulletin board" networks used by White supremacist groups (Kay, 1988) or their cable TV programs. In my view, these groups are not disconnected from the mainstream cultural reality of White racism in the United States (see Chapter 18), even if their love of violence seems to set them apart.

Part IV Information Technologies

In this section we introduce you to new technologies of communication that have rapidly made their mark on the way we live. A great deal has been written about these technologies and their impact, whether within rich countries or on poorer countries' prospects for economic development. In our view, what has been written has often consisted of hype and speculation, much of which is conveyed by the phrase "the information society." This phrase is used to conjure a future when seemingly all that happens is computerized, and a present in which suddenly almost everyone has been transformed into an "information worker." Municipal bureaucrats and their secretaries, telephone switch operators, research scientists, journalists, economists, microchip circuit assemblers, TV repair technicians, entertainers—all are redefined and lumped together and somehow trimmed into "the future," a clean, efficient twenty-first century laden with technological marvels and no pain. All we will want to know, all we will need to live, will be at our fingertips with a few keystrokes, summoned via satellite and flashing along the fiber optics.

Simultaneously, in the real world, the situation can be interpreted as being a good deal more somber. Governments and corporations are restricting the flow of information they value, pumping out the perspectives and "facts" they would have us value, and gathering more and more information about our activities for their own purposes. Microcircuit assemblers are contracting a variety of industrial diseases, and the circuits they make are being installed in missile nose cones.

Which of these perspectives is more valid? What evidence would you cite in support of one position or the other? The three chapters that follow provide basic information that can feed into your thinking on the subject. Those who already have substantial technical knowledge may want to skip some of these pages; others will find them a necessary basic introduction to the world of new communications technology. Remember the arguments by Sreberny-Mohammadi (Chapter 2) and Winston (Chapter 3) in Part I, especially their combined insistence on the interaction in earlier history between social and cultural forces and new communications technologies.

13 Computers and Communication

KAREN PAULSELL

We begin this section with Karen Paulsell's introduction to the computer as a communications instrument. A necessary first step in media studies today is to recognize that the communication and processing of data are forms of communication, just as media and interpersonal communication are. Even if no human being specifically originates or receives the information, and even if a computer automatically processes the data without a specific instruction to do so in each case, communication is still taking place through the medium of the computer. As Gandy pointed out in Chapter 11, the interface between audience data communication and media communication is developing extremely quickly, precisely via the computer.

Paulsell reviews some of the major ways computers are currently used in communications, especially in electronic mail (e-mail), conferencing, and data bases of various kinds. In turn, these applications raise questions of surveillance and privacy. She also notes the very heavy investment of the Department of Defense in computer hardware and software developments over the past 50 years. The implications of computers for the future, for good and for ill, are a major theme for all communications analysts. They are affecting all aspects of the ways we work for a living, as well as how the military prepares and wages war. They also, however, provide a medium through which we can foster strategies for peace, as in the PeaceNet organization discussed in Chapter 12.

Let us use this particular ambiguity to recall the importance of Winston's argument (in Chapter 3) that society and culture develop the technology of media, not the other way around. As Winston proposes, the technology always offers opportunities, it always has a radical potential, but whether that is realized hangs upon the pressures exerted by different groups within society. Media by themselves do not make anything happen.

The Computer's Beginnings

In the 1980s the microcomputer became the centerpiece of popular conceptions of the "computer revolution." But the evolution of the computer from a power-guzzling mammoth to a user-friendly laptop spans more than 40 years. The history of "computing machinery" takes us back to the last century. The first computing machines were built to tabulate the 1890 census; they were not computers, but electromechanical devices that could read the holes in punched cards and perform simple arithmetic. This technology was developed into a whole family of equipment to create, read, and perform math upon the little square holes punched in cards. Each punched card machine could perform one simple operation. (The corporation that spread this technology from a Census innovation to a world marketplace was the International Business Machines Corporation—IBM.)

Computers, however, perform a wide variety of operations under control of a program, that is, a set of fixed instructions. The first computer was developed to break Nazi military codes during World War II. It was quickly followed by other computers that were used for complex mathematical operations, including the development of trajectory tables for aiming artillery[1] and for computing the mathematics involved in the development of the atomic and hydrogen bombs.

Historically, computers have been a much-misunderstood technology. In 1958, IBM predicted that five large computers would satisfy the whole world's needs for data processing. And the microcomputer was not developed by any big corporation (although it has spawned many). The January 1975 issue of *Popular Electronics* deserves much of that credit, as do the Homebrew Computer Club and curious engineers and hobbyists working in basements and garages. By the end of 1975, an individual could buy a computer, plug it into his or her television set, and run Electronic Pencil, the first word processor (Donaldson, 1987).

This was the beginning of the so-called computer revolution. Computers escaped from the air-conditioned enclaves of corporations and research laboratories. Instead of only five, there are now many millions. Instead of merely performing bookkeeping and scientific computing, computers are performing a multitude of tasks.

There are thousands of potential computer applications. At least in research labs, the blind are "seeing" in new ways via computer, and computer-controlled body braces are helping paraplegics to walk. Computers are finding beds for homeless people in San Francisco, catching arsonists in Brooklyn, connecting Home Alert clubs to the Police Department in Santa Monica. But these are not the uses that push the development of computers. Most of these uses were possible long before service providers could afford computers and the expertise to run them.

Why Computers Have Developed

The two main forces that drive the development of computers in the United States are the needs of the biggest users (especially the military and the U.S. government) and industry competitiveness. The push to develop the first computers came from the military, which continues to generate new weapons that require innovation from the computer industry. The Department of Defense funds over half of all academic computer science research (Mosco, 1989, chap. 6). One example of military requirements pushing computer development involves the computer guidance devices in missile nose cones, where weight is of crucial importance. Weapons designers want smaller, more powerful computers to make smarter, lighter bombs that can go farther and be more discriminating in their choice of targets. Other enormous military expenditures on computer software and hardware continue to drive innovation. Wonders now being designed include robot tanks and electronic "pilot's companions" capable of firing guns and rockets in response to a jet pilot's eye movements. As these and other DOD-funded projects and research push the capabilities of computer hardware and software, some of the innovations find their way into commercial products and services. This occurs to such an extent that such funding is sometimes seen as a government subsidy to the private computer industry.

The second major force in the development of computer technology has been the computer industry's competitiveness on two levels: the international marketplace and the individual firm. In the international arena, the race between Japan and the United States has eclipsed news of the computer industries of Europe (most notably Germany, France, and Italy) and of the attempts of other countries to develop their own computing capacity. Computer technology now represents a multibillion-dollar business, and countries want the money spent on computers to stay within their own borders. No country wants to see a major, growing sector of its economy totally represented by imported hardware, software, services, and human expertise (see Chapter 15). Governments have subsidized their computer industries in a wide variety of ways, such as the French government's free provision of terminals (the Minitel) on demand to its citizens.

On the level of the individual firm, no single company competes in the full spectrum of computer products (microchips, computer components, laptop computers, microcomputers, minicomputers, mainframes, supercomputers, computerized games, software, services), but within a market niche the competition is fierce. Whether in price, speed, power, portability, ease of use, or some variety of special features, computer firms must innovate in order to compete.

The competition spreads beyond the computer hardware and software industry. Who wants to buy an unprogrammable VCR? Busy people want to program their microwave ovens to time dinner for their return from work (in their electronically fuel-injected cars). Banks have provided electronic tellers, banking from home, automatic payroll deposits, and other computerized services.

Implications for Culture and Society

The innovations brought about by these forces show no signs of slowing. As with any change in technology in society, the effects are not noticeable all at once. As individual consumers and individual companies make individually "wise" choices, these choices build into a sum that is greater than the parts.

The effects will be as pervasive as those of the automobile. At first, a car was a "horseless carriage," considered much cleaner than a horse because it left no droppings in the street. Today, we realize how the automobile has changed the shape of our cities, our relationships with each other, the places we live and work, the air that we breathe, the forests, and the ozone layer. If we could have foreseen the air pollution, the traffic jams, and the loss of open space, might we have opted for more mass transit and different city planning? Automobile manufacturers bought mass transit lines and dismantled them, the U.S. government built a multibillion-dollar highway system, all in order to promote the use of cars. This might make us wary: Why are some computer manufacturers so willing to give computers to schools, and what are the implications of federal grants to support computer research and development?

An invisible web is already building around us, one that few of us have directly helped to create. But our indirect participation is there: Every time we use a telephone, credit card, an electronic teller, or make a supermarket purchase, we are part of the web of computers that are tracking our transactions, tabulating summaries, and communicating with other computers. The web has not been designed as an entity: It has grown as the result of individual corporations, government departments, and citizens making decisions to use computers. The sum of these individual decisions, shaped only vaguely by government policies, has created a world that already has seen major shifts in many jobs and industries as a result, and will see many more.

Examples of this cultural shift are already evident, some of which will be noted below. Dependence upon electricity supply is one obvious result ("I can't give you that information now, the system is down"); freedom from political and economic oversight is another. However, let us now examine what is needed for computer communications to take place, and then look at some particular applications of computer communications.

The Technology of Computer Communications

At the simplest level, four things are needed for computer communications: (a) hardware—computers at both ends, plus a device to allow the computers to send data over a communications channel; (b) a software program for each computer; (c) a communications channel; and (d) standards for communication. If we used this list to describe two humans talking, we would say they both need ears and mouths (hardware); thoughts, words, and syntax (software); air to carry the sounds (a communications medium); and a set of rules for taking turns while talking (not the same as speech itself).

Hardware

Microcomputers contain the same basic parts as large computers. A lot of the parts are hidden away: The processor chip, the memory chips, and a lot of circuitry are tucked inside some sort of box. There is probably a slot or two indicating a disk drive. There is a keyboard and a screen, and cables to hook it all up together. Larger computers are much the same. They may consist of several boxes to hold their chips and components; they may be capable of having several users, each with a screen and keyboard; they may have tape drives or much larger disk drives than a microcomputer. Only in very specialized cases do computers differ from this basic pattern.

In addition to these basic units, a computer can be hooked up to a wide variety of other devices, such as a printer, a drawing tablet, a mouse (a small hand control that moves a tiny arrow over the screen and lets the user enter commands without using the keyboard), a tape drive, a large-capacity disk drive, a slide projector or slide camera, and a videotape or videodisc player. Just about anything that can be operated electrically can be turned on and off by computer.

Another other basic piece of hardware needed for computer communications is a device capable of sending signals over a communications channel. Most microcomputers use a modem (a word derived from *mod-*

ulator/demodulator) to transmit signals via telephone wire. If you listened to the transmission of these signals, you would hear only screechy static.

Software

Software is a set of instructions for what a computer is supposed to do. A program looks vaguely like an algebra proof. If you are writing with a word processor, the program waits for you to type a character, then displays that character in the proper place on the screen. You might type a special key or combination of keys that relay commands instead of words; then the software performs some special action (like printing or erasing). Communications software designed for microcomputers is capable of dialing phone numbers typed from the keyboard, of sending text typed at the keyboard out via the modem, and of taking the text that comes in over the modem and displaying it on the screen. The information that comes in over the modem from the remote computer can also be stored onto disk to be read or printed later.

Computers can also communicate without an immediate human source. For example, some computers are already programmed to make "junk phone calls" by dialing every possible local phone number and playing a tape (sometimes asking for push-button responses that are also gathered by the computer).

Communications Channels

Computer communications can travel in several ways. Between rooms, buildings, cities, or continents, they can travel over ordinary voice telephone lines, over leased computer circuits, or over special computer networks called "packet switching networks." Businesses with huge amounts of data to transmit from one office or branch to another will lease circuits. Some leased circuits are extremely high capacity, capable of sending data hundreds of times faster than an ordinary telephone line with a modem. An office with many computers may connect them by "local area networks" or LANs. Any person on the network can use any computer, printer, modem, or other device connected to the LAN.

Most computer users who dial up electronic mail systems or on-line data bases (both of which are discussed below) use packet switching networks. Computer communications tend to go in bursts or "packets." From the computer's point of view, it takes you a long time to type a request; then it sends you a rapid burst of data, which you read s-l-o-w-l-y; then you ask for another packet. Most of the time, the phone line is idle. Packet networks take advantage of this by having users share the long-distance portion of the phone line.

Most existing channels that carry computer communications were really designed for voice, especially at the local level. Big users are demanding better, more flexible, cheaper, and faster channels. Such networks are currently being designed and tested. One such plan is called the Integrated Services Digital Network (ISDN), which is designed to carry all electronic communication, high-definition television, telephone, and data to office complexes or affluent homes (see Chapter 14).

Standards

Computers could not communicate with each other without procedures. One of the most common computer standards is ASCII (pronounced ASKee), the American Standard Code for Information Interchange. You might think of ASCII as Morse code for computers. Each character to be sent has been assigned a number between 0 and 127. For example, A is 65, B is 66, a is 97, and b is 98. If I have a big mainframe and you have a tiny micro, all of our hardware and software will be different, but you can still log on and read my files: Our machines communicate in ASCII. Other standards or protocols set rules for which computer transmits first, and what the computer transmits, at what speeds. Certain standards apply to the way communications are transmitted by packet-switching networks. Standards agreements, including standards for ISDN, are devised by representatives from governments, the telephone industries, and telecommunications users in months (or even years) of international meetings.

Computer Communications Applications

The four components discussed above must exist for computer communications to take place. This section provides a quick look at just a few of the existing and developing uses of computer communications. With each application, one or two important areas of concern are raised.

Transaction Processing

Any type of business process in which payments change hands is a transaction. Computers now play a role in transactions from the electronic teller withdrawal to international electronic funds transfers involving millions of dollars, pounds, yen, and marks. Other types of electronic transactions include payroll deposits and utility bill payments.

Bankers regard the ability to communicate as the same thing as the ability to provide banking services. Banking is no longer just moving sacks of money and slips of paper: It is the transmission of electronic messages. These transactions travel over secured data lines, with many levels of checking for errors or tampering.

Computerized financial transactions are also used for currency trading—fortunes can be made or lost by buying and selling currencies at particular moments. Exchange rates can be tracked electronically, and buy or sell orders can be sent via computer. Transnational firms do this all the time to improve their currency holdings, for if the amounts are big enough, a fraction of a percentage point change in exchange rates can make a large difference up or down. For a Third World economy, these changes may influence such basic outcomes as the level of child malnutrition.

On-Line Data Bases

Computer data bases are like filing cabinets: They can contain virtually any type of organized information. Computers equipped with large-capacity disk drives can keep vast amounts of data that can be accessed in a few moments "on line." Programmed with sophisticated indexing and searching functions, they can find, compare, sort, and count the stored information. The kinds of information stored in computers and accessible over telecommunications links continue to grow. Much of it is private information stored by corporations or governments for their own use. Some types of on-line data bases are available, usually very expensively, to the public.

Many libraries subscribe to at least one on-line data base service. Bibliographic data bases are used by searching for a keyword or keyword combinations. For instance, a researcher looking for information on the use of computers by the FBI could use the words *computers* and *FBI.* If a print index had no entry for "computers, FBI," the researcher would have to compare the entries under both headings to find relevant entries. But an on-line data base would use one rapid computerized search to list all the articles that have both keywords. Also, most printed indexes contain only one year's worth of information; on computerized versions, the researcher can choose a range of dates.

Some on-line data base services store only references to articles or summaries of articles. Others, such as LEXIS (a legal data base), store and supply the full text of articles. This sounds terrific, but there are problems involved with such data bases. For example, preparing a legal case requires understanding all prior legal cases that provide precedents. LEXIS makes this easy—but it is very expensive to use. The creator of LEXIS has expressed doubts about what he created, knowing he had made the rich richer. He had created a service that a wealthy landlord's lawyer could afford, but the tenant's legal aid office could not.

Many computer data bases that store detailed information about individuals are meant for use only by certain personnel. Law enforcement officials and Department of Motor Vehicles workers, for example, use on-line data bases to track drivers and automobiles. The telephone company computer records for billing any nonlocal numbers called from a particular telephone. Insurance company computers contain records about their customers' health care.

In their separate and intended uses, most of these systems are relatively benign. But the potential for abuse is enormous, and some abuses have already happened. Law enforcement organizations check telephone records when looking for drug dealers, smugglers, or other criminals. While we might approve of most of these uses, such power can be abused. Issues of both personal privacy and political freedom are involved. The 1960s FBI campaign against the civil rights and antiwar movements is one example of such abuse. (For further discussion on this issue, see Chapters 6 and 11.) Computers do not create such policies, but they do make them much easier to carry out.

From the information kept on-line in various computers around the country, it would be very easy to develop an entire profile of a person and his or her activities. Data about phone calls, travel arrangements, police records, school history, doctors' visits, bank withdrawals, books purchased, and videos rented can be compiled into a profile. This profile could be of interest to potential employers, to a present employer contemplating promotion or firing, to opponents in a political race, to lawyers in a civil suit, and, not least, to advertisers. Often, it is impossible for an individual to know that anyone has such information about him or her.

Electronic Mail and Conferencing

Electronic mail, or e-mail, is a popular term for what a purist might call "computer-based messaging." Electronic mail's format is very much like that of a business memo. Paper memos are dictated, typed, photocopied, and distributed; then they are responded to in like fashion. With electronic mail, senders and receivers need not move from their desks. Electronic mail can replace many normal memos and telephone conversations, and often reduces interruptions for the workers who use it.

When someone (Debbie) wants to send a message to someone else (Kathy), she could type something as simple as "mail ksmith," adding a subject when the program asks for one, and then typing the body of the message. Below is a simple mail message as it might appear in Kathy Smith's electronic mailbox.

> Message 6 (4 lines)
> From: dmiller Fri Jan 20
> To: ksmith
> Subject: Marketing Meeting Time
>
> We'll have to reschedule the marketing meeting planned for 10 on Wednesday. Stu is away; he's due in at noon on Wednesday. Let's try for 3 pm instead, OK?

Computer conferencing is another electronic communications medium; it is more like conversation or a college seminar than an exchange of memos. In most computer conferences, someone starts a topic and other users read what has been written and then add their comments. Eventually, a topic can become a long chain of messages. Computer conferencing, since it provides a more structured pattern of interaction, is particularly good for group work situations, where several people are involved in working on a complex problem or project. The value of both electronic mail and computer conferencing obviously increases with the physical distance between the users.

Computerized messaging raises issues of security and privacy. We assume that our mail is private: When we write a letter, we assume that it is for the recipient's eyes only. But while a message is waiting on a computer mail system for its recipient to pick it up, anyone who is adept at cracking computer systems could conceivably read it. This is a serious problem for sensitive government traffic and also for confidential commercial traffic. Few businesses would use an electronic mail or computer conferencing system that might allow their competitors to eavesdrop on their discussions; this is one reason businesses prefer in-house systems, and set up many security safeguards. But computer protection is a dialectical art: As computers become more secure from "crackers," the crackers become more ingenious, and computer security again is increased by new software and hardware protection systems.

Another issue, still untested in the courts, is the status of the information stored in computers during criminal investigations. The Fourth Amendment to the U.S. Constitution protects citizens from "illegal search and seizure." The authorities must have just reason before they search your property or confiscate your belongings. But this protection does not extend to records kept about you by a third party, such as the telephone company or your bank. It is unclear whether this includes electronic mail messages or entries from private computer conferences stored in a remote computer. To make matters even more unclear, on-line computer data are usually copied—"backed up"—to tape as a safeguard against hardware failure. So even if all on-line information has been erased, copies of it might still exist on tape. Do the authorities have the right to subpoena those tapes?

Conclusions

The three computer communications applications described above were selected because they are easy to describe and very similar to existing human communications patterns. However, it requires quite a few keystrokes, and reasonable computer skills, for an on-line data base user to capture a particular piece of information and forward it as an e-mail message. It is still difficult to send e-mail from one electronic network to another—the user has to know the complicated routing. The networks are not integrated, and there is as yet no phone book for the world's e-mail.

Other applications are available, or are being planned, most of them mimicking already-existing noncomputer communications: Electronic shop-at-home services, news services, and on-line airline reservations are a few of these. The technical obstacles have been the low-volume "narrow" communications link—the telephone line—into most homes and offices; expensive technology, software, and services; and the amount of learning required. A social obstacle has been the relative slowness with which most people are willing to adopt new ways to communicate. Such slowness is infuriating to corporations that have tried—and failed—to mass market computer services for home users. Given the poor quality of these services, the high prices, and the general uselessness of most of the information provided, this "slowness" looks like wisdom and well-placed caution at present.

But improvement is under way in all computer communications: The hardware and software continue to become faster, cheaper, and more "user-friendly"; telecommunications networks of greater capacity will be put into place in the 1990s and beyond; and new international standards for e-mail and all levels of computer communications protocols are under study or in field trials.

We will see many more unanticipated effects. We will read headlines about computer "crackers" and breaches of computer security. Whole new kinds of crime will be committed electronically. We will see entirely new uses in medicine, education, and every other sphere of our lives. In glimpses, we will see the military, the Immigration and Naturalization Service, and the FBI deploying new applications.

So far, control over these uses has stayed with the few who have the financial clout to develop them. Few new applications are devised that do not involve profits for the creators. Whether the development of the computer communications future continues its lurching path or whether all the issues are debated and examined will depend on those who develop computer expertise, on our leaders and legislators, and on the interest, energy, and understanding of the public, whose lives are more and more affected by computers with each day that passes.

Further Questions

(1) Consider the different ways governments have subsidized the computer industry. How does the United States do it? How has France done it? How has Brazil done it? And Japan?

(2) Check on the impact computers have on employment, both in office work and in factories, where robots and computerized "just-in-time" component deliveries are increasingly important. Will the computer change the kinds of jobs available to us?

(3) How can personal computers—"micros"—be used for alternative communication? In Chapter 12, Downing discusses such networks as PeaceNet; other options also exist, such as "desktop publishing" and data base use; are there other uses?

Note

1. Before the computer, for each individual artillery weapon a table had to be calculated to set up the gun parameters for a wide variety of variables, including range, altitude, wind direction, and wind velocity. Hundreds of clerks with calculators were needed for each model of each new weapon.

14 New Communication Technologies: A Plug 'n' Play World?

DONNA A. DEMAC

This chapter explores the new transmission technologies that have been developed in recent decades, from satellites to fiber-optic cables to cable television and high-definition television. Satellites in particular have multiple applications, from military reconnaissance to effective communication and education programs in thinly populated areas such as Alaska or the Pacific Islands. One of the paradoxes of the situation is that the channels of communication seem to multiply astronomically, but the scarcity of good software programs or of creative television programming appears all the more striking by contrast.

Indeed, the hallmark of these technologies' applications seems to be their ambiguous character. Is high-definition TV an enhancement of domestic pleasure for the film buff, a means of guiding nuclear missiles more flawlessly than ever to their destinations, a key element in the technological race among Japan, Western Europe, the Soviet Union, and the United States, or a chance to develop less ambiguous remote sensing images? The answer is all four. But who will benefit the most from these four, the powers that be or ordinary citizens? This is the crucial question to bear in mind.

On June 11, 1979, Walter Wriston, then chair of Citicorp, gave a speech titled "Information, Electronics and Gold," in which he described how computers, satellites, electronic funds transfer, and high-speed fiber-optic telephone lines were eliminating the problems of space and time. "Whether we like it or not," Wriston said, "mankind now has a completely integrated, international financial and informational marketplace capable of moving money and ideas to any place on this planet within minutes." As the head of a multinational corporation with over 1,000 offices worldwide, Wriston argued that nothing should stand in the way of "an integrated economic and financial marketplace which government—and all of us—must learn to live with."

Not everyone is as ready as Wriston to embrace a world of advanced technology. No doubt computers, satellites, and the other technologies discussed in this chapter are having a dramatic impact on our lives. Homes, offices, hospitals, and schools fill up each year with more gadgets that people can plug in and play. Yet some argue that it is people, as much as the new gadgets, that are being "plugged 'n' played." Siegel and Markoff (1986) warn:

> If Silicon Valley represents the promise of a technological utopia, it also epitomizes the peril of an Orwellian world out of control. Slowly but surely the average American has unknowingly accepted the electronic mapping of his or her entire existence. (p. 7)

Others argue that computerized networks are intensifying society's more serious problems, including class divisions, threats to civil and human rights, and global warfare.

Where do you stand in this debate? Do you tend to equate new technologies with progress, or, instead, agree that people should be wary of being "plugged in and played"? The perspective taken in this chapter is that in order for society to reap the greatest benefit from the new technologies, we must look beneath the surface to their dark side.

Background: Deregulation of Telecommunications and Broadcasting

To understand the new transmission technologies, we need to understand (a) the transnational corporate economy as it is has developed over the past 40 years and penetrated almost every corner of the planet and (b) the technical possibilities opened up to corporations by melding with these new telecommunications channels (satellites, fiber optics, and so on) the computer's capacity to transform all video, data, and voice information into electronic pulses. It is against this dual background—the transnational economy and the computer-telecommunications hookup—that we need to understand U.S. policy on new information technology.

A third element is the revival in corporate and government circles of the belief that market forces must know best, and, notably, what is the best national communications policy. A key agent in the deregulation of telecommunications and broadcasting has been the Federal Communications Commission, which was set the task—especially under the Reagan administration, but even before then—of cutting back its own powers of intervention in U.S. communications policy, leaving them to be dominated by market forces.

A historic event occurred in U.S. communications policy in 1981, when the federal government and AT&T reached an agreement that allowed the long-established phone monopoly to enter the computer field, dominated by IBM. In exchange, AT&T gave up its monopoly over nationwide telephone service, spinning off its local subsidiaries into seven giant regional monopolies. These soon became powerful, profitable firms in their own right.

One consequence of the 1981 agreement, which went into effect in 1984, was to announce the interest of the United States in the global expansion of the telecommunications hardware and software industry. By unleashing AT&T to compete internationally, a shake-up in the equipment markets and regulatory customs of other countries was sure to follow (see Chapter 8).

Here in the United States, the breakup of AT&T began a long period of constantly changing rates for telephone service. Between 1934 and 1984, AT&T had held a monopoly in this sector and was required under the Communications Act of 1934 to offer reliable, affordable telephone service to all. After 1984, competition in the delivery of long-distance service among firms like AT&T, MCI, and Sprint brought down the cost of long-distance calls, but the savings to individuals were often canceled out by hefty increases in the costs of local service.

A second major change in communications policy involved the deregulation of broadcasting. Policies of the Federal Communications Commission were repealed or amended that had limited the amount of advertising, required stations to assess community needs on a regular basis, and set minimum standards for public affairs, news, and local programs. Faith in the infallible wisdom of market forces gave full priority to corporate rights to advertise over these other "public service" objectives. From 1981 to 1984, the following changes were made:

- *Radio* (January 1981): Deregulation eliminated ascertainment of community programming needs; limits on advertising time; guidelines on minimum hours of news, public affairs, and local programming; and requirements that stations keep program logs open for public inspection.
- *Television* (June 1984): Deregulation had the same effects as on radio.
- *Children's television* (December 1983): Recommendations that broadcasters schedule children's programs throughout the week, develop more educational programs, and schedule programs for specific age groups were eliminated.
- *Fairness Doctrine* (repealed, 1987): This requirement that stations provide programs on controversial issues of public concern and do so in a balanced fashion was eliminated.
- *Multiple ownership rules* (amended, August 1984): This change increased from 7 to 12 the number of AM and FM radio stations a company could own (from 7 AM and 7 FM to 12 of each); similar action was taken for television.

- *Sale of broadcast stations* (amended, 1984): This amendment changed the time period an owner had to hold on to a station from three years to one year. The objective of the old policy was to encourage continuity in attention to community interests; the new rule has resulted in rapid turnover and has enabled the concentration of media ownership.

As of 1990, there is little government policy for nationwide communications. Though the Communications Act of 1934 is still in effect, the earlier regulations have been repealed and few new policies have been established for computers, satellites, fiber optics, or the other advanced technology systems. Market forces are expected to construct policy by themselves.

Profiles of the New Transmission Technologies

This section provides a brief description of cable television, satellites, fiber optics, the Integrated Services Digital Network (ISDN), and high-definition television (HDTV). Though the technologies are treated separately here, it should be noted just how often they are used in combination with one another, and especially with computers. This is especially true when it comes to the information and communication networks of transnational corporations. Indeed, high-speed, high-tech systems that facilitate the movement of goods, services, and information are at the center of today's transnational economy. The fax machine is not included for specific comment because its operation is easy to understand and it has very quickly become commonplace, but it is one more example of this trend.

Computers

In Chapter 13, Paulsell has already introduced a number of major computer communications uses, but we need to begin by examining some further aspects related to labor and the economy. At the workplace, computer technologies have contributed to the plugged-in labor force. Secretaries now work on machines that monitor when they begin work, when they take breaks, how many keystrokes they type, and whether or not they meet their quotas. Telephone operators have been required to complete a phone call every 26 seconds. Supermarket checkout clerks work with optical character readers that compute the number of purchases they ring up in a given time period. In addition, computer technology has allowed companies to automate many jobs, deskilling and cheapening their value as many thousands of people a year have been replaced by machines.

One consequence of the reductions in the labor force is that consumers are often required to do more work to get the services they need. They go to phone stores to pick up phones that were once installed at their homes. They take their phones out to be repaired. They punch numbers in on their telephone keypads in response to automated recordings that replace human salesclerks. A computer error originating at a company or a bank often takes endless letters and calls to clear up.

The future factory will be dominated by computer data communication in many directions. *Robotics* is the term for computerized manufacture, which in today's factory has islands of computerized machines that make other machines. Soon we will see these islands linked up into an archipelago of intercommunicating producing agents. A microcircuit can register that the cutting edge on a robot's machine tool is wearing out and summon up the replacement just before it is needed. Indeed, "just-in-time" computerized parts delivery is already saving corporations very large sums indeed, through cutting out downtime spent waiting for replacements and materials to arrive. The very design of the product itself, once the specialized domain of the drafting office's skill, has now been wrenched away and is part of computer-aided design and manufacture (CadCam). All these data communications can cross oceans and continents as easily as they can cross a factory floor.

Cable Television

Cable television started out in the late 1940s as a technique for delivering broadcast signals to remote or mountainous areas that could not be reached by the existing broadcast stations. A powerful antenna would receive the broadcast signal and relay it to households via cable. By the late 1980s, most cities and towns across the country had cable systems that carried the regular broadcast channels in addition to over 150 cable program services. With cable, TV has moved from a time when most television viewers paid for television indirectly, through the cost of the products advertised, to direct payment of a monthly cable charge or pay-per-view channel.

Cable TV differs from broadcast television by providing a much greater number of channels. All cable subscribers get what is called the "basic tier." It includes the broadcast channels, "direct-access" cable channels that are often made available through provisions in the local cable franchise, and additional channels that require no extra payment by the subscriber. After signing on to receive the basic tier, cable subscribers have the option of receiving "pay TV" channels for which they pay an additional sum.

In 1984, Congress passed the Cable Communications Policy Act. This act divided up authority over cable systems between the federal and state or local governments. Specifically, it recognized the right of local governments to franchise cable systems. In addition, Congress said that local authorities could arrange for viewers to have direct access to putting out programs over the cable system, stating that this would further the goal of program diversity. (See the information on the Deep Dish network in Chapter 12.)

The endorsement of a public-access channel in each cable system is considered one of the few distinguishing aspects of this service. Cable has generally provided old movies, sports, music videos, and news. In other words, it has not lived up to its original promise of expanding the range of programs available to the public. More channels have generally not meant more diversity. System owners have quite often been less than cooperative in developing their public-access channels.

However, cable also raises the danger of a local information monopoly. As stated above, when it comes to broadcast stations, a single company is not allowed to own more than 24 radio and 12 television stations across the nation. In contrast to this, the owner of a cable system may control 30 or more channels in one community. And since, in virtually all places, there is only one cable system, this company effectively controls all the TV programs entering its community's homes. This situation becomes far more severe when one looks at the power of multiple system operators (MSOs). One of the biggest, Time-Warner, Inc., owns hundreds of cable systems nationwide, as well as a number of pay cable services. The latter gives it strong motivation to exclude other pay TV companies' products. The viewing choices available to many millions of Americans are thus determined by this one corporate conglomerate.

Communication Satellites

The idea of using satellites to transmit information dates back to an article published by British physicist Arthur C. Clarke in 1945. Clarke saw that a satellite parked in one particular orbit, called the geostationary orbit (GSO), 22,300 miles above the equator, could transmit to up to a third of the earth's surface. Three satellites would cover the entire globe.

It is generally acknowledged that the majority of satellites in orbit are used for military rather than civilian purposes. The "Star Wars" program (Strategic Defense Initiative), for example, is a military program that has attracted much public attention and is designed to take the arms race in space a major step ahead by developing ultra-high-speed satellite-carried weaponry (Manno, 1984).

Today Americans take for granted the use of satellites for long-distance telephone calls, weather forecasting, and broadcast transmission (e.g., for international sports events and "hot" news). In addition, hospitals, universities, farmers, large and small businesses, and the government depend upon satellites on a daily basis for the information they need. Also, satellites linked to computers and telephone lines have transformed global trade and finance. IBM's network, for example, reaches its 400,000 employees in 145 countries with a combination of satellites and telephone lines.

One of the most remarkable features of satellite communications is the possibility of direct TV communication across vast distances. Journalists, rock musicians, and high school choral singers have engaged in live meetings transmitted via satellite. In 1985, musicians in several countries joined together to stage the globally transmitted Live Aid concert to raise funds to address starvation in Africa. This program was so successful that, soon after, Farm Aid (a benefit concert to help small U.S. farmers) was transmitted via satellite from the United States.

During the 1960s, the United States committed itself to ensuring that as many countries as possible benefited from this powerful new technology. For the next decade, NASA made satellite time available to other countries on an experimental basis. One such project involved the Indian government's use of a NASA satellite in the 1970s to experiment with the transmission of educational television to hundreds of impoverished villages. This project was a success, and, from 1983, India had its own Insat satellite series, used for weather forecasting, data transmission, and education. Currently, the following countries own satellites: United States, Soviet Union, France, West Germany, Italy, People's Republic of China, India, Brazil, Indonesia, Japan, Canada, Mexico, United Kingdom.

In 1964 the International Telecommunications Satellite Organization (INTELSAT) was founded in order to coordinate satellite communication use across its member and user nations (in 1989 totaling, respectively, 110 and 165). In 1971 the Intersputnik organization was founded to fulfill much the same purposes, though mostly with emphasis on television and primarily serving the Soviet Union and its allies. Inmarsat organizes international satellite communication for merchant ships, and Cospas-Sarsat does the same for distress and rescue messages on the high seas.

Many developing nations have been concerned that the orbit used for satellite communications would be filled up by a handful of countries by the time Third World countries were in a position to launch satellites. In 1979, the largest international conference ever held took place under the auspices of the International Telecommunication Union in Geneva, Switzerland. Representatives of 145 countries attended, the majority from developing nations, although Western industrialized countries sent much larger contingents. The developing nations demanded that the rule of "first come, first served" be changed to provide equitable access to the orbit for all countries.

In the 1980s, two more ITU conferences took place. Each involved a month or more of intense negotiation. At the end, it was agreed that the "first come, first served" procedure would be altered to a scheme in which one slot would be reserved for every nation on the globe. Although this is a victory in principle for equity, as Hamelink shows in Chapter 15, many more policies need to be altered to develop true equity in world communication and information.

Many industrialized and developing countries use data provided by "remote sensing" satellites to obtain images of the earth, for pinpointing oil and mineral deposits, for mapping, for monitoring crops, and for disaster relief. Although most of this information is purchased from a few countries, during the next 20 years it is likely that an increasing number of countries will own their own remote sensing satellites.

This technology was originally developed for military surveillance, to observe troop movements and to photograph military installations. Then, in 1972, the United States launched LandSat, the first civilian remote sensing satellite. In the 1980s, LandSat's ownership was switched over to a private company (EoSat). In France, a company called Spot Image took the lead in turning remote sensing data into a profitable commodity. Since then, the Soviet Union too has been marketing some of its remote sensing images. Both the French and Soviet systems produce very high-definition images. This intensified the efforts of developing nations to get involved, due to concern that if they did not own remote sensing satellites they would be at the mercy of foreign companies for information about their own countries.

This technology is also being used by the media for coverage of major international events such as the Soviet Chernobyl nuclear plant disaster in 1986 and the tragic earthquake in Armenia in 1988. However, the sale of remote sensing images has prompted objections from the U.S. government, which claims that national security would be threatened if the media could provide pictures of its military installations in other countries.

Fiber Optics

As with other communication systems, a fiber-optic link includes a transmitter, a transmission medium, and a receiver. Fiber-optic cables consist of extremely pure, thin strands of glass through which voice, data, facsimile, and video transmissions are sent over beams of laser light.

Compared with typical copper telephone wires, optical cable is lighter, takes up much less space, and can carry more than 800 times as many phone calls.

Fiber-optic cables also compete with satellites. The main advantages of a fiber-optic cable over a satellite are that it is less affected by weather conditions and can relay a far greater volume of information. On the other hand, fiber cable is a point-to-point mode. It does not have the satellite's point-to-multipoint capacity to link many locations simultaneously.

Integrated Services Digital Network

The Integrated Services Digital Network is already in the planning stages; this is also sometimes referred to as "broadband" technology. ISDN involves a single telecommunications system for transmitting voice, data, and video, including HDTV. All of these formats would be merged into a digital format at one end for purposes of transit and then separated out again at the other end. The main benefit of this would be extremely fast rates of transmission—as much as 128,000 or more bits of information a second.

ISDN has been discussed in public mostly in terms of home installations. Much more likely is that it would initially be used by a central business district office block. U.S. corporations have invested very heavily in developing ISDN, so in some shape or form it will probably emerge before long. Yet the search for ways of sending more and more information of different sorts at faster and faster speeds will also intensify problems of privacy invasion, monitoring at the workplace, and the treatment of more kinds of information as commodities.

High-Definition Television

By the late 1980s there was also considerable discussion of this potential transmission technology. U.S. television sets offer a 525-line picture, but HDTV would provide 1,125 lines and a more realistic screen aspect ratio (5:3 instead of the current 4:3). The image would be much clearer, the colors better, the depth greater, the shape of people's faces more like their real shape. It would be like having a Cinemascope picture on a TV screen, except that the blurring of rapid sideways movements would probably continue as now.

Japanese and European engineers are said to be much closer to producing a workable HDTV system than are U.S. engineers. Thus the issue has also become one of catching up in the technology race. However, other methods of achieving similar results are being worked on; these are known collectively as advanced compatible television (ACTV).

The applications of any of these systems are not, it seems, primarily entertainment based. The cameras might, it is argued, save Hollywood productions a lot of money, since direct video shooting and editing are much less costly than film or film-to-video editing. Nonetheless, and more intriguing, the Pentagon is very interested in developing HDTV's military uses, most probably in remote sensing and missile guidance—so much so that it has loudly urged that antitrust laws be suspended to allow AT&T, IBM, and Motorola to do joint HDTV research. The Pentagon's own research funding agency, DARPA, has also spent many millions of dollars in funding HDTV development.

Conclusions

The pervasive involvement of the military in the development of much new technology is one example of the high social costs associated with the world of advanced communications technology. In general, there is a growing gap between the potential of technology to give people better control over their lives and the drive by others to use it for profit and centralizing control. This gap makes it all the more difficult to know if the introduction of new technology equals progress.

The risks associated with advanced technologies should lead more people to seek out information about how various technologies are applied in their own environments. Developments should be followed closely for the ways they affect the operations of government, the national economy and employment trends, and the standard of living throughout society.

Further Questions

(1) What can be done about the growing numbers of people who cannot gain admission to the "information age"? This includes those who cannot read, cannot afford a telephone, and certainly cannot afford the fees connected with data base access. It also includes all of us who are excluded from gaining access to electronically stored government information (see Chapter 6).

(2) Do you see a deepening division between skilled and unskilled work forces? Will we see the emergence of a high-tech minority and a mass of people whose work is drastically changed from automation and deskilling?

(3) What is involved in designing appropriate, socially beneficial uses of these technologies? What types of organizations should be involved? What is the government's responsibility?

15 Information Imbalance: Core and Periphery

CEES HAMELINK

In this chapter, Hamelink sharply reminds us that debate about new communication technologies tends to be a luxury that can be enjoyed in affluent countries of the West or the East—but rarely in the South. He provides us with figures that relentlessly hammer home the truth that the planet is in desperate need of a new information and communication order; that communications hardware and software are primarily to be found in the Northern Hemisphere; that attempts to challenge this imbalance, such as the UNESCO policies of the 1970s and 1980s, which reflected Third World nations' demands for equity in communications, have been for the most part harshly rebuffed.

When there are more telephones in Japan than in the whole of the continent of Africa; when the French government can give away computer terminals (the Minitel) to 4 million of its citizens, while Brazil can be assailed by the U.S. government for trying to develop its own computer industry through government regulations forbidding computer imports; then global communication inequity has clearly become an issue that demands a response from reasonable people and a farsighted resolution. The question remains open as to whether or not such a resolution is within the vision of the transnational communications corporations.

These issues of equity are also posed to some degree within the rich nations: As communications corporations in country after country are increasingly freed from government oversight, will they not move to skim the cream from the communications market and leave the poor, especially the elderly, to wonder how to afford telephone service? As data bases become more and more expensive to use, what prospect is there for critical—and generally underfunded—researchers to work with them to provide information of service to the public rather than to corporate capital?

All in all, the gulf between rich and poor in information and communication has rapidly become a reality; it is no longer only a situation predicted. This intensification of social divisions in the world as well as at home cannot but signal serious conflicts ahead.

In studies of international communication, a great deal of attention has been paid to the global imbalances between rich and poor countries in terms of flows of media products, such as news, television programs, and films (International Commission for the Study of Communication Problems, 1980; A. Smith, 1984). Far less attention has been paid to the overall imbalances in *information* that exist in the world economy between core and peripheral nations. *Core* nations are the rich, industrialized countries: the United States, Canada, Western Europe, Japan, Australia. The economic *periphery* consists of the poorer, predominantly rural countries of Africa, Asia, and Latin America, countries that are often referred to as the South or the Third World (the Soviet Union might be considered another center with its own periphery, but it is part of a different, although sometimes interlocking, system, and is not included here). The term *peripheral* as used here is not intended to imply that these nations are culturally peripheral or of peripheral human value; it merely indicates that they are economically peripheral within the global balance of power that exists at present.

This chapter will address three main questions: What do we mean by information imbalance? How did the information imbalance between the core and the periphery develop? How does this information imbalance affect the prospects for development in the periphery?

Information Imbalance in the World

Let us begin with some basic definitions: (a) Information imbalance essentially means that some countries have a great deal more useful information than others. (b) It also means that some countries have better information capacities—the ability to produce, record, process, and distribute information—than others. (c) This capacity is dependent upon access to information hardware processors, like computers, and carriers, like books. (d) It is equally dependent upon information software—the contents of information. (e) There are also many different forms of information. Such categories of information may include scientific and technical information, financial and trading information, resource information, military information, and political and current affairs information.

Let us look at the *information hardware* question first. Most of the world's hardware processors and carriers are installed in the core countries, and the technology that is basic to their manufacture and upgrading is designed, developed, and controlled by and in the core. In the international trading of information hardware, the United States and Western Europe have been the largest exporters, but they are now powerfully challenged by Japan and other Asian producers.

A few figures can vividly show the differential distribution of information hardware around the world. The data listed below were gathered by UNESCO (1989); the base year for these figures is 1984:

- Together, all the peripheral countries own only 4% of the world's computer hardware.
- Of the world's 700 million telephones, 75% can be found in the 9 richest countries. The poor countries possess less than 10%, and in most rural areas there is less than 1 telephone for every 1,000 people. There are more telephones in Japan alone (with a 1988 population of 121 million) than in the 50 nations of Africa combined (with a 1988 population four times that of Japan and a land mass more than 80 times greater).
- In 39 peripheral countries there are no newspapers, while in 30 others there is only 1. By contrast, Japan has 125 dailies and the United States has 168.
- In the United States a daily newspaper enjoys a circulation of about 268 copies per 1,000 people; in Japan the comparable figure is 562. The African average is 16.5 copies per 1,000.
- Europe produces an average of 12,000 new book titles every year. African nations produce fewer than 350. Europe has an average of 1,400 public libraries per country where the public has free access to information. African countries have an average of 18 libraries per country.
- The world average for radio set ownership is 330 per 1,000. In the core countries, the average is 990 (2,100 in the United States) while in the periph-

> ery it is 142. In 34 peripheral countries there is no television. While the world average for television set ownership is 137 per 1,000, the gap between rich countries and poor countries is wide: 447 sets per 1,000 for the former and 36 per 1,000 for the latter.

The peripheral countries are extremely interested in improving their manufacturing capacity to produce information hardware themselves; China is currently one of the largest producers of television receivers. Increasingly, poor countries see information processors and carriers such as computers and satellites as instruments to promote economic and social development, as factors of progress. African leaders in 1985 issued the Yamousoukrou declaration, which states: "One of the main keys to solving Africa's development problems lies in mastering the rational management of information in all its forms. This is therefore not only a positive force for regional and continental integration but also an essential condition for the survival of Africa within the community of nations in the 21st century" (from a 1986 report by the International Bureau of Infomatics).

There is already a considerable spread of capacity in information hardware manufacturing in a number of countries, including Brazil, India, South Korea, and Malaysia. India has achieved a significant growth in the domestic manufacturing of information hardware, estimating in its 1985-1990 technology development plan that the growth in computer demand would reach US $862.5 million. India aims to export advanced computer technology as well as to improving its telecommunications capacity.

The periphery is also becoming more important as an import market for information hardware, with Brazil, Mexico, Venezuela, Argentina, the People's Republic of China, Saudi Arabia, Hong Kong, and Thailand among the largest importers. But this importation is not without problems, since the international market for information hardware is tightly controlled by a very few suppliers on whom importing countries have to depend. As they often lack the necessary expertise to assess the hardware they require, they are often sold obsolete products.

The periphery also has problems in producing information hardware, which is usually based on a very narrow range of specialized goods. Investment in this production, moreover, comes mainly from large transnational companies, which target certain peripheral countries because of their authoritarian governments, economic incentives like tax privileges and low wages, and knowledge of English among the elites. Exports are mainly products made by transnational manufacturers in offshore production and assembly operations by their subsidiaries. A large proportion of this trade, in reality, consists of transactions inside a company, between its subsidiaries and its headquarters. The result of this process is that the core of the technical know-how remains under the control of the transnational company, and the peripheral country plays a minor role just in assembly. Thus, all in all, there is stark international inequality in information hardware production.

For *information software,* we can look at the volume and direction of information flows and the possibilities of generating, distributing, or accessing relevant information. International information flows are imbalanced, since most of the world's information moves among the core countries and less between the core and the periphery; very little flows among the countries of the periphery. Less than 10% of all telephone, telex, and telegraph traffic takes place between peripheral countries.

Flows between the core and periphery tend to be one-way. Estimates suggest that the flow of news from core to periphery is 100 times more than the flow in the opposite direction. Thus in the mid-1980s in international broadcasting, Europe broadcast 855 hours yearly to Africa, while Africa broadcast only 70 hours back. Imbalances are evident in television importation also, so that Western European countries import an average 33% of their programs, while African countries import 55% of total TV programs (UNESCO, 1989).

If we look at different kinds of information, we find other hidden kinds of imbalances. For the most part, the flow between core and periphery consists of "raw," unprocessed information coming from the periphery, while the core provides ready-made information packages, and—as with manufactured goods—the considerable value added by processing translates into higher costs for the periphery if it wants to buy its own information back in its processed form. One example would be remote sensing by satellites that digitally encode images of, say, the shoals of tuna off the coast of Nigeria. The image is free, but it requires sophisticated computer processing to be intelligible, and thus the processed information has to be bought at a high price.

In the field of *scientific and technical information* the imbalance exists also; only 3% of the world's research and development takes place in peripheral countries (National Science Foundation, 1984). Only 1% of the world's patent grants are held by nationals of peripheral countries, since in most of those countries the technology patents are held by a small number of transnational corporations. Most of the world's scientific and technical information is produced and owned by individuals and companies in the core.

Full access to *financial and trading information* is the privileged property of a few private enterprises in the core. Most of this information flows as computer data through the communications networks of large banks and as economic data through news agencies and newspapers. There are also the specialized financial data base services, such as AP/Dow Jones, Chase

Econometrics, and Reuters. Poor countries (like most ordinary individuals) are handicapped in accessing information about the complex and rapidly changing international finance system, are late in receiving information about rates of exchange and interest, and have little access to the international brokerage circuit or to the vast and expensive systems for distributing this information. Western industrialized countries, on the other hand, enjoy rapid access to financial and trading information. This means that in trade negotiations, for example, the peripheral nation is at a considerable disadvantage when bargaining, often having fewer skilled negotiators and less useful information.

Resource information is another area where the core has enormous advantages, mainly through data collection about global natural resources through remote sensing via satellites. This can be used to monitor harvests and for mineral exploitation with obvious benefits; for example, New York commodity traders can know more about imminent Brazilian coffee harvests than do the Brazilian coffee producers, and so can determine prices on the commodities markets. Similarly, international fishing companies know more about the whereabouts of tuna shoals than do the local fishermen off the west coast of Africa, and use this information to land the best catches.

In the field of *military intelligence* it is obvious that poor countries cannot hope to compete with the extensive and very sophisticated surveillance networks that the superpowers have developed. Both the United States and the Soviet Union have computer systems that collect and process billions of bits of information, so that the Soviets can monitor, record, and identify thousands of private conversations in the United States, and the United States can collect such seemingly trivial bits of information as the laundry lists of Soviet submarine crews. Satellite photography now allows the identification of objects just 12 inches in diameter from an altitude of 150 miles. U.S. spy satellites include the IMEWS and Keyhole-11, which provide very precise information about Soviet tests of strategic and tactical nuclear weapons. Increasingly, outer space has become a militarized zone, since it is estimated that about 75% of satellites launched over the past decade have been for military use. Listening posts also collect valuable military information. NATO posts in Turkey monitor Soviet armed forces' broadcasts, collect seismographic evidence on subterranean nuclear explosions, and monitor the movement of Soviet satellites via radar, while at the world's largest listening post in Menwith Hill, United Kingdom, the American National Security Agency monitors all transoceanic telephone and telex traffic to and from Eastern Europe (see also Chapter 14).

Rich countries also have great advantages in the field of *political information*, particularly in areas of psychological warfare, propaganda, and disinformation. Both the CIA and the KGB have elaborate networks for deliberate distortion of political information. Disinformation employs the fabrication and distortion of information to legitimate one's own operations and to delegitimate and mislead the enemy. The CIA has a lengthy history of disinformation activity, on which it is estimated that the agency spends $1 billion annually (Hamelink, 1986). Peripheral countries have little chance to correct or counter such disinformation.

There are also severe international imbalances in a more public form of information, *news*. The "big four" news agencies—Associated Press (AP), United Press International (UPI), Agence France Presse (AFP), and Reuters—largely control the international flow of verbal information, while Visnews and CBS News are the dominant sources of visual information. The average daily news production of the world agencies ranges from an output of 17 million words a day by AP to 3.3 million words by AFP (Mowlana, 1986). By contrast, the only international news agency with a particular interest in covering developments in the poor countries is InterPress Service, which puts out 150,000 words a day. World news is predominantly about events in the core. When the periphery is covered, there are usually some other news pegs at work, such as a link to some superpower conflict (Afghanistan/Nicaragua), a threat to core interests (Iran-Iraq War), a sensational drama (floods in Bangladesh, murder in Sri Lanka, famine in Ethiopia), a historical relation (news about ex-colonies), or some exotic sexual dimension. Thus much of the time the periphery is invisible, or it is presented in a distorted form. (For further discussion of news coverage of the Third World, see Chapter 21.)

Thus, overall, information flows across the world are imbalanced in terms of their *direction*, their *volume*, and their *quality*. The capacity to produce, distribute, and access pertinent information is very unequally distributed among the world's countries, and the core countries have infinitely more control over the software of the world's information than do the peripheral countries.

How Did Information Imbalance Develop?

A central factor that explains these global imbalances is the history of colonial expansion by European nations into the rest of the world. Before the fifteenth century, when European colonial expansion began, the countries of the periphery possessed elaborate trade and information networks. These routes originated in the ancient empires of Egypt, China, India, and Mesopotamia (more or less modern Iraq), and connected Asia, Africa, the Mediterranean, and the Pacific. The spice and silk routes linked Mesopotamia and Iran with India and China. Gold was extracted in West Africa and transported across the Sahara to North Africa and the Middle East by Tuareg tradesmen who possessed vast knowledge about the desert. Before Vasco da Gama's travels from Portugal in the fifteenth century, trading took place between what is now Zimbabwe and China (for Chinese pottery) and India (for gold and ivory). Before Captain Cook traveled to the South Seas, Melanesian and Polynesian seafarers had developed sufficient geographical information to make long voyages. While Europeans painstakingly charted Australia, the native Aboriginals already possessed extensive knowledge of the territories they had inhabited since ancient times. Although European historians often suggested (and still sometimes do) that indigenous peoples lacked useful information, extensive evidence points in the opposite direction.

By the mid-eighteenth century, however, an international colonial economy had materialized. Gradually, trade and information traffic was rerouted from exchanges among the periphery to flows between the core—Britain, France, Spain, Holland, Portugal, and so on—and the periphery. For example, the North African trade routes became obsolete through the slave trade across the Atlantic. This pattern is still reflected in contemporary communications, so that telephone calls between East and West Africa are routed via European capitals.

Beyond the rerouting of trade and information, new values and ideas—a new culture—were introduced to the periphery. Alongside the colonial traders and gunboats came missionaries intent on saving "primitive" souls and expanding God's kingdom on earth. In turn, they often set up the first foreign schools, in which the language, religion, and general culture of the European colonizers were taught to a small, select group of the colonized—by definition, those prepared to compromise with colonial rule sufficiently to allow them to enter such institutions.

Not everyone who passed through such schools precisely mimicked the colonists, but nonetheless these schools served to generate a whole new set of perspectives among the indigenous elites of the colonies. As generation succeeded generation, and a few individuals began to make their way to France and England and the Netherlands to study at universities there, graduation from such places became a mark of distinction acknowledged by many who had not achieved it. Graduates had played the Europeans at their own game and won. But in the process, European culture was coming to be prized, for many purposes, above the national culture or cultures. The well-worn path of Latin American students to U.S. or French universities tells the same story. Military education was also significant—at St. Cyr in France, at Sandhurst in England, and at numerous establishments in the United States. Many of the military takeovers of governments in peripheral countries have been led by graduates of military academies in the core countries.

Whether by the military path, the business path, or the government route, the people running the affairs of peripheral countries after independence were overwhelmingly drawn from the ranks of those who had passed through core educational systems. Indeed, the expansion of university education in the peripheral nations has mostly been based on models copied from core countries, the cultures of which have thus been perpetuated, in differing degrees, despite demands for authentic local models of education (see Chapter 19).

Once the colonial powers ceased to exert direct administrative control, beginning with Irish independence in 1920 and gaining momentum with Philippine and Indian independence in 1945 and 1947, this educational and cultural tradition became more important than ever. There was no longer a colonial governor, no longer a detachment of the army, no longer a White government administration to secure by force the continued economic profitability of the former colonies for business interests in the core countries. There was instead a cultural apparatus and inheritance that at some level kept most of the former colonies, via their own new rulers, within the ambit of their old masters.

Thus in the search for economic development, both the products and the new development models of the West were generally sought after by the new rulers. Equally, consumer products were sought after by the new elite, who could afford to buy them—from Mercedes Benz cars to Swiss perfumes to Scotch whiskey to French fashions. Media imports, especially television and film, were generic advertisements for Western consumerism, even if not a single commercial was included (in Chapter 19, Mohammadi investigates this process in detail).

The transfer of technology itself created similar problems. Information technology, for instance, was not primarily introduced to meet basic needs, but to support the expansion of transnational business. Studies on the deployment of telephony, educational television, and satellite communication suggest that while peripheral peoples do benefit from the introduction of such technologies, the primary beneficiaries are the foreign and national elites; frequently, also, the intended development objectives are not achieved, and serious balance-of-payments problems occur, as the hardware has to be paid for regardless (Clippinger, 1976). Importing information hardware also has consequences for software. Many foreign companies insist on "turnkey" projects that tie the delivery of the hardware (such as a television station) to the purchase of certain software (such as foreign television programming). This undercuts the local production of necessary software.

The international information market is dominated by fewer than 100 transnational companies that control over three-quarters of all the world's information hardware and software. These companies are interlocked and share financial interests (Hamelink, 1983). For example, General Electric, the fifth largest industrial company in the United States, with $49 billion in revenue and $3.4 billion in profit in 1988, has strong links with Citibank and Morgan Guaranty Trust, is interlocked with Honeywell as well as the Japanese electronics firm Toshiba, and now owns RCA and NBC.

With such a power base, the companies in the international "information-industrial complex" leave little or no space for peripheral countries to participate in these markets. This has important consequences for information imbalance. On the one hand, much information is produced for domestic markets, so that AP and UPI essentially produce news for the U.S. market, and their production is guided by that market's news demands. On the other hand, whenever the domestic market does not yield sufficient revenues, the information industry distributes internationally, as with the sale of television programs. For example, while the costs of producing a program such as *Dallas* may be covered by domestic sales, profit may come only with international sales. Thus overseas markets are important for generating profit, but have no say about content. International pricing of television programs and other cultural products can also vary greatly, so that the price can be as high as the market will bear or less than the competitive price of a local production, flooding the local market and undermining local production. However, a few peripheral countries are important cultural producers: India and Egypt produce films that are in demand, and Brazil produces successful soap operas.

All these processes mean that, despite their formal political independence, most peripheral countries still experience neocolonial relationships. The flow of cultural products, the transfer of technology, the role of national elites tied to core centers, and the mechanisms of the international market all work to maintain the advantage that the core countries already possess.

Does Information Imbalance Matter?

Information imbalance does matter, in a number of ways crucial both to the poor nations themselves and to the whole international system. First, the inadequate information capacities of most peripheral countries are a serious obstacle to their own efforts to combat poverty and other deprivations. Their capacity to provide warnings about dramatic weather conditions or to communicate about health and hygiene practices or the benefits of a new development program requires an extensive information system. The peripheral countries must be able to discuss their own priorities and provide their own information about raw material requirements, import/export relations, and technological and labor needs. Without information about resources, finance, and trade, peripheral countries are continuously at a disadvantage in negotiations with core countries, and this jeopardizes their survival as independent nations.

Second, the national sovereignty of peripheral countries is threatened when so much information about them is stored in data banks in other countries. If a country lacks information about itself, it is limited in the decisions it can make about its own future. If a foreign country possesses such information, as when a mineral-exploiting corporation holds information about mineral-rich peripheral countries, it means that decision making has been exported and national independence is undermined.

Third, information imbalance leads to the cultural integration of the peripheral countries in the culture promoted by the core. Imported cultural programming encourages consumerism and individualism, and diverts attention from any regard for the long-term needs of the country. Internal gaps develop as urban elites become part of the international economy while the rural poor get left behind. A nation needs cultural independence to develop its own language, forms of musical expression, literature, theater, educational system, suitable technologies, and what it chooses to preserve from its cultural heritage. Information imbalance thus undermines cultural self-determination. (Again, see Chapter 19 for a case study of this process.)

Improving the Imbalance: What Can Be Done?

How can the international information imbalance be improved? There are three major approaches. One stresses the interdependence of the world's nations and suggests that peripheral countries should be better integrated into the international economy so that they can then catch up through international transfers of finance, knowledge, and technology. The basic problem with this approach is that such international transfers and modernization policies often increase the dependence of poor countries and do not help them to resolve their basic problems of deprivation and poverty. This approach suggests that the core and periphery share mutual interests.

A second approach suggests that peripheral countries need greater bargaining power. They could pressure the core for fairer schemes and terms of trade, for cheaper transfers of technology, and for solutions to massive external debt problems. Bargaining strength can be developed if the periphery pools resources and energy, like raw materials. But these bargaining chips may be undermined by changes in the core countries, such as replacing human labor with robots and the production of synthetic products instead of products requiring natural raw materials.

The third approach suggests radical self-reliance (Hamelink, 1983). It suggests that poor countries disassociate themselves—delink—from international networks that hamper their development. Since isolated efforts by individual countries are doomed to failure, this kind of strategy demands collective effort across the periphery, which in itself requires the solving of many old and difficult conflicts among the poor countries themselves. It also requires a visionary leadership willing to forgo the immediate benefits of links with the core.

Conclusion

Information imbalance takes many forms, as has been discussed above. It is especially entrenched in the differential capacities for collecting, processing, and utilizing information between the core and the periphery. Redressing this imbalance cannot mean that all countries must end up with equally sophisticated levels of information processing, but it would mean that each country develops the level necessary for its independent survival as a sovereign nation. Information imbalance is a crucial part of international relations in the postcolonial world. Since so many vested interests are involved in this unequal situation, it will be a long time before it is resolved.

Further Questions

(1) Do the kinds of information imbalances described in this chapter exist within the domestic information situation inside the United States?

(2) Identify some major transnational corporations and map out their patterns of ownership and corporate linkages. Explore further the political and cultural implications of this international trend.

(3) Would it be a solution to the problems of information imbalance if the periphery countries were to delink from the international information market and develop their own alternative information resources? Apart from delinking, what other kinds of interactions between the core and the periphery would counteract the existing information imbalance?

Part V Mass Culture and Popular Culture

In this final section of the book, we introduce you to a series of studies written largely from cultural studies perspectives. From reading earlier chapters by O'Connor (Chapter 1), Ang (Chapter 10), and Downing (Chapter 12), you know that the area of cultural studies entails approaches to media that stress both the variety of influences upon communication and the interactive nature of the communication process. In other words, the concept of communication as an individualized, one-way transmission (Who says what to whom with what effect?) is rejected.

Instead, communication is argued to be a collective, two-way, and multiply determined process. Cultural studies analysts focus on how the elements of national and international culture are generated and developed, on the "culture industry," on active audiences, and most of all on the mutual influences between a nation's cultures and its media institutions. Culture is seen as constantly developing and conflictual, not as static or seamless. Cultural products are analyzed for the excitement and pleasure they evoke, for their reflection of our dreams and hopes, not only as sources of political confusion and control.

These last two ways of seeing culture do not exclude each other. A widely popular film that encourages racism needs to be understood not just for the ways it cues into those forces in our culture, but for the attractiveness of its total message. Contradictory elements in its message also need to be perceived, along with contradictory responses in its audiences. Only thus can we grasp the combination of factors that enable such a media text to reinforce the repression of people of color.

Finally, for U.S. readers, who are often barely aware of the cultural impact the United States has across the globe or of the cultural backdrop of other nations' responses to its planetary power, the international dimensions of cultural studies analysis are especially important. We begin, however, with a focus that strikes a sensitive nerve in every culture, but that promises to extend everyone's frontiers of awareness and enrich their understanding of communication and culture: feminist analysis.

16 Feminist Perspectives on Popular Culture

LANA RAKOW

A major error of perception is contained in the commonly used phrase "women and minorities." Women in most societies, including the United States, are slightly in the majority. This is because they are generally hardier at birth and live longer, though quite often in unenviable conditions in their later years. (The term "minorities" also has problems; see the introduction to Chapter 18.)

Thus by beginning this book's main section on cultural studies with Rakow's chapter on feminist perspectives, we are not just trying to be different. We are simply beginning with the female majority, on the democratic principle of majorities. To be a feminist means, to be sure, much more than just this basic recognition. At the same time, a feminist perspective is emphatically not something to which women alone may aspire. Furthermore, there are various feminist perspectives, not merely one. Nonetheless, in a book concerned with mass communication and mass culture, there is particular reason to recognize that the mass in question is composed more of women than of men, and to foreground a feminist analysis of the communication process.

One of the advantages of doing so is that insights produced in other contexts are often amply confirmed by specific research on women and mass communication. The frequency of stereotyped media images of women, which is the first of Rakow's themes, is a key example of an even wider process, namely, the way we allow media to define reality for us in oversimplified and often injurious ways. Furthermore, it would be a mistake to see these media definitions as affecting only men; women, too, are prompted, with varying degrees of effectiveness, to conform to many of these stereotypes. One need think only of the requirement many women feel to push themselves to be as thin as the average model to understand this point.

Rakow's other two themes also usefully underscore some of the main themes of this reader. Her analysis of how women have developed media to communicate their reality, especially in the history of the novel, emphasizes that media are not only there to be deployed by powerful corporate or government interests, but can be used by the "mass" public to communicate horizontally (a similar argument can be found in Chapter 12 and runs through many other chapters). Similarly, her analysis of women as audience supports Ang's discussion of the "active" audience (Chapter 10), which brings its own interpretations and imports its own meanings into its reception of mass media output, such as soap operas.

It doesn't take a communication scholar to identify some of the more obvious ways in which women have a different relationship to popular culture than men do. Think of the books you read, the films and television programs you watch or flip past, the music you listen to, the posters and advertisements you see, the magazines in the rack at the local convenience store. In terms of sheer amount of visual content, representations of women form a major part of popular culture. Women's faces and bodies appear in advertisements, on album jackets, in X-rated films and videos, on magazine covers, on product packages. When it comes to women and men as characters in stories on television, in film, or in books, however, the opposite is true. While television seasons and the products of the film industry and book publishing industries may vary at any one time, male characters generally far outnumber female characters in prime-time television, mainstream Hollywood cinema, and such publications as children's books. Finally, when it comes to which popular culture forms women and men enjoy and pay attention to, there is a difference as well. Women and men tend to watch and read different kinds of television programs, advertisements, books, and magazines, many of which are intentionally designed to appeal to either women or men.

Does it matter that women and men have different relationships to popular culture? Feminists think so. It is important to bear in mind that there are many kinds of feminists, with differing political perspectives, but in general feminists share a concern about women's position in society. Most are concerned with understanding how our present political, economic, and social system functions so it can be changed to one that is, at the least, more egalitarian, more cooperative, and not exploitative of people's labor and services. Most feminists recognize popular culture as critical to understanding our culture as well as to changing it.

Because feminists are concerned about popular culture does not mean that they universally condemn it or think of all popular culture as detrimental to women. As will become clear from the discussion below, women's relationship to popular culture is a complex one. Fortunately, feminist activists and feminist scholars have been working from various perspectives to illuminate the relationship. These feminists have pointed out that women are a central subject matter of popular culture intended for both women and men, that women have played central roles as consumers of certain popular culture products, and that, in some cases and in some time periods, women have been significant creators and producers of popular culture. This essay will take you through three general ways that feminists have looked at popular culture so that you can better understand the critiques that feminists make of it and the larger social system of which it is a part.

Women's Representations

Perhaps the most obvious connection between women and popular culture—and the most disturbing to feminists—is the use of women as subject matter in popular culture content. In fact, a renewal of the feminist movement in the 1960s (it is important to remember that a woman's movement has existed in this country, sometimes more or less visibly, for at least the past 150 years) was spurred by women's dissatisfaction with women's images and the portrayal of women characters in popular culture. Feminists have been concerned about the kind of images that are present in popular culture, what those images reveal about women's position in our society, the consequences of those images, and how such images have meaning for members of the culture.

Feminists often point to the publication of one particular book, Betty Friedan's *Feminine Mystique* in 1963, as the renewal point of the contemporary feminist movement. That book pointed out a great disparity between the fulfilling role of wife and mother that was being held up in the mass media, in particular represented by the fictional characters in women's magazines, versus the isolation and despair that real women felt in their own roles. Friedan pointed out that fictional women characters in women's magazines had been career oriented and independent prior to World War II, when women were wanted in the work force. After World War II, the characters gave up their career aspirations in favor of home and family, the stories coinciding with social pressures that discouraged women from being in the work force. In other words, Friedan was pointing out that the ideals of womanhood presented in popular culture do not represent the lives or the best interests of real women, but the interests of such groups as government and business.

While Friedan demonstrated that the career-mindedness of heroines has changed over time, other feminists have shown that women's images over the past century or so have more or less consistently portrayed the ideal woman as passive, domestic, and pretty (Wald, 1975; Weibel, 1977). The ideal woman has also been White and middle class. This is of particular concern to women of color, who have been either invisible in popular culture or portrayed as servants, savages, or victims, while being forced to measure themselves or be measured by others against a White standard. And of course, for the many women for whom being dependent and domestic is impossible or undesirable, these representations have also been offensive.

The ideal woman, passive and domestic, who has been portrayed in popular culture over the years makes sense, however, in light of the work of feminist historians, literary critics, sociologists, and others. As feminist scholars tell us, in the nineteenth century a new social order and new roles for women and men were coming into place. As the country moved from an agrarian economy to an industrial one, women and men came to be seen as appropriately belonging to "separate spheres." Men were thought to belong to the public world of wage labor and politics; women were thought to belong to the private world of home and family. He was to be the producer, she the consumer. Though this ideal never matched the lives or dreams of many women, it was nonetheless an ideal that found expression in much popular culture.

Communication researchers became interested in representations of women in popular culture during the 1970s. In fact, many of the researchers were feminists themselves, who were interested in studying the problem because of their own concern about women's place in society. Most of the research that was done during that decade and into the next was what could be characterized as mainstream social science research. Researchers were concerned about empirically documenting how many and what kind of female characters versus male characters could be found on television, in magazines, in the news, and in books. There was an interest in discovering the relationship between content and its effects on audience members. In particular, feminist researchers were concerned that children were learning that women should be dependent and that they have limited choices about their lives.

By 1980, a consistent and doleful composite picture of women's representation in the mass media had been documented by researchers. A book that cataloged empirical studies of women's images made a number of conclusions about women's representation in the mass media, including the following: that television commercials were much more likely to show women working inside the home and men working outside of it; that most women in television commercials were younger than men in commercials; that there were far fewer women characters than men in television content; that magazine advertisements and articles showed few women working; that in children's literature, male characters were more frequent and were shown in more roles than female characters; that women have historically had limited roles in films (Butler & Paisley, 1980).

This traditional social science research needs to be considered in relation to two trends that have been occurring recently. The first is a trend in research that calls into question the manner in which we think about media content and women's representations. The second trend is a change in media content itself, which might seem to have resolved the problems feminists have had about women's representations. Let's look at both of these trends.

Media criticism and research that is concerned with how women are represented in media content has itself come under scrutiny by other feminists. These other feminists are likely to have both politics and methodologies that are different from those of more traditional social science researchers. These new critics have been pointing out that there is a conceptual problem in criticizing women's images in media content. First, they argue, it is not simply the images that are the problem, but the entire structure of the media themselves. Even if the images were changed, some argue, the media would continue to belong to commercial enterprises that use the media for profit. Others argue the media would continue to be in the hands of men, who use it to tell stories that suit their purposes. Second, these feminists say, media content cannot be measured against some other "reality." Media content can never be some veridical account of life; it will always be a selection, construction, and representation of it. It is not reasonable, therefore, to insist that media content be more "realistic." The question is, rather, who should have the opportunity to create accounts of people and their lives and how such accounts function meaningfully for us. Third, other feminists have argued that changing media representations of women is difficult. Superficial changes can be made—for example, more women characters can be shown in more diverse roles—while the deeper problem of a sexist ideology remains untouched.

As this final point suggests, superficial changes in women's representations in media content have occurred, not coincidentally, over the period of the past two decades when feminism has been more visible and successful. However, this trend in media content should not be taken as evidence that feminist concern is now unnecessary. On the contrary, these changing images provide all the more evidence that a deep, underlying sexism still exists.

For example, it is possible to look at some print and broadcast advertising and surmise that women are no longer shown as domestic or dependent. Women are shown having careers; they are shown as sexually assertive. Men are even shown in some advertisements as caregivers for children. Surely, it could be argued, these examples show that women's roles have changed and media content should not be of concern to feminists. Feminists counter that argument with two responses. The first is that these images are a co-optation of the real changes that feminists have sought; that is, while feminists have been trying to change a structure and value system based on competition, individualism, and economic exploitation, advertising has translated the goals of feminism into those very values. The second response is that the representation of women still remains that of "woman," a symbol that is given meaning by its relation to a broad sexist code that transcends any one advertisement. One feminist, Rosalind Coward (1985), has written about how fashion photography in women's magazines has changed from the portrayal of the smiling, anxious-to-please model to the unsmiling, defiant model of contemporary photography (pp. 57-58). This new fashion look bears a striking resemblance to pornography, she observes. We could extend that analysis to an interpretation that sees the scowling face (in pornography and fashion photography alike) as belonging to a woman to be conquered, to be made submissive—hardly a change in women's representation that feminists applaud. Coward goes on to say that the female body remains the main object of attention in Western culture because, as the subordinate sex, women can be the "aesthetic sex," an empty term that takes on the values of a particular society at a given historical moment (p. 77).

Feminists who have been critical of traditional research on women's images and who feel we need a richer conceptualization of how images function have, like Coward, looked at the broader relationship of media content and culture to understand how images are given sexist meanings or how they function to locate women in a subordinate social location. Feminists who have taken up contemporary psychoanalytic theory, for example, particularly as developed in film theory, have looked at how "woman" functions as a construction of male fantasy (Mulvey, 1975).

Women as Creators

While most feminists have been concerned with how women are represented in popular culture, some feminists have been interested in recovering a history of women's creative efforts as writers, artists, performers, producers, designers, and communicators. They place a positive value on women's culture and their creative efforts, focusing on women's images of themselves and women's stories about their own experiences, rather than on men's images of women. They are interested in how women have managed to express themselves, despite all the constraints against them, and they are interested in why women's creativity has been overlooked or devalued—labeled "popular," for example, where a man's creativity might become part of "high" culture.

Feminists who are interested in women's creativity have uncovered a long and rich history. For example, one collection of stories about women writers in Great Britain traces the careers of women in the pre-Victorian period, women who were writing popular plays and even publishing magazines in a time period that was actively hostile against their doing such things (Adburgham, 1972).

One of the most important forms of popular culture for women, the novel, has been reevaluated, too. The novel has been one of the most available and popular means for women (White women in particular) to speak to other women. Josephine Donovan (1980) has noted that prior to the nineteenth century, women were not allowed to receive Latin rhetorical training and as a consequence did not have the tools to create public art (p. 216). With the rise of the vernacular and the rhetoric of the home, women had greater access to the means of literary creation. The novel, written in "plain" style rather than "high" style, was particularly appropriate for women to adopt for their own uses. It has even been suggested that a common "women's story" appealing to White, middle-class women found in contemporary novels can be traced back to nineteenth-century predecessors (Miner, 1984). Poor and working-class White women and women of color have had fewer opportunities and less access to means of creative expression, but nonetheless a Black women's literary tradition has been recovered, with themes, styles, and aesthetics reflecting a set of experiences very different from those found in White male literary convention (Smith, 1982).

Feminists have gone beyond simply retrieving this lost history, however. They have called into question two important factors affecting women's creativity: (a) the impediments that have stood in the way of women artists and (b) the standards used to judge creative efforts as art or not art, high culture or popular culture. Modern feminists have taken inspiration from Virginia Woolf's 1929 analysis of the circumstances that prevent women from being as creative as men. Woolf laid the blame on women's lowly economic position and their lack of the private space and uninterrupted time necessary for creation. It is necessary "to have five hundred a year and a room with a lock on the door if you are to write fiction or poetry," she concluded, a set of circumstances few women find themselves in (Woolf, 1957, p. 109). Tillie Olsen (1978) writes of not publishing a book until she was 50 because she was raising children and working outside and inside the home, a time when everything else had to come before her writing (p. 37). Women's material and social circumstances, their caregiving, and their accessibility to children, according to Olsen, silence them.

Art is not the product, then, of a genius who transcends society; it is a social product. We must understand "*who* becomes an artist, *how* they become an artist, how they are able to *practice* their art, and how they can ensure that their work is produced, performed, and *made available* to a public," according to feminist Janet Wolff (1981, p. 40). In other words, if we are to look at women's creativity, we must also look at the opportunities or lack of opportunities available to them, for certain groups have access to the means of creative expression more than others. This helps explain why so much of popular culture is composed of men's stories about women rather than the other way around.

The standards that are used to judge creative works must be examined as well if we are going to understand evaluations of women's creative efforts. Feminist literary critics have examined how women's works are often denigrated because they are not concerned with "universal" themes and problems, because they lack the originality of men's works, or because they are too popular—that is, they appeal to the "lowbrow." These standards have kept most women's works out of traditional canons of art and literature. Even in relation to other popular culture forms, women's forms—novels and soap operas, in particular—are accorded the lowest status by male critics, suggesting it is the connection of these forms to women rather than any intrinsic lack of merit that earns them this disdain (Modleski, 1982).

The connection between women artists and their work, given the context of a patriarchal, industrial capitalist society, however, is not always an easy one to understand, so it is necessary to be careful in drawing conclusions about media content created by women as unfettered, "authentic" creativity. For example, how do we understand Hollywood films directed by women, a television series scripted by women, violent romance novels written by women, popular music performed by women? Are these "women's stories"? Are they "authentic" expressions of women's experiences? Are they liberating or conservative (consider Cyndi Lauper's version of Robert Hazard's "Girls Just Want to Have Fun")? We cannot separate the creation of art from the complex industries that now control its production. It is difficult to assess what impact women artists could and do have on the cultural forms produced when they are working in a large system of constraints and rewards.

Women as Audiences

The most recent feminist attention to popular culture has been in relation to trying to understand the audiences of popular culture products. A basic principle for most feminists involves a tolerance and sympathy for the positions of other women and for the interpretations they hold of their own lives. It makes sense that feminists would feel this way; they are leery of others claiming to have a better perspective on women's own circumstances, since this is something men have done to women historically. Consequently, some feminists have come to reject the implicit or explicit scorn for the consumers of popular culture that has generally pervaded scholarly discussions of it. The consumers of popular culture have been seen as uncritical, as lacking good judgment and taste, as dupes of an oppressive ideology that keeps them in their place.

Research has just started in the past few years that will help us better understand how popular culture functions and has meaning for the women who read or view it. It is not surprising that attention has first been directed to soap operas and romance novels, the two forms of popular culture most associated with women. Feminist Dorothy Hobson (1982) has tried to understand the popularity of the British soap opera *Crossroads* by studying viewers in their homes as they watched the program, observing how the program fit into the structure of their home roles. While it has been commonplace to discount soap operas as escapism and to ridicule their fantastic plot lines, Hobson found that viewers were interested in resolutions to problems shared by women in the program and in real life (p. 149). Viewers are not passive recipients of the program, she concludes, but active creators of the text; that is, they strip the storyline to the idea behind it and construct an understanding of the skeleton left behind. Their sympathetic disposition to the serial leads to their transformation of the text into something relevant and meaningful to them.

Another study, this one of romance readers, came to a similar conclusion. Janice Radway (1984) conducted a study of a group of romance readers to understand why they derive pleasure from reading romance after romance. She found that these readers see their act of reading as a minor act of independence that allows them to assert their need for time and space away from the demands made on them in their roles as primary family caregivers. They view the heroines of the novels they prefer as independent and assertive, victorious over the hero because by the end of the novel he comes to accept the female world of love and human relations over men's public world of fame and success. The romance novel can be seen as a minor resistance to patriarchy, Radway concludes, though at the same time it restores women to their current role (by giving them enjoyment and time to themselves but not challenging the social relations of their own situations).

A similar tension between resistance to dominant meanings and incorporation of them has been found in research on girls who are popular music fans, conducted by a researcher sympathetic to feminism (Peterson, 1987). Female and male undergraduates were asked to write an analysis of Cyndi Lauper's rendition of "Girls Just Want to Have Fun." The researcher classified their responses into three interpretive positions: liberal individualists, those who saw the song as an expression of the entitlement of youth to the individual experience of pleasure; liberal feminists, those who saw the song as a way for women to redefine pleasure around their own interests in opposition to dominant cultural meanings; and teenyboppers, those who saw the song in relation to other practices such as dancing, talking with other girls, and dreaming of romance. Despite the fact that teenybopper culture has been dismissed by researchers as trivial, being a teenybopper gives girls the potential to resist dominant cultural meanings because of the possibility for them to mark out their own culture through a combination of activities.

There is much about how women respond to popular culture and use it for their own purposes that has yet to be understood. The challenge for feminists comes in respecting and not patronizing other women's understandings of their own lives even when those understandings differ from a feminist reading of them. On the other hand, research that takes women, not objects or texts, as the central focus of study presents feminists with opportunities to offer their feminist interpretations to other women. If there are points of tension between what the dominant culture says it is supposed to mean to be a woman and the alternative, resistant meanings that women might construct through their pleasure with popular culture forms, feminist research might be able to make those contradictions visible and available for women to critique.

Summary

By now it should be apparent that feminists have taken a diversity of starting points when looking at women and popular culture. A feminist perspective on popular culture does not simply mean declaring some cultural product to be sexist. Feminists take a broad look at how culture and art function together in order to understand better how women's subordinate status is inscribed in cultural forms as well as in their own lives.

Feminists have been concerned about how women are represented in popular culture, but we have seen how important it is not to assume or expect some simple correspondence between the images in popular culture and "reality," or between the images and the way people understand them. As important, feminists have been concerned about recovering women's creativity and about reevaluating the standards that label some things as "popular," meaning less worthy. They have been concerned about understanding how women read and understand popular culture texts, looking for points of resistance to dominant meanings.

There are, then, several perspectives, not just one, that feminists bring to popular culture, in the belief that understanding how popular culture functions in our society will help us to change it.

Further Questions

(1) Examine current cultural consumption among your peers. Are the tastes and patterns of use markedly different for males and females? Is there more differentiation for some media than others, and what can we learn from that?

(2) Research the numbers of women employed, and the positions they occupy, in major print and electronic media. How would you assess the overall status of working women in the media?

(3) Compare certain products (music videos, television programs, films) produced by women to those produced by men. Are there differences of theme, orientation, image? Could the audience tell the gender of the producer? How might that affect the way they react to the product?

17 Advertising and Consumer Culture

DOUGLAS KELLNER

Some critical analysts focus mainly on the political economy of media, as discussed in Chapters 4 and 5 of this volume. Others concentrate overwhelmingly on cultural studies, as in this section. Kellner tries to fuse these perspectives together, examining not just the economic basis of U.S. broadcasting and the press—advertising—but also advertising's impact in creating a consumerist culture that seems at times to envelop us all.

The intellectual source of much of his critique is a group of German intellectuals who were forced into exile, mainly to the United States, by the Nazis' accession to power in 1933. Based originally at a short-lived research institute in Frankfurt University, they are the founders of what has become known as the Frankfurt school of critical theory. Their view of contemporary mass culture has been highly influential since. They are noted for their insistence on how mass-produced contemporary culture provides us with substitutes for feeling, for love, for curiosity of the mind; on how it manipulates our anxieties about ourselves; and on how it caters to a fraction of our intelligence and effectively sells us short as human beings.

Perhaps nowhere is this argument more plausible than in mass advertising. Kellner mercilessly dissects the ridiculous—but still potent—advertising messages that play upon our fears and uncertainties about how to present ourselves socially, how to behave in public and in private. (The pressure on women to be as thin as models, cited in our introduction to Chapter 16, is a case in point.) Kellner also analyzes the fashion industry, which is advertising's principal commercial bedfellow. These are pervasive components of our everyday cultural lives, of how we are pulled and tugged about by these corporate forces, unless we live as hermits in the wilderness. Even when we refuse to conform to the dictates of fashion and advertising, we are aware at the same time that we have resisted their pressure.

Furthermore, in sustaining an ongoing pattern of high spending and consumer debt, two economic objectives are realized. One is that mass-produced items always find buyers, which means the economy is less prone to crisis and collapse, in contrast to the 1930s when between a third and a quarter of Ameri-

---

Author's Note: I would like to thank the editors as well as Steve Best, John Harms, and Robert Goldman.

cans were out of work. No one wants that experience repeated, but, at the same time, the consumer products that have been sold most intensively are often dangerous and polluting, namely, cars and cigarettes. Auto and road construction, oil, and tobacco corporations improve their balance sheets, the economy seems stable—but what about our lungs, our limbs, our lives, the balance sheet of our physical and social health?

The second economic objective realized is work discipline. A currently popular bumper sticker says, "I owe, I owe, it's off to work I go." People moonlight to meet their consumer debt payments. Few people really relish Monday mornings. Yet our culture tells us we can enjoy ourselves to the limit—of our ability to work.

In 1986 more than $102 billion, or roughly 2% of the U.S. gross national product, was spent on advertising (Association of National Advertisers, 1988). When one considers that an equal amount of money is also spent on design, packaging, marketing, and product display, one sees just what is squandered on advertising and marketing. Only eight cents of the cosmetics sales dollar goes to pay for ingredients; the rest goes to packaging, promotion, and marketing (Goldman, 1987, p. 697). Advertising commands a tremendous amount of resources and talent and is a crucial component of the capitalist economic system.

The expansion of marketing and advertising was originally the result of mass production. By the early years of the twentieth century, industrial capitalism had perfected techniques of mass production. The assembly line, scientific management of the labor process, and the emergence of the modern corporation revolutionized production and made possible the creation of new mass consumer goods. New modes of advertising, marketing, packaging, and design helped produce the mass consumption necessary for the purchase of all these new commodities.

By the 1920s, corporations, advertising agencies, and market research organizations began planning ways to "produce" consumers (see Chapter 11) and to promote consumption as a way of life in the United States (Ewen, 1976, 1988). Individual resistance to new products had to be broken down, and individuals had to be convinced that it was acceptable to purchase goods that they had previously produced themselves and that it was morally justifiable to consume, to spend money, and to gratify desires. Previously, puritan work and savings ethics and a morality of delayed gratification prevailed, so advertising had to convince individuals that consumption was now a morally acceptable route to happiness and satisfaction.

Advertising also attempted to create problems and fears to which commodities were a solution; thus, for instance, unless individuals bought products to combat their bad breath or body odor, they would not be socially acceptable. In this way, a "commodity self" emerged in which different products allowed individuals to communicate different aspects of "their" personalities that could be shaped by using the right products and producing the right images. Advertising tells us that new commodities will make us happier, more popular and successful. Fashion in turn provides the constant cycle of new products, styles, and images that keep consumer demand at a high level. Advertising tells us that to be "with it" and up to date we must be fashionable; we must buy and exhibit all the latest products and fashions. Advertising and fashion also promote a worldview complete with ethics, politics, gender role models, and a sense of appropriate and inappropriate daily social behavior. These two industries thus have crucial economic and socializing functions in creating consumer demand, shaping behavior, and inducing people to participate in and thus reproduce consumer society.

This chapter will examine some "mainstream" approaches to advertising as information and then present critical theories of advertising and fashion that provide more complete analysis as to how these two processes function to produce consumers and integrate individuals within the consumer society. It will show how broader social values can be "read" from advertising content, and concludes with some criticisms of consumer culture and some proposals concerning how to minimize manipulation by the advertising and fashion industries.

Advertising: Information or Persuasion?

Mainstream writers essentially defend the institutions, life-styles, and values of consumer capitalism, and apologists for the advertising industry interpret it as a form of information that provides consumers with up-to-date news concerning commodities and the impetus necessary to maintain a high level of production and affluence (Konig, 1973, p. 29). Likewise, defenders of the fashion industry claim that it too merely provides a constant turnover of new products and styles that meet consumer needs for novelty, change, and desire for style. They argue that fashion "opens up, with all its new developments, new horizons, enriches and diversifies life and makes it more attractive; it also acts as a powerful stimulus to the economy" (McClure & Fulton, 1964, p. 21).

In most standard textbooks and theories, fashion and advertising are therefore presented as beneficial aspects of an innovative and dynamic consumer society that provides individuals with the goods and styles that they themselves desire. Thus in "A Statement of Advertising Principles" defined by the Advertising Federation of America, one reads, "Good advertising aims to inform the consumer and help him to buy more intelligently" (Ulanoff, 1977, p. 22). Another defender of the industry takes the same position: "Advertising is an integral part of business. Its primary function is to sell products, services, and ideas by informing the public of their good points and their availability" (Harms, 1989).

Yet advertisers also admit that they are attempting to persuade buyers to purchase certain products, and divide buying motivations into "rational" and "irrational" behaviors (Switkin, 1981, p. 66). In the words of one mainstream theorist, while informative advertising aims to appeal to reason and provides "reasons why" individuals should purchase products, by contrast "advertising that addresses itself chiefly to the emotions, rather than to reason or intellect, is called human interest copy. This kind of advertising is based on appeals to . . . emotions to which the average person reacts" (Switkin, 1981, p. 4).

Little advertising is purely "informative." There are informative ads in the classified sections of newspapers, but television ads are mainly image based, creating associations between products and desired conditions, such as happiness and success. Advertising is persuasive, relying on emotional appeals, dramatic or comic images, and manipulation of basic fears and desire.

Reading Advertisements Critically

Learning how to read advertising critically thus provides individuals with important tools for interpreting contemporary American culture and avoiding manipulation. Ads are complex texts, the images, words, framing devices, and structures of which attempt to influence individuals into accepting certain values and role models and into adopting certain lifestyles.

In order to sell their products, corporations undertake campaigns to associate them with positive and desirable images. Thus in the 1950s, Marlboro undertook a campaign to associate its cigarette with masculinity and with being a "true man." Previously, Marlboro had been packaged as a mild, women's cigarette, and the "Marlboro man" campaign attempted to capture the male market with images of archetypal and culturally familiar characters such as the cowboy, with its connotations of masculinity, independence, and ruggedness. Thus consumption of the product was associated with socially desirable traits, here masculinity. For decades, the Marlboro cowboy has been the central symbol in Marlboro ads. Yet, in the 1980s the cowboy has become a relatively small figure, overshadowed by images of snow, trees, and sky. Why this shift from masculine cowboy to images of nature?

All ads are social texts that respond to key developments during the period in which they appear. As the health hazards of smoking became more widely known, a mandatory health warning appeared on all packaging and advertising. "Light" and low-tar cigarettes are also responses to the health concern, so too Marlboro ads now feature images of clean, pure, wholesome nature, as if it were "natural" to smoke cigarettes and as if cigarettes were a healthy, "natural" product. The imagery is itself "light," white, green, snowy, and airy, often showing horses gamboling in snow or water, trying to associate cigarettes through the process of "metonymy," or contiguous association, with these natural elements. This glosses over the fact that cigarettes are an artificial, synthetic product, full of dangerous pesticides, preservatives, and other chemicals.

The Marlboro ads also draw on images of tradition (the cowboy), hard work, domesticating animals, and other values, as if smoking were a noble activity sanctioned by tradition. The images and text create a symbolic construct that tries to camouflage the contradictions between the "heavy" work and the "light" cigarette, between the "natural" scene and the "artificial" product, and between the rugged masculinity of the Marlboro man and the "light" cigarette. In fact, this latter contradiction can be explained by the marketing ploy of suggesting to men that they can both be highly masculine and smoke a (supposedly) "healthier" cigarette, while also appealing to "independent-minded" women who might enjoy smoking a "man's" cigarette that is also "lighter" and "healthier."

A 1989 Marlboro ad features the gnarled hands of an old cowboy holding a lighted cigarette. The subliminal message is that you too can smoke and live to a ripe old age (whereas the "real" person who played the Marlboro cowboy for many years had just died of cancer after giving many interviews warning of the dangers of smoking). It thus invites the consumer to a pleasurable experience and subliminally tries to allay fears that the experience is a dangerous one that might actually be life threatening.

Thus ads offer symbolic gratifications to consumers and try to associate their products with socially desired values. The well-known Virginia Slims advertising campaign, with its slogan, "You've come a long way, baby," tries to denote social progress for women, associating this progress with the right to smoke. Many of these ads try to visualize the positive change for women. They often depict the bad old days when, for example, a working women lights up a cigarette and angers her boss, contrasted with the modern beautiful Virginia Slims woman confidently and happily holding a cigarette in her hand. The ads connote a message of progress, linking Virginia Slims to the "modern woman" who has progressed from oppressed servant of men to independent subject of her own life. The appearance of the 1989 Virginia Slims woman contributes to this message; for example, her hair is teased, her makeup is perfect, her smile is dazzling, and her clothes are flamboyant, with mismatched earrings, connoting independence, style, and nonconformity. A red hat, carelessly tossed back over her shoulder, a gold bracelet, an exotic short shirt, all are carefully contrived to effect an image of individuality, daring, and sexuality.

It is interesting to compare the contemporary Virginia Slims woman with the earlier images. As recently as 1983, the Virginia Slims woman was much more conventionally pretty, more conservatively attired, and less flamboyant and sexy. The shift in image reflects changes in cultural ideals and the new "yuppie" emphasis on high fashion and individuality, as well as the collapse of moral taboos about women's sexuality. Also, during the Reagan 1980s there was increased emphasis on wealth and luxury, reflected in the new image. Thus ads sell not only products but social values and ideals.

The Virginia Slims woman is very slim, like her brand name, maintaining the powerful cultural pressure on women to achieve this socially desirable trait. In fact, Lucky Strike carried out a successful advertising campaign in the 1930s that associated smoking with weight reduction, and Virginia Slims plays on this tradition. The connection of smoking and slimness is far from innocent and has contributed to eating disorders, faddish diets and exercise programs, and a dramatic increase in anorexia among young women, as well as rising cancer rates. As Judith Williamson (1978) points out, advertising "addresses" individuals and invites them to identify with certain products, images, and behavior, and this is most powerful for women.

Advertising sells its products and view of the world through visual and verbal rhetorics, design, and layout, to which tremendous psychological research, artistic resources, and marketing strategies are devoted. Advertising, fashion, and consumerism are of crucial importance in producing the needs, values, and daily behavior that dominate our lives in the United States.

Fashion and the Manufacture of Image

To keep a high level of consumer demand in place, the advertising and fashion industries have to persuade consumers to change deep-rooted habits, to throw away old products and to buy new ones continually. Advertising and the fashion industry thus combine individuality and conformity in curious ways. Individuals consume and pursue fashion to individuate themselves, yet do so in order to be socially accepted—to fit in and be popular. Moreover, mass-produced goods and fashion are used to produce a fake individuality, a "commodity self," an "image."

In today's society, corporations, politicians, and individuals are all obsessed with image (Boorstin, 1962). Much magazine advertising is therefore devoted to stylish images, whether of clothes, cosmetics, automobiles, or liquor. Clothes ads show the "proper" image for specific social groups and classes. Upscale magazines directed toward the upper class and the upwardly mobile feature luxury items and high fashion as an essential part of a successful life-style. General-readership magazines and some specialty magazines sell less expensive mass-produced products that are promoted as magical roads to romance and popularity for middle- and working-class audiences.

Figure 17.1 projects to upscale male readers that they must have a variety of fashionable clothes in order to be popular and sexually successful. The sexist caption at the top—"So Many Women / So little Time"—appeals to the busy young man on the make. The nine images of different clothes and different women equates the two, projecting the idea that women are available for "consumption" in the same way new jackets are. Figure 17.2 highlights the message that in a competitive world a man must be well dressed and fashionable. The motto at the top—"The Survival of the Trimmest"—plays on the Darwinian thesis of the survival of the fittest in a dangerous and violent world. The menacing talons of the eagle at the top of the picture reinforce the image of danger. The young man in the center is coded as a hunter with a lethal crossbow and arrow, ready for the kill. The color of the exotic background of the desert and animals is a golden hue that provides a surrealistic aura to the scene. It signals to the attentive reader that the ad is an allegory of life in a competitive capitalist society, the jungle in which only the fittest survive, and it is the clothes that are the young man's "weapon." The sensual language and the phallic bow make it unclear exactly what the man's prey is. Indeed, despite their careful crafting, ads remain minitexts open to different critical readings if closely examined.

Television, Advertising, and Fashion

Television is one of the most ubiquitous and influential promoters of advertising and fashion. TV advertising is expensive, sophisticated, and ever more frequent during an era in which the deregulation of television allows the networks to show as many ads as they desire during a given time period. Television ads are typically 60-, 30-, 15-, or even 10-second dramatizations of the value of consumerism as a way of life and the joys

and benefits of the consumer society. TV ads frequently adopt the conflict-resolution structure of television programming. Situation comedies and action/adventure programs present problems and conflicts and then offer solutions that celebrate traditional values, institutions, and author-

ity figures. Similarly, in advertising a problem is shown, the commodity is offered as a solution, and happiness is the outcome.

Classic television ads presented problems like "ring around the collar" and "tired blood" and commodities that would solve these problems. They portrayed numerous sagas of young men or women unable to get dates because of bad breath or unappetizing hair, magically transformed into highly attractive and successful sex objects through the mouthwash or shampoo advertised. Television advertising is especially suitable for portraying such magical transformation and metamorphosis, building on fantasy imagery borrowed from myths, fairy tales, or contemporary media. Television is our primary storytelling medium, and ads provide brief narrative dramas that vividly present the agonies and ecstasies of life in the consumer culture.

Television stands at the center of our symbol system and provides mythic and ritualistic celebrations of dominant values and institutions (Kellner, 1982). Thus ads can be read as capitalist morality plays that celebrate dominant values, specific modes of action, and the "good life," much as medieval morality plays celebrated Christianity. Anheuser-Busch's "The night belongs to Michelob" ads of the late 1980s used high-tech, fast-paced imagery to associate the beer with a modern consumer life-style of cars, dance clubs, bars, and urban street culture. The images were dazzling, the editing was fast, and the pictures were tracked with loud music and Michelob slogans. The ads thus sold both beer and the fast life in the fast lane, linking Michelob to the paradise of consumer capitalism. During the late 1980s we were also treated to nightly incantations that "the heartbeat of America [is] today's Chevrolet." The cars sped through attractive landscapes and showed individuals, couples, and families enjoying the mobile and fun-filled life made possible by their cars. These ads equated owning and driving a car with being a real American, and used patriotism to try to persuade U.S. citizens to buy "American" cars rather than "foreign" models (as if the two were clearly distinguishable any longer).

TV ads are highly sophisticated, highly creative, and produced with the newest high-tech instruments and aesthetic strategies. Tremendous amounts of time, talent, and resources are devoted to producing such images, which are typically more expensive than programming. Networks receive from $150,000 to more than half a million dollars for each prime-time ad spot. Indeed, television programming itself is little more than bait for viewers who are sold to advertisers. One of the gigantic swindles perpetrated on the public today is that commercial television is free, that advertising pays for network television. In fact, consumers pay for the programming through higher prices for the goods they purchase. Many television series, like *Dallas, Dynasty,* and other prime-time soaps, are themselves advertisements for wealth, luxury, fashion, and a high-consumption life-style (an argument developed in Chapter 24 of this volume).

In a way, advertising is the art form of consumer capitalism, and it runs the gamut of aesthetic forms, from nitty-gritty realism to fantastic surrealism. As Goldman (1984) has argued, certain ads promote an idealized version of American history and the institutions and values of corporate capitalism as they try to huckster their products. For instance, McDonald's ads frequently contain images of small-town America, family life, middle-class affluence, and integrated Americana that surround the images of the Big Macs and Macmuffins that they are trying to sell. Other ads promote American ideology by equating consumerism with "freedom of choice" (e.g., between light and regular beer) or tell you to be an "individual" by buying this or that product. Note that individuality and freedom are here defined in terms of possession, consumption, and style, as opposed to thought, action, dissent, rational behavior, and autonomy, which were the basis of previous definitions of individualism promoted by the Founding Fathers and nineteenth-century individualists such as Thoreau, Emerson, and Whitman.

Critical Perspectives on Consumer Culture

Threats to individuality, democracy, and community from consumer culture were a primary focus of a group of critical social theorists known today as the Frankfurt school. These social theorists, who included Max Horkheimer, Erich Fromm, Theodor Adorno, Leo Lowenthal, and Herbert Marcuse, were forced in the early 1930s to flee Nazi Germany and emigrated to the United States (Kellner, 1989). While in exile they developed one of the first systematic critical perspectives on advertising, fashion, and the consumer society.

In a 1938 article, "On the Fetish Character of Music and the Regression of Listening," Adorno (1938/1980) offers some critical perceptions on the newly emerging consumer culture in the United States, written in powerfully condensed language:

> The couple out driving who spend their time identifying every passing car and being happy if they recognize the trademarks speeding by, the girl whose satisfaction consists solely in the fact that she and her boyfriend "look good"; . . . before the theological caprices of commodities, the consumers become temple slaves.

For all the couple's apparent freedom and enjoyment, Adorno argues, they are actually slaves to the ever-changing demands of the fashion industry's new commodities, which act like a capricious and tyrannical deity of old.

In a later work by Adorno and Horkheimer, *The Dialectic of Enlightenment*, written in 1947, the authors analyze the way that mass culture and communication produce consumers for the "culture industries" (see Adorno & Horkheimer, 1947/1972). Their experiences in Europe sensitized them to the danger that the manipulative techniques of advertising and propaganda in the consumer society could be developed to usher in some version of fascism in the political sphere:

> The ruthless unity in the culture industry is evidence of what will happen in politics. Marked differentiations such as . . . magazines in different price ranges, depend not so much on subject matter as on classifying, organizing, and labelling consumers. Something is provided for all so that none may escape; the distinctions are emphasized and extended. The public is catered for with a hierarchical range of mass-produced products of varying quality. . . . Everybody must behave (as if spontaneously) in accordance with his previously determined and indexed level, and choose the category of mass product turned out for his type. Consumers appear as statistics on research organization charts, and are divided by income groups into red, green, and blue areas; the technique is that used for any type of propaganda.

Culture was no longer a form of creative expression but a standardized manufactured product, almost indistinguishable from the advertising that surrounded it:

> The assembly-line character of the culture industry, the synthetic, planned method of turning out its products (factory-like not only in the studio but, more or less, in the compilation of cheap biographies, pseudo-documentary novels, and hit songs) is very suited to advertising. The effect, the trick, the isolated repeatable device, have always been used to exhibit goods for advertising purposes. . . . Advertising and the culture industry merge technically as well as economically. In both cases the same thing can be seen in innumerable places, and the mechanical repetition of the same cultural product has come to be the same as that of the propaganda slogan. In both cases the insistent demand for effectiveness makes technology into psychotechnology, into a procedure for manipulating men. In both cases the standards are striking yet familiar, the easy yet catchy, the skillful yet simple; the object is to overpower the customer, who is conceived as absent-minded or resistant. (p. 123)

Twenty years later, Marcuse (1964) argued that consumer culture produced "false needs" that induced individuals to buy into a consumer life-style. He was among the first to argue, as I have above, that the individuality offered by consumer culture is a pseudo-individuality, constructed and promoted for the purposes of manipulation and social control. Thus to be genuinely free and individual, one must free oneself from a whole system of pleasures, consumption, and entertainment administered by the power structure. According to Marcuse:

> Political freedom would mean liberation of individuals from politics over which they have no effective control. Similarly, intellectual freedom would mean the restoration of individual thought now absorbed by mass communication.

Not only is the consumer society based on a tremendous waste of resources and talents, but corporate control of the economy has made the United States look alike all over: Drive down any street in the United States and you will see generic America in the form of filling stations selling the same brands of gas, fast-food chains selling the same junk food, video stores renting the same (quite small) selection of films, and chains of other types selling the same goods everywhere. Through quasi-monopolies, advertising, price fixing, mergers, and other corporate developments, giant corporations have come to dominate economy and society in the United States. While enjoying less variety and diversity of goods, the consumer must pay for the entire corporate infrastructure and advertising and packaging, actually subsidizing the very industries that indoctrinate and exploit us.

Conclusion

Manipulation by the advertising and fashion industries can be avoided. Generally, generic products of the same or better quality can be had, and at lower prices. We can resist the machinations of fashion, choosing our clothes and other products on grounds of usefulness, durability, value, and actual need, instead of allowing ourselves to be manipulated by advertising. We must also learn to read and decipher advertising, to see through the hype so that we can analyze and criticize advertising's persuasive techniques. Corporate propaganda aside, advertising is a parasitic industry and a tremendous social drain. By the late 1980s, $100 billion was spent per year on advertising—far more money than was spent on schooling. Advertising is a disgraceful waste of resources, talent, and time. Eventually, citizens of the United States are going to have to question seriously the priorities, values, and institutions of consumer capitalism if we wish to preserve the democracy, freedom, health rights, and individuality to which we pay lip service.

Further Questions

(1) Collect a set of ads for a particular consumer item. Do they all use the same set of images and myths to market the product? Can you discover the intended audience by examining the way advertising is constructed, or by knowing in which media channel the advertising was located?

(2) Monitor the depiction of gender or ethnicity in advertising. Do the images and the social roles change over time? Does advertising create social trends or reflect already-existing patterns?

(3) How can we better educate consumers? What alternatives to advertising could be developed that would provide information without the hard sell?

18 Racism and the American Way of Media

ASH COREA

Racism is as integral a dimension of U.S. culture as advertising, and it has even deeper roots. There is a curious view that racism more or less vanished with the success of the civil rights struggles against segregation and for voting rights of the 1950s and 1960s. This claim lies somewhere between hypocrisy and willful blindness to everyday realities. It is not only in the United States that White people exclude Black people from opportunity, but the "American Dream" of a fair deal for all citizens is exposed as a cynical myth given that discrimination and disadvantage assigned by skin color are so systematic. Native Americans, African-Americans, Asian-Americans, and Latinos have current experiences of racism to relate, not just stories from bygone years, even though these experiences also have a continuity with the years of slavery and colonial subjugation.

Communicating racism, both in mass media and in the everyday conversations fed by the mass media, sustains it as an active cultural, and therefore political, force. Corea examines the way media, especially television, continue to stereotype both majority and minority, by means of some thought-provoking contrasts. She proceeds to summarize both the history of media portrayal of African-Americans and their very limited presence in positions of influence in media institutions. At the close of her argument, she addresses the significance of the widely popular Black-cast Cosby Show to ask whether U.S. television, unlike the leopard, has changed its spots.

Although Corea's analysis focuses on African-American experience, a considerable amount of what she points out can be applied to the experiences of other so-called minorities in the United States, such as Latinos. One of the problems with the term "minority" is that people of widely differing backgrounds and cultures are lumped together because of one factor: the readiness of White people to discriminate against them. And because they are labeled minorities, they are effectively marginalized and set apart from "mainstream" social life. The fact remains that collectively we are speaking of up to a quarter of the population, about 50 million human beings, whose origins in Africa, Latin America, and Asia make them part of the non-White majority of the planet.

USA, anno 1957

For the twenty-first century, how we communicate concerning this issue and how quickly U.S. mass culture adapts to this reality are of pressing importance. Where do U.S. media stand?

Many writers argue that media merely reflect what is happening "out there." What is more, on television African-Americans, women, and White men seem to have the same opportunities that exist in the society. Eddie Murphy can mock Stevie Wonder and other African-American celebrities, Mr. T can be charming to little White children, Bill Cosby can make it to the top of the ratings, Geraldo Rivera can make the headlines, Connie Chung can draw top newscaster salary. So it must be true: Everyone has the same opportunities.

However, in the United States the overwhelming factor that defines the position a group will occupy is color. Education, wealth, occupation, gender, and religion are also part of the picture, but nevertheless, to be an African-American normally means occupying the bottom strata. This in turn limits access to the benefits produced within this society. As a group, African-Americans compete with other groups discriminated against, such as Hispanics and Native Americans, for the honor of being at the bottom. Gender does intervene in this matrix: Women occupy a lower position when compared to men. But in this complex array of factors four clear points emerge.

First, White men occupy the apex of the hierarchy in the United States, in terms of both power and status. Second, White women earn lower salaries (on average, two-thirds those of White men) and have much less political influence. Third, African-American men have less political influence still and are paid substantially less than White men. Finally, African-American women earn less than the other three groups, although they have greater access than African-American men to very low-paying jobs such as babysitting, fast-food restaurant work, and cleaning. They have the very least political power.

For those citizens of the United States who have difficulty believing the evidence before their own eyes, seemingly endless studies have documented this pattern in detail, from Gunnar Myrdal's *An American Dilemma* (1944) through the series of reports issued in 1989 by the Special Committee on Children, Youth and the Family of the U.S. House of Representatives.

So far, then, it has been suggested that there is in reality, if not in TV reality, a distinct relationship between color and access by certain groups to wealth and power. These groups are further subdivided by gender, with White men at the apex, followed by White women and then African-American men. At the very bottom are African-American women. A similar analysis would generally be valid for Latinos, Native Americans, and Asian-Americans.

As the discussion now moves to a consideration of how media, in particular television, relate to this reality, the following three questions should be kept in mind:

(1) Do African-Americans and White Americans occupy the same positions within the controlling structures of the media?
(2) Does television portray African-Americans and White Americans as being equal with each other and coexisting in a multiracial environment?
(3) What factors are there that could militate against African-Americans and White Americans receiving equal treatment on television?

African-Americans and Employment in Media

Consider the following statement by an African-American TV executive who was asked about the operation of power in the television industry:

> Positions of real power have been in the past, and continue to be, reserved for a network of white males who all know each other, run the industry, and occasionally allow a token number of White women to preside with them over the decision making process. (Massing, 1982, p. 44)

One could dismiss this TV executive's statement as sour grapes. However, in 1986 a report titled *Minority Broadcasting Facts* was released by the National Association of Broadcasters, and in it were the following figures on the numbers of general managers of commercial TV stations who were non-White: 9 African-Americans and 5 Latinos. There were also 4 African-American TV station managers. Yet in the United States there are nearly 1,300 commercial TV stations. Clearly, then, African-Americans are not overwhelmingly represented in the controlling structures of television.

The Federal Communications Commission also released an equal opportunity trend report in 1988 that outlined ethnic minority employment in television and cable over the period 1983-1987. Ethnic groups were subdivided between males and females, and also between categories of employment. During 1987 the overall number of people employed was 176,159, compared with 160,967 for 1983. The proportion of minority professionals increased a little, from 15.3% in 1983 to 16.2% in 1987, or 28,590 in all, mainly due to a few more Latino professionals. The 1987 percentages for minorities subdivided by gender were as follows: 4.2% African-American women; 4.7% African-American men; 2.2% Latinas; 3.4% Latinos. However, the figures also showed that ethnic minorities were underrepresented in the top four groups, which jointly account for about 85% of all positions: officials and managers, 10.6% (3,832); professionals, 14.7% (8,006); technicians, 19.8% (6,345); sales workers, 10.0% (2,391). According to Dr. Edward Wachtel (1986) in a report titled *Television Hiring Practices,* issued by the Office of Communication of the United Church of Christ, if we were to look more closely at these categories we would see that they serve to mask the real underrepresentation of African-Americans in the power structure of the electronic media. Wachtel suggests that a more accurate picture would be given by matching of minority employment with salary, because that would provide a more adequate picture of the real situation. Is a "sales worker," for example, an executive selling ad spots to corporations, or that executive's typist?

So in answer to the first question posed we can draw the following conclusion. Ethnic minorities such as African-Americans exhibit a minimal presence in the upper echelons of influence in television, especially in the three big networks.

TV and African-Americans: Hostility, Apartheid, or Avoidance

Television, argues Michael Winston (1982), from its early stages, either was directly hostile to African-Americans or ignored them: "It was to be 'white' not simply, as newspapers were, in its employment practices, but in its projection of American life, insofar as it reflected American reality at all" (p. 177).

In spite of the civil rights movements of the 1940s, 1950s, and 1960s, in spite of the Black power movements of the 1960s and 1970s, there still exists among many White people an underlying belief in and image of the United States as essentially a White country. African-Americans are seen as being peripheral to the growth and development of the United States. Essentially, African-Americans are stereotyped as "a problem" in an otherwise harmonious country. For example, in urban America to be a mugger is synonymous with being African-American or Hispanic. The immediate image we accept as the norm is that of Whites being mugged by African-Americans and Hispanics.

How did this belief that all African-Americans are potential muggers originate and become so embedded in the culture? Although a leading Black communications scholar in Britain has traced out the genesis of the image in British media (Hall et al., 1978), the full story is yet to be told for the United States.

Let us, however, refresh our memories on how television handled the incident of the jogger who was raped and viciously beaten in Central Park in 1989. By contrast, consider the media treatment of the so-called preppie murder, which occurred in the same park in 1987.[1]

In the television news coverage of the former incident, viewers were informed that the jogger was an investment banker, which immediately set the tone that she was a worthy person. Next, they were informed that the attack occurred in the part of Central Park that borders Harlem, a predominantly poor African-American and Latino neighborhood. Viewers were bombarded with the details of how the woman was brutally beaten, raped, and left to die by these cruel African-American and Hispanic young thugs. One particular young man was singled out as being from a good family, with a bright future and doing very well at school. There was in general, however, a dearth of information about the conditions and environment of these young African-Americans, while there was an implied and shared assumption that all African-American men are liable to be violent, cruel, and vicious muggers, the kind of people who would predictably perpetrate such a crime on decent White women.

We should pause, however, to ask about the young White man who, in 1987, raped and murdered a White woman in Central Park—an incident the press labeled "the preppie murder." He was portrayed as a fine, upstanding young man who, under the influence of drugs and alcohol coupled with sexy provocation from the young woman, lost his head and accidentally strangled her. Television did not dwell with the same intense attention on the victim, or on the barbarism of this act. Instead, they presented the viewers with extenuating circumstances that would enable them to understand that this was not a premeditated crime, but just an unforeseen accident. (If only the dead girl's body could itself become an "accident.")

By contrast, the young men who raped and beat the jogger (who narrowly survived the incident) were not shown as having any circumstances that might extenuate *their* barbarous behavior. Attention was not focused on the harsh poverty of much of Harlem as an extenuating factor, justifiably or not, nor—more to the point—did the media trouble to ask the basic question of what kinds of individuals most of the young men were. The television coverage did not dwell on how some of these young men had been terrorizing the residents in their apartment buildings for months on end. It was not until the White woman jogger was mugged that these residents experienced some respite from the terror and harassment they had endured without any police protection or interest. Only White victims seemed to count.

Why were these two incidents treated so differently by television, especially given that in the preppie case the White woman was dead, while the jogger survived? Color. In the Central Park incident it was African-Americans attacking fine, respectable Whites, not a "preppie" behaving "out of character." Television viewers were presented with well-established categories that they took for granted and accepted as real.

On the other hand, the Central Park preppie murder was unreal. Young, wealthy, White men did not murder respectable White women. Therefore, the woman was at fault. She must have been a quasi-prostitute, loose, asking for it, deserving of what happened to her. Otherwise she would not have been killed by a White man in Central Park.

Viewer outrage against the attackers of the Central Park jogger was phenomenal. There were suggestions that they should be castrated, locked up and the keys thrown away, given the death sentence. The preppie murder did not evoke such an avid response. The situation was presented as being unclear as to whether the suspect actually did commit the murder. On television he was shown leaving court with his parents and lawyer. A Catholic bishop was wheeled out as a character reference.

Indeed, the whole tone of the proceedings on television lacked the "hang 'em high" lynching response meted out to the attackers of the Central Park jogger.

Were these two incidents treated the same by television? No. Both crimes were hideous, and the attackers should be punished. However, one victim was dead, while the other, though badly beaten and raped, was alive and recovering. Why are the African-Americans more deserving of punishment than a White murderer? We can subscribe to that position only if we accept the established belief that African-Americans are violent, uncontrollable, and uncivilized, or if we consider it obvious that they require more punishment regardless of what crimes they have committed.

These two violent incidents are important because they illustrate that African-American and White American offenders are not portrayed as being equally deserving of punishment. The television treatment of both events was presented within a context that relied on accepted racial belief about African-Americans. That belief can be stated as follows: African-Americans have an inherent tendency to mug, rape, murder, and otherwise disrupt the normal orderly processes characteristic of White society in the United States of America (the preppie murder notwithstanding).

To move to more everyday TV, let us examine the virtual apartheid that exists in most television situation comedies. African-Americans and White Americans are not portrayed as living or interacting harmoniously. Sitcoms are either African-American or White American (rarely the former, until the success of *The Jeffersons* and then *The Cosby Show*). Also, as Gray (1986) observes, many all-Black sitcoms have not stirred from stereotyped and demeaning portrayals. He comments on the patronizing, even contemptuous, assumptions behind a series like *Diff'rent Strokes*, which was integrated in the formal sense, but centered on a White man adopting two Black boys. In fact, television has invariably followed the successful formula from radio, which presented African-Americans in a demeaning manner. Television, according to Professor J. Fred MacDonald (1983), became "visualized radio: the enactment for viewers of story lines and stereotypes that had proven successful for decades on radio" (p. 7). The influence of film and its generally racist portrayals was also of considerable importance (Nesteby, 1982).

In general, as TV developed, African-Americans either were portrayed as simple, happy, uneducable buffoons, or they were ignored. A classic example of their being ignored is the fact that many Vietnam War documentaries scarcely included or mentioned them, even though African-Americans were greatly overrepresented in the fighting compared to their numbers in the population.

A different but very important example is to be seen in the development of art in the United States, especially music, where African-Americans have also played a central role. Television, radio, and the music industry have managed to take over the cultural forms produced by African-Americans—such as blues, jazz, and swing—without their actual participation. The original swing bands were those of Duke Ellington and Count Basie, yet it was bands such as Glen Miller's and the Dorsey Brothers' that were dubbed the "Kings of Swing." Some readers might argue that Duke Ellington and Count Basie were recognized by TV as being talented and great musicians, but was it just coincidental that the Glenn Miller Band and the Dorsey Brothers Band received much more time on radio, television, and film?

If it was coincidental, why has there never been an African-American musical star with his or her own musical television series, with national syndication and a national advertising sponsor who would willingly buy the series? For example, in 1956-1957, the *Nat King Cole Show* premiered on NBC. In spite of the efforts of NBC and the show's popularity, the show never found a national sponsor. None of the conglomerates wanted to be closely identified with a "Negro program." Cole himself wrote after this experience that "racial prejudice is more finance than romance" (MacDonald, 1983, p. 62).

Thus regardless of whether we are discussing the presentation of African-Americans in a barbaric situation such as the crime committed against the Central Park jogger, or in sitcoms, or in TV documentaries about the Vietnam War, or the cultural appreciation of music in this society, there is one compelling factor that we cannot ignore: the presentation of African-Americans as marginal in this society. There is no parity between African-Americans and Whites on television. Apart from some TV commercials full of instant cheerfulness around food or drink, African-Americans and White Americans are not shown as living in an integrated society, where they interact as friendly equals, respectful of each other's needs and tolerant of each other's differences.

Racist Stereotyping on TV: From Amos 'n' Andy to Cosby

To understand the long roots of these problems in U.S. television, we have to begin with *Amos 'n' Andy*, which was initially a very popular radio show and then was transferred to television. The *Amos 'n' Andy* radio formula originated with racial stereotypes derived from White vaudeville entertainers performing in "blackface," that is, with their faces painted with caricatural African features. On radio, the characters of

Amos and Andy were played by two White comedians, Freeman Gosden and Charles Correll. Gosden, who was from South Virginia, attributed his mastering of "Negro dialect" to having been raised by an African-American housekeeper. He also had from childhood a close friend called Snowball, who lived in his household as the boys grew up. According to Gosden, Snowball was the source of his humor for the show. According to Barlow (in press), the blackface characters that Gosden and Correll developed for radio into *Amos 'n' Andy* were fairly typical of the prevailing minstrel stereotypes in White popular culture. Amos was the classic "Uncle Tom" stereotype, while Andy was the "coon." Both exhibited characteristics that were easily recognizable in White culture.

The stereotypes that Gosden and Correll portrayed on radio in the 1920s and 1930s served a variety of purposes in the social and political arena of the epoch. The characters of Amos and Andy were identified as having no education and, by definition, no intelligence. African-Americans did not have the vote in 1938, when this radio program was at its zenith. The implication that White Americans derived from this program was very crude: African-Americans are grossly ignorant and uneducated. Therefore, to give them the vote, decent jobs, political power, would be tantamount to reducing American democracy to a racial injustice—to Whites.

In 1951 *Amos 'n' Andy* premiered on television with African-American actors instead of Whites in blackface. How did African-Americans respond to this presentation of themselves on White television? This episode is important, not only in the development of the racial politics of American television, but also in the acknowledgment that audiences can be active, not merely passive, in their responses to media. The National Association for the Advancement of Colored People (NAACP) sought an injunction to prevent CBS from putting the program on television. Several groups sensitive to the African-American struggle for civil rights condemned *Amos 'n' Andy* as an affront to social achievement. The Michigan Federation of Teachers called the TV series "a gross and vulgar caricature of fifteen million Negro citizens of our country" (MacDonald, 1983, p. 27). Several eminent African-Americans blasted the show, describing it as the slow and steady poison of 20 years on radio, which was now transferred to TV. The African-American *Pittsburgh Courier* led a campaign to have the show pulled.

One question that must not be ducked is why African-Americans agreed to portray themselves and their race in such a demeaning manner. The answer is simple: job opportunities. African-American actors were overwhelmingly excluded from TV and film except as infrequent guest stars on variety shows or as "walk-ons" (usually in the role of house servants); very rarely were they stars in filmed or live drama. Examples of this exclusion are legion. The great singer Lena Horne was originally allowed only as far as a film soundtrack, while a White actress mouthed the words on camera. Paul Robeson, the distinguished actor, thinker, and political campaigner, appeared as co-lead in a film glorifying British colonialism in Africa (*Sanders of the River*). Hattie McDaniel, attacked by some African-Americans for her role as maid to Scarlett in *Gone with the Wind*, snapped that she would rather earn $7,000 a week acting a maid than $7 being one. *Amos 'n' Andy* provided regular employment for 142 African-Americans who were paid a handsome salary and had a chance to develop their careers.

However, the purpose of this discussion is to demonstrate that the television industry quite consciously developed a program written, produced, and directed by White men that broadcast a stereotypical projection of African-American life. Has there been a radical change in the media industry since then as far as African-Americans are concerned? Quite frankly no, despite appearances that might seem to be to the contrary.

During the 1970s, African-Americans achieved increasing visibility in news coverage because of the political events of that era. Although the political upheavals in the 1960s and 1970s resulted in a few more African-Americans being able to participate in TV, the overall numbers in any part of the production process, as actors, producers, camera operators, or executives, have not risen significantly. Contributions of African-Americans to television since the 1970s should not be casually dismissed. However, the manner in which they have been treated on TV despite their contributions has been very dishonorable and disrespectful of their sensibilities.

We should acknowledge that African-Americans have gained a significant market as actors and actresses in TV commercials and also public service announcements. But major producers still continue to avoid employing the many talented African-Americans outside the advertising sphere. Some of the stereotypes that are still very active in producers' minds are depicted in Robert Townsend's comic yet serious feature film, *Hollywood Shuffle.*

The issue is how to interpret greater visibility. African-Americans are more visible on television, and are not as subjected as they were in the *Amos 'n' Andy* era. In 1988 one of television's top four White House journalists was Cable News Network's Bernard Shaw, an African-American. Nevertheless, despite these individual gains, African-Americans as a group do not have the same degree of opportunity as do White people as a group in the television industry. The key example that might be cited against this interpretation of the trends is *The Cosby Show,* which is

immensely popular but has an all-African-American cast. We turn now to a presentation of two contrary positions on whether this show has reversed the image of African-Americans on television.

Professor Marc Crispin Miller (1988) argues that *The Cosby Show* owes much of its immense success to advertising, because the Huxtables' milieu is "upbeat and as well stocked as a window display at Bloomingdales" (p. 69). The Huxtables are successful, wealthy, comfortable, and African-Americans. Within their environment the atmosphere is comfortable, without any serious discord, a far cry from the racial caricatures of *Amos 'n' Andy*—maybe. But, according to Miller, Cliff Huxtable's image represents a threat combined with a reassurance. In spite of his dark skin and physically imposing stature, he has an agreeable persona that should alleviate the fears of Whites. Nevertheless, says Miller, many Whites continue to have the mugging nightmare, and are terrified that one day African-Americans will steal their worldly possessions. Therefore, *The Cosby Show* has renovated the image so that there appear to be no feelings of animosity toward Whites from African-Americans, and so that all the old injustices seem to have been rectified. This type of reassurance, Miller states, is needed by White Americans because they are both spatially and psychologically removed from the masses of poor African-Americans. In other words, *The Cosby Show* offers White Americans a view of reality that is reassuring and acceptable, just the way they want it to be—no guilt, no fears.

However, let us also consider Downing's (1988b) contrary analysis of *The Cosby Show*, in which he argues that the reasons for its popularity cannot be reduced to one variable only, such as its soothing effect on White America. His position is that it has a different function for African-American audiences from its function for White audiences, and also that its positive effects for White audiences are related to its mixing together multiple strands of professional achievement, family life, antisexist positions, and humor, together with an attack on racism that is not preachy. Be that as it may, the TV reality of *The Cosby Show* is not the norm for most African-Americans in this society. On the other hand, it does portray African-Americans with dignity in a medium that has generally failed to do so.

At the same time, it has to be acknowledged that *The Cosby Show* is a celebration of the virtues of the upper-middle-class life-style that can be achieved through the education system (to which Bill Cosby himself feels a strong commitment; he recently gave $20 million from his earnings to a college for African-American women). Both parents in the show are professionals: He is an obstetrician; she is a lawyer. This has to be placed in a sobering context: Data from the late 1980s indicate that the number of African-Americans enrolling in colleges has dropped significantly. Given the limited scope for African-Americans on television, *The Cosby Show* is a refreshing though limited change of pace.

Conclusions

Throughout this discussion, aspects of how television portrays "reality" while making African-Americans invisible, or segregating them, have been examined. The U.S. version of apartheid is as evident in TV as it is in city neighborhoods. At the same time, when African-Americans do appear, their presentation generally fits the racist culture of this society like a glove. It is especially the case that the absence of African-Americans in positions of authority in the television industry has contributed to their lack of influence over their media roles and portrayals.

Further Questions

(1) How have other groups been portrayed in U.S. media, such as Latinos, Native Americans, Asian Americans, Arabs, Jews? What are the similarities of the portrayals of these groups to those of African-Americans? What are the differences?

(2) To what would you ascribe the relative success of African-American women novelists, such as Toni Morrison and Alice Walker, in having their work published during the 1980s? Are African-American women seen as less threatening than African-American men? Is their subject matter seen as safe? Does these novelists' success represent a breakthrough, to be followed by others?

(3) What are the lessons of the protest against *Amos 'n' Andy* for the active audience in its relation to media authorities? Do you know of other protests against racial stereotyping?

Note

1. These observations on the contrast between media presentations of the two attacks in Central Park are based on research in progress. They were framed before a similar event occurred in Boston late in 1989, when an African-American man was falsely charged with fatally shooting a pregnant White woman and wounding her husband. A harsh media-police blitz descended on African-Americans in Boston before it emerged that the wounded man, who later committed suicide, had himself been the killer.

19 Cultural Imperialism and Cultural Identity

ALI MOHAMMADI

Just as cultural studies and political economy are two approaches to media studies that often seem to be pulling in opposite directions, so, too, international communication frequently seems to be off on its own. This chapter offers important insight into the way culture and communication operate internationally, not just within the space of one country. In doing so, it brings together the approaches of international communication, political economy, and cultural studies.

The first reality that demands attention is that this planet's history since about 1500 is marked by the way certain countries—such as Spain, Britain, France, Russia, the United States, and Japan—have invaded and dominated other nations in pursuit of profit and power. Other empires have done the same, but not on the unprecedented scale of these countries. That is the core of today's international relations (see Chapter 15).

In turn, a significant part of those international relations consists of cultural and communication relations. Some critical researchers have argued that the national cultures of the Third World are virtually on the way to extinction as a result of Western, especially U.S., cultural imperialism, with media influence at the cutting edge of the process. Others have attacked this view as overly conspiratorial, as though the Western countries were plotting to sabotage the independence of these nations, and have stressed that cheap TV series from the United States, for example, may be the only way an impoverished nation can fill its television schedules. They also accuse the critics of being too snobbish in their tastes, noting that many U.S. television series are enormously popular outside as well as inside the United States.

Mohammadi seeks to move beyond these generalized positions to identify both the influence of Western culture and the birth of its counterpart, cultural resistance and the communication of cultural identity. He does so by examining Iran. Throughout the decade of the 1980s, as Sreberny-Mohammadi shows in Chapter 21 of this volume, Iran was portrayed in U.S. media as an enemy nation, as was the United States in Iranian media. In the decades before that, ironically, the governments and media of both nations were extremely positive about each other.

Iran and its Neighbors. From Contemporary World Atlas
© Copyright 1990 by Rand McNally & Company, R. L. 90-S-45.

These stereotypes have left many Americans confused and bitter, with no understanding of the seemingly sudden switch in Iranian attitudes from 1979.

Mohammadi explains the effect on Iranians of many decades of systematic Western cultural influence, a process actively supported by the shah's government up until 1979. In turn, he underlines the active cultural resistance this process provoked among many Iranians. He also analyzes the colossal impact of alternative media in developing this cultural resistance, while at the same time acknowledging how for some groups this resistance fused with religious fundamentalism, which tragically left Iranians in general subjected to the obscurantist version of Islamic belief of the Khomeini regime. This outcome was specific to Iran, but in other ways Iran serves as a very clear case study for the cultural dynamics in many other Third World nations.

International Powers and National Cultures: An Uneven Contest

One description of the world we live in is "postimperialist." Much of world history from 1945 has centered around the struggles of subjugated peoples to extricate themselves from the European empires of the nineteenth century and to create the newly independent nations of Africa, the Middle East, and Asia. But the economic dominance of the West has meant that, despite being politically independent, many nations of the Third World find themselves still tied in very complex ways to the dynamics of Western industrial societies. Hence these Third World nations find it very difficult to pursue their own definitions of, and paths to, independent development. These new ties are different from the older ties of imperialism. The new kinds are often referred to as ties of *dependency*, and "cultural imperialism" has been analyzed as one major form of dependency. The purpose of this chapter is to analyze this new cultural imperialism and to show the vitally important role that communications technologies and flows of cultural products have in keeping planetary ties of dependency alive.

This process will be illustrated through a detailed examination of one Third World country, Iran. Although at the turn of the twentieth century the British and the Russians competed for influence in Iran, and the United States played a major role in Iranian affairs, helping to reinstate the shah in 1953, Iran was never directly colonized. Iran tried very deliberately to use communications for a particular development strategy, one strongly supported by the West, but found that the costs were greater than the benefits. This is a case study with powerful implications for other Third World nations and for mainstream—noncritical—communications analysis.

What Is Imperialism?

The essence of imperialism is domination by one nation over another. That relationship might be direct or indirect, and might be based on a mixture of military, political, and economic controls. There have been many different forms of imperial relations throughout world history, from the Greek and Roman empires to the Persian, Moghul, Chinese, Ottoman, and many others. But the forms of empire that have had the greatest impact on our contemporary world are the European, American, and Japanese forms of empire that prevailed through the nineteenth century into the twentieth century. Even European domination went through various stages. There were relationships that were more purely economic or "mercantilist," as in the early Portuguese empire, where the European power essentially extracted the resources it required, whether gold or ivory or slaves, from the dominated territory. Often such relations required military conquest at the outset and a continued military presence to enforce the economic exploitation.

By the end of the nineteenth century, a new form of relation had been developed that was based on the formal conquest, annexation, and administration of territories by the imperial powers. As Hobsbawm (1989) summarizes the process:

> Between 1880 and 1914 . . . most of the world outside Europe and the Americas was formally partitioned into territories under the formal rule or informal political domination of one or the other of a handful of states: mainly Great Britain, France, Germany, Italy, the Netherlands, Belgium, the USA and Japan. (p. 57)

About one-quarter of the globe's land surface was distributed or redistributed among a half dozen states, ushering in the age of imperialism based on colonial rule. This form of direct political and administrative domination helped to create a truly planetary capitalist economy in which economic transactions and flows of goods, capital, and people now penetrated into the most remote regions. The world was fundamentally divided into strong and weak, advanced and backward areas (Hobsbawm, 1989).

There were many different reactions to and consequences of imperialism, both within the "mother" power (such as movements for democracy, for socialism, and for women's rights) and within the Third World, where revolution—as in Mexico between 1910 and 1920 or in China at the beginning of the twentieth century—or growing anticolonial movements for liberation—as in India—began to develop. Since 1945, the world has been defined by these struggles against imperial domination and the success of independence movements in the creation of "new," independent political nations in Africa, Asia, and the Middle East. Thus, for example, India freed itself from the British in 1947, Indonesia liberated itself from the Dutch in 1960, Zaire was freed from Belgian domination in 1960, and Algeria became independent from the French in 1962 (Harris, 1987).

This process of political independence might appear to be the end of the story, but in fact it is only the start of a new global dynamic that we might label the process of *cultural imperialism* or *cultural dependency*. When the colonial powers packed their bags and removed their nationals from administrative positions directly running the government and the economy, that was not the end of their influence. Often they left behind a European language, as the "lingua franca" of the country's new governing classes. They left behind European values and attitudes, including religion, ways of organizing public life, styles of politics, forms of education and professional training, clothing styles, and many other cultural habits, none of which had existed prior to colonial domination. All of these phenomena continued to have effects long after the formal, direct, political rule of the colonies was ended, and have created a new kind of model of domination called *neocolonialism*. In turn, neocolonialism has sparked new kinds of struggles to eradicate this enduring cultural and economic influence in the Third World. Let us look at the constitution of this Third World and then examine how cultural issues came to be such a central focus in current international politics.

Where Is the Third World?

The term *Third World* is itself a phenomenon of the divisions in the world since World War II. The United States and the Soviet Union were allies against fascism during the war, but immediately after its conclusion the realignment of "democratic countries" versus "communist countries" took place. Then the Cold War, which is still in a process of thawing, divided the world into two camps or worlds, each of which had its own sphere of economic relations, political influence, and military arrangements (i.e., NATO versus Warsaw Pact). Rivalry and competition between the two superpowers have brought the whole world to the edge of war on certain occasions, as in the 1950-1953 Korean War, the 1962 Cuban missile crisis, and the 1973 Arab-Israeli War.

The Third World is a label applied to the new independent countries of the South, which are also referred to as the *nonaligned nations*, countries that are not interested in supporting either of the superpowers in their regional or international conflicts. The nonaligned movement was started at a huge international convention of the nations of the South in Bandung, Indonesia, in 1955 and is a formal organization of independent nation-states. *Third World* is a much looser term, and actually covers over a great deal of difference in level of economic development and political outlooks among the nations of the South; it is a useful shorthand, however, so we will continue to use it here (Harris, 1987).

Cultural Identity in the Third World

It was the independence movements in the developing world that made many people aware of the cultural dimensions of colonial domination. Many leaders in the Third World have paid serious and continuing attention to the issue of cultural freedom. For example, one of Gandhi's major concerns while he led India's independence movement was how to create an independent national identity that could unite the Indian people, who were scattered over 750,000 villages and spoke many different languages. Concerned about how to foster national unity in the face of the legacy of British cultural domination, Gandhi once proclaimed:

> I do not want my house to be walled on all sides and my windows to be stuffed. I want the culture of all lands to be blown about my house as freely as possible but I refuse to be blown off my feet by any one of them. (in Hamelink, 1983, p. 26)

In a major echo of Gandhi's concern, at a key 1973 meeting of the heads of states of the nonaligned nations there was a formal joint declaration that the activities of imperialism were not limited to the economic and political domains, but encompassed social and cultural areas as well, imposing a foreign ideological domination on the peoples of the developing world. Many in Third World nations were becoming aware of the superiority of the advanced world, in communications technologies but also in communications software, the news, entertainment, and other cultural products that the technologies transmitted, and that, as a result, their own national cultures and identities had become threatened (Harris, 1987).

It is not very hard to recognize that the continuation of Western dominance over Third World nations, even after their formal independence, was based partly on advanced technologies, including communication technologies. But it was also based on an ideology, accepted in many parts of the Third World, that there was only one path to economic development, which was to emulate the process of development of Western industrial capitalist societies.

In the 1960s, when certain Third World nations did not appear to be developing economically as quickly as they had been expected to, Western analysts began to develop models and theories of development and to explain the "blockages" to development that they thought prevented Third World countries from developing links to Western ones. One of their arguments was that Third World countries lacked investment capital, so the World Bank was established. Some argued that Third World countries lacked skilled entrepreneurs and professionals, so various educational scholarships, exchanges, and training programs were established to bring the necessary expertise to developing countries. But one of the most powerful models, widely adopted in Third World societies, dealt with the role of communications in development, as propounded by U.S. theorists Daniel Lerner and Wilbur Schramm (in Pye, 1963).

Modernization Theory: Development as Westernization

"Modernization" theory held that underdeveloped nations had not yet experienced an industrial revolution, but through proper savings and investment a "takeoff" into industrial growth could take place. For this investment process to work, the right attitudes were very important; for the right attitudes to develop, there needed to be the same mix of political and economic structures that had worked in Western industrialization. Prominent among these structures were said to be mass media (Mohammadi, 1976).

In the early 1950s, Daniel Lerner conducted a study in various Middle Eastern countries, including Turkey, Lebanon, and Iran. He argued that the growth of literacy and the operation of electronic media both played decisive roles in the modernization process. The media were multipliers of the "mobile personality," a frame of mind that was no longer mired in village traditions but was open to new influences and insights—even, without specifying the matter, to U.S. influences and perspectives. He recommended a basic minimum media infrastructure for all developing countries. Media would convey the appropriate contents to promote economic consumption and political participation among hitherto static and traditionalist peoples in supposedly stagnant and disconnected rural communities (Lerner, 1958).

The changes in attitudes, expectations, and values proposed would create a welcoming rather than a suspicious response to U.S. and other Western encroachments on traditional cultures, for investment in development, including communications infrastructure, would have to include external as well as internal sources, and that investment required the right kind of political and cultural climate, with a welcoming government, welcoming businessmen, and congenial cultural forms.

What was valuable in the traditional culture was defined, effectively, as anything that did not impede the growth of Western capitalist endeavors; what had to change culturally was anything that interfered with this process. Clearly, Lerner never defined the issue as cultural imperialism sabotaging cultural identity. For him, mass media were automatically progressive. We, however, have to stand back from his policy-oriented studies and face that very question.

To begin to answer it, it is instructive to examine a major Middle Eastern nation, at the heart of the U.S. and Western oil-related strategy in the region, namely, Iran. Despite or perhaps even because of its contentious relations with the United States since 1979, Iran particularly merits study—not least because Lerner's theories were put into practice there in a more thorough way than in perhaps any other Third World nation, as part and parcel of the last shah's strategy of pro-Western modernization. Iran is also an instructive case study because it was never directly colonized, so examining the impact of Western culture in Iran shows vividly how neocolonial subordination and cultural inferiority can be fostered from a distance, without the elaborate machinery of colonial rule.

The Case of Iran

Iran (formerly Persia) is located on the southern border of the Soviet Union and stretches south to the Persian Gulf. It borders Turkey to the northwest and Afghanistan and Pakistan to the east. It had in 1989 a population of over 45 million. From the geopolitical viewpoint the strategic location of Iran between East and West is very crucial. Iran's political system up to 1979 was monarchical dictatorship, but then 2500 years of kingship was terminated by the Iranian revolution under the leadership of Ayatollah Khomeini (for further information on Iran, see page 299).

Media and Development in Iran

Through a close look at the process of development in Iran we can see a clear pattern of dependent economic development that was centrally based on the export of crude oil and raw materials, with expansion linked to foreign investment. This economic dependence provided the basis for political and military dependence both in technological and human expertise. In the 1970s businessmen from all over the world waited in Tehran hotels to clinch multimillion-dollar deals of all kinds. Slowly, too, the media in Iran tried to convince people of the benefits of modernity and created new needs that consumer durables could satisfy.

Prior to World War II, Iran did not have a national broadcasting system. Iran's first radio transmitter went on the air in 1940. Radio programs were limited to evening broadcasts that consisted of the national anthem, major messages from government, news, and some Persian and Western music. In the early days of radio, loudspeakers and radio receivers were hooked up in various parts of Tehran, the capital, and people were very excited by this unprecedented form of communication. When the national anthem was played, people would rise and stand still. This was one of the first modern symbols of Iranian nationhood, broadcast over electronic media imported from the advanced world. Slowly, radio was used to maintain political control, to spread the ideological rhetoric of modernization, and to prepare Iranians for the neocolonial relationship that would strengthen after World War II.

In 1959, the last shah of Iran was persuaded by an imaginative urban entrepreneur to allow the establishment of commercial television. The entrepreneur was the son of a rich businessman whose wealth was based on importing Pepsi Cola from the United States. This first television station was allowed to operate for five years tax free while it developed commercial television and promoted the expansion of a consumer market, as in the United States. The family who controlled the television monopoly also controlled the importation of most television receivers, possessing the franchise for RCA products in Iran.

Television became a multiplier of Western and consumption values. These were overtly displayed in the advertisements for new consumer products and were also embedded in the depiction of a Western life-style carried by American films and television series such as *I Love Lucy* and *Bonanza.* Private television supported the monarchy's strategy of capitalist development. After some studies were undertaken, and worried that the Baha'i religious sect was monopolizing television, the shah decided to take over private television and transform it into a government-financed and -operated service. In 1966 National Iranian Television started broadcasting (its first message was from the shah, of course), and among the first test week's programming was a broadcast of the shah's birthday celebration. Soon radio was amalgamated with television to create National Iranian Radio and Television (NIRT). Consumerism was still encouraged through advertising, but, more important, NIRT tried to foster support for the regime through the glorification of the monarchy and support for modernization, maintaining the state ideology. Every royal activity was broadcast and the glorious history of 2500 years of Persian monarchy celebrated wherever possible, but the media also propagated the idea that the shah's major concern was to modernize Iran along the lines of the countries of Western Europe; television nightly news began with images of dams and new buildings, the physical symbols of development.

Radio and television were given substantial government budgets, so that coverage expanded rapidly. From 2 television transmitters in 1966, the number rose to 88 by 1974, and coverage increased from 2.1 million people to 15 million of both urban and rural populations, over half the country; radio coverage was almost universal (Mohammadi, 1976). By the mid-1970s, NIRT had became the second-largest broadcasting network in Asia, after NHK of Japan. Thus most of the nation was connected through broadcasting, linking small villages with major urban centers, and creating a novel national audience.

Yet, at the same time, literacy levels remained low, particularly for women, and there were not enough primary schools to accommodate all children of school age. Publishing and the press were strictly censored, so there was little choice among the dull daily newspapers, which thus had very low circulations. One commentator wryly noted that "if Iran continues on its present path, it will be the first nation in the world to have nationally spread television before a nationally spread press." Thus Iran seemed to leap over the stage of literacy and print development, moving almost directly from a traditional oral culture to an electronic one.

Even a brief glance at Iranian mass media in the mid-1970s would have indicated that the broadcast or published materials were not designed to preserve national culture or to raise the level of public education. Rather, they promoted the alluring manifestations of Western culture, with little consideration of the urgent needs and demands of Iranian society; they did little more than amuse and entertain their audience. One international study made in 1975 revealed that of 11 developing countries studied, NIRT had one of the highest levels of imported television programming, including Western feature films—78% of all television content—and broadcast the lowest percentage of serious programs—only 22% of total broadcast time. Typical imported programs included *Baretta, Star Trek, Marcus Welby, MD, Tarzan,* and the soap opera *Days of Our Lives.* When homemade programs were aired they became extremely popular, but much domestic programming was rather anemic because of actual and self-censorship. The prevailing policy seemed to disregard the cultural implications of importing so much Western media content, which carried Western life-styles, gender roles, consumption values, and so on. And while, for many developing countries, the economic argument that it is much cheaper to buy foreign programming than to produce your own had some justification, NIRT's large budgets didn't support such an argument. It seemed to be safer for the regime to allow lots of Western entertainment to be imported than to allow possibly critical homemade programs to appear (Motamed-Nejad, 1976).

The rapid expansion of broadcasting was a central element of the shah's ambitious development project, as he tried to use the communications media to help bring about the change from a traditional to a modern society. But it failed because the modernization process did not go far enough; indeed, the strategy has been described as "pseudomodernization," a desire for the superficial style of modernity without the deeper structural changes that true development requires. For example, the government, through the mass media, talked about modernization but failed to provide adequate and coherent national health care or education. It spent millions in developing NIRT, but failed to electrify large areas, so many rural people ran their televisions and lighting from small portable generators. It talked about improving working conditions, but would not allow labor unions to operate. It established many universities, but would not allow free exchange of ideas or free access to written materials. Iranian writers, artists, and broadcasters all had to fit in with the prevailing rhetoric of modernization, and no criticism was allowed. The security system of SAVAK (the shah's secret police) was waiting for any oppositional voices to be raised. Severe political repression thus blocked popular participation and discussion of social needs, the heart of political development.

Those in the educated middle class felt frustrated about the lack of political participation and the lack of cultural freedom, which allowed importation of American television but blocked the production of good, critical, indigenous programs. They felt frustrated as the political concerns of the state interfered in the legal system, the educational system, and the broadcasting system, undermining professional practices and independence. They felt the pinch of rampant inflation in the 1970s, with house and car prices rocketing, and watched as foreign "experts" were favored over Iranians with comparable skills.

The traditional middle classes, particularly the bazaar merchants and the clergy, were threatened by this Westernized mode of development. The economic position of the bazaaris was being undermined by large multinational corporations and agribusiness, while the social authority of the clergy was threatened by secular education and the media. They were also horrified at the effects Western values were having on the fabric of Iranian society. For example, the system of dating and marriage shown in the imported Western programming was totally in contradiction with the Islamic tradition of marriage, in which parents play a very significant role in selecting suitable spouses and dating of any sort without the presence of a relative is not allowed. Khomeini had been speaking out since the 1960s about the negative impact of Western values, and warned that the media were propaganda vehicles for Western imperialists who were trying to undermine Iran. Some religious authorities publicly denounced watching television, and others declared that having a television was a sinful act. The city of Qum, which is the equivalent of the Vatican for Iranian Shi'ite Moslems, actually banned television during the shah's reign.

From 1976, helped by President Carter's human rights policy, both the secular opposition and the religious opposition began to use a variety of small media to voice their objections to the regime. Professional groups such as lawyers and writers wrote "open letters" to the shah, demanding an end to regime intervention in the process of law and greater freedom of expression. The religious opposition also began to mobilize, and developed a communications system quite independent from the big media of the state to politicize the people. The leaders used the national network of mosques and bazaars to preach their Islamic identity against the dependent Westernization of the shah. When Khomeini left his isolated place of exile in a small village in Iraq for the outskirts of Paris in 1978, he became the focus of much Western media attention. Also, the religious network transmitted his speeches across the international telephone lines to Tehran, and within hours thousands of audiocassettes of his voice were available on the streets of the capital and were carried to other cities and villages for all to hear—a new international electronic pulpit. In a still very oral culture, where the clergy possess considerable social authority and are used to addressing ordinary people on a regular basis at the mosques, this was a very powerful form of communication.

A popular movement against the shah began to grow, and when demonstrators were killed through regime violence, the Islamic mourning pattern of the seventh and fortieth days gave the demonstrations a religious rhythm. Gradually, political groups—communist, socialist, nationalist, democratic—banned by the regime resurfaced, and countless photocopied leaflets began to circulate, setting out analyses, making political demands, organizing demonstrations. Thus certain small media, particularly audiocassettes and leaflets, were used very effectively in the Iranian popular mobilization, another example of alternative media use described by Downing in Chapter 12. These small media are interesting because they are so easily reproduced, making it extremely difficult for any regime to block their circulation. When the military tried to maintain order and took over NIRT in November 1978, the personnel went on strike, so for three months radio and television were run by the military while the professionals produced underground newspapers debunking the regime news.

Thus a combination of religious authority and small media mobilized some of the largest demonstrations of recent history, bringing together modern and traditional groups united in hostility to the pattern of Westernized development of the shah, combining a mixture of economic discontents, political frustrations, and cultural concerns into a single slogan, "Down with the shah." In January 1979, the shah left "on holiday," never to return, and in February, Ayatollah Khomeini established the Islamic Republic of Iran.

Conclusion

The communication and development model failed to understand the historically different cultural contexts of Third World societies; as applied to Iran, it served to bring the West into Iranian living rooms and allowed Iranians to compare themselves with Westerners, exacerbating existing economic, political, and cultural frustrations. The model failed to pay attention to political development or less quantifiable aspirations such as equality, justice, freedom, identity, and even happiness. In the context of Iran, the communications and development processes seemed to suggest that Western patterns of life and attitudes were the only ones of value, to be imitated by Iranians, and that indigenous Iranian culture had little to offer. The process created not only great gaps of wealth between an urban elite and rural poor, but also a deep sense of cultural inferiority, which the clergy effectively used to mobilize people against the regime.

Frantz Fanon (1967) presents a vivid image of the effects of Western cultural products on the people of the Third World:

> Young people have at their disposition leisure occupations designed for the youth of capitalist countries: detective novels, penny-in-the-slot machines, sexy photographs, pornographic literature, films banned to those under sixteen, and above all alcohol. In the West the family circle, the effects of education and the relatively high standard of living of the working classes provide a more or less efficient protection against the harmful action of these pastimes. But in an African country, where mental development is uneven, where the violent collision of two worlds has considerably shaken old traditions and thrown the universe of the perceptions out of focus, the impressionability and sensibility of the young Africans are at the mercy of the various assaults made upon them by the very nature of Western culture. (pp. 157-158)

Although written about a different cultural context, these words could also be applied to Iran. The development strategy in Iran was undermining the very basis of cultural identity and the traditional values of Iranian society. The rapid change from small-scale self-sufficiency to commodity production for the markets, the neglect of channels for political participation, and the blocking of self-expression and indigenous cultural development undermined the harmony and tranquility of cultural life. The process of development, by definition, upsets the pattern of life that went before, but in the West that process went hand in hand with the basic values and cultural patterns of those societies. In Iran, as in much of the Third World, development was replaced by a mimetic Westernization, a copying of the superficial elements of the modern West without the fundamental political and social changes required. Economic dependency, as in the spread of montage industries that merely assemble consumer technologies developed elsewhere (thus not helping an independent economic sector to grow), was supported by cultural dependency, in which mass media broadcast news and cultural entertainment programs more attuned to the markets of industrial nations or regime needs than to the cultural habits of the Iranian people.

Iran is a unique example of a Third World country that implemented the communication and development model to accelerate the process of modernization, and the model failed dramatically. Communications can help people to find new norms and harmony in a period of transition; in the Iranian case, however, the effect was totally the reverse.

The Iranian experience makes us question the powerful media/powerful effects model of communication. The shah could control all the media, but he couldn't produce political legitimacy. And Iranians could watch a lot of American programming and still prefer their own values. Thus both the communications and development model—which suggested that media could play such an important, positive, role in economic and political development—and the cultural imperialism model—which said that media were carriers of Western values that would swamp Third World cultures—are too one-dimensional, as the Iranian case has shown.

The rhetoric of revolution included slogans against Westernization, consumerism, and the idea of self-determination, expressed in the slogan "Not East, nor West, only Islam." The tragedy of Iran is that while cultural identity may be an important appeal against the forces of Westernization, it alone does not guarantee broader progressive social values such as freedom and justice, which were fundamental demands of the popular movement. Also, religious identity was felt by many to be their cultural identity, not anticipating the rigid fundamentalism that has ensued, and there is new concern that traditional Iranian culture and its music and dance are suppressed. Many have been killed or imprisoned, many others have left Iran. The Islamic Republic has thus bitterly disappointed many hopes, and inherits many of the old problems that the shah did not solve. Analyzing the global context in which modernization and popular reaction took place at least helps to explain the deep dilemmas of development that confront Third World nations.

Further Questions

(1) Has the pattern of importation of Western media products changed significantly in Third World countries over the last ten years?

(2) What kinds of relationships are there between traditional cultural forms and television? Find examples of First World and Third World cultural traditions that have been preserved and even developed through television. Find examples of traditions that have been destroyed.

(3) Media simply absorb time that might otherwise be spent on traditional cultural habits. What might those be and what impact in terms of time, social relations, and habits have media had in First World and Third World societies?

20 The Production of T.V. News

RICHARD GRUNEAU
ROBERT A. HACKETT

One of the main reasons many people become interested in media studies is because of the way news is presented. Not only is this information very important to a fast-moving modern society, not only has it helped to transform and unify many nations that previously consisted of scattered communities with little knowledge of one another's doings or concerns, but in many cases critical scholars have been galvanized into research by noting how issues have been simplified and distorted in the news. Herman (Chapter 4) and Robinson (Chapter 5) argue in this volume that distortion is a product of the patterns of ownership of media and, beyond that, of the organization of the U.S. political economy as a whole. Schulman (Chapter 7) analyzes how media professionals are influenced to toe the line in the production of news programs.

Gruneau and Hackett take the analysis one stage further, to examine the cultural codes by which TV news bulletin items are put together to "create reality." (The title of one classic study of British broadcast news is Putting "Reality" Together; *Schlesinger, 1988.) They select one news episode for a concentrated and detailed analysis, namely, the departure from the United States of a planeload of Soviet immigrants back to the Soviet Union. The event was so clearly contrary to popular perceptions—that is, that almost every Soviet citizen would love to emigrate to the United States if they could—that it is easy enough to accept its "newsworthiness," or its selection from the mass of events that could have been in the news that day.*

Gruneau and Hackett explore the ways in which news presentation processed this minor but dissonant event, in the general direction of making it less upsetting to conventional wisdom and smoothing out its provocative dimensions. In so doing, they point out some of the standard cultural codes and procedures that operate in the construction of news, which includes in this case the reassurance to the national audience of the abiding value of being American. Thus although the returnees constituted a foreign news item on one level, they represented a domestic news question on a deeper level: Are we or are we not the most desirable nation on earth, especially as judged against our rival superpower?

Gruneau and Hackett's analysis then explores how it is that an event becomes "news," and reveals the powerful roles of both cultural and production values in the news process. This raises questions once again about the validity of journalistic claims to objectivity.

One area of controversy in television news is the problem of bias. Individuals and groups on the political right (an example from the 1980s would be the lobbying group Accuracy in Media) claim to detect a persistent left-wing bias in news accounts. Other people (for example, the liberal media watchdog group FAIR) claim the opposite—that television news reinforces and reproduces an essentially conservative viewpoint.

Television news has also been subject to strong criticism from politicians who claim that news accounts always accentuate the negative aspects of government policy. Other critics argue that responsible journalistic reporting has become a casualty of the network's relentless quest for profit. Informed news broadcasts, we are often told, have become transformed into mindless "infotainment." Yet millions of people continue to watch television news on a regular basis and, as confused or cynical as people may be, they nonetheless get much of what they know about the world on a day-to-day basis from television newscasts. Most people generally appear to accept the authority of television news and rarely subject it to any serious reflection or critical analysis.

We want to raise questions about the claims to actuality, realism, and journalistic authority made by television news, but we do not want to be confined by the usual debates about news bias. A much better starting point is to think of the news as something that is socially and culturally produced within organizations, subject to a complex set of pressures and limits existing within American society as a whole.

Television News as a Social and Cultural Product

Television news represents itself to us as a neutral conveyer of "real events" that are "shown" and then commented upon. In the words of one old news cliché, TV news tries to provide "a window on the world." This image of TV news is built out of a chain of widely shared assumptions, that there is an "event" or a "problem" (e.g., a political convention or an airliner crash) that happens somewhere in the world and that TV news reports on that problem and tells/shows us what happened. The "window on the world" is thus constructed out of an assumed link between two separate and discrete things: really existing events, and reports about them. This is reinforced both in the language of televised news programming itself and in the way people speak about TV news in everyday conversation. For example, people speak constantly of news "coverage" of real events, and newscasters work hard to achieve the immediacy of "live" reportage, with "on-the-spot" reports and remote cameras to bring the viewer the pictorial "proof" of the event's existence.

Yet there are a number of reasons television news "coverage" should be viewed neither as a separate and distinct process easily distinguishable from the "events" or "problems" being reported nor as a neutral conveyor of these events or problems. First, TV news always involves a process of selection of which events to report, which to leave out, which aspects to highlight, and which to downplay. The world is teeming with "events," "problems," and "stories" of interest and relevance. A wide range of items of human interest, scientific discovery, heroic action, political intrigue, scandal, economic development, and social and political change could be "covered" every day. But not all of these items qualify as "news" to American television broadcasters. It is important to ask why some things are selected rather than others.

Herbert Gans (1980) has identified the major "news values," the criteria of newsworthiness, of American journalism. They include the following: timeliness, political importance, a further development in an ongoing story, involvement of individuals rather than abstract structures or institutions, conflict, involvement of powerful people or celebrities, drama, geographical and cultural proximity, negative events, scope or size and potential impact of event, visual interest, relevance to some deep-rooted cultural theme, novelty, violation of social order, and human interest. Some of these news values counterbalance each other (e.g., news is a blend of the familiar and the unexpected). If a story is short on some news values, it must make up for it with others to be worthy of inclusion on network news. In other words, what constitutes news is defined against background assumptions about what is normal, routine, and hence not news. These assumptions reflect widespread—but not necessarily valid—agreement about the way the world works, or cultural common sense.

Television news also involves a complex process of visual and narrative *presentation*—for example, choosing what sort of images, language, camera positioning, lighting, and story line to use to translate "what happened" into a suitable television news item. Television cameras do not simply present an object or event in a completely neutral way; rather, they situate us in a particular position or location *in relation to* that object or event. A good example is the case of the strike, riot, or political protest.

Camera placement behind or among the strikers, rioters, or protesters, looking out at the police, positions the viewer much differently from camera placement among or behind the police and looking out at the protesters. Similarly, the use of close-ups and long shots, different types of graphics, rhythms of shot lengths and styles of editing all play a role in presenting news from a particular viewpoint. The linkage of verbal commentary to this viewpoint reinforces a set of preferred meanings and usually unconscious viewer positioning.

The point is that television news is not something set apart from the real world or the seemingly neutral voice of journalistic authority. On the contrary, television news is noticeably shaped by the very world that it purports to cover objectively. In the United States, the structures of the "free-market" economy and liberal-democratic political system combine with persisting and changing features of American popular culture to provide a context that sets significant limits and exerts powerful pressures on the production of television news.

Pressures and Limits on the Social Production of Television News

Some of these limits are dealt with elsewhere in this book. The manner in which powerful ideologies shape the political environment is examined by Herman (Chapter 4), Schulman (Chapter 7) shows how professional values create conservative pressures on journalists, and Sreberny-Mohammadi (Chapter 21) explores ethnocentrism and imbalance in international news coverage. Here we consider how the economic realities surrounding news production influence the selection and presentation of news.

In the United States news is a business and, for television, journalism often becomes indistinguishable from show business. Most television news production in the United States is produced by organizations with a mandate that has very little to do with the dissemination of public information; rather, these organizations exist to sell audience viewing time to advertisers for profit. As Daniel Hallin (1987) notes, this gives television news a rather unique character: "a key political institution as well as a seller of detergent and breakfast cereal."

News programs contribute directly to a network's profit-making process through ads shown during news programs, or indirectly as an element of a network's own self-marketing to prospective advertisers and viewers. Competition for news viewers has led the networks to adapt traditionally accepted journalistic practices to the conventions of camera work and editing more typically associated with television entertainment.

As a primarily visual medium, television has difficulty accommodating complex and detailed verbal narrative. But it can shock and surprise with its speed and immediacy, and its images can personalize a story in ways that cannot be duplicated in print. Television news achieves its popularity by playing to its visual strengths of *immediacy* and *personalization,* but the visual and narrative style adopted is that of the action drama, the commercial, and the variety show: short shots, fast-moving coverage, visual variety at the expense of narrative sophistication and detail. The race for ratings has also meant "coverage" that plays to perceived popular sentiment and fashions a style of coverage produced with an eye to offending the smallest possible number of viewers.

Technical innovation and escalating costs have also been an important part of competition in the area of news production. News today dazzles us with its technical sophistication—its capacity to seemingly take us anywhere in an instant and receive reports from journalists around the globe. However, this introduces extra pressures on news coverage; the significant investment in remote camera crews, on-the-spot reporting, satellite feeds, studio equipment, and salaries means that commercial news organizations require a continuous flow of "low-cost" news items to finance the more exotic ones. Furthermore, news media cannot take many risks with investigative or speculative items that take up large blocks of airtime, cost a lot to research and produce, and may not, ultimately, prove popular with viewers.

All of these economic constraints predispose network news programs to gear much of their production to "coverage" of events that are, on the basis of past experience, high in predictable news values. Crime, violence, and scandal are proven news items, as are such officially staged events as press conferences, political conventions, and organized demonstrations. These pressures give obvious advantages in headline making to organizations and groups with sufficient resources to plan and stage such events. Boorstin (1985) emphasizes the staged character of such occasions by referring to them as "pseudoevents."

News selection and presentation is also influenced by a vast array of organizational pressures and limits arising from the structures of the journalistic workplace and people's allegiance to long-standing professional conventions of filming, editing, and reporting. When television journalists are asked how they decide what to cover, and how to cover it, they often make vague references to journalistic "news sense," even suggesting that an instinct for recognizing news and knowing how to present it is something one is born with. Really what is involved is the process of acquiring a set of professional and social skills—some learned through professional training but many acquired informally by exposure to the conventions and styles of TV news coverage, working with other reporters and production personnel, and conforming/negotiating with senior production personnel (see Chapter 7). All of this goes on in the context of the economic and technical pressures and limits noted earlier. Thus news values and conventions of news presentation are learned informally, yet they become so habitual and seemingly instinctive that they guide television news production with scarcely a moment's conscious reflection on the part of the producers.

Many television analysts have suggested that it is useful to think of news values and conventions of presentation as a set of codes (e.g., Fiske & Hartley, 1978; Hartley, 1982). These codes represent the collective sense among television news personnel about what matters most in the world, what is going to change things the most, what viewers presumably want to know about or will be interested in, how they like it to be shown, and what types of narrative structure will most appeal to them. These codes are not always explicit or consciously held, but they nonetheless tend to be widely shared by professional personnel and their audiences.

Representation and Ideology: Some Conventions of Television News

A close examination of a single television news item can tell us a great deal about the conventions and representational practices typically employed in television news production, and can illustrate how the limits and pressures discussed previously are evident in the content of a specific television news story. The item we have chosen to examine was aired by CBS on December 29, 1986, and dealt with Soviet émigrés who, after coming to the United States, had decided to return to their homeland. Table 20.1 provides a shot-by-shot description of the verbal and visual components of this item.

Representational Practices

Just as there are rules of grammar for speaking English "correctly," there is a visual "grammar" of TV news. Any major violation of these rules would disrupt the expectations of the regular news viewer and might be viewed as amusing or jarring, not quite right. How is this demonstrated in our sample story?

TABLE 20.1: Verbal and Visual Components of a CBS News Item (December 29, 1986)

Shot Number and Type	*Duration (in seconds)*	*Number of Subjects*	*Description of Shot*	*Verbal Commentary*
(1) close-up	19	1	Anchorman speaks to camera at left of screen. In upper right of screen, a graphic of U.S. and Soviet flags, with words GOING HOME superimposed. U.S. flag is dominant in terms of color and position.	*Newscaster:* Since 1981 about 35,000 people have emigrated from the Soviet Union to the United States. Nearly all of them have stayed but many have had a hard time in this country. Today, about 50 of them went home to Russia. CBS News correspondent Wyatt Andrews was there when they arrived.
(2) close-up	6	2	Man with arm around woman, faces down, to right of screen.	*Correspondent:* If the Russians who returned had anything in common it is
(3) medium shot	3	2 and others	Man and woman embracing, facing each other at right angle to camera.	that they were desperately homesick for friends and family.
(4) extreme close-up	4	1	Woman in fur hat, facing to left of screen, crying.	Some had tearful tales of loneliness and fear of crime.
(5) medium shot	6	2 and others	Focus on two men behind media paraphernalia, photographers in foreground.	Most had tried to carve out homes in New York City and were escaping that as much as rejecting the United States.
(6) close-up	6	1	Man, holding boy in arms, speaking to front right.	*Russian, anon:* In general I felt alien, totally alien to the, to the United States. I decided to go home.
(7) close-up	7	1	Man, holding boy in arms, speaking to front right.	*Second Russian, anon:* I missed my mother, my relatives, my friends, my culture, my city.

(continued)

TABLE 20.1: (*Continued*)

Shot Number and Type	*Duration (in seconds)*	*Number of Subjects*	*Description of Shot*	*Verbal Commentary*
(8) medium shot	2	1	Artist Cleaver faces two other people, their backs to camera.	*Correspondent:* Artist Valery Cleaver could not make a living
(9) close-up	2	1	Artist speaking.	selling art in the competitive New York market.
(10) medium shot	3.5	2	Girl seated on airport bench, facing left of screen, next to small boy.	His 16-year-old daughter Karina disliked the materialism of her teenage
(11) close-up	13	1	Karina speaking toward front right of screen.	friends.
(12) close-up to medium shot	3	3 and others	Several men walking single file through crowd, toward front left of screen.	*Correspondent:* To Soviet authorities it was propaganda theater.
(13) long shot	2	4	Two men in gray suits, one speaking through a bullhorn, facing camera.	Officials stage-managed the returnees,
(14) medium shot	2	1	Man with bullhorn, facing camera.	granting them visas to be on the same flight
(15) long shot	3	crowd	Émigrés and media people.	and diverting them to a room full of foreign correspondents
(16) close-up	2	1	Man taking photo, toward lower front screen. Focus on his hands and the camera.	before émigrés and even cleared customs.
(17) medium shot to close-up	5	1 crowd	Woman walking through the crowd.	The Soviets intended this as a lesson—that emigration does happen in reverse.

(18) medium shot	15	1	Correspondent speaking directly to camera. His name and *CBS News* are supercaptioned below.	The homecoming demonstrates another lesson about the East and West the Soviets never intended. It is, that any American who wants to leave the country has the right to just go, while Soviet citizens do not have that right. The émigrés had to use the freedom of America in order to leave it.
(19) medium shot	5	2 and crowd	Couple embracing at right angles to camera.	The show of propaganda is a reminder that American freedom isn't for everyone.
(20) medium shot	2	2	Facing away from camera, two people wave.	Freedom to an American can look wild and uncertain to a
(21) medium shot to close-up	4	2	Man with arm around woman, walking toward front left of screen. Woman mops brow, tearfully.	Russian homesick for a more predictable and familiar Soviet life.
(22) medium shot	2	1	Man in gray suit speaks through bullhorn, facing camera but slightly to left.	Not everyone who yearns to be free
(23) long shot	5	crowd	People slowly walking out airport exit, backs to camera.	always learns to be free. Wyatt Andrews, CBS News, Moscow.

- The first set of codes pertains to *the pacing of the item*. Fiske (1987) has noted how in the rapid pace of commercial television programming the average length of shot is approximately 7 seconds. Here, in an item about two minutes long, there are 23 separate camera shots, with an average of just over 5 seconds per shot. This pace reflects the competitive nature of commercial TV, the need to attract and hold the interest of mass audiences whose attention span is assumed to be low, and mimics the fast pace of TV commercials, which are typically only 30 seconds long.
- It is easy to overlook that *each report is "introduced,"* and the context or frame set, by an "anchorperson," usually male, who sits at a desk (a cultural symbol of authority), who can apparently summon at will the impressive technology of television (graphics, film reports, satellite interviews), and who is a familiar personality in his or her own right—a point of identification and reassurance for the viewer—and someone who anchors both the flow of the program and the viewer's own sense of reality. Helping the anchorperson to set the stage is an electronically projected graphic, which not only categorizes the topic, but also suggests an interpretation.
- *Only the anchorman and the reporter are "permitted" to address the camera* directly, to make eye contact with the viewer, as it were. While there are technical reasons for this (interviewees would find it confusing to face the camera rather than the interviewer, for instance), it does add to the apparent authoritativeness of the journalists—and to our impression that they, rather than the politicians, witnesses, or spokespersons they interview—are speaking to, and for, the ordinary viewer. Furthermore, the item supports newscaster authority by awarding the newscasters the two longest single shots. The third-longest shot is of the Russian girl Karina, but her point is not elaborated upon or reinforced in the script.
- In the sequence of shots, *there is a kind of rhythm*: Close-up shots tend to be followed by longer-range ones, and vice versa. Long-range shots are used to establish the scene or transfer to a new one; close-ups are used for interviews or to convey emotion. The sequence avoids "jump cuts," whereby one person suddenly appears to move from one part of the room to another, or a portion of his or her speech has been noticeably edited out. In the interviews, two of the three people are not identified by name at all; one other (Karina Cleaver) is named orally by the reporter, but her name is not spelled out in "super-captions" at the bottom of the screen. Such omissions are clues to the status of people interviewed: They are not important or famous in their own right, but are used simply to illustrate the theme(s) of the story, and are substitutable for each other.
- The item illustrates how *TV news narrative has a dramatic structure* very different from that of traditional print journalism. This is partly dictated by the nature of the television medium, which must hold all the viewers' attention through time. This narrative structure is also dictated by the mass audience of millions of Americans, which is geographically and socially diverse. To engage their attention, TV news has adopted the practice of telling virtually self-contained stories, with an introduction that poses a

central theme or paradox, a middle in which characters and scenes are used to develop that theme, and a conclusion that temporarily offers a resolution of the initial question or problem—sometimes in the form of a visual moral lesson. Here, the moral is not that the United States is the cause of the émigrés' return, but rather that the cause is their inability to "learn to be free." So television news works hard to contain, or minimize, unanswered questions or challenges to dominant values.

Ideological Manifestations

We noted earlier how the competition for audiences pressures news production to gear itself to the predictable and familiar, since anything else might be upsetting or confusing and may cause viewers to switch channels. That is why, as Hallin (1987) notes, "television, contrary to the mythology about its immense power, rarely takes the lead in anything; rather, as a shift (in popular mood, political consensus) occurs, television follows cautiously behind" (p. 41).

For much of this century, Americans have viewed the Soviet Union with suspicion and alarm. The "American way of life" has been widely portrayed as superior to life in the Soviet Union in every respect. To be sure, American attitudes toward the Soviet Union have never been completely monolithic, and since the heyday of the Cold War there have been several minor "thaws" and "freezes" in American public opinion about the Soviet Union. This news item, aired during the middle of Ronald Reagan's second term, positions itself in accordance with the perceived dominant political mood of the day. It reflects a journalistic assumption that during the Reagan era, Cold War attitudes once again constitute the ideological "middle ground" to which most news is designed to appeal.

The positioning of news toward the ideological middle ground is motivated by more than the fear of losing audiences, for there are a wide range of unique political pressures that set limits on the range and types of political discourse perceived to be appropriate in television news production. To some extent these limits are generated from the heavy dependence of network news on powerful representatives of national institutions—especially the president and his spokespersons, other cabinet officials (e.g., the secretaries of state and of defense), and a handful of leading members of Congress. Not only are these people routinely allowed to speak on network news, but, in more subtle ways, they influence the language and terms of reference of political reporting (see Chapter 5). Their influence is powerful in establishing limits to "acceptable" political debate, definitions of what count as political problems, and their potential solutions. Network news organizations are sensitive to these dominant political actors because they fear unfavorable legislation, but also because methods of news gathering are highly dependent on such sources, who can potentially deny access to information or newsworthy events. Thus to challenge the credibility and authoritativeness of these sources consistently would be to undermine the credibility of the networks' own news-gathering procedures.

However, these political limits are not rigidly applied. The statements of officials, even the president, are usually set in context by TV journalists (whose first allegiance is to their pursuit of audiences, not to the president) and even official news sources rarely speak to viewers directly. To maintain credibility with an American audience that always maintains a degree of "little guy" populist sensibility, network news cannot be seen as a mere mouthpiece for the administration. There is a striving for the appearance of balance and objectivity and, however illusory this may be, it creates a potential space for the expression of alternative and "nonofficial" interpretations of events.

Our sample CBS item on Russian émigrés is an unusual item for national evening news. Nobody famous is even mentioned, so what makes it newsworthy? A clue is given by the graphic that introduces and "frames" it. The phrase "going home" is a common and emotional experience to which we can all relate—human interest. But the U.S. and Soviet flags tell us it is about much more than this. This story is about U.S.-Soviet relations. National honor is at stake, for what national symbol is more cherished than the flag? Yet this is not a relationship between equals. The Soviet flag is dull in color, and is lying prone, pointing perspectivally toward the "horizon," over which looms the Stars and Stripes, brightly lit, in strong color definition. This graphic invokes the popularly held Cold War "common sense" that the two countries are adversaries, in which each gain for one side is a loss for the other, and that overall the United States enjoys moral and technological superiority. The newscaster's opening statement likewise draws on that common sense—everybody "knows" that the Soviet Union is such a repressive system that many of its citizens are itching to flee to the United States, the land of freedom and opportunity. But when you think seriously about them, some of these assumptions are very much open to debate.

American citizens undoubtedly enjoy a range of individual freedoms and a level of material well-being not widely available in the Soviet Union. But is the United States truly a land of freedom and opportunity for the poor and for ethnic minorities? The mechanisms of political censorship in the United States are described in Chapters 4 and 6. Perhaps the unbridled individual freedoms of "American life," including the right to sell pornography and to own automatic weapons, undermine collective rights to personal safety and respect? Perhaps the Soviet experience even offers us some lessons—in such areas as education, health and child care, local government, and science and the arts; in personal warmth, the commitment of friendship and family, the dynamics of the unofficial culture.

The cheap point scoring that naturally flows from the zero-sum perspective—"throwing dead cats at each other," as Premier Kruschev put it to President Kennedy—provides no guidance as to how shared problems might be solved. Alternative perspectives are barely evident in U.S. network news, which dramatizes and implicitly celebrates dominant American preconceptions of the world.

This story is newsworthy, then, because it involves national prestige, superpower relations, and human interest, and because it violates viewers' expectations of how the world works. Why *did* a group of Russians decide to go home? The story creates a problem for TV news: It is too newsworthy to ignore, but it demands to be explained in a way that avoids fundamentally challenging common sense—the presumed superiority of the American way of life. That puzzle is posed in the anchorman's introduction, and then is addressed immediately by the correspondent, both of whom work very hard to contain and minimize the story's potential as a damaging critique of the American way by using a number of rhetorical devices:

- *The introductory narrative* implies that such an event is occurring only "today" out of all the years "since 1981," and it involves only "about 50" out of 35,000 emigres. In fact, as we can tell from other similar TV news stories at different times, this event is not unique.
- *The report's credibility* is enhanced by the provision of the appearance of balance and objectivity—critiques of the United States are included in the report. However, every major criticism of the United States is from a Russian, who is either interviewed directly or paraphrased by the correspondent. The correspondent does not take the initiative to amplify or expand upon these critiques; nor does he "embed" them in his own narrative as taken-for-granted assumptions. The reasons for the Russians returning home are "particularized"—that is, they are presented to avoid any general critique of American values or society. They are leaving the United States for personal and emotional rather than rational or political reasons: They are fearful, tearful, desperately homesick (reinforced by the visuals of hugs, crying woman, and tearful reunions). Or they are rejecting not the United States as such, but the grime and crime of New York City—a contrast that implies that New York is not part of the "real" America and that appeals to a nostalgic populist image of the "real," wholesome, agrarian, America.
- The returning *Russians are "marginalized,"* presented as atypical and as failures. The artist couldn't cut the mustard in the "competitive" New York market; the émigrés "had not learned to be free."

- *There is no suggestion* in the item that the Russians are returning because they regard the U.S. political or economic system as inferior to that of the Soviet Union. Instead, they seek a return to a "predictable and familiar Soviet life." In another network item on a similar event (ABC, February 23, 1987), the émigrés are returning not to the Soviet Union at all, but to "mother Russia."
- *The one statement that borders on a general critique* of U.S. materialist, consumerist values is Karina's interview. However, the correspondent does not expand this critique. Instead, he immediately changes the narrative line to accuse the Soviet authorities of staging "propaganda theater," a verbal claim given credence by the visual shot of a gray-suited man speaking through a bullhorn. This device turns the tables on the Soviets, deflecting attention away from the critiques of U.S. life, and advancing a critique of the Soviet Union. It also suggests this is a "pseudoevent," staged specifically for the media, something that wouldn't "really" happen but for the machinations of Soviet authorities—and this is used to discredit or delegitimate the Soviets' intended message. But in fact, a great many of the stories we see on TV news are such staged pseudoevents (news conferences, presidential speeches, photo opportunities with the president and visiting heads of state, even street demonstrations). The difference is that on this occasion, it served the rhetorical purposes of the TV journalists to call attention to that fact. In addition, the concept of "Soviet propaganda" is juxtaposed to "American freedom," which becomes the major theme of the last half of the item. It invokes stereotypes regarding the two nations, uncritically equating "freedom" with the United States; the phrase "wild and uncertain" regarding American freedom refers to the myth of the western frontier, which also served President Reagan well in his rhetorical appeals for the Strategic Defense Initiative.

Some Concluding Remarks

One can see how even a single two-minute item on returning Russian émigrés opens up a vast field of questions regarding the codes of television news coverage in the United States. So what should we make of all this? We argue that network news gravitates toward an assumed political and ideological consensus, and works hard and actively to pull the meaning of events, which it apparently only "covers," toward the consensus. That consensus can shift and change over time, but network news tends to follow and retard such changes, rather than to lead and provoke them.

Network news is far from seamless, and is open to a wide range of interpretations and readings by viewers. Yet the social production of network news in the United States is subject to profound and varied pressures and limits that greatly shape what it is that Americans come to see as "news" on television. The codes of television news tend to generate preferred meanings in news items that articulate and reproduce a hypothetical "common sense" about the world and the place of the United States in it. In addition, television news in the United States tends to position viewers into specific roles, here as an American who "knows" and understands a freedom that cannot be grasped by the Russian émigrés. The viewer is invited to share with the correspondent a position of superior knowledge, in contrast to people whose knowledge is only limited and partial. The Russians *feel* (they are homesick) but they do not *know* (the benefits of "real" freedom).

It is no longer sufficient simply to complain about problems of bias in discussions of television news, as if the news could ever become truly "objective." Rather, we need to develop a much more comprehensive and analytic viewpoint to understand the whole process of news production and consumption, its limits and pressures, its ideological manifestations, and its possibilities to be something more than it currently is.

Further Questions

(1) Using the method described here, explore the "commonsense" assumptions buried within other news stories. What are some of the assumptions found in stories about the homeless, drug abuse, political activists, and so on?

(2) Compare television coverage of news events with print coverage. Are the rhetorical devices and "commonsense" assumptions very different?

(3) Find alternative (political, ethnic, women's) news channels; how do their representational practices compare with those described in this chapter?

21 U.S. Media Covers the World

ANNABELLE SREBERNY-MOHAMMADI

For many years, most Americans were used to thinking of themselves as mercifully detached from the rest of the world and its conflicts. The United States joined in World War I reluctantly in 1917, three years after its beginning, and joined World War II equally reluctantly in 1941, two years after the war had commenced in Europe and Asia. Staying away from the battlefield is not irrational in itself on most occasions, but the issue for our purposes is that insularity—often termed isolationism—has been a marked feature of U.S. popular culture. One of the many reasons for the Vietnamese victory over the United States in 1975 was the widespread feeling here that Americans were getting killed for no good purpose thousands of miles from home. The cruel irony is that, as Robinson notes in Chapter 5, the American elite has rather consistently intervened on the world stage, sometimes, as in the case of Vietnam, dragging a largely unwilling public after it.

Yet the United States is less and less able to pretend that it is an independent actor on the world stage, despite its enormous military might and technical advance. It is part of a web of rich nations that have their own priorities, and it has an extensive series of client nations in the Third World, most of which are anxious to assert their own independence from it, at least from time to time. Our lives as Americans cannot escape these developments, and they will increase as time goes on.

For this reason, international news is of the highest importance. If it is well constructed, it can help us adjust intelligently to the new position of the United States and indeed to anticipate likely changes in the world. In particular, it might help the American public to outgrow its habit of allowing Washington and Wall Street to make foreign policy, and to increase the number of independent commentators and critics in that area of life. The tragedy of lives lost in the Vietnam War—55,000 Americans and 1,000,000 Vietnamese, not to speak of the maimed—are but one instance of why this awareness matters.

In this chapter, Sreberny-Mohammadi traces out a number of the problems in conventional international news presentation in U.S. media. She shows us other dimensions of the communication imbalance between North and South already explored by Hamelink in Chapter 15, here contrasting the considerable quantity of information available in the affluent United States with its frequently poor quality of news presentation. Again, as a case study of the processes in question, she selects Iran, a nation that from 1979 on has stirred passionate anger inside the United States and that therefore constitutes a particularly illuminating example of the negative impact of international news coverage, and of the ways it has typically failed to inform us adequately.

Television as the Major International News Source

McLuhan and Fiore (1968) have claimed that developments in electronic media and telecommunications have made the world into a "global village." Yet while the possibilities exist for receiving letters from aunties in Australia and phone calls from boyfriends in Britain, for most people across the United States, the domestic mass media—especially television—are the major source of information about international events in far places. The way in which the media, particularly television, select and interpret events, what they focus on and what they omit, helps construct a public opinion. This public opinion may be educated—not only knowledgeable about the sequence of events but also fully informed about why events occurred, the goals of national and world leaders, and the domestic and global implications of events—or it may be poorly informed, invited to see only dramatic moments rather then long-term processes, and developing a gung ho mentality toward the "national interest" rather than appreciating the intricate interactions of most foreign policy issues. This is of special importance for the United States, which as a global superpower has many kinds of international relations that the American public needs to comprehend.

International news coverage is a controversial and contested area of media production. Almost all professional journalists and many media analysts claim that international news coverage in the United States, like its domestic equivalent, is objective, truthful, and unbiased, and that what they report is "the way it really is." It is argued that if there is more news about one area than another, it is because the American people are more interested in certain places than in others, it is easier to report from some parts of the world than from others, and if certain developing countries want a better press, they should hire Madison Avenue public relations firms to improve their image abroad (see Chapter 20 for further discussion of news values and "objectivity").

Many critical news analysts have argued, on the other hand, that U.S. media coverage of international issues focuses on the sensational and the negative, news of the "coup and catastrophe" kind; that there is an unbalanced focus on Western industrialized nations, Japan, and the Soviet Union, while whole continents remain invisible; that international news tends to be shallow and oversimplified, concentrating on personalities and pronouncements of governments rather than exploring how issues affect ordinary people; and that international news coverage fragments complex problems into isolated events without providing explanation and analysis of their causes.

One of the first issues to be sensitive to is the problem of definition. For example, our terms seem to separate "international" news neatly from "domestic" news coverage. But in fact the bulk of U.S. international news reporting concerns U.S. relations with another nation, and it is generally true that international news is defined in terms of the interests of the nation where it is broadcast or published.

Second, only very few nations are regularly covered in international news reporting. A study of the most frequently mentioned nations in U.S. network news coverage in the period 1972-1979 produced only 20 nations that were mentioned in more than 2% of international news stories, hardly extensive coverage (Larson, 1982). Most of those countries were the politically or economically powerful nations, such as the Soviet Union, Great Britain, France, the People's Republic of China, Japan, and West Germany. Most of the rest were countries involved in wars or major conflicts, so that South Vietnam was the single most frequently mentioned nation from 1972 through 1975 and Middle Eastern nations such as Israel, Egypt, Lebanon, and Iran received substantial television news focus especially from 1976 to 1979. This means that much of the world remains invisible to us if it is not involved in some "newsworthy" and telegenic conflict.

It is useful to explore this dynamic further for U.S. media by examining the coverage of one country in detail. Since the 1979 Islamic Revolution in Iran and the subsequent seizure of hostages in the U.S. embassy in Tehran captured overwhelming media attention, and since there was such an intimate relationship between U.S. government policy on Iran and U.S. media coverage, it is a highly instructive case study for pinpointing some typical problems in U.S. foreign reporting (Dorman & Farhang, 1987).

A Brief Profile of Iran

Iran has been a national entity and a monarchy for more than 2,500 years, dating back to the empire of Cyrus the Great. It lies at the crossroads of Europe and Asia, and has suffered numerous invasions: by Greeks, Mongols, and Arabs. Despite these invasions, Iran has retained a strong sense of national identity and cultural traditions. Although historically Zoroastrianism was the prevailing religion, Islam came to Iran at the time of Mohammad, and a Shi'ite version of Islam has become the dominant religion, covering 98% of the population.

At the turn of the twentieth century, Iran underwent a constitutional revolution, pressured by a new secularly educated middle class and sections of the clergy, which tried to limit the powers of the shahs (the monarchs) and to develop a framework for democratic participation, without much success. Reza Shah, who took the throne in 1925, wanted to modernize Iran along Western lines, including dress and other cultural patterns, and allowed the British to supervise the development of the oil industry.

His son, Mohammad Reza Shah, was forced into exile by a popular movement in the early 1950s, led by Mossadeq, that wanted both to nationalize the oil industry and to ensure the democratic process as guaranteed by the Constitution. The shah was returned through a coup in 1953, orchestrated by the British and Americans, and became a royal despot, controlling political and cultural life, imposing censorship, and organizing a secret police.

It was not until the 1970s that a real mass movement grew again against political repression, rapid Westernization, and lopsided economic development. This movement involved many sectors of the Iranian population, such as university professors and students, the professional middle class, traditional bazaar merchants, and the urban poor. Gradually, however, religious slogans overtook secular demands and Ayatollah Khomeini became the charismatic figure to bind such a mass movement together. The shah was overthrown in January 1979 and an Islamic Republic was established in February of that year.

Like many Third World countries, Iran's economy was dominated by a single export product—in its case, oil. Because of its rich oil deposits and its key strategic location, the United States and other Western powers, together with the Soviet Union, were very closely concerned with Iranian affairs, and had been throughout the twentieth century.

U.S. Television Coverage of Iran: 1970-1987

Iran enjoyed very good relations with the United States after the coup of 1953, received substantial military aid from the United States, and began to play a crucial role as a regional power in U.S. strategy in the Middle East. Thus Iran might have been expected to receive considerable media attention; but that was not the case. Until the end of the 1970s, Iran received a remarkably low level of news time, just over 5 minutes a year on weekly network newscasts, and the coverage was correspondingly narrow in perspective. The focus was either on the persona of the shah, exemplified in the pomp and splendor of his lavish coronation in 1971, or on oil, which fueled the rapid economic modernization the shah was trying to impose on Iran. The shah was portrayed as an insightful monarch, trying to drag his backward population into the twentieth century, and, in any brief attention to the repressive political system, the shah's dictatorship was justified as necessary for economic development to take place.

Almost no attention was paid to the living conditions of ordinary rural people, the bulk of Iran's population, whose conditions hardly improved—except for the addition of television run on generators!—and even declined, as self-sufficient agriculture gave way to international agribusiness. Almost no attention was paid to the fast and ungainly growth of Tehran, its traffic, pollution, and inflation, and the rapidly increasing divide between the conspicuous consumption of the urban rich and the lack of electricity, medical care, and schooling for the illiterate rural poor. Almost no attention was paid to human rights abuses, such as the absence of free speech, the impossibility of free political organization and debate, the control of trade unions, and the torture and murder of political opponents. Almost no attention was paid to the universities or to the plight of academics, intellectuals, artists, and writers unable to practice their professional and creative lives in the prevailing political conditions.

Why was this the case? Essentially, it was because U.S. government and corporations supported the shah, maintained only narrow channels of communication with Iranian government sources and supporters, and ignored the signs of looming political trouble even when they became pronounced. As late as December 1978, with millions of demonstrators on the streets of Iranian cities, President Carter was still calling the shah "an island of tranquility in a sea of troubles."

The media followed the lead of the political system. International news coverage is the area where political influence in news presentation is the strongest and where the adversary relationship between media and government and any notion of "fairness" are at their weakest (see also Chapter 5). In their coverage of international events, the news media are more likely to present the perspectives current in the State Department and/or National Security Council than any other interpretation, and the "national interest" operates as an important criterion in selecting, and as a crucial value in interpreting, events as news. This means that the question, How does this event affect the United States? blots out any independent attempt to understand the internal dynamics of a situation, the main actors, and their motivations.

Thus the U.S. media were blind to numerous signs of dissatisfaction and lacked the sources to explore these. Like the State Department and National Security Council, the media had not cultivated sources among crucial social sectors like bazaaris, university professors, or oil workers, who would have provided very different interpretations of what was happening in Iranian society. The narrow network of government sources created an illusion that the shah might be facing some temporary difficulties but enjoyed an essential stability, and they succeeded in so persuading and thus blinkering both U.S. politicians and the major mass media.

Alternate views and analyses of the popular movement were available, however. There were the reports of Amnesty International and PEN International; lengthy articles in *Le Monde* by Maxime Rodinson, long a student of the Middle East; articles in *MERIP Reports*, an alternative magazine on Middle East affairs; and reports on the World Service of the BBC, whose correspondent lived in Iran and had built up an extensive and varied network of contacts. Alternate sources of information and interpretation are almost always available to those who are interested enough and know where to look to find them. The media pay limited attention to mainstream academic journals such as *Foreign Policy* and *Foreign Affairs* but almost never examine radical periodicals or the reports of small research institutes, whose alternate perspectives thus rarely penetrate into mainstream media coverage.

A lack of independent analysis, the acceptance of prevailing government views on foreign policy issues, and the ignoring of other sources of information color international news coverage, but production and economic pressures compound the process. International news coverage is increasingly expensive and does not regularly attract enormous audiences. In fact, were it not for FCC stipulations about "social responsibility" and the necessity for a minimum level of such news coverage, it is possible that for financial reasons international news coverage would disappear from general broadcasting and become the province of specialized news channels such as CNN on cable television. Economic pressures and audience priorities have steadily depleted the number of correspondents based abroad. This has implications for the ability of a correspondent to cover an international issue adequately. A correspondent might cover a Latin American economic issue one week and then fly to the Middle East to cover a military story the next, preparing for the assignment by reading what competing media have written. The correspondent is unlikely to be fluent in the relevant languages and so will be totally reliant on interpreters; he or she will lack a network of sources built up over time and so will be reliant upon officials and public figures and their perspectives; he or she will not be familiar with operating in highly policed societies to build access to and trust with alternative sources.

The damaging implications of such limited coverage of Iran came when the popular revolutionary movement burgeoned rapidly in 1977-1978 into some of the biggest mass demonstrations in Iranian history. U.S.

government officials and major media were at a loss for explanation, hence their recourse to the easiest one, that the stubborn and backward Iranians were rebelling at being thrust into the twentieth century and that the protests were a reactionary movement against progress. U.S. media reports spoke of mobs running riot, as though there were no legitimate political reasons for action, while the shah was never referred to as a dictator or despot. Thus, far from objective reporting of "both sides," the media in the main adopted the political perspective of the shah, the U.S. proxy in the Gulf region and a major player in U.S. foreign policy.

But beyond the political blinkers manifested by the media lurks a deeper cultural mythology and ethnocentrism, displayed in the detail and nuance of the verbal and visual languages of television. Cultural mythologies can be found in all media systems and are often at their most pronounced in international news reporting; U.S. coverage of Iran is merely one vivid case of a very widespread phenomenon. News language, whether international or domestic, supplies subtle and not-so-subtle value-laden terms that constitute an interpretive framework for the audience. Thus it is important to examine media use of such terms as *terrorist, fanaticism,* and *crisis,* which can be contrasted with *freedom fighter, commitment,* and *conflict.* The terminology often derives from the prevailing political atlas, especially as articulated by the president of the day. Thus, for example, "terrorists" are always by definition tiny groups or individuals acting by themselves without popular support—never governments, whether Iranian, Israeli, or other.

In the Iran coverage, media language helped to stress cultural differences. Iranians were described in highly colored terms—"black-robed mullahs" (are we ever told of "black-robed bishops"?), the "turbaned" Khomeini, the "veiled" women—so that the indigenous cultural habits and religious practices were presented as bizarre, alien, and clearly reactionary, while the "modernizer" shah was portrayed as a strong ruler who had to be tough to develop such a backward people. The verbal code was supported by an even more effective visual code. It was common for references to Iran to be supported visually by pictures of either Royalist soldiers sporting weaponry or citizens marching in demonstrations, which served to suggest metonymically that the entire population was in a constant state of extreme political mobilization. Thus the ever-mobilized Iranian demonstrators in a news photograph came to stand for the whole population of Iran.

What was revealed in the coverage as the greatest omission of U.S. political and media analyses was any understanding of Shi'ism as the religious practice and cultural worldview of most Iranians. Nor was any sense provided of the loss of cultural identity precipitated by the pattern of modernization under the shah (see Chapter 19). Hence the very superficial labeling of Khomeini and the religious perspective that developed as "fanatical" and "reactionary," rather than as revolutionary and courageous—which the demonstrators doubtless were in their unarmed opposition to the shah and his huge secret police and army. The inability to see the Iranian revolution as a popular movement, uniting many different sectors of Iranian society mobilized for a number of political, economic, and cultural reasons is exemplified by the dominant media question in the postmortem on the Iranian revolution, which was "Who lost Iran?" The assumption was that Iran was a quasi-colony, a possession to be "lost" by the United States, rather than an independent nation in the midst of a painful and violent process of social change.

The Hostage Crisis

This narrow ethnocentrism was highlighted further in 1980 throughout the 444 days of the "hostage crisis," when the Iran story became the single most intensively covered story on all three television networks and in print media. Indeed, nightly coverage of this crisis, involving 53 American hostages, equaled and even surpassed average nightly coverage of the Vietnam War, which at one point involved over 500,000 U.S. troops. Watergate and presidential campaigns are the only other contenders for such intensive yet long-term focus. Media coverage, especially when the leading U.S. newscaster, Walter Cronkite, counted each day in his nightly newscast, become a collective public ritual.

It is important to ask why this was the case: Why did this particular event qualify for such massive media attention (Adams & Heyl, 1981)? There was the obvious "newsworthiness" of the event—a "crisis," a highly unusual set of events, relevant to a large audience—and there was a strong "human interest" angle. But there were other factors besides. It was an almost perfect televisual drama (Altheide, 1981), with all the necessary ingredients of a cultural and media myth. It offered a simple plot with two opposing sides, the "good guys" and "bad guys" readily visualized through images of blindfolded hostages and concerned families who were contrasted to the turbaned mullahs and angry crowds. It also directly involved the president of the United States, responsible both for U.S. policy vis-à-vis Iran and for allowing the fallen shah to enter the United States for medical treatment.

The coverage would undoubtedly have been very different if Iran had not permitted, rather than fostered, media attention. As it was, Iran somewhat effectively managed to use the media to speak directly to the American people, creating a new debate that "media diplomacy" was taking the place of more formal diplomatic channels, which had actually been broken. Within the "news as entertainment" mold the hostage crisis provided a political soap opera that occasioned collective national outrage, frustration, unity, nationalism, and, finally, with the safe return of the hostages, euphoria. The net effect was to create and maintain a public perception of a menacing world in which the United States must stand tough and where America's allies welcomed Reagan's reassertion of America's prestige.

So what is wrong with this coverage, you might ask? Isn't that what really happened? To answer this, we need to look not only at what was presented and how it was constructed, but also at what was *not* said. First, the hostages were immediately presented as innocent individual victims rather than as U.S. government officials in military or foreign service positions, who could be viewed as representatives of relations between the United States and the shah. Iranian accusations about espionage out of the embassy were not responded to. Similarly, little attention was paid to Iranian demands for the return of the shah and his wealth to Iran (in marked contrast to the critical attention given to demands for return of the wealth of Ferdinand and Imelda Marcos to the Philippines). The shah was generally portrayed as a sick and harassed man, and little attention was paid to the history of political repression and growing economic inequality under his rule. Again, there was little attention to the role of religion in Iran, although religious leaders and religious rhetoric were by then dominant, and little attempt was made to explain why Iranians followed Khomeini, who was presented as an aged fanatic.

Thus any historical and political reasons the Iranians had for their actions were ignored, and the entire chain of events was labeled as the work of fanatical and lawless Moslems. As Altheide (1981) summarizes, "The Iranian situation was reduced to one story—the freeing of the hostages—rather than coverage of its background and context, of the complexities of Iran, of alternative American policies, and of contemporary parochial politics in a world dominated by superpowers" (p. 155).

While many Americans do not understand why there was a revolution or why the hostages were taken, they did come to "know" that Iran was an "enemy" of the United States, a "terrorist" state filled with Moslem fanatics. Thus news helps to create and perpetuate cultural myths about other peoples, labeling friends and naming enemies (Keen, 1987). By denying legitimacy to any Iranian position, any basis for negotiation or solution was denied; foreign policymaking was and is stalled.

Middle East coverage in 1987-1988 was taken up with the Gulf War, the name given to the fight between Iran and Iraq, and the increasing American involvement in that situation. Although the lengthy war included the use of chemical weapons, massive missile attacks on cities, and international sales of often obsolete military hardware as well as military intelligence, it garnered only limited media attention. Media interest increased only when the United States sent its warships into the Persian Gulf in 1987. Again, most Americans would be hard-pressed to explain what the war was about, and what either side wanted, beyond some crude and unsympathetic labeling of the protagonists.

The point of this analysis is not to condone Iranian government actions or to support the Islamic Republic. The point is to show that the news media's basic desire for dramatic and visual stories with readily comprehensible plots and identifiable actors creates stereotypes, labels, and impressions that remain long after the particular event has ended. There is growing interest in how the media and our culture depict and define "others," and there is considerable evidence (Said, 1979, 1981) of the very limited, narrow, and stereotypical image of the Orient that runs through Western literature, analysis, and now news. The focus of this chapter has been the Iranian example, but a similar argument could be made about the media's coverage of many other foreign issues.

Conclusion

Such issues are relevant not only to U.S. media but to international news coverage in much of the world. There appears to be a worldwide skewing in the pattern of international news reporting, no doubt partly influenced by the structure of news materials available from the big international news agencies such as Associated Press and Reuters. Every national audience receives most news about its local region, so that Africans read most about Africa, Latin Americans about Latin America, and so on. A second tier of "consistent newsmakers," essentially North America and Europe, regularly receive considerable news media attention across most media systems, deemed newsworthy by dint of their power alone. The third tier is made up of the "current hot spots," those areas of the Third World that are currently enduring some kind of crisis. There remain important "areas of invisibility" in many media systems, usually the areas of the Third World where no major "crisis" is supposedly unfolding, and Eastern Europe, until *glasnost'* (Sreberny-Mohammadi, Nordenstreng, Stevenson, & Ugboajah, 1984). This old pattern meant very unequal news attention to different parts of the world, an apparent disinterestedness in more positive news of development or the slow processes of social change, and an inability of the news to explain most crises in relation to their causes.

If we are to be invited to see the Third World as "crisis ridden," then we also need to know why that is the case. If indeed there is some sense in which Third World nations are less politically or economically stable than those systems of the more developed world, that in itself demands explanation. Presumably the newness of many Third World nations, their only comparatively recent independence from the grip of colonialism, and the difficulties of creating a new national identity in societies generally divided along racial, ethnic, and religious lines are all relevant factors. We are rarely reminded that many of the nation-states of Europe are only just over 100 years old, that the unifications of Italy and Germany and the establishment of the United States were conflict-filled and violent processes, and that racial and ethnic issues are by no means solved in more industrially advanced countries, such as the United States or the Soviet Union. Nor is much background provided on how current competition and conflict among the superpowers are often played out on the battlefields of the Third World.

That superficiality and sensationalism suit the U.S. networks better than in-depth reporting and analysis is shown by a final example. There was considerable network coverage of an airplane hijacking in the summer of 1985 when a TWA plane was taken to Beirut and the "hijackers" organized press conferences; audience ratings increased and the networks garnered increased revenues. The ABC crew, which had been based in Lebanon for some time, had built up a network of contacts and information sources, and spoke Arabic. They were thus privileged to special interviews, arrived first at events, and generally provided the best coverage of the tense and complex set of events, which included historical and political analyses of the ongoing conflicts in Lebanon and the wider Middle East. The ABC crew, instead of being commended for their excellent coverage, were removed from Beirut and assigned to other duties, because the corporation felt they had become "too involved" with the situation they were covering.

So news values such as "crisis" reporting, production variables like the demand for good visuals, and a lack of time in network news to give more than the bare bones of factual detail mean that although a "story" like the Iranian revolution gets a lot of screen time, it is not told in a way that would allow the American audience to understand the causes behind and the implications of the events they view. Thus the audience is left with more vague impressions than information, with some stereotypic cultural notions of friends and enemies rather than a more critical awareness of the real issues and conflicts.

Negative media stereotypes may be pernicious at a domestic level, maintaining unequal relations of race and gender, and can become globally dangerous at an international level, fueling cross-national misunderstanding, mistrust, and conflict. As the ties between nations become more complex and multifaceted, and when many apparently domestic problems turn out to have international dimensions, an informed U.S. public opinion can help to create a rational, informed, and peaceful foreign policy. A less informed public opinion based on stereotypes and prejudices is more likely to support hostile relations, as with Vietnam, Iran, and Nicaragua, rather than peaceful coexistence.

Further Questions

(1) Construct a "news map" from a week of current news coverage. Does it fit the model presented here? What is different, and why?

(2) Identify critical, alternative news channels and compare their coverage of some international news issue with that of the television networks. What are the areas of omission and commission in both kinds of media?

(3) Compare U.S. news geography with the "worlds" of British, French, or other foreign news systems. Do we inhabit the same world?

22 Popular Music and Mass Culture

IAIN CHAMBERS

Music is a central aspect of all popular cultures, and has become the single most important force sustaining the medium of radio in the television era. It is a fascinating form of communication; it often operates without words and frequently manages to flow across cultural boundaries and delight the ears of people who do not understand one word of the lyrics. Yet at the same time musical tastes often reflect social background, from opera to "easy listening," from salsa to reggae.

The production of music is a heavily corporate activity, with huge record companies, major promotional budgets, and close links to radio and TV. Some commentators talk about the "packaging" of popular music. Chambers, using a personal, even "musical" style of writing, introduces us to some of the complicated patterns of influence that make up the development of popular music. Some of these flows of influence are international, crossing from the Caribbean and Afro-America to England and back again to the United States. Some of them could be defined as unauthorized borrowing and transformation (see Chapter 18), such as the conversion of African-American rhythm and blues of the 1940s and 1950s into smoother versions more "palatable" to White Americans.

This approach is an interesting contrast to the dismay of the Frankfurt school at U.S. popular culture in their own day. It casts a different perspective on the contradictory relations between popular music as an alternative medium of expression and the corporate packaging that profits from it, often takes the cutting edge from it, but also makes it widely available.

Understanding these flows of influence and adaptation not only helps us understand the development of musical culture, but also points us to similar processes within cultural development in general. Not only is culture a contested area of human interaction, but in this era it is never still. The reciprocal relation between culture and communication—one might speak of their virtual fusion—is both complex and absorbing.

A Short History of "Apache"

In 1960, an English instrumental group, the Shadows, released an instrumental called "Apache." The twangy Fender guitar sound of the bespectacled Hank B. Marvin (preceding the similar-sounding Ennio Morricone scores for the Clint Eastwood-Sergio Leone spaghetti westerns by some years) rose to number one in the British Top Ten. In 1974 the tune was again recorded, this time in the Caribbean by the Jamaican disco group the Incredible Bongo Band. It subsequently became popular in New York's Harlem, where its drummed rhythms were regularly folded into the cut-up sounds spun by the Jamaican DJ Kool Herc on his system (Hebdige, 1987). In 1981 the tune reappeared yet again, this time providing the base motif for a rap by the Sugarhill Gang. In the space of 21 years, "Apache," from its beginnings in a White pop group in England, had traveled, via Kingston and an early sound system in Harlem, to the hot summer streets of New York, there to emerge out of the speakers of a "boogie box" and provide the pulse for the latest in Black urban culture: hip-hop, break dancing, and rap.

It is perhaps worthwhile to reflect at length on the circuitous history of this particular sound. The music, recorded in a London recording studio as homage to an imaginary "America," ends up circulating in the most diverse cultural situations: the England of Cliff Richard, a mythologized Elvis Presley, and those greasy-haired, proletarian dandies known as "teddy boys"; disco music in the tropics (also the home of Bob Marley and the simmering "ridims" of reggae); the sound graffiti of New York's "wild style" in the early 1980s.

Rock and Romance: An Aesthetics of the Everyday

All this can be said to demonstrate the "plastic" potential of contemporary popular music: It is a product that can be bent into different shapes, whose surfaces can be readily inscribed by diverse emotions. The music comes to be less an isolated object—a record, a sound on the radio—and more an open-ended process that "sounds out" the potential of our circumstances, temporarily pushing back their immediate limits to reveal a further grasp of the possible. As sound and suggestion it is multidimensional. Set down on vinyl and tape, memorized on video, it provides an open archive of the sound track of our lives.

But there is little time for nostalgia here. A "hit," whether that means the Top Ten or a particular club selection, will last only some weeks, a fresh "sound" not much longer. In the velocity of use and consumption, sounds must constantly be recreated, rediscovered, recycled. In what is increasingly turning into a global soundscape, different sounds and musical ideas are raided, lifted from the past, and existing styles and genres increasingly drawn in, contaminated, and cross-indexed. Whether it is break dancing in Paris or soul music in Glasgow, the production of

Japanese techno-pop in Los Angeles or electric African music in New York, the metropolitan repertoire is literally "scratched" together in a continual mix.

The classic example of such cross-cultural "scratching" comes, appropriately enough, from the scratch and graffiti environment of New York's hip-hop culture in the aptly named "planet rock." Here we encounter different sounds—Kraftwerk, Ennio Morricone, Captain Sky, the Soul Sonic Force—electronically mixed together by Afrika Bambaata into a planetary collage. But the mixing, cut-up, "scratching" metaphor has potentially an altogether wider application: It can include the whole of rock music and contemporary popular—and not so popular—culture (Chambers, 1988).

So, if the history of "Apache" demonstrates, as its critics never tire of reminding us, the power of the mass media seemingly to penetrate every corner of the world, it also illustrates that it is ultimately a network that is also full of holes. It is a "leaky system," as Enzensberger (1970) described the media, never wholly susceptible to the decisions made by company executives, record producers, radio and television programmers, or musical journalists. In other words, alongside the millions of records and the millions of dollars of Madonna or Michael Jackson, there exist more diffuse and local connections. There, in the altogether less public world of cultural and sexual investments, stylistic and musical subcultural followings, changing dance-floor fashions, club hits, and minority, regional, and ethnic tastes, we find both the slippery semantics of contemporary rock music and the mobile sources of its perpetual revitalization.

In fact, the very history of rock music, and behind it, of the blues, R&B, and later soul and more recent urban Black sounds, is a history that emerged from the margins of the culture industry; from what, in the early 1950s, was considered the scandalous cultural miscegenation of the music of poor rural Whites and Blacks (hillbilly and R&B), in turn promoted by the promiscuous distribution of records and the cavalier attitudes of small radio stations anxious for novelty and local audiences. Elvis, and even less Little Richard or Chuck Berry, would not have been welcomed or even initially accepted by the self-elected arbiters of taste who usually made decisions for national radio, television, and record companies. It was local radio airplay and the success of these singers in the recently recognized youth market—the world of the "teenager"—that eventually convinced the diehards and fuddy-duddies of the adult, "square" world to give this music space. To put it simply, it was a particular audience, in Elvis's case around a local recording studio and radio station in Memphis, rather than major media corporations, that opened up such a possibility. While today its earnest tones seem to verge on parody, the obvious stakes in the game are all graphically recorded in Elvis's movie *Jailhouse Rock*. What then happened often turned out to be another story. There are individual victims. In Elvis's case, once RCA (and Colonel Parker) got their hands on his career, his subsequent music was largely imprisoned within an increasingly dull, play-safe, corporation logic. However, the story fundamentally remains open.

Those margins, today invariably caricatured and amplified through detailed (often grainy "realist" black-and-white) retro-chic imagery and soft-focus nostalgia (the Levi's jeans ads in recent years, for example), have continued to provide the source of the everyday, and overwhelmingly masculine, romance of rock music. Moving, usually to an up-tempo beat, from Elvis Presley to Prince, from the promise of "life, joy, kicks, darkness, music" (as Jack Kerouac said in *On the Road*) to the lonely, T-shirted driver of the burnt-out American dream (for example, Bruce Springsteen), popular cultures both Black and White, usually public and male, have set out to conquer symbolically the signs, sounds, and streets of their present. *West Side Story*, as Dick Hebdige (1987, p. 111) has noted, is the archetypal video of rock culture. In this scenario even the figures of Madonna and Michael Jackson represent more ambiguous and potentially more "open" situations than that of mere commercial manipulation. The sounds and signs represented by the stars slide *into* and *across* the everyday surfaces of experience, making innumerable points of contact, some obvious, others altogether unsuspected. But to explain the seductive and simultaneously ubiquitous sense of the music, and to understand better why the hit-making machinery is ultimately more complex and unpredictable than previously presumed, we need now to extend our horizon.

Popular Culture: Who's Zoomin' Who?

In 1964, the German philosopher and critic Herbert Marcuse, who was then living in the United States, published an influential and radical critique of contemporary society titled *One-Dimensional Man*. The idea of reality being flattened out and reduced to a single dimension by consumerism, monopoly corporations, and the capitalist mode of production has, like many other radical ideas, today become part of an extensive consensus (this argument is developed by Kellner in the context of advertising in Chapter 17). Here the answer to the question, Who makes the hits? is straightforward. It is the record companies who sign the groups, organize production and markets, and manufacture the stars to ensure a suitable commercial return on their investment. They are the "hit makers." The music, suitably adorned with the latest novelty and image, is merely the sound track of a consolatory consumerism, as satisfactory and as significant as absentmindedly switching on the radio or lighting up a cigarette. These metaphors regarding consumer culture are those of Marcuse's one-time Frankfurt school colleague Theodor Adorno (1959), for while Marcuse later changed his mind about certain aspects of mass culture, particularly the liberating aspects of rock music, it has been Adorno's ferocious criticism of popular music and the "culture industry" (heavily tinged by the direct experiences of Nazi Germany) that has fundamentally contributed to the formation of a common sense among critical scholars on the question of mass culture over the past 40 years.

What is striking in all this is the rapid consensus formed between radical and conservative critics in their agreed verdict of the "masses" as being mere dupes of a programmed consumerism. The consumers are passive victims, mindless bearers of useless goods; seduced by advertising to follow market forces blindly. The traditional intellectual may well look to "innate genius," the arts and the opera house, and the radical to the grass-roots expressions of the "folk," but both see eye to eye in their condemnation of "mass culture" for being a contradiction in terms, for being a vulgar exhibition in a commercialized sham, a gaudy exhibition of nonculture.

This idea of consumerism as an aberration, as an unnatural growth on society's "real" needs and a "genuine" life-style, of tastes being manipulated and "hits" manufactured, carries us into the altogether wider critique of modern mass culture as a whole. Our critical response to rock music, how we understand its sense and place in our lives and the contemporary world—who, in other words, lies behind the "hits"—is therefore bound up with how we approach and appreciate these wider realities.

I do not want to suggest that commercial manipulation and attempts to implant, construct, and channel cultural tastes and desires do not go on. They do. But, and I would insist that this is worth emphasizing, it turns out to be a far more open, or leakier, system than most critics of mass culture are willing to admit. If contemporary culture, its commercial organization and procedures, can be thought of as a net that attempts to capture and direct our tastes and habits, it is also, like any net, full of holes. These holes represent other possibilities that, from the point of view of the record or media industry, are unplanned and unexpected. Elvis, disco, punk, hip-hop, and salsa music were not planned in a corporate boardroom. That people have sought to transform such events into a lucrative money-go-round is undeniable. But I would suggest that this fact alone does not exhaust the cultural sense of the music or the particular connections and meanings formed around it.

To understand this argument a little better we shall take one further step. The next section presents a discussion of the importance of "authenticity" in popular music.

Two Versions of "Authenticity": The "Original" Cut and the "Dub" Mix

Buried deep inside the criticisms and condemnation of "mass culture" is an underlying belief in the idea of "authenticity." Use of the word *authenticity* implies that there exists the possibility of a *direct* relationship between our actions and our ideas, that the former express something that is essentially immediate and natural. It is against this particular measure of the "truth" that modern culture is found to be wanting, to be fundamentally "false," and therefore "unnatural." Continually mediated by the mass media, commerce, and consumerism, modern culture represents the "inauthentic" world of an indirect and "falsified" existence. But this second world, for all its faults and contradictions, is ultimately the contemporary social one that we know. And, when all is said and done, it is in this second world, through and across its everyday textures, that we also come to experience and explain our circumstances. It is the only world that we inhabit and can know.

In linking the idea of authenticity to culture there is a clear attempt to impose already-established standards. The categories are, in an important sense, presocial. Rather than experiment with the potential of our present and elaborate there a sense of aesthetics and authenticity, most critics of mass culture have sought to identify and explain it according to preconceived values that are apparently immune to the contaminating flux of the immediate world. It leaves us with a rather abstract sense of culture, and one that is unable (and fundamentally unwilling) to connect to the textures and possibilities of many of its contemporary forms. Against the idea of culture as a timeless abstraction we can propose the perspective of a living, changing, historical construction. We might suggest that there is nothing "natural" or eternal about culture. It is a social artifact. In fact, the history of developments in popular music has continually demonstrated both that it is mutable and that as a historical product or construction it is more open-ended, and therefore more complicated, than its critics presume. It has already been briefly noted how, supported by record player, jukebox, transistor radio, and ghetto blaster, a record like "Apache" acquired a flexible, polyphonic presence across time and in different cultures. These connections were neither instigated nor necessarily foreseen by the record industry. In fact, the particular trajectory of this piece of music was plotted by local operators—a disco band, a DJ, a rap crew looking for a fresh rhythm, a diverse sound, a new twist, a new possibility in the musical spiral.

It is the *reproducible* quality of the music that keeps this possibility alive. The centrality of the idea of reproduction, so crucial to both the production and aesthetics of rock music and contemporary culture in general, was first elaborated in an important essay published in 1936 by the German critic Walter Benjamin. In *The Work of Art in the Age of Mechanical Reproduction* Benjamin (1936/1973), studying the impact of the new mass media, especially cinema, on the perception of art, argued that artistic "aura," in which the "presence of the original [painting] is the prerequisite to the concept of authenticity," was waning (p. 222).

There were two strands to this notion of aura. One was religious: Medieval pictures were almost all of religious scenes, and were meant to communicate a sacred awe to the public. The second was economic: A painting grew in market price, so it became vital to owners to be sure of possessing the original. Only the original had the real message, the aura. Yet with twentieth-century reproductions of paintings, and the decline of religion, this whole mystique of the original aura was called into question. The process of reproduction, the industrialization of aesthetic production through thousands, even millions, of identical art prints, photographs, records, film negatives, tapes, cassettes, and simultaneous television programs explodes such an idea of authenticity and its idea of the "original." "To ask for the 'authentic' print makes no sense" (Benjamin, 1936/1973, p. 226). For Benjamin, this was positive; it took the communication of important ideas out of the claws of religion and the wealthy, and democratized it.

If it is ultimately impossible to return to a preindustrial, prereproductive, world of art, the suggestion that emerges from Benjamin's discussion is that it is necessary to seek an alternative and concrete sense of authenticity in the present conditions of cultural production. This can be illustrated with a contemporary example. In the recent novel *White Noise*, by American writer Don DeLillo (1985), the narrator advances the hypothesis, after a trip to visit a historical barn during which he is eventually frustrated by the crowds photographing it, that the more a sound, style, object, or image is reproduced, quoted, sampled, and photographed, the more an "aura" accumulates around it and hence the more "authentic" it becomes. The situation has been turned inside out, as it were; it is no longer the unrepeatable rite of the original gesture—the grainy texture of Van Gogh's brushwork or Caruso's voice—but the secular and social quantity of subsequent reproductions (in prints or records in the cases of Van Gogh and Caruso) that now reproduces an aura. (I myself have not read this novel. I am recycling a description I came across in an Italian newspaper, using it to further "authenticate" my "own" discourse—although proprietary rights, like DJ cut-ups and sound sampling, become pretty weak at this point.) *Authentic*, in this sense, no longer refers back to a particular point of "origin" or "tradition," but rather toward the "truth" of a particular set of historical circumstances; the song, the painting, the photograph, the novel is not "authentic" to an "original" but to the complex and shifting possibilities of its (re-)production in the present-day world.

Going back to rock music, what does this mean? Well, if tastes remain unpredictable, the technology employed in its production is ultimately even more difficult to monitor. Pop music is a child of this technology. Formed inside the historical developments of record, radio, recording studios, and recording tape, its cultural possibilities have consistently been involved in exploring the continually changing context of sound reproduction. It is a context that, while involving vast sums of money and national and transnational corporations, also involves elusive sounds and an increasingly accessible technology—both highly exposed to unsuspected uses and developments. The most basic tools of reproduction—the recording turntable and microphone—can unexpectedly become musical instruments in their own right in the dub, scratch, cut-up, and mix environments of contemporary urban Black music.

The blank cassette, tape recorder, and Walkman, not to mention the imminent growth in individuals sampling the soundscape and creating digitized sound archives via the personal computer, have, as Frith (1987) has argued, "given fans a new means of control over their sounds; they can compile LPs and radio shows for themselves, use a Walkman to carry their soundscapes around with them. . . . Records are being replaced not by tapes as such but by other leisure activities; music is being used differently and in different, more flexible forms" (p. 73). Frith shows how the recording—and culture—industry is continually being remade and reorganized under the impact of social and cultural forces that are clearly beyond the threshold of the industry's immediate control and manipulation.

Thus the potentially "open" nature of the music, the fact that it can acquire a "sense" in different historical contexts, is therefore fundamentally due to different cultural explorations of the increasingly flexible technology of reproduction. In the mid-1950s this meant Elvis Presley working on his "sound" in a tiny recording studio in Memphis; 35 years later it can range from a multidubbed Michael Jackson record to a talkover artist, with simply a microphone in hand, inventing rhymes to a reggae beat at an all-night party in Brixton, London.

In this common network we finally discover the heterogeneity of the possible: Hispanic culture, salsa, zoot suits, and Ritchie Valens ("La Bamba"); London Punjabi pop and hip-hop culture (Pathi, 1986); urban dandies, including teddy boys, mods, and casuals, styling-up for street fashion; Italian disco mixed into Chicago dance music, "a reminder that House is neither precious about its 'black' identity nor parochial in its taste" as Cosgrove (1986) notes; as well as less public, less observed, domestic rhythms and female identities. Here, then, in the complex investment of social and cultural energies, where the sounds, signs, and sensations of music, gender, class, ethnicity, subcultures, and styles become shared metropolitan constructs, coded cultural stratagems for producing a temporary sense of delight, a pleasurable appropriation of circumstances, ultimately lies the dynamic enigma of the hit-making machinery. It is here where the hits finally have their home.

A Final Comment

It is the 1990s, not 1956. Elvis, Buddy Holly, Sam Cooke, and Jackie Wilson are dead; the Beatles' LPs have all been re-released as compact discs. The retro-recycling fashion of so much of today's music tells the story. In the TV, radio, film, and advertising worlds of "light entertainment" and "popular music" it is rock that lies at the heart of a musical consensus; its presence is everywhere, from advertising jingles to film scores—it is now a *hegemonic* genre. This concept of hegemony was first developed by the Italian communist leader Antonio Gramsci while in a fascist jail in the 1930s (see Gramsci, 1971). Rather than appeal to the simple idea of ideological domination, economic impositions, or co-optation, it seeks to suggest the complex process whereby power is exercised by consensus so that particular processes, relationships, ideas, and realities come to be accepted in every walk of life—in other words, are taken for granted, become part of our common sense, pass for "normal," and are therefore rarely challenged (see Chapter 1).

There is certainly no longer a struggle over establishing rock's commercial, aesthetic, and cultural legitimacy. But, of course, it remains only one version of the possible. Inside the spread of rock's increasingly global syntax, heterogeneous dialects, rhythms, and accents continue their struggle to emerge. In a shared electronic network, diverse cultural proposals—ethnic, sexual, regional, gendered—continue to invest in the reproduction of sounds their desires, hopes, loves; in other words, their sense of the "authentic" and the possible. Culture may well be made within these historical limits, but it does continue to be made.

Further Questions

(1) Trace out some historical and cultural maps of current musical styles. How easy is it to identify the sources of cross-fertilization in music?

(2) Advertising is a powerful appropriator of music (for example, Nike running shoes used the Beatles' "Revolution" in their television commercials). Examine current television advertising to identify the sources of musical themes. How does this fit the model of "authenticity" suggested in this chapter?

(3) How do musical classifications by radio stations and commercial retailers affect public access to popular culture? Are there other structures that serve to differentiate and divide the listening audience?

23 Cinema and Communication

RON MOTTRAM

Curiously enough, many mass media courses omit the consideration of cinema. Yet, at least from the era of Charlie Chaplin and Buster Keaton, film has been a mass medium par excellence in the United States, and similarly was actively developed on a mass level in the Soviet Union from soon after the 1917 revolution. Television effectively imported the cinema into the home. For the first TV audiences, it was like having their own personal theaters. The picture was not so well defined, the sound was not so clear, but these were acceptable reductions in quality for not having to travel or pay, since most people did not realize that what they paid for goods included the cost of TV advertising and of continuous programing on an increasing number of channels.

Nonetheless, the cinema continued to exert its attraction. Many independent broadcast television and cable stations serve up a basic diet of older or newer films, and situation comedies and serials are only an adaptation of forms drawn from film, theater, and popular literature.

Traditionally, cinema studies specialists have developed their own terminology, founded on the enthronement of film as one of the arts and their frequent contempt for "mass" media. This is yet another example of the enduring "high culture/low culture" division that O'Connor criticizes in Chapter 1. The consequence is that film specialists have focused almost entirely on the film as a text, dissecting the film as a work of art using artistic standards. Sometimes the film's director would be analyzed, as a novelist or a poet might be in literature, but quite omitting the creative contributions of camera operators, sound engineers, and the small army of specialists needed to make a major film. The context of the film as a communication has been effectively ruled out as unimportant, thus obliterating the audience, the culture, politics, and economics.

Mottram does not jettison analysis of the traditional "cinema studies" kind. His first area for comment is on film as art. But to that he adds two further dimensions, namely, the film industry and the language of film. The film "industry," an expression derived from the Frankfurt school's term "culture industry," points to the collective nature of film production, including its business dimension and the huge Wall Street investment that a major "spectacular" requires. (A classic study of Hollywood by Powdermaker, 1960, termed it "the dream factory.")

The language of cinema is a more difficult concept, since it involves learning the often difficult terminology of semiotics (see Chapter 1). Briefly, semiotics is a mode of communication analysis that focuses upon signs and how they convey meaning. Signs could be anything from red roses given by an admirer, to children's toys that express gender roles (soldiers for boys, dolls for girls), to trendy clothes, to grim, daunting prison architecture. For the semiotician, our culture is drenched with signs, and the task is to try to unpick the detailed mechanisms that enable them to convey meaning or meanings to us. A film is a complex assemblage of signs. It is constructed partly according to the traditions of producing meaning via signs in the cinema (or film "language") and partly—in the case of an innovative film—by experimenting with new signs or by producing variations on older signs. Thus understanding that film communicates via particular ways of deploying signs, different from the ways a theatrical play or a piece of music deploys signs, is an important element in understanding how film works as a mass medium.

Some Basic Considerations

By 1885, when the Lumiere brothers gave their first exhibition of projected motion pictures in Paris, the camera was a fixed fact of modern culture. But their presentation was something significantly different: The photographs moved, time passed; reality had somehow transferred itself to the screen. The Lumieres called their apparatus the *cinematograph*, from the Greek words *kinematos* (motion) and *graphein* (to write). "To write in motion" was both a scientific definition, stemming from the nature of the apparatus itself, and a linguistic analogy, comparing the use of the apparatus to the act of writing. Today, three terms predominate in English: film, cinema, and movie. All refer to the same phenomenon but have, for some critics, different connotations.

Naming is the first step in creating a theory, a system by which the nature of the thing can be described. The great French critic Andre Bazin (1967) asked the basic question that was implied in the first name given the medium and its machines and has been at the heart of all discussion of the aesthetics and uses of film: What is cinema? Closely linked to this question is the problem of how the medium functions in the complex cultural context of which it is part. From the very beginning, film has been a tool of scientific investigation, an entertainment, an investment, a means of documentation, a channel of communication, a shaper of opinion, a determiner of taste, and an artistic object. In fact, it can be all these at one time.

There are three principal functions all films serve: the artistic, the industrial, and the communicative. As art, some films have narrative structures, that is, they present a series of causally connected events that help construct a story. Others are nonnarrative, organizing their material for tasks that are informational, rhetorical, or purely aesthetic. As industry, films are items that are part of the economic production of a society and must be considered in relation to other products. As communication, they are an important part of the system by which individuals and groups send and receive messages.

The artistic function (Bordwell & Thompson, 1986) concerns the nature and organization of the formal elements of the medium: composition, color, sound, montage (the order of the separate shots), lighting, decor, camera placement and movement, performance, and the ordering of space and time. Film as art demands that the medium be considered in relation to painting, sculpture, photography, dance, theater, literature, and music. For any individual film to be art, one might say that its artistic function must be dominant, despite the other functions that may also be present.

The exact nature of a film's industrial function is that films are products of human labor and are commodities to be consumed. In capitalist systems profit is the basic motive that operates in the commercial film industry, and the kind of films that can be made are determined largely by their potential for making a profit. Organizations and individuals who invest in films do so for the same reasons they invest in any other commercial venture. In socialist systems with state control of the film industry, films are normally made if they are considered to fulfill an acceptable social role. Of course, in both capitalist and socialist systems, films are made that do not conform neatly to these generalizations. Independent cinema, for example, often avant-garde in tendency, is essentially not profit producing or is only marginally so. Even within the official cinemas of both systems there is some room for films that are nonconforming in style, subject, or political statement. In American cinema, films such as Stan Brakhage's *Anticipation of the Night* (1958) and Michael Snow's *Wavelength* (1967) were made almost entirely independent of commercial considerations, while Warren Beatty's *Reds*, a very expensive product of the capitalist film industry, is unorthodox in style and surprisingly sympathetic to the American communist movement and the Russian Revolution.

Perhaps the most powerful function of film is the communicative (Lotman, 1976; Wollen, 1976). Since its inception, film has been used to reach large numbers of people with a message that was meant to influence their actions and thinking. No less a shaper of mass opinion than Lenin, the great intellectual leader of the Russian Revolution, is reputed to have said: "For us, film is the most important art." This belief found practical expression in an extraordinary body of films made in the Soviet Union in the decade immediately following the revolution. During the political ferment of those years, film led the way in spreading the message of the new social order and in bringing that vast country, made up of so many diverse nationalities, to a revolutionary consciousness.

Other countries also have understood this power and have used film to advance their own cultural and political interests, especially in time of war. In the work of Soviet directors Eisenstein (*Strike, Battleship Potemkin, October*), Pudovkin (*Mother, The End of St. Petersburg, Storm over Asia*), Dovzhenko (*Arsenal, Earth*), and Vertov (*A Sixth of the World, Man with a Movie Camera*), and Nazi filmmakers Riefenstahl (*Triumph of the Will, Olympia*) and Hippler (*The Eternal Jew*), political cinema reached its zenith of expressive power between the world wars. With World War II came a flowering of political cinema in the United States, well illustrated by Frank Capra's series *Why We Fight*. American social documentaries of the 1930s (*The River, The Plow that Broke the Plains, The Land*) also served specific political goals, linked, for the most part, with the programs of Roosevelt's New Deal.

Film is used by institutions other than government to provide information or spread ideas. Business, educational, and philanthropic organizations often use this medium for public relations, to sell products, raise money, and influence voting choices. Even artists and intellectuals send messages that are meant to enlighten, convince, entertain, or stimulate in some direction the audiences for which they are intended. The communications couched in artistic and entertainment forms are often the most effective and the most subtle in their influences. Finally, all films are cultural and social documents that help communicate the times in which they were made even if they were never intended to do so.

These three functions of film are interdependent and embedded in a total context of culture, economics, and technology. Films reflect the cultural codes of the society in which they are produced, which often makes it difficult for individuals to understand fully the films of another country or era. They also are the products of different economic systems with different aims, creating different relationships with audiences. The rapidly changing technologies of the medium help determine the types of films that are made by providing new possibilities of expression for the filmmaker and by making possible the creation of new audience tastes and expectations. The introduction of sound, the advent of color, and the integration of video and computer systems, for example, have all profoundly affected what has been done with film and what audiences will accept.

Whether a film is thought of as an individual work of art, an industrial product, or a message in a mass communications system, the problem arises of how it is understood by the audience. To help in understanding this process, it is useful to consider some simple distinctions between personal and mass communications. The first and most obvious difference is that the sender of the message in film is communicating with a mass rather than with an individual. Second, the medium of communication comes between the sender and the receiver of the message. Third, in a personal communication a particular language is the carrier of the information. Each intervening medium of mass communication, including film, also has a language. In order to understand the communication, therefore, one must understand the language.

To call film a language is not a new idea: The concept dates back at least 50 years and was given its first extensive treatment by the Russian filmmaker Sergei Eisenstein (1969). Since natural language is such a powerful communicating system, it readily suggests itself as a model for examining other media of communication. However, not all the characteristics of natural language can be found in film. For example, there is no real equivalent of past- or future-tense verbs. Film exists in the present tense, even though the ideas of past and future can be created by means of flashback and flashforward. However, the experience of these sequences occurs in the present as much as the sequences set in the present. In other words, scenes of the past or future are only understood intellectually as representing the past or future.

There are other differences between natural language and film language. Every language is made up of two parts: the language system, that is, the rules of grammar and syntax and the lexicon of meanings; and speech, the individual use of the system. It is clear that in film the second of these occurs: There are individual films, individual uses of the "language." Is there, however, a general language of film? Are there rules that govern how the various elements of the film language can be put together? Are there rules that assign fixed meanings to camera positions, lighting techniques, shot transitions, and editing strategies? Despite attempts to find such meanings, there do not appear to be any. If film is a language, then, it must be a language without a language system; it must be more like speech, inventing itself as it goes along.

Yet if film has a self-inventing language, how can films be intelligible to large groups of people? Film may not actually have a set of rules that govern it, but it does have three characteristics that function as if they were rules: (a) Film material is organized according to certain conventions that have developed over the years and that have become so common that audiences expect them even if they are not often consciously aware of them; (b) photographic images look so much like reality that they can be understood in similar terms: and (c) films incorporate other languages and languagelike systems, such as natural language itself, gesture, and dress code, that add preestablished meanings to the film. These three characteristics add a stability that allows films to be understood without actually having fixed rules for their construction.

The complex of conventions, photographic reality, and cultural codes as a substitute for the language system permits a consideration of film at least as a quasi-language. It also demands that filmic images not be thought of as the equivalent of reality, no matter how much they may seem to be. To confuse them with reality obscures the fact that the image is always a substitute or a sign for reality.

Like all signs, the image signs that make up film have two parts: the signifier and the signified. The signifier, the physical part of the sign, is the specific form of the image itself, its expression. What is signified is the conceptual content, what is referred to by the image. Unlike the word signs that make up natural language, the signs of film are visual. They have a natural and inherent link between signifier and signified rather than the essentially arbitrary link between the letters of a word and its meaning (which could be totally different in another language). It is this natural relationship between signifier and signified that causes the film image to be confused in viewers' minds with the reality it represents. The word *apple*, for instance, refers to a concept of a type of fruit, while a photograph of an apple refers to a specific piece of real fruit. This difference points to both the strength and the weakness of the film sign (Wollen, 1976). As a concrete representer of the material world, film has an almost elemental power, but its capacity to communicate ideas is severely limited because in order to do so it must overcome its extreme concreteness.

However, film does have the ability to go beyond this to become a subtle and effective means of communication. Film images do not have to restrict themselves to literal "denotative" meanings, but can be associative, suggestive, or even symbolic, that is, "connotative." These images may actually achieve a degree of conventionality that would allow them to have the precision of words. However, the more loaded with meaning film images become, the more possible and necessary it becomes to "read" films, to learn to decode their language signs in an informed and alert manner. This must be done, of course, within the overall cultural, economic, and political context that made the film possible in the first place.

A Very Brief History of Film in Europe and the United States

Film was born of an unholy alliance between art and commerce, with invention and scientific curiosity as midwife. In the United States it was the brainchild of the Thomas Edison organization, another scientific wonder from the Wizard of Menlo Park; in France it came from the Lumiere brothers, manufacturers of photographic equipment (Allen & Gomery, 1985). In both cases it was a product to be manufactured and marketed. Yet the films the Lumieres produced to go along with their machine, mostly short and straightforward documents of the people and events of the time, had an artistic merit and purity of expression that cannot be denied. The films of the Edison Company, though more compromised by the demands of popular entertainment and by Edison's attempt to monopolize the early film industry, also contributed to the aesthetic development of the medium.

The history of the audience in relation to these events has not been widely researched. It is known that the first audiences could not always make a distinction between the lifelike moving images and life itself while they were involved in the experience of viewing. Naively, they reacted to film of a train pulling into a station as if it might run over them. Many of the early narratives apparently presented problems of understanding the plot and character relationships, and, in response, film exhibitors provided lecturers who helped explain the action as it unfolded on the screen. Within a short time, however, there was a large and experienced audience for the new medium and a vigorous international trade in motion pictures. American audiences, for example, could regularly and routinely see films from France, Italy, Denmark, Germany, and Great Britain.

As the number and types of films increased, so did their complexity. In France the former theater manager and stage magician Georges Melies began to produce elaborate fantasies as early as the turn of the century. Using techniques of theatrical scene design and construction, he turned established literary works, such as Cinderella and Jules Verne's *A Trip to the Moon,* into highly successful "features" running to almost 15 minutes. Other producers went in a more realistic direction, constructing sets that attempted to imitate the physical look of the world and often taking their cameras outdoors. By the beginning of World War I, audience tastes had become more limited, and the expressive Melies fantasies had essentially given way to naturalistically rendered melodramas.

The best representative of the trend toward and development of realistic dramas in the period before World War I is the American director D. W. Griffith, best known in some circles for his spectacle *The Birth of a Nation.* From his first film, *The Adventures of Dollie,* through such works as *The Lonely Villa, A Corner in Wheat, The Lonedale Operator, The Battle, The Painted Lady, A Girl and Her Trust,* and *The Musketeers of Pig Alley,* he developed a complex narrative organization, a sophisticated editing technique, and an essentially naturalistic acting style. He also made extensive use of real locations and stories drawn from history and current events.

Within 15 years of the first projected motion pictures, film had established itself as a significant industry in both Europe and the United States. There was expansion of both domestic and foreign markets, the rise of the feature-length film, the development of the star system, and the growing dominance of U.S. film in the world industry, encouraged by the disruption of European production caused by World War I.

Between 1910 and 1920, U.S. film production began to shift from the East Coast to the West. European filmmaking struggled to survive amid war and profound political change. By 1920 the last of the powerful monarchies had fallen. Germany entered a period of economic disaster and a difficult experiment with democratic processes. Russia swept away the monarchy and set out on a path of socialist revolution. Film, however, flourished in both nations during the 1920s. In Germany, defeat, economic hard times, and new political freedoms combined to transform both audiences and filmmakers as they sought to come to terms with a changing culture. In the Soviet Union a new generation of filmmakers came forward consciously to create a cinema free of conventional bourgeois ideas. Both national cinemas evolved new forms to respond to their new social and historical conditions.

American cinema meanwhile was building the industrial and artistic foundation for "Hollywood." The shift to the West Coast was completed, and the studio system was established. The great producing organizations that were to dominate U.S. filmmaking for the next 40 years and that were to become brand names to general audiences around the world laid the foundations of their power and influence. They also made the transition to sound. This change had to be financed by the New York banks and brokerage houses, and it forever shifted the economic decision making of the industry into the hands of business. But this change also made the financial foundation of the industry more solid and helped establish the dominance of Hollywood.

Film-going became a habit that was fed by a constant stream of popularly oriented genres featuring highly publicized stars. The consistency of these films, both in style and subject, could be counted on: For the most part they were reassuring to audiences at a time when the potential alternative to reassurance was the growth of social protest against the Depression conditions of the 1930s. A consistent set of narrative procedures developed that included chronological development of the plot, single point of view of the action, psychological motivation of the characters that essentially divorced them from any real social context, naturalistic acting, realistic rendering of sets and costumes, traditional dramatic structure, and endings that resolved all the issues raised in the course of the story. These are characteristics drawn primarily from the nineteenth-century novel; they present an image of a world that is stable and easily understandable, but they are not very illuminating of the world in which the audience actually lived. This style, which has since been labeled "classic," was the dominant mode in all countries during the period. Its effectiveness is attested to by the fact that much of contemporary filmmaking still uses the same techniques for the same purposes.

In 1939 the nations of the world once again plunged into global conflict, taking film with them. The need for war propaganda had the additional effect of giving new life to documentary uses of film. As the war was covered on film, a new appreciation for the photographing of reality emerged, and this impulse carried over to the postwar period. The first significant manifestation occurred in Italy with the rise in 1945 of what became known as *neorealism*. A generation of Italian filmmakers, fed up with the falsity of studio productions during the fascist years, took to the streets with their cameras and constructed dramas around the everyday problems of the working class. Socially committed, open to new narrative forms, and willing to confront both audiences and the political structure, these filmmakers demanded that film no longer evade the truth of the times and pacify audiences in the process.

Even the Hollywood industry, the most commercially entrenched of all, received a dose of this new realism in the appearance of what is known as *film noir*, tough, urban-oriented films that were not afraid to reveal some of the nastier aspects of American life in their fictional explorations of crime, psychological aberration, political corruption, and national psychosis. During the 1950s there also arose a strong, independent, avant-garde cinema and, for a short time, an attempt to create a viable semicommercial alternative to Hollywood that critic and filmmaker Jonas Mekas has dubbed the "New York school of filmmaking."

Following in the aesthetic wake of the Italian neorealists, a new generation of French critics turned filmmakers set out in the late 1950s to reinvent the cinema. Although drawing on the past, they made films that swept away most of the conventions of the classic cinema and that pointed in a new direction that younger filmmakers throughout the Western world were eager to follow. Although this *new wave*, which included Resnais, Truffaut, and Godard, encountered critical hostility, audience resistance, and industry rejection, it made a surprisingly rapid transition to a degree of success. Ultimately, the innovations of the new wave became the backbone of modern European cinema.

Following the French example, new film movements emerged in England, Italy, Germany, Poland, Czechoslovakia, Yugoslavia, and Hungary. A renewal had also begun in the Soviet Union in the mid-1950s, shortly after the death of Stalin, and continued into the 1960s. In the United States the most interesting work was done completely outside the commercial cinema by independent filmmakers operating through their own distribution cooperatives and centered primarily in New York and San Francisco. The films of this modern cinema offered a viewing experience quite different from that of the classic cinema. The audience was not encouraged to identify with the characters, nor was it supposed to accept the film as if it were life itself rather than a representation of life. The films demanded an acknowledgment that the audience was engaged in an interaction with a film and that through this interaction the world was being explored. The necessary relationship between film and viewer was not a passive but an active one, and the world described was not the closed, simple one in which all conflicts and problems could be resolved by the end of the last reel. The new cinema was—and is—open-ended, complex, and often unsettling.

Further Questions

(1) Film industries have developed around the world. Find out about the history of cinema in Third World nations such as Brazil, Egypt, and India; explore film in Japan and Australia, too. What are the similarities and differences in the development of film in these countries compared with the processes described in this chapter?

(2) Examine the current film listings in your area. What is the most prevalent genre of film? How many of the films available to you are foreign? How many directors are women or members of ethnic minorities?

(3) How have television and video had an impact on the film industry?

Select Filmography

The films included here are examples of the genres of films discussed in the text. They are among the best known and most readily available in the United States. The names of the films' directors follow the titles.

- Lumiere Brothers (1895-1896)
  Workers Leaving the Lumiere Factory
  Arrival of Express at Lyons
  The Falling Wall
- The Edison Company
  The Life of an American Fireman (1903), Edwin S. Porter
- Early European Cinema
  Pioneer Films (1895-1896), Max Skladanowsky, Germany
  A Trip to the Moon (1902), George Melies, France
  Rescued by Rover (1905), Cecil Hepworth, Britain
  Don Juan's Wedding (1909), Heinrich Bolten-Baeckers, Germany
  Quo Vadis? (1912), Enrico Guazzoni, Italy
- German Films of the 1920s
  The Cabinet of Dr. Caligari (1919), Robert Weine
  Nosferatu (1922), F. W. Murnau
- Soviet Films of the 1920s
  Battleship Potemkin (1925), Sergei Eisenstein
  Mother (1926), Vsevolod Pudovkin
  Man with a Movie Camera (1929), Dziga Vertov
- Hollywood Films of the 1920s-1930s
  The General (1927), Buster Keaton
  It Happened One Night (1934), Frank Capra
  Stagecoach (1939), John Ford
- Italian Neorealism
  Rome—Open City (1945), Roberto Rossellini
  Bicycle Thieves (1948), Vittorio DeSica
- American Film Noir
  The Maltese Falcon (1941), John Huston
  Kiss Me Deadly (1955), Robert Aldrich
- American Avant-Garde of the 1950s-1960s
  The Wonder Ring (1955), Stan Brakhage

A Movie (1958), Bruce Conner
Scorpio Rising (1963), Kenneth Anger

- New York School of Filmmaking
  The Quiet One (1949), Sydney Meyers
  On the Bowery (1956), Lionel Rogosin
  Guns of the Trees (1961), Jonas Mekas
- French New Wave
  Hiroshima Mon Amour (1958), Alain Resnais
  The Four Hundred Blows (1959), Francois Truffaut
  Breathless (1959), Jean-Luc Godard

24 Myths In and About Television

SARI THOMAS

In this chapter, Thomas sets out to puncture a series of popular propositions about television and U.S. culture. Some of these are widely accepted definitions of the function of television; others are commonly expressed judgments of the messages of television.

To begin with, she attacks the notion that television is simply entertainment and therefore of no particular consequence one way or the other. Against that view, she argues that TV is a powerful educational force, a significant source of orientation. She further proposes that television does not communicate commercial messages in advertisements alone, but that its entire output is saturated by economically oriented messages in favor of the status quo—dominated, it may not need observing, by the corporate establishment. This first section of her argument should be read in close conjunction with Chapters 10 and 11, on media audiences, for it presents a third angle of vision on the difficult problems of interpreting audience responses to media, and of relating media content to the political economy.

In the second part of her argument, Thomas proposes that far from TV being antibusiness, as some have claimed, for example, in its portrayal of corrupt businessmen in popular serials such as Dallas or Dynasty, the medium is actually a potent support for certain myths that sustain the business order. Her argument here supports Kellner's analysis of advertising and consumerism (Chapter 17), with the difference that she locates consumerist pressures squarely within the entertainment/education diet of television, not simply in the advertisements.

Beyond the myths of consumer culture, however, are other myths of social mobility, that all individuals can advance as far as they want up the economic ladder if they work hard. This "American dream" is a source of continuing inspiration to many who migrate here. Simultaneously, it is a message to the majority still at the foot of the ladder that they have not exercised sufficient ingenuity to make use of the opportunities presented them, that they are lacking in drive. In reality, people achieve very little upward mobility compared to their parents, with the exception of a few sports or entertainment stars, and even these stars' careers are usually lush for only a few years. But the notion that the dream can become real nourishes positive feelings about the nature of the society and self-blame if, despite your efforts, you do not achieve it. The dream is a source of political and social stability.

The Myths About Television

For decades, critics have bemoaned the state of commercial U.S. television. In general, they say that programming is low-level, unimaginative pabulum. They argue that it serves only two purposes: to entertain a mindless audience and to create a marketing forum through advertisements in which to sell products and services to that mindless mass. It is assumed that these two functions, in combination, are the key mechanisms by which the sellers—network, corporation, and agency executives—get rich.

Although everyone might not hold such a harsh view of television, the two assumptions underlying this view are pretty much taken for granted by most members of our society. These assumptions can be spelled out as follows: (a) Television is an "entertainment medium," and (b) television's primary mechanism for economically supporting the established elite is through "audience commoditization." Audiences are thought to be "commoditized" through a multistep process: First, they are provided with "free entertainment" (the programming) and, next, research is conducted to find out what programs are watched by whom. Advertisers are then sold time slots within appropriate entertainment periods, where they, in turn, sell products and services to targeted audiences. Thus TV viewers become packaged commodities purchased by advertisers (Smythe, 1981).

In this chapter I will refer to these two assumptions stated above as the primary myths *about* television. The term *myth* is used here to represent any belief in a culture that is so ingrained in and pervasive among members of the society that, for the most part, what the belief asserts goes without question. In other words, the accuracy of the information contained in a myth is not, on an everyday level, very important. A myth is accepted *as a given*. Thus these two interrelated assumptions are understood as "the way things are" about television. Clearly, if you are a network executive, advertising executive, or sponsor, you will probably approve of the system as a positive example of capitalism at work. If you are a parent, educator, or political activist, you might be antagonized by the "mindless entertainment," the corporate greed you think is behind it, or both. Nevertheless, whether you approve or disapprove of the system on these terms, you also ultimately accept the above-mentioned myths about television: that it is mindless entertainment that supports capitalism by packaging audiences.

This chapter represents an attempt to clean the slate somewhat. Rather than argue for or against the system represented in the two myths, I will question the validity of the myths themselves. Is TV primarily an "entertainment" system? Is television's major contribution to capitalist economy made primarily through selling audiences to advertisers and, in turn, products to audiences?

The Myth About Entertainment

Whatever "entertainment" is—apparently the same phenomenon that induces people eagerly to cringe during *The Exorcist*, weep while reading *Love Story*, or cheer while boxers inflict brain damage on each other—television seemingly does provide it. But, when people watch TV, is "entertainment" the only or even the major result of the viewing experience? Let us assume, instead, that TV provides the primary adult-*educational* experience.

Statistics show that sleeping is the only activity in which the average American indulges more than television viewing (let alone combined media use). It is ironic that these two most popular activities—sleeping and watching TV—are commonly viewed as being similar in nature and effect. That is, we are led to believe that at least two-thirds of the average American day is spent in one form or another of vegetation. While it is probably true that the average person *believes* that most viewing time is spent in the pursuit of entertainment, relaxation, or escape, perhaps there is actually a lot more going on during those thousands upon thousands of viewing hours.

Whatever their conscious motivation, when people watch television, they watch stories (drama or news) showing how "things" work. Television especially provides a window on many matters with which most of us have relatively little or no real-life experience: How police or lawyers operate; what life is like in New York, Miami, Shanghai; what rich people do at the dinner table; and thousands of other pieces of information come to us almost exclusively from television and, to a lesser extent, other popular media. When we are confronted with this information, it is very unlikely that we regard the information as "education"; we would hardly equate TV viewing with listening to a lecture in a classroom. Yet the two experiences may not be that far apart. In fact, the "educational" material coming from television stories probably has more to do with the business of ordinary life—values and ideas involved in our everyday judgments—than does the educational material in most formal classroom situations. Moreover, we may be more receptive to TV information than that from classroom lectures precisely because we do not view TV stories as education. Indeed, it is unlikely that we would acknowledge or even recognize the source of much TV-gained information because its entrance into our store of knowledge is so subtle. This is why so much mass communication research on the effects of TV is very problematic; researchers often interview people in the mistaken assumption that they can articulate the *full* meaning of their viewing experiences.

This picture of "TV as education" is not a popular one. When the "educational" component of television is introduced into the debate, it typically appears in only three contexts: discussions of children, violent crime, and concerned or curious citizens. That is to say, "learning" from television is predicted for innocents, sociopaths, and those adults deliberately choosing to be informed through news, public affairs, and documentaries. In terms of the third group, the fact that we persist in drawing a line between so-called information and entertainment programming attests to this assessed division in function; that is, we assume that "entertainment" programming is *not* informative.

In the 1950s and 1960s, when communication as a discipline was being established, the "hypodermic" model was popular (for more about this and other models, see Chapter 10). It represented a "strong effects" theory, claiming that the mass media directly and uniformly inject passive audiences with their messages. However, as studies grew, researchers documented the fact that all people did not get all their information directly from the mass media. Rather, specific individuals would learn things from the media and pass that information on to other people who had not shared the original media experience, in what became known as the "two-step flow" (Katz & Lazarsfeld, 1955). Thus, because some information coming from the media is filtered and indirect, it seemed important to examine not only what messages the media were sending, but also what people were doing with mediated information after it was disseminated. Researchers found that different people chose to attend to different media, demonstrated preferences for different things within the media, and, overall, showed varied patterns of interaction with the media. These findings led to "uses and gratifications" theory (Blumler & Katz, 1974), a much weaker media effects model, arguing that individuals employ and derive benefits from the media differentially. The history of mass communication research shows swings between "strong" and "weak" effects models, but, overall, those theories arguing against powerful effects and for weaker ones have been the most popular among both scholars and the general public.

Let us begin to interpret the relationship between effects theory and "entertainment." The weaker effects models present us with some puzzling evidence. Although researchers have accumulated considerable data showing that different people indeed do interact differently with the mass media, it is premature—in fact a leap of logic—to conclude that people walk away from the mass media with unique, individualized knowledge. Two findings need to be examined. One is that people do attend differently to the media, identify with and like different things, and interpret the meaning of certain media events differently. But the second major finding is that there are a very limited number of preferences, identifications, and, most important, interpretations that arise regardless of how many individual "interpreters" have been studied. Essentially, the few variations in media interaction that do occur can generally be linked to broad sociodemographic differences rather than to unique individual psychological distinctions.

Scientific evidence alone cannot explain the popularity of "weak effects" theories that stress differences in individual psychology. However, the popularity of such theories may lie in their ability to be translated into the politics of autonomous individualism (Elliot, 1974; Messaris, 1977). Models that stress how each person uses the mass media to fulfill his or her own needs, like the uses and gratifications approach, are highly compatible with the meritocratic philosophy of American capitalism, which holds that an individual's choices and actions will supposedly yield his or her status in the overall social structure. In general, in the United States we like theories that stress our individual differences and emphasize the control we have over our own destinies.

Widespread belief in meaningful uniqueness and self-control helps keep the economic system going, but it doesn't necessarily mean that the belief is correct. We should also see that the myth of television "entertainment" serves this larger orientation very well. It is a myth that allows us to believe that we are in control of what we learn and know.

The Myth About Where the "Business" of Television Is Located

From a psychological perspective it is generally believed that people use television to fulfill their own individual needs and that these needs lie largely within the realm of entertainment and relaxation. From an economic perspective, it is generally believed that while this source of entertainment is ostensibly free, its hidden costs are great, charging for that "free entertainment" in the everyday marketplace. Both these perspectives, the psychological and the economic, separate "entertainment" from some other commodity. From a psychological view, the distinction is between "entertainment" and "information," while in terms of economics, "entertainment" is made separate from "advertising." Economic interpretations typically relegate the "business" part of television to advertising (see Chapter 17), and it is rare that the "entertainment" *itself* is understood to be commercially effective, and a major component in the economics of both television and the larger world. More liberal economic interpretations acknowledge that the content of the "free lunch" (the "entertainment" programming) tends to reinforce the status quo so that it complements the audience-commoditization process. However, this complementariness is traditionally viewed as indirect and vague with regard to the creation of bourgeois consumerism and social-order maintenance.

It would be intellectually pointless to discount the importance of advertising and corporate structure in television's contribution to capitalism. The argument here is twofold: First, "cultural reproduction"—the continuing attempt to reproduce the existing society—is the primary industry of all human societies. All social institutions, including the mass media industry, are but subsidiary firms for the "parent corporation" of culture production. What this means is that popular creations (whether material or symbolic) will generally reinforce the rules and values of the overall system. Put another way, we must look for the possibility that all major cultural artifacts and activities contribute, at different levels and in different ways, to the coordination and sustenance of the established system.

Second, the mythology in television programming reinforces American corporate structure as powerfully as, if not more powerfully than, the more obvious mechanisms of packaging audiences and selling commodities. While television commercials largely sell specific products to a commoditized audience, television "entertainment" serves, in part, to sell the audience on the *general process* of capitalism. Therefore, the teaching of this general process (of earning, buying, and selling) is a *prerequisite* of audience commoditization and an essential contribution to the preservation of American capitalism.

To speak of the mythology *in* U.S. television is to speak of many things. This is not to suggest that the views and values represented on TV are various and conflicting, but rather that, like Proteus, they take many mutually reinforcing forms. Given the discussion thus far, there are two sets of myths *in* television "entertainment" that are most relevant: myths of labor and consumption, and myths of social mobility. The first set includes direct lessons about commercial issues, and the second provides the broader, stage-setting material for life in a commercialized system. Taken together, this mythology is instrumental in creating economic sensibilities that neatly serve the interests of the corporate elite and its reigning social structure.

Labor and Consumption in Television

Theberge (1981) argues that businessmen on American television come in one of three categories: crooks, con men, or clowns. He asserts that "business" is represented negatively to the American viewing public, but there are three problems with this conclusion. First, it can be argued that negative images of businesspeople on TV can be confused with negative images of *rich* businesspeople and that it is wealth, not business per se, that is stigmatized. (Negative images of wealth are discussed below.) Second, it is also important to suggest that television's portrayal of businesspeople represents idiosyncratic images of individuals rather than a systemic characterization of business. That is to say, bad businesspeople on TV are typically shown to be uniformly bad people. J. R. Ewing of *Dallas*, for example, is not simply an evil businessman, but an evil person in all facets of his life, including business. Of course, it would be telling if TV businesspeople were malicious and unlawful at work while loving and honest family members, friends, and lovers, but this is not the case—at least not on TV. Thus it is difficult, again, to claim that business in particular is under indictment. Third, the specific TV portrayals of businesspeople are not necessarily the only, or the most important, means by which social messages about labor and consumption are conveyed. If we turn our attention to the seemingly mundane filler of TV drama—those trivial or background events that permeate "entertainment" programming—we see a number of things happening that very much contradict the supposedly negative images of business, commercial transaction, and so forth. These events may be, at least partially, accounted for in the nine myths described below.

Myth 1: The Inconsequence and Invisibility of Everyday Spending

The world of U.S. television is pretty moneyless. Of course, characters engage in activities that require money in real life, but on television, the monetary transactions are rarely included, and when they are, payment is typically a fleeting and unconscious gesture. Every night on television dozens of scenes are played out in restaurants, nightclubs, taxicabs, and so forth, but the fact that these things cost money invariably becomes an issue only when comedy or crime is involved. A man, for example, may do some serious gulping (accompanied by an uproarious laugh track) when he discovers his date has chosen a restaurant where he can barely afford a salad.

The neglect of everyday spending on TV would probably be dismissed by writers as necessary editing of irrelevant material; however, since there are many other trivial events dramatized, one might question the function of this particular omission. It might be interpreted that viewers are being shown the pointlessness of seriously considering what is part and parcel of everyday costs. Like the spending of TV characters, our spending should remain unconscious, invisible, and inconsequential. If spending is not invisible, it is probably a laughing matter.

Myth 2: Excess Money Is to Be Spent

The invisibility of spending on TV refers to money and credit-card handling, the normal, everyday transactions requiring payment that are typically overlooked in the television world. Thus the act that for many is problematic, if not painful, is often ignored. However, that money is spent by television characters—especially regular folk—is often implied.

What we often see on television are the results of spending—the products bought, the consumerism. Moreover, except for special instances that will be detailed below, the purchase of products usually occurs in dramatic contexts where a working- or middle-class character accumulates some extra cash. For example, when Roxanne, a secretary on *L.A. Law*, makes a sizable sum on stock deals, she is immediately seen sporting new, expensive clothes and a new car. Indeed, when the money, obtained through insider-trading tips, is confiscated, we find that she is dead broke. In a made-for-TV movie, a previously poor writer hired at high salary by a scandal tabloid immediately exchanges her new (and projected) bank balance for luxurious home and fur; an alternative, such as depositing her money in a college account for her young son, is not a choice written into the script. In almost all cases of this type, if and when the character runs short of funds, the plot text usually addresses this problem as new and totally separate from the character's failure to save.

In general, what we see on television are otherwise normal characters living to the ends of, or beyond, their means. Security and savings do not seem to be a part of most fictional game plans. When characters do save, it is typically with a future purchase in mind. In fact, the portrayal of the relationship between children/teenagers and money is especially poignant in this regard. When younger characters need funds, it is invariably shown that their savings are close to nonexistent. For instance, almost every show featuring children has produced one or more episodes where the children must jointly collect their funds to accomplish something important, such as replacing a broken household valuable before the parents return from a trip. Typically, the "wealthiest" of the children can contribute something on the order of $1.06. Moreover, on most shows featuring children and teens, grandmother's birthday check is usually committed to a future purchase before it even arrives. I do not mean to suggest that one should expect children (or adults) to have huge sums of cash on hand, but rather that the television message suggests total and constant moneylessness among the working and middle classes as a standard state, as well as the acceptability of credit debt.

Myth 3: The Desire for Excess Accumulation of Capital as Deviance

No discussion of a "money is to be spent" theme would be complete without the mention of that myth's corollary: There is something wrong with those individuals bent upon accumulation rather than expenditure. On television, this moral bears most heavily on those characters who are currently without considerable wealth (although Western culture also tells comparable stories in relation to the materially endowed, e.g., stories of Scrooge and Midas). Moreover, television speaks to other problems endemic to wealth, as will be discussed later.

For the present, this myth is most typically manifested in comedy programs featuring a character whose deep interest in making and accumulating money is supposed to appear as obsessive and, thus, becomes the butt of jokes. In recent years, *Family Ties*'s Alex Keaton is a clear incarnation of this myth. Alex is hardworking, intelligent, and reasonably moral in his choices, yet his profound interest in accumulating capital is portrayed as both strange and comic.

Myth 4: Celebration Is a Material Event

A lot of the time, TV characters have special reasons to be happy. There are classic causes of celebration (birthdays, anniversaries, and so on) and less classic ones (solving a crime case, reconciling interpersonal differences, exceptionally nice weather). When TV characters celebrate anything, the revelry inevitably involves spending money, so that celebration becomes operationally defined as a commercial event. In fact, characters' happiness with something seems to be directly proportional to the money that will be spent in its honor. If the celebration involves reconciliation—"making it up" to someone—then the character's sincerity can be measured by how much the "making up" will cost. As the first myth would suggest, celebration spending is typically done unflinchingly. For example, without careful deliberation, *L.A. Law*'s Ann Kelsey purchased a tremendously expensive wristwatch for her fiance, with whom she had been fighting. As might be expected, such grandiose gestures are typically shown to achieve the desired effect; on television, this is one context in which good characters can "be bought." We are shown an equation where spending equals love and respect.

Myth 5: Spending Defeats Depression

There may be a gender-coded corollary to the "celebration as material event" myth: Spending is antidepressive. While male characters usually turn to their work when saddened (a relationship discussed below), depressed TV women often go shopping. Although television may not be the primary forum promulgating the notion that commercial consumption helps beat the blues, many incidents in fictional programming certainly reinforce this line of action. In an episode of *Cagney & Lacey*, for instance, Mary Beth Lacey, in a context of feeling inadequate, chooses to buy herself a "smart" hat to help alleviate her insecurities.

Myth 6: More Consumption Yields Better Treatment

In TV contexts where spending is expected (restaurants, shops, hotels, and the like), those characters (presumably) spending a great deal receive excellent treatment. This is not to say that those who refrain from spending a lot are invariably mistreated or that the excellent treatment afforded big spenders is never given begrudgingly or with scorn. The staff in the series *Hotel*, for example, is incredibly pleasant to all guests. Of course, just staying at this luxury-class establishment would usually involve considerable expenditure. The point here is that on TV, spending demands at least superficial respect.

In a society characterized by its size and impersonality, television shows offer what appears to be a certain route for acquiring respect. Rich gangsters and corporate potentates may ultimately be shown to suffer in other ways, but one thing they usually do not suffer is lack of eager subordinates. Moreover, while it may not always be the case that TV's small tippers, cheapskates, and nonspenders are harassed, it is not uncommon to find them reviled or the butt of jokes. Disrespect (e.g., haughty insolence from a sales clerk) meets TV's nonspenders often enough to create a standard of expectation. Thus viewers are shown that "good" treatment might be directly proportional to the money they give.

Myth 7: Cheap Is Vulgar

While homespun philosophy may argue that the simple things in life are what count, and while TV characters may even mouth such sentiments, the portrayal of vulgarity is, more often than not, characterized by cheapness in deed or demeanor. An episode of *Dynasty*, for example, showed the then semivillainous Sammi-Jo eating corn dogs (and other fast food) in an impromptu "picnic" in the Carrington mansion. While the tone of such a scene could have been created as endearing or charming, this one was not. Sammi-Jo was characterized as vulgar; the "ladies" of the show dine at elegantly set tables with respectable food.

Ironically, television does sometimes indicate the vulgarity of spending, but it is important to realize that such dramatizations are usually confined to spending by the rich. It may be shown, for example, when a typically evil or buffoonish rich character flaunts his or her wealth through lavish tipping. Good rich characters (the few there are) are rarely portrayed as ostentatious; these may be the only characters for whom the "less is more" doctrine is shown to work positively. When lavishness is enacted by the middle and working classes on television, these acts are generally shown as kind and generous behavior.

The myths articulated above are omnipresent foliage in the scenery of U.S. programming. Myths concerning work and consumption also abound in typical stories. To recite each fully would require a much longer text, but the two myths that follow should adequately suggest the pattern to which the general ideology subscribes.

Myth 8: Satisfaction Must Be Earned

This myth mutates in a variety of social contexts. It may emerge, for example, as "Idle wealth breeds evil" or "Easy money is dangerous," but, collectively, such myths proclaim that hard work is the only key to understanding and appreciating the meaning and marvel of money. Thus *Hill Street Blues*, for example, showed us a young Black police officer winning substantial money in a lottery and then encountering many more (serious) problems than those existing in his life prior to this "run of luck." Similarly, the boy who works every day after school earning money to restore a dilapidated car is probably going to beat the rich kid (with his fancy foreign wheels) in the finale's big race. The philosophy also extends to nonmaterial issues. A TV romance plagued with difficulties in its early stages has better chances for meaningful survival than one that seems smooth sailing from the start. Actually, such "nonmaterial" parables can be interpreted as metaphors for the fundamental money-earning lesson. In any case, that satisfaction must be *earned* teaches workers to appreciate the current fruits of their labors and to feel assured that they have properly paved the way to appreciate riches they might accumulate. However, since it is all too possible that, in real life, labor will largely beget more labor, another lesson typically accompanies the one teaching that "satisfaction must be earned," as the next myth shows.

Myth 9: Work Is Inherently Satisfying (Especially Real Work)

When one examines the major differences between "good" and "bad" characters on TV, proportionally a higher number of "good" characters hold legitimate jobs. Moreover, of all working characters, the "good" ones are more likely to find satisfaction in their professions beyond the acquisition of money and power. The contrast between *Falcon Crest*'s Angela Channing (a not nice character who is forever scheming and taking part in new power plays in the wine business) and Chase Gioberti (a decent character who is continually concerned about his vineyard) exemplifies this division. It is, of course, eminently important to teach "labor as its own reward" to a real world of inequitable compensation and false meritocracy. Indeed, this lesson is most powerfully conveyed by portraying already-wealthy characters driven to experience the reality of their ownership, as shown, for instance, in *Dynasty*'s very rich Dex Dexter, clad in work clothes and hard hat, laying oil pipeline. From the other side, several television plots per season revolve around a middle- or working-class character willingly forgoing "promotion" or job advancement involving more money but less "honest" work. Both Steven Keaton of *Family Ties* and Kate of *Kate & Allie* have, for example, rejected job advancement for the sake of honorable considerations. In fact, basically good characters are often moved to give away ill-gotten riches (as when the very poor janitor in *Frank's Place* anonymously leaves thousands of criminally obtained dollars at an orphanage and thankfully resumes his post as janitor). These types of portrayals suggest that the value of work is not ultimately to be measured in the material payment received.

The above nine myths are among the many specific lessons on television encouraging the precise kind of work and spending habits benefiting the U.S. economic structure as it is currently calibrated. The myths of social mobility that follow are geared to a broader understanding and rationalization of the worker's place within that system.

Social Mobility in Television

In the United States, wealth and power are not evenly distributed, yet the relatively impoverished masses work very hard keeping the system afloat. Three interrelated messages regularly dramatized in U.S. television serve to make this system of imbalanced conditions acceptable to those who might otherwise find cause to object.

Myth 1: There's Room at the Top

This first message emerges in television's distorted portrayal of the socioeconomic structure—that is, real-life statistics are distorted. Content-analysis research has borne out time and time again that the world of television is dominated much more by middle- to upper-class people than is American real life. Poorer people are simply not represented too often. Similarly, the occupations of television characters tend to lean far more to the professional, if not glamorous, side of the employment spectrum, whereas the masses of everyday workers who are needed for the overall real-life system are not proportionally portrayed.

While such "misrepresentations" might be "explained away" in a variety of ways (Thomas, 1986), it can be argued that the relatively heavy-viewing American public is being taught indirectly that wealth is more plentiful than it really is. High school seniors might be more inclined to apply to Harvard if they believe there are 5,000 openings rather than 800. In the maintenance of the social order, widespread belief in a roomier upper echelon might also suggest that the possibilities of upward social mobility are good. This sort of message, then, sets the stage for social mobility myth 2.

Myth 2: Anyone Can Achieve

Another theme popular in U.S. television is that, given the wide-open arena suggested in social mobility myth 1, anyone has a decent chance of accomplishing upward social mobility. Considering the continuing characters of U.S. TV drama, the majority of those who are wealthy or "better off" are portrayed as not having been born that way. Some have worked their way up (e.g., George Jefferson, Jonathan Hart, the Huxtables), some have married money (e.g., Krystle Carrington), and some have vastly compounded a smaller fortune (e.g., Blake Carrington). TV news and interview programming similarly recounts such stories by chronicling events such as Sylvester Stallone's or Roseanne Barr's climb to fame or the awarding of grand sums to formerly poor lottery winners.

In all, television may give us the decided impression that upward social mobility is quite feasible; however, this is not where television's ideological "story" ends. The ending is not always a happy one, and characters most definitely fall. The third social mobility myth makes the equation complete by indicating where trouble may be found.

Myth 3: It's Not So Great at the Top

As described, television suggests that there is a wide-open area for upward mobility to which everyone has a decent chance to ascend. These myths provide hope for the future, but they are not necessarily sufficient for the present. A message that can temper immediate hostility is dramatized in the third myth—that it's not so great at the top. This message may be translated in several ways, such as "Money doesn't buy happiness," "You can live on love," and "Wealth/power corrupts."

In daytime-television serials, the poorer families usually display a loving harmony that is in stark contrast to the interpersonal conflicts found within the very wealthy families. During prime time, misery and constant trauma await the Ewings of *Dallas*, the Carringtons of *Dynasty*, and the like, but the Waltons, the Ingallses, and others of their ilk are essentially at peace (Thomas & Callahan, 1982). Indeed, one of the reasons that nighttime serials may concentrate on the rich is that serialization requires "running" problems—serious complications—that can continue from episode to episode. Such problems on television are largely confined to the wealthy. Poorer or middle-class people are usually placed in contexts (often comedic) in which their problems can be resolved in half an hour.

Made-for-TV movies also keep this myth alive by presenting many sentimental stories of poor people surviving in loving harmony. Similarly, many scenarios—particularly in docudramas—show characters who cannot find happiness in supposed wealth and success (e.g., variations on the "poor little rich girl" theme). Often these movies take viewers into the world of glamour, power, and wealth, and portray that terrain as insidiously treacherous. It seems that the only happy wealthy characters on TV are those who live below their means while doing good deeds (e.g., *Diff'rent Strokes*'s Mr. Drummond or Commissioner McMillan of *McMillan and Wife*) and/or those who enrich their lives by risking death weekly (e.g., Jonathan and Jennifer Hart).

Again, the message in question is not limited to TV fiction, but appears quite regularly in news and documentaries. Sonny Von Bülow is still technically alive in a coma, but this high-society matron's sad destruction—allegedly by the hands of her baron husband—received coverage hundreds of times more powerful and lengthy than that given to the numerous other victims of violent crime. In recent years, the murder of the wealthy "Scarsdale Diet doctor," Herman Tarnower, by the headmistress of a socialite school was one of the few stories that competed with the Von Bülow saga. Barbara Walters interviewed all the relevant players; the network news took viewers into the very exclusive Newport, Rhode Island, and Scarsdale, New York, estates to query neighbors and show the "trouble in paradise." Clearly, it is not that we are taught especially to mourn Sonny Von Bülow or Herman Tarnower or people like them; rather, the lesson is that wealth has an unseemly side, no matter how atypical the object lesson may be.

Collectively, what the three myths of social mobility provide is a rationalization for lives that are less than glamorous, powerful, or wealthy. While viewers are taught to have hope if wealth and its concomitants are what they really desire, they are simultaneously instructed to be grateful for the prices they don't have to pay.

A Final Note

In recent years, much attention has been paid to the problems involved with pay television and VCRs. What is happening, it is asked, to the "business of television" when viewers can watch for hours without being confronted with advertisements or when they can electronically "zap" the commercials? Clearly, if the concern is with the selling of specific products and/or the welfare of specific companies, such questions are pertinent. However, to the extent the concern is with a general decommercialized broadcasting system—a concern with the possible elimination of bourgeois consumerism—then such worries would seem to be unfounded. American "entertainment" television, with or without commercials, contains a very rich economic lesson plan, as has been detailed in the list of myths presented here.

In a sense, the myths *about* television—that it is mindless entertainment, the only persuasive moments of which occur in advertisements and candidate debates—conspire with the myths *in* television. Capitalism is sold in our living rooms on a daily basis. However, in a society wary of the hard sell, the most persuasive educational forum is probably one that seemingly offers only relaxation and choice.

Further Questions

(1) Are some groups in the television audience—such as men or women, recent immigrants or long-term-citizens—more likely than others to accept the myths discussed in this chapter?

(2) What, if any, experiences have you had that contradict these myths? How do people deal with these potential contradictions between real life and televisual reality?

(3) Are these myths stable over time? Does current programming reflect any new or alternative myths?

25 Sport and the Spectacle

MICHAEL REAL

With Real's analysis of sport and media in the United States, we reach the final insights of this volume—last, but not least, for sports are of passionate concern to vast numbers of people, and are followed these days more through television than in personal attendance. Along with music, sport engages the great majority of the public. Understanding mass communication without attention to sports coverage is practically impossible. Many popular newspapers, whose readership is often despised by elitist cultural critics, are bought for the sports coverage much more than for the news pages, which are hardly glanced at most days.

Real analyzes the appeal of media sports and of sport in popular culture overall in terms of certain myths. His use of the term myth is different from that of Sari Thomas in Chapter 24. Thomas uses it to denote a popular belief based on weak or nonexistent foundations in reality. Real uses the term to denote the power of certain beliefs in our imagination and daily lives. Thomas uses myth in the sense of an unfounded viewpoint; Real uses it in the sense of a culturally established belief. Both use the word to pinpoint a strong formative influence.

Real distinguishes between conventional cultural analyses of sport, which simply see it as a good training in how to behave properly in life in general, and critical approaches that stress the conflict expressed in sport, whether between the management and the players or in the endorsement of violent behavior or through the near exclusion of women. Most of his argument, however, is devoted to exploring the excitement and pleasure that sport offers its audiences. Real proposes that, whether in the process of identifying with a player or a team or in the enjoyment of suspense and tension ("liminality"), competitive sport is a mixed form of communication, like so many others commented upon in this volume. It offers release at the same time that it provides confirmation about the status quo, a fantasy of achievement against the odds as well as an acknowledgment of the conflicts built into everyday social relations.

"The thrill of victory—the agony of defeat." Few experiences in life are sweeter than the taste of a well-earned victory in a sporting event. Even vicarious participation in a great victory can bring incredible exhilaration.

Through the mass media, millions and even billions of viewers, listeners, and readers are brought immediately into the experience of a great sports performance. The emotional power of the gymnastic perfection of an Olga Korbut, Nadia Comenici, or Mary Lou Retton, especially as enhanced by slow-motion video and musical sound track, can take your breath away or bring tears to your eyes. The fans of the New York "Miracle Mets" in 1969, through a decade of intense suffering with baseball's most miserable team, knew what it meant to feel a triumph was "earned." The feelings of sheer joy, of intensity, of hope, of energy and control, of discipline, of expressiveness can carry immense power, even to a spectator at home. Of course, the more negative feelings of defeat, of having a victory snatched away, of performing miserably under pressure of rejection, and of dejection are also part of such sports.

What has critical communication research taught us of the central meaning and value of these experiences of a sports event received through the media of mass communication? What are some of the contending positions on how media and sport relate to the broader society? What kind of critical concepts does cultural studies bring to the study of the sports media phenomenon? How does "mythic analysis" take us inside the social experiences and internal meaning of these ritual experiences of sport spectacles on media? To revert to the style of our subject matter, "Stay tuned, sports fans, for answers to these and other exciting questions right after these announcements."

Contending Positions: Critical Versus Conventional

Cultural studies analysis generally regards the media experience as a text to be analyzed, whether a Shakespearean stage production, an episode of *The Cosby Show,* or a major league ball game. The cultural studies approach is an approach to media analysis that examines ideological signs and cultural structure found in the media text. Media scholars Stuart Hall (1980) and James Carey (1989) illustrate how cultural studies can draw effectively on other intellectual sources concerned with human culture. This approach is eclectic in sources but becomes specific in the topics and sites it examines.

When a cultural studies approach is used to examine the topic of sports and media, it takes the subject apart as if it were an exotic and previously unknown tribal ritual in a foreign land. Rich in myth and ritual, the sports media wonderland provides a revealing text for cultural studies analysis. Myths and rituals take the dominant tendencies in a culture and crystallize them into a popular and repeatable form through which members of the culture can celebrate their common values. Michael Jordan mythically represents super-hero flight and achievement; an NBA game ritually celebrates such ideals and more.

In contrast to the cultural studies approach, conventional theory approaches the issue of sports and media primarily in terms of quantifiable data. The basic questions of conventional theory concern phenomena, especially behavior changes, that are physically measurable and individually located. How many individuals viewed one television program? Is the cost of 30 seconds of advertising time justified by resulting changes in consumer behavior? What were the payments from networks to teams? These are more administrative (Lazarsfeld, 1941) and conventional (Smythe, 1981) styles of media research. This mainstream tradition of American behavioral science and ideology has generally dominated media studies in the United States for the past half century. Conventional research asks these smaller questions of more limited significance and answers them very precisely. Critical research, such as cultural studies analysis, asks larger questions, answerable only through careful use of data, observation, reasoning, analysis, and criticism. Why do so many watch? Who profits from media sports? What values are reinforced or suppressed?

Theories of sport and society parallel the distinction between conventional and critical theory. Conventional theories of the relationship between sports and the social order avoid criticism. They emphasize instead the usefulness of sport in preparing youth for socialization into the culture and the value of sports interests as recreational and entertainment outlets. An extreme form of this theory appears in the gentlemanly mythology to which Pierre de Coubertin, founder of the modern Olympic Games, and others have subscribed. In this view, sport teaches manly virtues and provides general vigor among the populace, useful in work, school, business, and warfare.

Critical cultural theories of sport and society emphasize more the conflict side of sports competition and its social impact. Whatever positive social integration sports accomplish, they also injure people, create antagonisms among fans, encourage passive consumption, place owners against players, allow male domination, in some cases endorse violence, and contribute to other negative consequences. The pressure to win has abolished the traditional Grantland Rice motto, "It matters not if you win or lose, but how you play the game." Instead, coaches admonish players with "Show me a good loser and I'll show you a loser" or "Nice guys finish last."

The following analysis draws data from conventional theory and then utilizes a cultural studies approach to define and explain the fundamental dimensions of human experience and culture at work in mass-mediated sports events. Cultural studies analysis explores sports media in terms of their cultural importance, personal and collective identity, archetypes, liminality, and related mythic and structural dimensions.

Myth and Ritual in Media Sports

The massive spectacles of the Super Bowl, the World Series, the NBA play-offs, the Olympics, college football, Wimbledon tennis, and World Cup soccer each comprise texts replete with signs, codes, myths, and ideology. Each takes in many millions of dollars from television revenues and dominates national sports news for days or weeks. These dominating cultural celebrations, and their multitudinous lesser counterparts, are central expressions and forces in our society.

Media sports provide dominant myths in modern culture. In any culture, myths first provide a perceptual system that produces the common social understandings; media sports concretize the "common sense" of our culture. Second, myths present exemplary models showing a single life history as an archetype and pattern for imitation; media sports provide heroes. Third, myths present binary oppositions and conflict negotiation as they reduce history to intelligible patterns; media sports locate us in space and time through whichever teams we cheer on. Media analysts Breen and Corcoran (1982) conclude, "The analysis of the mythical dimension of telemediated messages allows us to more fully appreciate how we are shaped into what our culture considers to be moral creatures by both the form and content of television programming" (p. 133).

Cultural Importance

The first noteworthy feature of the text of media sports is the obvious importance that natives place in this ritual activity. Rituals are the repeated activities that act out myths. Just as important native rituals come to dominate for a few hours or days or weeks the life of a traditional village, so the televised football, baseball, basketball, hockey, or other major game takes on central importance for whole communities and regions during specific periods. Fans schedule their lives on certain days, especially Saturdays or Sundays, around televised sports. They wear team colors when feelings are intense, at home as well as in the stadium. They spend valuable time and money reading sports pages to stay informed and in touch with their teams and stars. As Bob Edwards (1987) summarizes, "Many Americans are obsessed with sports. They follow their favorite team with racing hearts and trembling wallets."

The economics of media sports illustrate the central importance of these mythic rituals to our culture. Samuelson (1989) estimates that Americans spend more than $60 billion annually on sports, between 1% and 2% of the gross national product. That figure includes spectator sports that we watch ($7.2-$8.2 billion), recreational sports that we play (($46-$48 billion), and sports gambling ($7.4 billion lost on $56 billion bet). Media access to and promotion of sports are central to all those figures. One television network, CBS-TV, entered the 1990s with $2.2 billion in rights contracts to major sporting events; this included $1.1 billion for four years of major league baseball, $543 million for the 1992 and 1994 Winter Olympics, $450 million for three years of professional football, and $50 million and $56 million, respectively, for a year of professional and college basketball. Being a star in media sports in America means receiving a temporary income in six or seven figures. Sports pages are the first-read part of the print media for many. A vast amount of resources, technology, money, energy, and time in America is given over to mediated sports.

Personal Identification with Competitors

Sports fans invariably root for one side in any competition. They identify with teams, players, regions, or whatever, so that outcomes take on personal significance for them. Mythic rituals in tribal and ancient cultures played this same role. The individual joining in the chant and dance around the ritual fire was united with the entire history and role of this group of people. Social psychology has pointed out how personal identification with a group occurs when the self-identity of a person takes on the frame of reference of the larger group. This "generalized other" of group identity then becomes the norm for social activity. Thus when a fan cheers the Chicago Bears or New York Yankees or Los Angeles Lakers, that person takes on an additional identity and frame of reference beyond her or his immediate physical existence. A fan identifies with a competitor and cares about the outcome; the result is "us against them." As uses and gratifications research points out, we use media to serve both cognitive and affective needs (Blumler & Katz, 1974). Sports fans identify with "their" teams or stars and, through media, acquire information and understanding about them and feel emotional identification with them.

Heroic Archetypes and Exemplary Models

Media sports center attention on specific individuals, who, through this process, become larger-than-life heroes and models for successful conduct. Just as in ancient Greece Theseus conquered the Minotaur and became a hero to all Athens, so Don Larsen in 1956 pitched a perfect game no-hitter in the seventh and final game of the World Series, becoming the hero and toast of all Yankee fans and a historic idol to the sports-loving public. An earlier Yankee, Babe Ruth, became one of the all-time great sports legends through his home-run hitting and colorful career. Still another Yankee legend, Joe DiMaggio, not only set the majors record by hitting safely in 56 straight games, he also went on to marry (however briefly) another media legend, Marilyn Monroe; he later took on iconic significance with a mention in Paul Simon's song "Mrs. Robinson" and with appearances in Mr. Coffee television ads.

Carl Jung (1968) examined in detail the power of archetypes to reveal and control human psychology and life. Sports today in our mass-mediated culture provide superstar *archetypes* to spur the imagination and dominate the ideals of youth and adult alike. In the age of super media, celebrity is not always a positive experience. At times these sports heroes seem to feel like Prometheus of Greek legend, bound to a high, craggy rock for having brought fire down to humans. Sports lets fans see not only great deeds but also the deflation of heroes in their bad moments, the failure of authority in crisis—a reassuring experience for common people all too aware of their own limitations. Subconsciously we may reflect, "If Mike Tyson or Wade Boggs or Pete Rose cannot control his personal life, perhaps my life is not so bad." Sports pages today examine the heroes in minute detail, warts and all, outlining details of greedy contracts, after-hours drug abuse, and undisciplined sex lives, but sports heroes and their motivating power over others live on.

Fewer female than male heroes are held up for emulation in current mass media, but women have received increasing coverage in sports media and have won some well-publicized competitions. The famous "battle of the sexes" in 1973 pitted a mouthy 55-year-old ex-Wimbledon champion and tennis hustler, Bobby Riggs, against female tennis champion Billie Jean King. Riggs had publicly charged that women tennis players were inferior and overpaid and that, even at his age, he could beat the best of them. On Mother's Day, he had managed to triumph over Margaret Court. King then accepted his challenge and, in front of the largest live audience ever to attend a tennis match and a vast television audience in 36 nations, resoundingly defeated Riggs 6-4, 6-3, 6-3. In so doing, mythically King became a modern Atalanta, able to compete with men in their own games as had that fleet-footed maiden of ancient Greece. Princess Atalanta had been promised by her father as a bride to the winner of a lengthy footrace, but Atalanta herself entered the race and won, retaining her independence. Also following Atalanta, King was forced later to endure widely reported criticisms without once retreating in embarrassment.

Fans become one in spirit with the great warriors of sports and rise with them to unimagined heights or fall tragically, dashed on the rocks. In either case, they are taken far beyond the desultory limits of routine, everyday life.

The Adventurous Quest

The great quest of Jason for the Golden Fleece and the wanderings of Odysseus provide prototypes for the adventurous quest of athletes for the laurel wreath of victory. Predictable, easy victories carry little impact, but true struggle and deserved success have epic power. When Roger Banister became the first runner to break the once thought unreachable goal of a four-minute mile, millions felt as one with him as they heard of it on the radio or read it in the newspaper. Humans can overcome limits. Our seemingly fantastic quests can come to fruition.

Vicariously through the media the sports fan shares the athlete's quest to overcome personal limits, to perform flawlessly, to defeat the opponent, to achieve the trophy. A Kevin Mitchell home run, a Dwight Gooden strikeout, a Tom Watson putt, a Steffi Graf serve, a Sugar Ray Leonard knockout—each can inspire wild cheering and remain etched in memory.

The adventurous search for achievement is basic to the human search for meaning, and media sports can carry us off on that quest each season, each day, each hour.

Marking Space and Time

The formation of historical and geographical markings gradually establishes our crucial sense of location in place and time. Who we are is intrinsically wrapped up with where we sense we are. Traditionally, myth and ritual have played central roles in defining human place and time. The "sacred" places and times of tribes in Australia defined a most important sense of identity for members of Aboriginal society. Geographically, Olympus was where the Greek gods dwelt, Mecca is the pilgrimage center of Islam, and the Vatican is the home of worldwide Roman Catholicism. In terms of time, the sabbath marks a day of worship and withdrawal from normal activities of work, while the holy season designates a period of commemorative observances during which fasting precedes feasting, and the worship service sets aside certain moments and hours of the day as sacred.

In a secular culture, "special" times and places are increasingly marked off by media. The ritual darkness and popcorn of the movie theater, the exuberance of a rock concert, the togetherness of family television viewing—these become the special times and places where routine, regularized human existence is broken into by a higher power.

Media sports also provide spatial orientation. Today the sources of geographical pride in a school, a city, even a country are often found in sports teams and events. Romanian gymnasts and Ethiopian runners mark the identity of those countries. Chicago is the Bears, Bulls, Hawks, Sox, and Cubs; Pittsburgh is the Pirates and Steelers; Boston is the Celtics and Red Sox. UCLA will forever be the school where John Wooden won nine NCAA basketball titles. Nebraska and Oklahoma would secede from the union if college football were abolished. Try to imagine Notre Dame without football. Citizens may not take pride in their political representatives, their educational system, their business community, their transportation or public services, but insult their sports franchises and you may well have a fight on your hands. The stadium, field house, and whateverdome are the sacred destiny of pilgrims and the center of public attention for quasi-holy rituals.

Time is similarly marked off by sports events. The high holiday of American media is the Super Bowl, followed by other secular celebrations such as the World Series, NBA and NCAA finals, Stanley Cup, Triple Crown, Masters' tournament, and championship fights. *Seasons* refers as much to sports seasons as to annual weather cycles in contemporary discourse. Media-distributed sports have become psychosocial centers of gravity, the fulcrums around which social and personal life are organized.

Binary Oppositions

The influential French anthropologist Claude Lévi-Strauss (1967) argued for the importance of identifying the fundamental two-sided conflicts, or binary oppositions, in traditional myth and ritual. In competitive sport there is one fundamental binary opposition, that between winning and losing. All competitive athletic preparation, strategy, and effort rises from that fundamental dichotomy.

There is an overlapping binary distinction between individual and team sports and typical gender patterns in sport. Female sports have traditionally been individual. Tennis, swimming, ice skating, golf, and gymnastics come to mind. But the dominant media sports in the United States have been team sports—baseball, basketball, football, and hockey, among others. This distinction directly correlates with the obvious underrepresentation of women in media sports. Women participate in individual sports, which are less dominant in male-managed American media. And women are partially excluded from the "team" experience in sports that is often an ingredient in success in business and the corporate boardroom.

Another binary distinction, moving right from classical Marxism onto the sports pages, is the conflict between owners and workers. Who should receive the greater rewards, those who invest the capital in the business side of sports or those who supply the labor? With television dollars creating inflation, both sides can become absurdly wealthy, albeit players often for only brief periods. Player strikes in major sports have made sports pages read like financial pages. NFL owners cite the hefty $120,000 average annual salary of players, while the players' union notes the short (3½-year average) career in the league. Sport mythology attempts at times to "transcend" this conflict by claiming "the game and fans shouldn't suffer" from labor-management disputes, as if the sport event itself were a fiction without real people making it work. The material reality is that one group labors and one group invests capital, and their interests conflict.

The eminent Scandinavian social philosopher Johann Galtung (1982) extends the problem of binary oppositions to argue the negative consequences of sport in its "deep structure." He finds that, whatever its professed ideals, sport competition serves to impose Western cultural structures and standards of space, time, knowledge, nature, and relationships. Cohesive, less differentiated, traditional societies learn from sport the more aggressive, competitive, fragmented, instrumental, exploitative style of modern sports provided by mass media. In Galtung's view, sports in their deep structure are not value-free recreation but a training field for Westernized life-styles and value systems, sometimes perpetuating cultural domination and even promoting nationalism and militarism.

A less obvious binary opposition in media sports distinguishes between playing and spectating. Classically, sports were heralded for all their benefits of health and fitness to participants. But in the twentieth century, media have made vicarious access to sports the more prevalent and accessible form of involvement. This mediated form of involvement in sport eliminates the benefits for physical health and reduces them to psychic, emotional, and social benefits. While these benefits exist, they leave the possibility of fans' leading an objectively passive and unhealthy life-style while fantasizing themselves into a false self-image of action, vigor, and victory. Alas, the sports couch potato does exist.

Another distinction can be made between live attendance in the arena and media participation. Arena attendance carries with it an environment of crowds, expressive behavior of cheering and booing, and physical movement to and at the game. Media participation, however, isolates the fan from the event and its crowd. The media fan may share viewing with a small social group and cheer a bit, but, for him or her, the event comes packaged with announcers, on-screen statistics, replays, and other "enhancements" of the arena experience. The two experiences are different. Fans sometimes make efforts to combine them. One can find spectators in arenas with radio earplugs, binoculars, and television sets to add on the media experience. Television viewing can take place in large social establishments, such as sports bars, where fan behavior and crowd interaction begin to resemble the arena environment.

Another valuable distinction, though not truly a binary opposition, is the clarification of differences between print and electronic forms of sports communication media. Electronic media allow instantaneous, real-time participation in a sport through television or radio. Print media allow delayed re-presentation of sports events and facts through newspapers, magazines, and books. The latter excel at providing digests of highlights, standings, averages, schedules, and similar data and features, but electronic media capture the narrative sequence and dramatic tension of the actual sporting event while it happens. The purposeful information seeker is best served by daily newspapers and *Sports Illustrated,* but the flexible thrill seeker will likely prefer ABC and ESPN. Rader (1984), in his otherwise excellent history of sports and television, argues that television, with its abundance and commercialism, has reduced and trivialized the earlier richness of the sports experience. In fact, the various media mutually support each other in sports coverage, and fans usually follow a mixture of electronic and print media.

Experiencing Liminality in Media Sports

Like traditional myths and rituals, media sports play a role in defining status and negotiating differences among people. Tribal leaders, ritual priests, initiated adolescents, prominent warriors, women elders, protected young—these and other categories of tribal society have their status ritualized and reinforced in the special festivals and celebrations of the village, which may also mark changes from one status to another.

According to anthropologist Victor Turner (1969), "liminality" is the crucial transition stage during ritual. During liminality, participants are in limbo, being neither what they were before nor what they will be afterward. The liminal stage thus provides a sense of possibility, magic, and power unavailable anywhere else in social life. For example, when an adolescent is initiated into adulthood, there is often a ceremony of transition during which the group of initiates is isolated in a remote spot, is stripped of childish signs and made naked, is scarred or painted, undergoes trials and tests, and exists for a time as no longer children but not yet adults. It is a time of heightened awe and emotional intensity from which participants will emerge permanently changed.

The media experience in general, and mediated sports in particular, possess some of these qualities of liminality. The sports fan can achieve this state, this experience, either meagerly and on a trivial level in undisciplined chasing after games or powerfully and consummately in entering knowingly and totally into the sequence of a powerful sporting event.

Imagine the transcendent power experienced by a New York Giants fan in the storybook 1951 pennant race. The hated cross-town rival Brooklyn Dodgers led by 13½ games on August 11. Suddenly the Giants put together winning streaks of 16 and 10 games. They managed to win their final 4, while the Dodgers were struggling to win only 3 of their last 7 games. The two teams ended the season tied. The Giants and Dodgers then split the first 2 out of 3 play-off games. Finally, in the third and final game, it was the last half of the ninth inning and the Dodgers led 4 to 1. With one out, one run in, and two men on, Bobby Thomson came to bat. The Dodgers brought in bullpen ace Ralph Branca. On his second pitch, Thomson homered into the lower left field seats of the Polo Grounds, giving the Giants a tumultuous 5 to 4 victory with his "shot heard 'round the world." Thomson's hit was the fantasy of every youthful sandlot player. The Giants' victory was the magical dream experience of every team locked in near-hopeless do-or-die travail. From the liminal insecurity of the pennant race, the Giants fan emerged transformed and transcendent, never again to lose that unparalleled memory.

The well-prepared and attentive sports fan can savor in varying degrees many such moments. The "miracle on ice" of the 1980 U.S.

hockey team in the Lake Placid Winter Olympic Games was a classic. The underdog, inexperienced American team pulled off a series of last-second victories culminating in the wild final game triumph that left Al Michaels screaming, "Do you believe in miracles?" and a joyous nation limp with incredulous exhaustion. Bob Beamon's miracle long jump in the 1968 Olympics impossibly broke the world record by more than two full feet. Secretariat won the Triple Crown in horse racing with decisiveness and grace never to be forgotten.

Unfortunately, the immature and unbalanced sports fan may emerge from the liminal experience a dangerous, even psychotic, individual, as soccer deaths and grandstand fistfighting constantly remind us. The liminal experience is powerful, a trial as well as a transformation, and not all emerge transcendent.

Conclusion

Like religion, sports have been used for political purposes, to prepare nations for war rather than to prevent warfare and other destructive behavior. Sports can be no more healthy than the general culture and ideology of which they form a part, and as a form of mythic and ritual behavior, must also be controlled by reason. Critical thinking through cultural studies and mythic analysis opens up many of the inner dimensions of the experience of sports and media. Conventional research and data provide a shell of information that is necessary but somewhat rudimentary. Understanding sports, media, and spectacle reveals both details and generalizations about our specific culture and our general humanity. This can protect us from damage and excess as well as enhance and extend our appreciation.

Further Questions

(1) How does the media packaging of sport, with commentary and technology, change the nature of the spectator experience?

(2) Why are certain sports popular in the United States, such as football, not popular elsewhere? What cultural factors are at work here?

(3) What is the economic power of television in the Olympic movement and in other sporting events?

Epilogue

Our essential tasks in compiling this reader have been to select areas of current communications research and inquiry and to present each as an arena of debate, not of fixed knowledge. In each chapter different perspectives and problems about some area of media have been raised. In a sense, the more we know, the more there is to explore and question.

We also hope that you now have some sense of why a critical, questioning stance is necessary, and of the importance of some of the problems that need to be posed. While we have mapped out many major issues, there are many other areas we have not addressed and questions we have not raised. You can develop your own agenda of issues and research projects, using the suggestions at the end of each chapter and developing your own.

One last comment: It is also important to think about what it is you are invited to think about and know while in college. What counts as the "curriculum," what subjects can you study, what perspectives are you introduced to? And, by implication, what subjects do not count, what topics do not appear in your syllabi, what perspectives are rarely discussed? Why is this? Because the university also reflects interests and positions of different groups in society, and what they have come to value over time. But what is useful or important knowledge in a society also alters, and is often the subject of debate and controversy. Currently at many campuses across the United States debates are taking place about integrating more materials written by women and people of color, and cross-cultural perspectives, into different areas of the curriculum. Knowledge is not a fixed truth, nor is it neutral. What is defined as "knowledge," as established fact, often tends to support particular interests, and so it is always important to ask, *Why* should we know this, and whom does such knowledge serve?

We could ask, Who benefits from communications research? Does academic research "help" the industry, the audience, or no one at all except the academics themselves? Does this matter? We are not arguing that all knowledge must be directly practical, or even that all perspectives are equally valid and important. We are inviting you to think and talk about how universities package knowledge and the relationship of different groups to that knowledge, especially in the field that we are most interested in, media studies. Even think how publishers package knowledge, what a textbook means by way of fixing in students' minds what is "reasonable" to say, and what "unreasonable," and whether in this book we have covered the most important and relevant issues. We obviously think so, but that is a valid topic of critical debate!

Now perhaps you understand better how the media are connected with economic forces, political processes, and cultural values and products in our society. We hope that this book will be the beginning of many interesting debates for you, not the end.

Glossary

affiliate: In this context, an affiliate is a local television station that contracts with one of the networks to take its programs plus the commercials the networks have attached to them. An affiliate is not necessarily bound, as are the networks' own stations, to use their entire programming. In the 1980s, certain major cable operators, such as Cable News Network and Turner Network Television, began to develop similar network-affiliate relationships with cable stations across the United States. These businesses were called *multiple system operators* (MSOs). See also Chapter 14, on new communication technologies.

agenda-setting: In general usage, an agenda is the list of items, usually in order of priority, to be discussed at a committee meeting. It is also any list of topics to be addressed. The agenda-setting approach sees news media as powerful because of their ability to define for us which events are most important, and are therefore news, and which are not. Are women's rights important? Is the environment important? Are traffic fatalities or the love life of a TV star more important? Which gets prominence in news media coverage? People who see the media as having an agenda-setting function say this: News media power is based not so much on how the media interpret events to us as it is on the sheer fact that they can set our agenda of things to think about in the first place. See also gatekeepers and Chapters 4, 7, 20, and 21.

anarchism: This is a political philosophy, and also a type of political activism, the modern origins of which lie in mid-nineteenth-century Europe. Anarchists typically believe that power should be decentralized so that government can be close enough to people for them to exercise effective control over their representatives. They do not, in spite of what is often claimed, advocate anarchy in the sense of chaos. Socialist anarchists are opposed both to the capitalist economic system and to centrally organized government, including communist government. Many anarchists are not socialists. There is not a great deal of uniformity of belief among anarchists. See also communism, Marxism, socialism, and Chapter 12.

audience: The audience has been defined four ways: (1) as a mass, (2) passively, (3) actively, and (4) economically. (1) As a mass, the audience is understood as a collection of individuals whose primary connection is to the media, not to each other by way of friendship, family, or work ties (see mass). (2) The passive sense, rather close to the mass sense, indicates that people simply soak up whatever the medium offers them. In strong versions of this view, the media are seen as all-powerful over the audience. (3) The active sense indicates that people make up their own minds about what the media present them with, often generating their own interpretations of the media text. In strong versions, the audience is seen as able to bend the media text to its own outlooks and concerns. (4) The economic definition sees the audience simply as consumers, people whose attention the media "delivers" over to advertisers so that corporations can make their sales pitches. See also negotiation, reception theory, uses and gratifications, and Chapters 10, 11, 17, 19, and 24.

cable: (1) Cable is a communication transmission technology that primarily uses land lines, thus improving the quality of TV reception. Cable stations increasingly use fiber-optic cables, which are highly accurate and very fast, and can deal with very large volumes of traffic at a time. This makes them invaluable for any form of computerized transmission. Cable can also link up with satellites. (2) This term is also used to refer to the corporations and stations that are in the business of cable transmission to the 57% of U.S. homes that, as of 1989, were cabled. See also affiliate, network, and Chapter 14.

capital: In economic analysis, capital may mean (1) savings, of a firm or individuals; (2) a sum of money invested; (3) the wealth of a corporation in money, machines, property, land, shares, or bonds (all bar labor power); (4) the value that labor produces on behalf of the corporation; (5) the long-term economic and political strategy (i.e., over decades and even centuries) of capital owners taken as a class, whether in a nation or among transnational corporations. The first three uses of the term are common in conventional economics; the latter two are used in critical and Marxist political economy. See also capitalism, corporation, cultural capital, and Chapters 4, 5, 11, and 17.

capitalism: This term is defined in several ways: (1) an economic system distinguished from feudalism and slavery by the fact that those who work are legally entitled to walk off the job when they choose (even though immediate financial hardship often keeps them from doing so); (2) an economic system defined by its competitive and efficient nature, which pushes each corporation to reinvest part of its profits in developing new methods of production and new products; (3) an economic system defined by its combination of innovation, expansion, and skillful but often merciless exploitation of labor; (4) the general way of life and cultural patterns of a capitalist society, such as the reduction of all aspects of living—health care, wildlife, creativity, information—to the price they can fetch. Definitions 1 and 2 are most common in writing favorable to capitalism; definitions 3 and 4, in writing critical of it. Today capitalism is overwhelmingly a global economic system. See also corporation and transnational.

censorship: This is the practice of forbidding publication or broadcasting of certain views, words, and/or images. The source may be governments or other agencies, such as religious authorities, workplace managements, or school boards. Censorship may operate through vetting a text before it goes out ("prior restraint") or through various forms of punishment after the fact (threats, demotion, firing, fines, imprisonment, closing the newspaper or broadcast station, execution). See also self-censorship and Chapters 4 and 6.

class: This term describes a group of people defined in one of two ways: (1) by their similar social and financial standing (as in *middle class*), or (2) by their mutual relationship in the economic process (e.g., whether they plan manufacturing and banking and direct the economic process or carry out the process). The latter sense is integral to Marxist approaches, where the relation between the corporate classes and the working classes is seen as influencing all spheres of society, including culture and communication. Some analysts have seen this influence as very tight, others as much looser. See Chapters 1, 4, 5, 11, 15, 17, 22, and 24.

commodity: Anything that becomes an object to be sold, be it food, sex, recreation, cars, or drama, is a commodity. Some critical analysts (e.g., Kellner, Chapter 17; Gandy, Chapter 11) argue that modern capitalism reduces all aspects of life to commodities to be bought and sold, the process of "commoditization."

communication: (1) A classical model of communication is that of the transmission process, using the analogy of the electrical circuit. "Who says what by which channel to whom?" is a standard version, which tends to imply that communication is individualized and one-way, that is, not interactive. (2) A second model defines communication as a sharing process, necessarily based upon a common culture and its codes if it is to take place at all. (3) A third model focuses upon the processes and institutions—mainstream and alternative—by which communication is produced, which stresses the cultural production of mass communications.

communism: This term can be used to refer to (1) the political belief in the practical possibility of moving toward a fair and equitable economic and political system, originally based on the analyses of Marx and Engels; (2) the political and economic institutions of the Soviet Union and nations strongly influenced by that model; or (3) the varying left-wing political parties and movements in favor of either of the above in countries without Soviet-type institutions. See also anarchism, capital, capitalism, Marxism, socialism, and Chapters 4 and 9.

community: A community may be formed by (1) a group of people defined by their common recognition of their mutual geographical bonds (e.g., a village or city neighborhood) or by their professional or cultural interests (e.g., journalists, computer hackers, sports fans); or by (2) a group of people claimed to have mutual bonds (e.g., "the international community," "the financial community"), who are in fact generally in some form of conflict with each other. This use of the term often masks, deliberately or unthinkingly, these conflicts.

consumer society/consumerism: People who buy products are consumers. Some critical analysts have argued that modern capitalist economics is powered by the attempt to get us to consume more and more, whether we really need to or not, and that both advertising and consumer credit (e.g., use of credit cards) are part and parcel of the same drive. See Chapters 17 and 24.

copyright: This is the legal right of the creator to control who makes money out of his or her cultural invention—a TV series idea, a computer program, a book, a song—by copying it. As more and more cultural products are stored digitally in computers, and as more and more photocopy machines are available, policing this right has become extremely difficult.

corporation/corporate: A corporation is a firm, usually a giant firm, sometimes producing many different things, sometimes almost monopolizing one product area. Many media corporations are also involved in other areas, such as General Electric, which owns NBC and its affiliate TV and radio stations along with many other firms in other sectors. For a long time in the United States, AT&T monopolized telephones and IBM monopolized computers, and both are still dominant forces in these areas. The term *corporate* is often used to distinguish between nineteenth-century capitalism, when there were many small firms competing with each other, and twentieth-century capitalism, which has been dominated by giant firms. See also transnational, and Chapters 4 and 5.

critical: As used here, this refers to questioning established opinion, querying both knowledge and the sources of knowledge, and refusing to take "authoritative views" as the last word. See also critical theory and the Preface.

critical theory: As used in this volume, this term refers to the perspectives associated with writers Theodor Adorno, Max Horkheimer, Herbert Marcuse, and others (sometimes known as the Frankfurt school). They tried to blend Freudian and Marxist perspectives into a critical analysis of contemporary capitalism, especially of its tendency to encourage conformist, bland communication and thinking in society at large. See Chapter 17.

cultural capital: This is a term coined by French sociologist Pierre Bourdieu to describe the cultural resources of the middle class, such as effective schooling, artistic taste, and knowledge. See also Chapter 1.

cultural imperialism: Imperialism is the conquest and control of one country by a more powerful one. Cultural imperialism signifies the dimensions of the process that go beyond economic exploitation or military force. In the history of colonialism (i.e., the form of imperialism in which the government of the colony is directly run by foreigners), the educational and media systems of many Third World countries have been set up as replicas of those in Britain, France, or the United States and carry their values. Western advertising has made further inroads, as have architectural and fashion styles. Subtly but powerfully the message has often been insinuated that Western cultures are superior to the cultures of the Third World. See also identity and Chapters 15 and 19.

cultural studies: Developed by Stuart Hall in Britain and James Carey in the United States, this critical approach to communication analysis argues that culture is an all-embracing dimension of communication, but retains major interconnections with political and economic forces. See also Chapter 1 and all chapters in Part V.

culture: This term is used in a series of different senses, for which see Chapter 1.

dependency: This is the state of many developing countries according to the argument that even after former colonies became politically independent in the middle decades of the twentieth century, they continued to be economically and culturally dependent on the Western powers, and therefore heavily under the latters' influence, not least in media and communications hardware and software. See Chapters 15 and 19.

deregulation: This is the process by which governments reduce their controls over broadcasting and telecommunications, whether by relaxing restrictions on broadcast station ownership, by compelling monopoly communications institutions (e.g., the old AT&T telephone monopoly or French state broadcasting) to break up into separate firms, or by yet other measures. The term does not mean that government stops regulation altogether. See Chapter 14.

determination/to determine: This is the process in which one event is caused by, or significantly influenced by, another. For example, in Chapter 4, Herman asks whether the ownership pattern of the U.S. media "determines" how they present the news.

discourse/discursive: This can be (1) a speech or (2) an argument or position, logical or otherwise, that has a number of interconnected views and assumptions built into it. Examples include religious discourse, engineering discourse, and sports discourse. The term focuses especially on the verbal expression of a particular position or argument. As used by French analyst Michel Foucault, it also signifies the public mode of talking about an issue (e.g., crime or sexuality), which also tends to change over time. See also ideology and text.

disinformation: This term is used to describe communication that purports to be accurate and truthful, but that is in fact constructed to mislead. See also information, propaganda, persuasion, and manipulation.

elite/elitist: The elite is a small group of people in control of society as a whole, or of one segment of it. The term implies more homogeneity of outlook and policies than does the term *class*. The adjective implies the snobbish life-style and arrogant attitudes common within an elite.

empirical: This word describes any analysis carried out on actual situations, past or present. Critical researchers require this analysis to be shaped by an explicitly stated theory or theories; this is one of the factors that differentiates their approach from that of empiricist researchers, whose theoretical assumptions are sometimes implied rather than carefully worked out.

empiricist: Not to be confused with *empirical*, this term describes a very common approach to the study of human society in U.S. universities, so much so that other approaches often seem rather offbeat by comparison. In its simplest forms, the empiricist approach proceeds by (1) setting up certain categories of media output or audience reaction, and taking them as fixed; (2) counting how many items can be reckoned as falling within these categories; and then (3) drawing conclusions from the figures. The model for this procedure is drawn from a popular image of what physicists or chemists do in their scientific research, with the aim of making social research less subjective and more reliable—although that image has often been challenged as untrue to actual procedures in the physical sciences. A brief though oversimplified illustration would be if some members of the TV audience were to be asked, "Did you like this program a lot, a little, not at all, don't know, no response?" and their answers were then to be counted up, put in percentages, and taken as straightforward fact. Critical scholars usually argue that this kind of research tends to avoid deeper issues and complexity, and produces only superficial and trivial results.

ethnography: This is a research method, used mainly in anthropology, that is increasingly being used in communication research to study and map other cultures in detail. It usually involves living with another cultural community over a period of time and systematically observing its way of life. People working in the cultural studies tradition consider a very important problem to be how we can properly know other cultures. See also Chapter 10.

Federal Communications Commission (FCC): This agency was originally founded as the Federal Radio Commission in 1927; its present title dates from 1934. It is the U.S. government's primary body through which to establish communications policy.

feminism: This is a social philosophy, and also a type of political activism, with its modern roots in the women's voting rights movements of the nineteenth century. Its contemporary roots in the United States are in both the women's liberation movements of the 1960s and the massive involvement of women in the work force since 1950. Feminists are committed not only to equal rights for women in all spheres of life, private and public, but also to developing and communicating women's perspectives on all issues against male-dominated understanding of life—for example, on war and militarism, or on the value of sensitivity and nurturing in everyday relations. One does not have to be a woman to be a feminist. See also Chapter 16.

gatekeeping/gatekeepers: This approach to news media sees editors in particular, and journalists in general, as deciding what is newsworthy and what is not, controlling the flow of news, selecting its priorities (agenda-setting), and rejecting news issues they do not rate as significant. As Herman notes in Chapter 4, this approach—while pointing us to many important aspects of journalistic training and decision making—generally omits the analysis of media ownership and how this may affect news output. See also Chapters 4, 5, 7, 20, and 21.

hardware: This is a general term that covers all physical communications equipment, from earphones to mainframe computers, from satellites in space to TV sets. Its corollary is software.

hegemony: A general term for dominance or control, *hegemony* has also been used more specifically by Italian social theorist Antonio Gramsci, who has been influential in critical cultural studies. As used by Gramsci, it signifies all the means of ideological leadership and dominance that a capitalist class and its allied classes, such as major landowners or professional and managerial classes, exert over wage workers. It operates together with the coercive controls of the police and military, which are deployed at those points where ideological hegemony breaks down and political movements erupt into rebellious activity. This hegemony operates through such institutions as education, religion, and the media, but not with any absolute or permanent force. See also state and Chapter 1.

identity: Two types of identity are of concern here: personal, psychological identity—the bundle of factors that make up an individual—and cultural identity. Cultural identity generally rests upon a common language, a shared history, a series of values or principles that are generally held to be important in living one's life, and some major symbols (e.g., the

U.S. flag, the Japanese emperor system, or the French Revolution) that are seen as expressing all these factors in a condensed form. However, cultural identity need not be national; also common are regional cultural identities (e.g., the U.S. South or Midwest, or Quebec in Canada), ethnic minority cultural identities, and social class cultural identities. These different identities can intersect in complicated ways. Furthermore, to add to the complexity, some scholars have argued that identity, personal or cultural, does not mean a single unified awareness of oneself or one's culture. Indeed, these varied identities are not mutually excluding, but may all be valued in different contexts. See also Chapters 1 and 19.

ideology: This term has been used to connote both (1) a clearly defined and somewhat obnoxious and irrational viewpoint, tenaciously held by its proponents, and (2) the complex of ideas in society and their expression in social institutions, whether the military or the arts or the courts, which in turn dominate the way we live and how we understand the world around us. See also Chapter 1.

imperialism: See cultural imperialism.

informatics: A term used more in Europe than in the United States to refer to information policy and information technology; see both below.

information: As used here, this term refers to (1) a set of data or (2) electrical signals sent along a cable or through the air. See also disinformation, information policy, and information technology.

information policy: Policy regarding information is made up of government rules on (1) how open or secretive government should be with the public and (2) access to information hardware and its applications, including such issues as privacy from computerized surveillance and selling sophisticated hardware to other competitor nations.

information technology: This is a general term for computer-based communications technology, involving computer capacity for memory storage, data processing, and communication. See also Chapter 13.

Marxism: This term refers to the version of critical social analysis pioneered in the nineteenth century by Karl Marx and Friedrich Engels. It emphasizes the relations between social classes in the economic sphere as highly influential in all other social and cultural processes. Some of Marx and Engels's most famous followers pushed their argument much further, to claim economic forces as the sole determining factor in human history. Marx himself is famous for having declared that he was not a Marxist. The term also refers more generally to the state philosophy of communist countries. See also anarchism, communism, and socialism.

mass culture: This is a term used to refer to the general public's culture; it is often used with contempt. See also Chapter 1.

mass media: This term refers to media that reach many people, or the masses (also called mass communication); it may be thought of as the opposite to interpersonal communication.

mass society: Although it refers simply to the whole of a society, this term usually signifies that citizens have been reduced to separate individuals, "atomized," so to speak, and subjected to centralized one-way mass communication without the ability to communicate or organize with other people. Fascism was the clearest example, but some writers have pointed to the period of regimented political and commercial ideology during the first Cold War and the McCarthy era in the United States as an instance as well. See also Chapters 4 and 12.

media: This term, which is the plural of *medium*, has come to mean communications media specifically in many contexts: press, broadcasting, cinema, photography, video, satellites, cable, computers, photocopiers, fliers, billboards, and so on—both the physical objects and the organizations that activate them. It can also refer to virtually any object or activity as long as it carries some kind of symbolic meaning: children's toys, a wrestling match, a mathematical equation, a building, a flower. This much wider sense of the term is especially associated with French semiotician Roland Barthes.

myth: Two meanings of this term are relevant here: (1) a religious and/or heroic story expressing deeply held beliefs and emotions (see Chapter 25) and (2) an unfounded but widely accepted account of social, economic, or political reality (see Chapter 24).

negotiation: In communications analysis, this means that different understandings of reality are haggled over between different sets of people. The intended message of a TV situation comedy might be to encourage people to laugh at prejudice and bigotry as outmoded and foolish, as in the TV classics *All in the Family* with Archie Bunker (United States) or its British original *Till Death Do Us Part* with Alf Garnett. In fact, many audience members in both countries took these series as giving the green light to their own bigotry. They negotiated its officially intended meaning, in this case drastically. See also Chapters 10 and 16.

network: This term refers to a group of radio or television stations linked together; in the United States, ABC, CBS, and NBC are the three major broadcast networks, although Rupert Murdoch's Fox Television has been attempting to become a fourth, and various cable operators have also been endeavoring to establish effective networks. See also affiliate and telecommunications network.

orality: This term refers to the phase in the development of human communication before the full development of writing systems, when only a tiny handful of people, usually in royal courts, communicated with writing. Cultural history was therefore dependent upon the memorization of myths, poetry, and legends rather than upon being able to check written data. During this time almost all communication was conducted face to face.

persuasion: This is the process of trying to influence other people in a particular direction, by using words, images, sounds, or their combination. The dividing lines between persuasion and propaganda and information are often set by the person using the term, rather than by some absolute, generally agreed-upon criterion. This is because persuasion is thought to be acceptable, whereas propaganda and disinformation are thought to be unethical. Propaganda is something other people engage in producing, not something one admits to creating. See also disinformation and propaganda.

political economy analysis: This is an approach to social and communications analysis that stresses the interaction of political factors and economic institutions in determining communications or other processes. In critical communications research this approach is often set up as an opposing approach to cultural studies, although in this reader we have representatives of both positions, as in Chapters 1 and 4. See also cultural studies.

propaganda: This is the attempt to convince other people by systematic packaging of information and manipulation of their emotions, often in a rather crude and unconvincing form to the intelligent audience. In fact, this common definition masks the difference between crude and sophisticated propaganda, the latter sometimes referred to as persuasion. The dividing line is often hard to draw. See also persuasion and disinformation.

public service broadcasting: In a number of countries (e.g., Britain and Canada), broadcasting has been organized through a government corporation. In turn, this corporation has been set up at partial arm's length from the government's control of its output. The broadcasters are supposed, as professionals, to maintain independence from the government and other powerful interests, and to provide the public with a balanced diet of news, culture, education, and entertainment. This was defined as "public service" broadcasting, and is the opposite of commercially based broadcasting, as in the United States, where profit making determines program making and policy. The public service philosophy sees broadcasting as a unique national resource that cannot be deployed in the nation's best interests simply by market forces. Under pressure from corporate media interests, however, this broadcasting philosophy has been under increasing attack. See also Chapter 8.

qualitative research: As applied to communications studies, this is research that concentrates on analyzing how meanings are conveyed or not, or how power operates in communication, without any attempt to study these with the aid of mathematics or statistics.

quantitative research: This is research that uses mathematics or statistics to pursue analysis. In fact, some communications research is done mixing quantitative and qualitative approaches; there does not have to be exclusion of the one by the other. See also empiricist and ethnography.

rationalization: This is the attempt to impose some rational order on a disordered situation. As used by the adherents of the Frankfurt school, this term signifies the unstoppable tendency of capitalism to blot out any human values save those of the economic market and the priorities of the power structure. Thus for Marcuse, Nazi death camps were the ultimate example of this negative rationality, with their efficient, scientific gas chambers and ovens to annihilate millions of human beings.

reception theory: This is a position that holds that the audience is active, bringing its own values and experiences to viewing television or reading. Thus women may react more negatively to their TV portrayal than men, and ethnic groups may be more angry about the ways newspapers represent them than the ethnic majority. These variations, of course, are very much in evidence within these groupings, not just between them. The emphasis in reception theory on what the audience does with media output sets it in direct opposition to the mass society approach. See also audience, negotiation, uses and gratifications, and Chapters 10 and 16.

representation: This refers to the processes by which reality is conveyed in communication, via words, sounds, images, or their combination. Many critical scholars in cultural studies will argue that in fact the representation is the reality for all practical purposes. Many in the political economy mold will argue that reality cannot be simply in the mind, but makes its presence felt upon us in differential access to wealth, health care, power, and other areas of life, whether we are ready to acknowledge it or not. This is yet another round in a familiar battle among Western philosophers that has been going on since Plato and Aristotle, about how we can or do understand reality. Rather than dismiss it as pointless abstraction, you should try to think through each position carefully and why it is that people often adhere to one or the other: What are the advantages in insight that each brings?

rhetoric: In modern everyday use, this term refers to the persuasive and sometimes empty language of politicians, official spokespersons, advertising, and other communication sources. It is also the name of the study of persuasive language, dating back to Aristotle and ancient Greece. See also Chapter 2.

self-censorship: This takes place when media employees anticipate what the government, the authorities, or their editors will not wish to have communicated to the general public and decide to keep silent themselves to avoid making waves. Even in countries with censorship agencies, self-censorship is the most effective mechanism through which media output is censored on a daily basis. See also censorship and Chapters 5, 6, 7, 9, 20, and 21

semiotics/semiology: This is the study of how signs of any kind work in society to communicate meanings. There are American, French, Italian, and Russian traditions of semiotic analysis, which do not always overlap. An important point of difference among semioticians is whether they focus strictly on dissecting the signs within a particular text, perhaps of a film or TV show, or whether they take the cultural codes of the film's context into account as well. See also Chapters 1 and 23.

socialism/socialist: This is a general term for the movement since the late 1800s for a more just and humane social order, and the different arguments and policies framed to that end. It is also used to describe political parties, in or out of government, that adopt this social order as their official goal but submit themselves to elections rather than establishing themselves by armed mass revolution (the classical credo of communists). See also anarchism, communism, and Marxism.

software: This term refers to the creative products in communications, such as computer programs, TV series, and film scripts. Its corollary is hardware.

South: This is a general term for the less economically developed countries of the planet, from their location in the Southern Hemisphere. It was coined to avoid some of the often negative connotations of the term *Third World.*

state: This term has several meanings: (1) one of the constituent units of a system having a federal government (e.g., the United States, Brazil, India, Mexico, Nigeria); (2) an independent nation; (3) the armed forces, judiciary, police forces, courts, and prisons that collectively maintain order in favor of the capitalist class (from classical Marxism). A theoretical use of the term in later Marxism, especially following Gramsci, includes communication institutions, such as the media and education, and government intervention in the capitalist economy (e.g., via the FCC) as part of the definition. This use tends to blur the distinction between public/governmental and private/business, perhaps reflecting the tendency of governments to intervene more and more in society during the twentieth century.

structure: This is a very common term in social science. Sometimes a society or an organization (e.g., a newspaper) is compared to the structure of the body—bones, veins, nerves, muscles, organs, skin. The interdependence of all the parts and their interrelated growth are therefore what is emphasized. Less frequently the image of a bridge is used; a combination of opposing forces keeps the structure from collapsing. One way or another, the term prompts us to ask what the main elements or forces are that keep a particular society or communication institution in operation, and how they combine with each other. Alternatively, what are the elements at war with each other? See also culture and system.

subculture: This term applies to a group that represents a variant on a mainstream culture, whether merely a modified version, an opposed version, or one with little connection to the mainstream at all.

system: This is a very common term in social science. It signifies structure, but usually with the added implication that the structure is one that is functioning smoothly, not one that generates conflict. Sometimes this term is also used to alert our attention to the interaction between a social institution, such as a telecommunications corporation, and its environment of other corporations, customers, the government.

telecommunications: This includes any form of electronic information transmission, using computers, telephone, telegraph, fax, cable, satellite, or microwave. The term is often reserved for nonbroadcast transmission, but it does not have to be.

telecommunications network: This is a system that links two or more points for electronic information transmission, usually involving the use of computers and telephone lines and/or satellites. See also Chapters 13 and 14.

text: This term often refers specifically to written communication, but it is also a general term for any communication, written or visual. This second meaning is used by researchers who focus upon texts' numerous strands of meaning and implied meaning. The Latin word for *woven together* is its origin.

theory: This term refers to a body of principles that attempt to develop clear, logical explanations for things. For example, a theory of media impact on the audience should try to define as clearly as possible which type of media output, and which types of audience (young, older, men, women) are involved. In the study of communications there are often competing theories, so that part of learning the subject means learning how to evaluate the strengths and weaknesses of a particular theory or theories. The everyday sense of the term involves abstract and irrelevant speculation about things, but that is not the sense intended here. There is no substitute, in serious study of communication, for the careful theoretical analysis of communication processes. Deeper understanding is otherwise impossible.

Third World: This term was originally developed to signify (1) the less economically developed nations, and (2) the irrelevance of the Cold War between the West (the First World) and the Soviet bloc (the Second World) to their development needs. Often today this is considered a negative term in the West because of what is seen as implied contempt for these nations' problems of poverty and instability, supposedly their own fault entirely. It also blurs over the enormous variety of cultures in the Third World. See also South.

transnational: This term describes a giant corporation that is based in one country (typically the United States, Japan, or a Western European nation) but operates in many others. There are many such in the latter part of the twentieth century, and quite a number of them are media transnationals. Major examples at the time of this writing are Rupert Murdoch's News Corporation, AT&T, IBM, Saatchi & Saatchi Advertising, General Electric, and Sony. See also Chapter 8.

uses and gratifications: This is a term used to denote a type of media research very common in the United States in the 1950s and 1960s, and very influential since, which stressed the audience's views and preferences as determining what impact broadcasting had on them (and, by implication, on other media as well). The research methods used to study the uses made of broadcasting, and the gratifications audiences received from it, were largely empiricist. See also audience, reception theory, and Chapters 10 and 24.

References

Adams, W. C. (Ed.). (1981). *Television coverage of the Middle East.* Norwood, NJ: Ablex.

Adams, W. C., & Heyl, P. (1981). From Cairo to Kabul with the networks, 1972-1980. In W. C. Adams (Ed.), *Television coverage of the Middle East.* Norwood, NJ: Ablex.

Adams, W. C. (Ed.). (1982). *Television coverage of international affairs.* Norwood, NJ: Ablex.

Adburgham, A. (1972). *Women in print: Writing women and women's magazines from the restoration to the accession of Victoria.* London: George Allen & Unwin.

Adorno, T. W. (1980). On the fetish character of music and the regression of hearing. In A. Arato & E. Gebhardt (Eds.), *The essential Frankfurt school reader.* New York: Continuum. (Original work published 1938)

Adorno, T. W., & Horkheimer, M. (1972). *Dialectic of enlightenment.* New York: Continuum. (Original work published 1947)

Alexander, W. (1981). *Film on the left: American documentary film from 1931 to 1942.* Princeton, NJ: Princeton University Press.

Allen, R., & Gomery, D. (1985). *Film history: Theory and practice.* New York: Knopf.

Altheide, D. (1981). Iran vs. U.S. TV news: The hostage story out of context. In W. C. Adams (Ed.), *Television coverage of the Middle East.* Norwood, NJ: Ablex.

Althusser, L. (1970). Ideology and ideological state apparatuses. In L. Althusser, *Lenin and philosophy.* London: New Left.

Altschull, J. H. (1986). *Agents of power.* New York: Longman.

Ang, I. (1985). *Watching* Dallas: *Soap opera and the melodramatic imagination.* New York: Methuen.

Archer, J. (1973). *The plot to seize the White House.* New York: Hawthorne.

Aristotle. (1967). *The "art" of rhetoric* (J. H. Freese, Trans.). Cambridge, MA: Harvard University Press.

Aronson, J. (1972). *Deadline for the media.* Indianapolis: Bobbs-Merrill

Association of National Advertisers. (1988). *The role of advertising in America.* New York: Author.

Bagdikian, B. (1983). *The media monopoly.* Boston: Beacon.

Bagdikian, B. (1987). *The media monopoly* (2nd ed.). Boston: Beacon.

Bagdikian, B. (1989). The lords of the global village. *The Nation, 248*(23), 805-820.

Ball, H. (Ed.). (1984). *Federal administrative agencies: Essays on power and politics.* Englewood Cliffs, NJ: Prentice-Hall.

Barber, J. D. (1987, November/December). Candidate Reagan and "the sucker generation." *Columbia Journalism Review,* pp. 33-36.

Barlow, W. (in press). *Sounding out racism: The radio industry.* Washington, DC: Howard University Press.

Barnouw, E. (1978). *The sponsor.* New York: Oxford University Press.

Barthes, R. (1973). *Mythologies.* New York: Hill & Wang.

Bausinger, H. (1984). Media, technology and daily life. *Media, Culture and Society, 6,* 343-351.

Bazin, A. (1967). *What is cinema?* (2 vols.). Berkeley: University of California Press.

Beaver, F. (1983). *A history of the motion picture.* New York: McGraw-Hill.

Beniger, J. (1986). *The control revolution.* Cambridge, MA: Harvard University Press.

Benjamin, W. (1973). *The work of art in the age of mechanical reproduction: Illuminations.* London: Fontana/Collins. (Original work published 1936)

Bennett, W. L. (1988). *News: The politics of illusion.* New York: Longman.

Bennett, W. L., Gressett, L., & Haltom, W. (1985). Repairing the news. *Journal of Communication, 35,* 50-51.

Berger, A. A. (1982). Semiological analysis. In A. A. Berger, *Media analysis techniques.* Beverly Hills, CA: Sage.

Berger, J. (1972). *Ways of seeing.* Harmondsworth: Penguin.

Bernstein, D. (1988, October). And that's the way it isn't. *In These Times,* pp. 12-18.

Beville, H. M., Jr. (1985). *Audience ratings: Radio, television and cable.* Hillsdale, NJ: Lawrence Erlbaum.

Blumer, H. (1950). The mass, the public, and public opinion. In B. Berelson & M. Janowitz (Eds.), *Reader in public opinion and communication.* Glencoe, IL: Free Press.

Blumler, J., Brynin, M., & Nossiter, T. (Eds.). (1988). *Broadcasting structure and finance in Western Europe.* New York: Oxford University Press.

Blumler, J. G., & Katz, E. (Eds.). (1974). *The uses of mass communications: Current perspectives on gratifications research.* Beverly Hills, CA: Sage.

Boorstin, D. (1962). *The image.* New York: Atheneum.

Bordwell, D., & Thompson, K. (1986). *Film art: An introduction.* New York: Knopf.

Bourdieu, P. (1984). *Distinction.* Cambridge, MA: Harvard University Press.

Braestrup, P. (1977). *Big story.* Boulder, CO: Westview.

Brecht, B. (1983). Notes on the use of radio. In A. Mattelart & S. Siegelaub (Eds)., *Communication and class struggle* (Vol. 2). New York: International General.

Breen, M., & Corcoran, F. (1982). Myth in the television discourse. *Communication Monographs, 49,* 133.

Broder, D. S. (1988). *Behind the front page.* New York: Simon & Schuster.

Brown, J. D., Bybee, C., Wearden, S., & Straughan, D. M. (1987, Spring). Invisible power: Newspaper news sources and the limits of diversity. *Journalism Quarterly, 64,* 45-54.

Burgelman, J. C. (1986). The future of public service broadcasting: A case study for a "new" communications policy. *European Journal of Communication, 1*(2).

Butler, M., & Paisley, W. (1980). *Women and the mass media: Sourcebook for research and action.* New York: Human Sciences Press.

Carey, J. W. (1989). *Communication as culture.* Boston: Unwin Hyman.

Carroll, P. (1974, January/February). Mutiny in Greensburg. *Columbia Journalism Review,* pp. 39-42.

Cassirer, E. (1946). *The myth of the state.* New Haven, CT: Yale University Press.

Caute, D. (1978). *The great fear.* New York: Simon & Schuster.

Chambers, I. (1988). *Popular culture: The metropolitan experience.* New York: Methuen.

Clippinger, J. H. (1976). *Who gains by communications development studies of information technologies in developing countries.* Cambridge, MA: Harvard University, Program on Information Technologies and Public Policy.

Cockburn, L. (1988). *Out of control.* New York: Atlantic Monthly Press.

Condee, N., & Padunov, V. (1989). The Soviet cultural underground in the 1980s. In S. Siegelaub & A. Mattelart (Eds.), *Communication and class struggle* (Vol. 3). New York: International General.

Conway, M. D. (Ed.). (1967). *The writings of Thomas Paine* (Vol. 1). New York: AMS.

Cosgrove, S. (1986, August). The DJs they couldn't hang. *New Musical Express, 9.*

Coward, R. (1985). *Female desires: How they are sought, bought, and packaged.* New York: Grove.

Curran, J., & Seaton, J. (1985). *Power without responsibility: The press and broadcasting in Britain.* London: Methuen.

de Bens, E., & Knoche, M. (Eds.). (1987). *Electronic mass media in Western Europe: Prospects for development* (report of the FAST Programme for the EC). Brussels: D. Reidel.

DeLauretis, T., & Heath, S. (Eds.). (1980). *The cinematic apparatus.* New York: St. Martin's.

DeLillo, D. (1985). *White noise.* New York: Viking/Penguin.

Demac, D. (1985). *Keeping America uninformed.* New York: Pilgrim.

Demac, D. (1988). *Liberty denied: The current rise of censorship in America.* New York: PEN International Center.

DiMaggio, P. (1982). Cultural capital and school success: The impact of status culture participation on the grades of U.S. high school students. *American Sociological Review, 47,* 189-201.

DiMaggio, P., & Useem, M. (1978). Cultural democracy in a period of cultural expansion: The social composition of arts audiences in the United States. *Social Problems, 26,* 180-197.

Donaldson, R. (1987, Spring). An incomplete history of micro-computing. *Whole Earth Review, 54.*

Donovan, J. (1980). The silence is broken. In R. Broker & N. Furman (Eds.), *Women and language in literature and society.* New York: Praeger.

Dorman, W. A., & Farhang, M. (1987). *The U.S. press and Iran.* Berkeley: University of California Press.

Downing, J. (1984). *Radical media.* Boston: South End.

Downing, J. (1985). The Intersputnik system and Soviet television. *Soviet Studies, 37*(4), 465-483.

Downing, J. (1986). Government secrecy and the media in the United States and Britain. In P. Golding, G. Murdock, & P. Schlesinger (Eds.)., *Communicating politics: Mass communications and the political process.* New York: Holmes & Meier.

Downing, J. (Ed.). (1987). *Film and politics in the Third World.* New York: Praeger and Autonomedia.

Downing, J. (1988a). The alternative public realm: The 1980s anti-nuclear press in West Germany and Britain. *Media, Culture and Society, 10*(2), 163-181.

Downing J. (1988b). *The Cosby Show* and American racial discourse. In G. Smitherman-Donaldson & Teun A. van Dijk (Eds.), *Discourse and discrimination* (pp. 46-74). Detroit: Wayne State University Press.

Downing, J. (1988c). International communications and the Second World: Developments in communication strategies. *European Journal of Communication, 4*(1), 99-119.

Downing, J. (1988d). Soviet media coverage of Afghanistan. *Journal of Communication, 38*(4), 5-32.

Downing, J. (1989). Ethnic radio broadcasting in the United States. *Howard Journal of Communication, 2*(2).

Downing, J. (in press). Latino media in Greater New York. In S. Riggins (Ed.), *Minority languages and cultural survival.* Chicago: Aldine.

Drinnon, R. (1980). *Facing west.* New York: Meridian.

Dyson, K., & Humphreys, P. (1986). *The politics of the communication revolution in West Europe.* London: Frank Cass.

Edwards, B. (1987, November 10). *The morning edition* (radio program, National Public Broadcasting).

Eisenstein, S. (1969). *Film form.* New York: Harcourt Brace.

Elliot, P. (1974). Uses and gratifications research: A critique and a sociological alternative. In J. G. Blumler & E. Katz (Eds.), *The uses of mass communications: Current perspectives on gratifications research* (pp. 249-268). Beverly Hills, CA: Sage.

Englund, S. (1975, January/February). Censorship a la mode. *Columbia Journalism Review,* pp. 32-38.

Enzensberger, H. M. (1970). Constituents of a theory of the media. *New Left Review, 64*, 13-36.

Epstein, E. J. (1973). *News from nowhere.* New York: Random House.

Euromedia Research Group. (1986). *New media politics.* London: Sage.

European Economic Community. (1984). *Television without frontiers: EEC green book.* Brussels: Commission of the European Communities.

European Institute for the Media. (1988). *Europe 2000.* Paris: Author.

Ewen, S. (1976). *Captains of consciousness.* New York: McGraw-Hill.

Ewen, S. (1988). *All consuming images.* New York: Basic Books.

Fabre, M. (1963). *A history of communications.* New York: Hawthorne.

Fanon, F. (1967). *The wretched of the earth.* Harmondsworth: Penguin.

Federal Communications Commission. (1988). *Broadcast and cable employment trend report 1987.* Washington, DC: Author.

Fishman, M. (1980). *Manufacturing the news.* Austin: University of Texas Press.

Fiske, J. (1982). *Introduction to communication studies.* New York: Methuen.

Fiske, J. (1987). British cultural studies and television. In R. C. Allen (Ed.), *Channels of discourse.* Chapel Hill: University of North Carolina Press.

Fiske, J., & Hartley, J. (1978). *Reading television.* London: Methuen.

Foner, P. (Ed.). (1950). *The life and writings of Frederick Douglass* (Vol. 2). New York: International.

Foote, J. S., & Steele, M. E. (1986, Spring). Degree of conformity in lead stories in early evening network newscasts. *Journalism Quarterly, 64*, 19-23.

Forgacs, D. (1989). *A Gramsci reader.* Cambridge, MA: Belknap.

Frith, S. (1987). The industrialization of popular music. In J. Lull (Ed.), *Popular music and communication.* Newbury Park, CA: Sage.

Galtung, J. (1982). Sport as carrier of deep culture and structure. *Current Research on Peace and Violence, 5*, 2-3.

Gans, H. (1974). *Popular culture and high culture.* New York: Basic Books.

Gans, H. (1979). *Deciding what's news.* New York: Vintage.

Gans, H. (1985, November/December). How liberal are the media? *Columbia Journalism Review.*

Gitlin, T. (1980). *The whole world is watching: Mass media in the making and unmaking of the New Left.* Berkeley: University of California Press.

Gitlin, T. (1983). *Inside prime time.* New York: Pantheon.

Gitlin, T. (Ed.). (1987). *Watching television.* New York: Pantheon.

Gleason, A., Kenez, P., & Stites, R. (Eds.). (1985). *Bolshevik culture.* Bloomington: Indiana University Press.

Goldman, E. (1969). *Anarchism and other essays.* New York: Dover.

Goldman, R. (1984). We make weekends: Leisure and the commodity form. *Social Text, 8*, 84-103.

Goldman, R. (1987). Marketing fragrances: Advertising and the production of commodity signs. *Theory, Culture and Society, 4*, 691-725.

Goldstein, T. (1985). *The news at any cost.* New York: Simon & Schuster.

Gouldner, A. (1976). *Dialectic of ideology and technology.* New York: Seabury.

Gramsci, A. (1971). *Selections from the prison notebooks* (Q. Hoare & G. Nowell-Smith, Trans.). New York: International.

Gray, H. (1986). Television and the new Black man: Black male images in prime-time situation comedy. *Media, Culture and Society, 8*, 223-242.

Habermas, J. (1979). The public sphere. In A. Mattelart & S. Siegelaub (Eds)., *Communication and class struggle* (Vol. 1, pp. 198-201). New York: International General.

Halberstam, D. (1979). *The powers that be.* New York: Knopf.
Hall, P., & Preston, P. (1988). *The carrier wave: New information technology and the geography of innovation, 1846-2003.* London: Unwin Hyman.
Hall, S. (1980). Cultural studies: Two paradigms. *Media, Culture and Society,* 2(1).
Hall, S., et al. (1978). *Policing the crisis.* London: Macmillan.
Hallin, D. (1986). *The "uncensored war": The media and Vietnam.* New York: Oxford University Press.
Hallin, D. (1987). We keep America on top of the world. In T. Gitlin (Ed.), *Watching television.* New York: Pantheon.
Hallin, D. (1989). *The "uncensored war": The media and Vietnam* (2nd ed.). New York: Oxford University Press.
Hamelink, C. J. (1983). *Finance and information.* Norwood, NJ: Ablex.
Hamelink, C. J. (1986). *Militarization in the information age.* World Council of Churches.
Hamilton, E. (1940). *Mythology.* Boston: Little, Brown.
Harms, J. (1989). *Advertising and the forms of mass communications: An immanent critique.* Unpublished manuscript.
Harris, N. (1987). *The end of the Third World.* Harmondsworth: Penguin.
Harris, R. (1983). *Gotcha! The media, the government and the Falklands crisis.* London: Faber & Faber.
Hartley, J. (1982). *Understanding news.* London: Methuen.
Havelock, E. (1963). *Preface to Plato.* Cambridge, MA: Belknap.
Havelock, E. (1986). *The muse learns to write.* New Haven, CT: Yale University Press.
Hebdige, D. (1987). *Cut'n'mix.* New York: Comedia/Methuen.
Hebdige, D. (1979). *Subculture: The meaning of style.* London: Methuen.
Hendricks, G. (1961). *The Edison motion picture myth.* Berkeley: University of California Press.
Herman, E., & Brodhead, F. (1986). *The rise and fall of the Bulgarian connection.* New York: Sheridan Square.
Herman, E., & Chomsky, N. (1988). *Manufacturing consent: The political economy of the mass media.* New York: Pantheon.
Hersh, S. (1983). *The price of power.* New York: Summit.
Hertsgaard, M. (1988). *On bended knee: The press and the Reagan presidency.* New York: Farrar, Straus, Giroux.
Hilgartner, S., Bell, R. C., & O'Connor, R. (1983). *Nukespeak: The selling of nuclear technology in America.* New York: Penguin Books.
Hobsbawm, E. (1989). *The age of empire 1875-1914.* New York: Vintage.
Hobson, D. (1982). *Crossroads: The drama of a soap-opera.* London: Methuen.
Hoffman-Riem, W. (1988). National identity and cultural values. *Journal of Broadcasting and Electronic Media, 31*(1), 57-72.
International Commission for the Study of Communication Problems. (1980). *Many voices, one world.* Paris: UNESCO.
Jezer, M. (1982). *The Dark Ages.* Boston: South End.
Jhally, S., & Livant, B. (1986). Watching as working: The valorization of audience consciousness. *Journal of Communication, 36*(3).
Jowett, G. (1976). *Film: The democratic art.* Stoneham, MA: Focal.
Jung, C. J. (1968). *Man and his symbols.* New York: Dell.
Kagarlitsky, B. (1988). *The thinking reed.* New York: Verso.
Katz, E., & Lazarsfeld, P. (1955). *Personal Influence.* Glencoe, IL: Free Press.
Katz, E., & Wedell, G. (1978). *Broadcasting in the Third World.* Cambridge, MA: Harvard University Press.

Kay, J. (1988). *Communicating through electronic bulletin boards in the white supremacy movement: Creating culture via computer* (Laase Communication Research Center Report 88-7). Lincoln: University of Nebraska.

Keen, S. (1987). *Faces of the enemy.* New York: Harper & Row.

Kellner, D. (1982). Television, mythology and ritual. *Praxis, 6,* 133-155.

Kellner, D. (1989). *Critical theory, Marxism and modernity.* Cambridge: Polity.

Kenez, P. (1985). *The birth of the propaganda state: Soviet methods of mass mobilization, 1917-1929.* New York: Cambridge University Press.

Kennedy, D. M. (1980). *Over here: The First World War and American society.* New York: Oxford University Press.

King, E., & Schudson, M. (1987, November/December). The myth of the great communicator. *Columbia Journalism Review,* pp. 37-39.

Kleinsteuber, H., Siune, K., & McQuail, D. (1986). *Electronic media in Western Europe: A handbook.* Berlin: Campus Verlag.

Konig, R. (1973). *A la mode.* New York: Seabury.

Laing, R. D. (1971). *Knots.* Harmondsworth: Penguin.

Larson, J. F. (1982). International affairs coverage on U.S. evening network news, 1972-1978. In W. C. Adams (Ed.), *Television coverage of international affairs.* Norwood, NJ: Ablex.

Lazarsfeld, P. (1941). Remarks on critical and administrative communication research. *Studies in Philosophy and Social Science, 9,* 2-16.

Leiss, W., Kline, S., & Jhally, S. (1986). *Social communication in advertising.* New York: Methuen.

Lerner, D. (1958). *The passing of traditional society.* New York: Free Press.

Lévi-Strauss, C. (1967). *Structural anthropology.* Garden City, NY: Doubleday.

Lichter, S. R., Rothman, S., & Lichter, L. (1986). *The media elite.* Bethesda, MD: Adler & Adler.

Liebes, T., & Katz, E. (1986). Patterns of involvement in television fiction: A comparative analysis. *European Journal of Communication, 1,* 151-171.

Lindlof, T. R., Shatzer, M. J., & Wilkinson, D. (1988). Accommodation of video and television in the American family. In J. Lull (Ed.), *World families watch television.* Newbury Park, CA: Sage.

Logan, R. K. (1986). *The alphabet effect.* New York: William Morrow.

Lotman, J. (1976). *Semiotics of cinema.* Ann Arbor: Michigan Slavic Publishers.

Lull, J. (1982). How families select television programs: A mass- observational study. *Journal of Broadcasting, 26,* 801-813.

Lull, J. (Ed.). (1987). *Popular music and communication.* Newbury Park, CA: Sage.

Lull, J. (Ed.). (1988). *World families watch television.* Newbury Park, CA: Sage.

Macdonald, J. F. (1983). *Blacks and White TV: Afro-Americans in TV since 1948.* Chicago: Nelson-Hall.

MacDougall, K. A. (1975). Up against the *Wall Street Journal.* In R. Pollak (Ed.), *Stop the presses, I want to get off!* New York: Dell.

MacDougall, K. A. (1988a). Boring from within the bourgeois press: Part One. *Monthly Review, 40*(6), 13-25.

MacDougall, K. A. (1988b). Boring from within the bourgeois press: Part Two. *Monthly Review, 40*(7), 10-25.

Marcuse, H. (1964). *One-dimensional man.* Boston: Beacon.

Manno, J. (1984). *Arming the heavens: The hidden military agenda for space, 1945-1995.* New York: Dodd, Mead.

Marx, G. (1988). *Undercover: Police surveillance in America.* Berkeley: University of California Press.

Massing, M. (1982, November/December). Black-out in television. *Columbia Journalism Review*, pp. 38-44.

Mast, G. (1981). *A short history of the movies* (3rd ed.). Indianapolis: Bobbs-Merrill.

Mattelart, A., & Siegelaub, S. (Eds.). (1983). *Communication and class struggle* (Vol. 2). New York: International General.

Mattelart, A., & Siegelaub, S. (Eds.). (1989). *Communication and class struggle* (Vol. 3). New York: International General.

McClure, L. W., & Fulton, P. C. (1964). *Advertising in the printed media*. New York: Macmillan.

McCrum, R., Cran, W., & MacNeill, R. (1986). *The story of English*. New York: Viking/Penguin.

McLuhan, M. (1963). *Understanding media*. London: Methuen.

McLuhan, M. (1964). *Understanding media*. New York: Mentor.

McLuhan, M., & Fiore, Q. (1968). *War and peace in the global village*. New York: McGraw-Hill.

McQuail, D. (1986). Commercialization. In Euromedia Research Group, *New media politics*. London: Sage.

McQuail, D. (1987). *Mass communication theory: An introduction*. Newbury Park, CA: Sage.

Medvedev, R. (Ed.). (1984). *Samizdat' Register I*. New York: Pathfinder.

Messaris, P. (1977). Biases of self-reported "functions and gratifications" of mass media use. *Et Cetera, 34*.

Mickiewicz, E. P. (1981). *Media and the Russian public*. New York: Praeger.

Mickiewicz, E. P. (1988). *Split signals*. New York: Oxford University Press.

Miller, M. C. (1988). Cosby knows best. In M. C. Miller, *Boxed-in: The culture of TV* (pp. 69-78). Evanston, IL: Northwestern University Press.

Miner, M. (1984). *Insatiable appetites: Twentieth-century American women's bestsellers*. Westport, CT: Greenwood.

Modleski, T. (1982). *Loving with a vengeance: Mass-produced fantasies for women*. New York: Methuen.

Mohammadi, A. (1976). *Development-support communication and instructional learning centers for rural areas in Iran*. Unpublished doctoral dissertation, Columbia University.

Moore, R. (1988). The Constitution, the presidency and 1988. *Presidential Studies Quarterly, 18*(1), 56-57.

Morley, D. (1986). *Family television: Cultural power and domestic leisure*. London: Comedia.

Morone, J. G., & Woodhouse, E. J. (1989). *The demise of nuclear energy? Lessons for democratic control of technology*. New Haven, CT: Yale University Press.

Mortensen, F., & Svendson, E. N. (1980). Creativity and control: The journalist betwixt his readers and editors. *Media, Culture and Society, 2*.

Mosco, V. (1989). *Pay-per society*. Norwood, NJ: Ablex.

Mosco, V., & Wasko, J. (Eds.). (1988). *The political economy of information*. Madison: University of Wisconsin Press.

Motamed-Nejad, K. (1976). *Communication and westernization*. Tehran: College of Mass Communication.

Mowlana, H. (1986). *Global information and world communication*. New York: Longman.

Mulvey, L. (1975). Visual pleasure and narrative cinema. *Screen, 16*, 6-18.

Myrdal, G. (1944). *An American dilemma*. New York: Harper & Row.

National Association of Broadcasters. (1986). *Minority broadcasting facts*. Washington, DC: Author.

National Science Foundation. (1984). *Communications technology and economic development*. Washington, DC: Author.

Nesteby, J. R. (1982). *Black images and American films, 1896-1954: The interplay between civil rights and film culture*. Lanham, MD: University Press of America.

Niane, D. T. (1965). *Sundiata* (G. Pickett, Trans.). London: Longman.

O'Connor, A. (in press). The problem of cultural studies in the United States. *Critical Studies in Mass Communication.*

Ogle, P. (1977, January). Development of sound systems: The commercial era. *Film Reader, 2.*

Ohman, R. (1987). Doublespeak and ideology in ads: A kit for teachers. In D. Lazere (Ed.), *American media and mass culture.* Berkeley: University of California Press.

Olsen, T. (1978). *Silences.* New York: Delacorte/Seymour Lawrence.

Ong, W. (1982). *Orality and literacy.* New York: Methuen.

Paletz, D., & Entman, R. (1981). *Media power politics.* New York: Free Press.

Parenti, M. (1986). *Inventing reality: The politics of the mass media.* New York: St. Martin's.

Pathi, D. (1986, March). Punjabi goes pop. *The Face.*

Pearce, J. (1982). *Under the eagle.* Boston: South End.

Perry, L. (1984). *Intellectual life in America: A history.* New York: Franklin Watts.

Peterson, R. E. (1987). Media consumption and girls who want to have fun. *Critical Studies in Mass Communication, 4*(1), 37-50.

Postman, N. (1984). *Amusing ourselves to death.* New York: Viking/Penguin.

Powdermaker, H. (1960). *Hollywood: The dream factory.* Boston: Little, Brown.

Propp, V. (1968). *Morphology of the folktale* (2nd ed., rev.). Austin: University of Texas Press. (Original work published 1930)

Pye, L. (Ed.). (1963). *Communications and political development.* Princeton, NJ: Princeton University Press.

Rader, B. (1984). *In its own image: How television has transformed sports.* New York: Free Press.

Radway, J. (1984). *Reading the romance: Women, patriarchy and popular literature.* Chapel Hill: University of North Carolina Press.

Radway, J. (1987). Interpretive communities and variable literacies (commentary on T. Lindlof, Media audiences as interpretive communities). In J. Anderson (Ed.), *Communication yearbook 11.* Newbury Park, CA: Sage.

Ramsaye, T. (1926). *A million and one nights.* New York: Simon & Schuster.

Real, M. (1989). *Super media: A cultural studies approach.* Newbury Park, CA: Sage.

Remington, T. (1988). *The truth of authority.* Pittsburgh: Pittsburgh University Press.

Riffe, D., Ellis, B., Rogers, M. K., Van Ommeren, R. L., & Woodman, K. A. (1986). Gatekeeping and the network news mix. *Journalism Quarterly, 63,* 315-321.

Rosengren, K. E., Palmgreen, P., & Wenner, L. (Eds.). (1985). *Media gratifications research: Current perspectives.* Beverly Hills, CA: Sage.

Said, E. (1979). *Orientalism.* New York: Random House.

Said, E. (1981). *Covering Islam.* London: Routledge & Kegan Paul.

Samuelson, R. (1989, September 4). The American sports mania. *Newsweek,* p. 49.

Schiller, H. (1976). *Communication and cultural domination.* White Plains, NY: International Arts and Sciences Press.

Schiller, H. (1971). *Mass communication and American empire.* Boston: Beacon.

Schiller, H. (1984). *Information and the crisis economy.* Norwood, NJ: Ablex.

Schlesinger, P. (1988). *Putting "reality" together* (2nd ed.). London: Methuen.

Schramm, W. (1988). *The story of human communication.* New York: Harper & Row.

Seiter, E., Borchers, H., Kreutzner, G., & Warth, E. (Eds.). (1989). *Remote control: Television, audiences and cultural power.* London: Routledge, Chapman & Hall.

Shanor, D. (1985). *Behind the lines.* New York: St. Martin's.

Sepstrup, P. (1989). Research into international television flows. *European Journal of Communication, 4*(4).

Shaw, D. (1989, February 3). Leftist reporter's boast raises a ruckus. *San Francisco Chronicle.*

Siegel, L., & Markoff, J. (1986). *The high cost of high tech.* New York: Harper & Row.

Sigal, L. (1973). *Reporters and officials.* Lexington, MA: D. C. Heath.
Smith, A. (1984). *The geopolitics of information.* London: Faber & Faber.
Smith, B. (1982). Toward a Black feminist criticism. In G. T. Hull, P. B. Scott, & B. Smith (Eds.), *All the women are White, all the Blacks are men, but some of us are brave.* Old Westbury, NY: Feminist Press.
Smith, G. S. (1984). *Songs to seven strings.* Bloomington: Indiana University Press.
Smythe, D. (1981). *Dependency road: Communications, capitalism, consciousness, and Canada.* Norwood, NJ: Ablex.
Sreberny-Mohammadi, A., (1990). The power of tradition: Communications and the Iranian revolution. *International Journal of Politics, Culture and Society,* 3, 3.
Sreberny-Mohammadi, A., Nordenstreng, K., Stevenson, R., & Ugboajah, F. (1984). *Foreign news in the media: International reporting in 29 countries* (Reports and Papers on Mass Communication No. 93). Paris: UNESCO.
Stamps, C. H. (1979). *The concept of the mass audience in American broadcasting.* New York: Arno.
Switkin, A. (1981). *Ads: Design and make your own car.* New York: Van Nostrand Reinhold.
Taylor, M. (1989, February 3). What's all the fuss? the writer asks. *San Francisco Chronicle.*
Temple, R. (1986). *The genius of China.* New York: Simon & Schuster.
Theberge, L. J. (Ed.). (1981). *Crooks, conmen and clowns: Businessmen in TV entertainment.* Washington, DC: Media Institute.
Thomas, S. (1986). Mass media and social order. In G. Gumpert & R. Cathcart (Eds.), *Inter/media.* New York: Oxford University Press.
Thomas, S., & Callahan, B. P. (1982). Allocating happiness: Television families and social class. *Journal of Communication, 32.*
Toop, D. (1984). *The rap attack: African jive to New York hip hop.* Boston: South End.
Tuchman, G. (1978). *Making news.* New York: Free Press.
Tunstall, J. (1977). *The media are American.* New York: Columbia University Press.
Turner, V. (1969). *The ritual process: Structure and anti-structure.* Ithaca, NY: Cornell University Press.
Ulanoff, S. (1977). *Advertising in America: An introduction to persuasive communication.* New York: Hastings.
UNESCO. (1989). *World communication report.* Paris: Author.
Wachtel, E. (1986). *Television hiring practices.* New York: United Church of Christ, Office of Communication.
Wald, C. (1975). *Myth America: Picturing women 1865-1945.* New York: Pantheon.
Webster, F., & Robins, K. (1986). *Information technology: A Luddite analysis.* Norwood, NJ: Ablex.
Weibel, K. (1977). *Mirror, mirror: Images of women reflected in popular culture.* Garden City, NY: Anchor.
Weiss, M. J. (1988). *The clustering of America.* New York: Harper & Row.
Williams, R. (1961). *The long revolution.* Harmondsworth: Penguin.
Williams, R. (1974). *Television: Technology and cultural form.* London: Fontana.
Williams, R. (1977). *Marxism and literature.* New York: Oxford University Press.
Williams, W. A. (1980). *Empire as a way of life.* New York: Oxford University Press.
Williamson, J. (1978). *Decoding advertisements.* London: Marion Boyars.
Wilson, K. (1988). *Technologies of control.* Madison: University of Wisconsin Press.
Winston, B. (1985). A whole technology of dyeing: A note on ideology and the apparatus of the chromatic moving image. *Daedelus, 114*(4).
Winston, B. (1986). *Misunderstanding media.* Cambridge, MA: Harvard University Press.
Winston, B. (1987). A mirror for Brunelleschi. *Daedelus, 116*(3).

Winston, M. R. (1982). Racial consciousness and the evolution of mass communication in the United States. *Daedelus, 111*(4), 171-182.

Wolff, J. (1981). *The social production of art*. London: Macmillan.

Wollen, P. (1976). *Signs and meaning in the cinema.* Bloomington: Indiana University Press.

Wood, E. M. (1988, January/February). Capitalism and human emancipation. *New Left Review, 167.*

Woolf, V. (1957). *A room of one's own.* New York: Harcourt Brace Jovanovich.

Zinn, H. (1980). *A people's history of the United States.* New York: Harper & Row.

About the Authors

Ien Ang teaches in the Department of Communication, University of Amsterdam, and is author of *Watching Dallas* and *Desperately Seeking the Audience: Viewership is Known.*

Iain Chambers teaches cultural studies in the English Department of the Instituto Universitario Orientale, Naples, Italy. He is author of *Urban Rhythms: Pop Music and Popular Culture; Popular Culture: The Metropolitan Experience;* and *Border Dialogues: Journeys in Post-Modernity.*

Ash Corea works in women's health in New York City and has produced alternative radio programs for and about women.

Donna A. Demac is a lawyer and teaches at New York University. She is author of *Keeping America Uninformed* and *Liberty Denied: The Current Rise of Censorship in America* and editor of *Tracing New Orbits.*

John Downing teaches in the Communications Department at Hunter College, City University of New York. He is author of *The Media Machine* and *Radical Media* and editor of *Film and Politics in the Third World.* He also serves on the editorial board of *Discourse and Society.*

Oscar H. Gandy, Jr., teaches at the Annenberg School of Communication, University of Pennsylvania. He is author of *Beyond Agenda-Setting* and coeditor of *Proceedings from the Tenth Annual Telecommunications Policy Research Conference.*

Richard Gruneau teaches in the Department of Communication, Simon Fraser University, Vancouver, Canada. He is author of *Class, Sports and Social Development* and editor of *Popular Cultures and Political Practices.*

Robert A. Hackett teaches in the Department of Communication, Simon Fraser University, Vancouver, Canada. He is author of *The Press and the Politics of Peace.*

Cees Hamelink teaches international communication at the University of Amsterdam, the Netherlands, and is President of the International Association for Mass Communication Research. He is author of *Finance and Information*, *Cultural Autonomy in Global Communications*, and *The Technology Gamble.*

Edward Herman teaches in the Annenberg School of Communication, University of Pennsylvania, and is a Director of the Institute for Media Analysis. He is the author of *The Real Terror Network* and coauthor of *The Washington Connection* (with Noam Chomsky), *Manufacturing Consent* (with Noam Chomsky), *The Rise and Fall of the Bulgarian Connection* (with Frank Broderick), and *The "Terrorism" Industry* (with Gerry O'Sullivan).

Douglas Kellner teaches in the Philosophy Department at the University of Texas, Austin, and is author of *Herbert Marcuse and the Crisis of Marxism* and *Critical Theory: Marxism and Modernity.*

Denis McQuail teaches mass communication at the University of Amsterdam and is an editor of the *European Journal of Communication.* He is the author of *Mass Communication Theory* and coeditor, with Karen Siune, of *New Media Politics.*

Ali Mohammadi teaches in the Media Studies Program at the New School for Social Research in New York and has written on culture and communications in Iran, and on Iranian exiles.

Ron Mottram teaches cinema in the Department of Theater at Illinois State University. He is the author of *The Danish Cinema Before Dreyer* and *Inner Landscapes: The Theater of Sam Shepard.*

Alan O'Connor teaches in the Communication Department at Ohio State University. He is the author of *Raymond Williams: Writing, Culture, Politics,* and editor of *Raymond Williams on Television.*

Karen Paulsell is affiliated with the Community Memory Project in Berkeley, California. She is treasurer of the Union for Democratic Communication.

Lana Rakow teaches in the Communication Department, University of Wisconsin—Parkside, and is coeditor, with Cheris Kramerae, of *The Revolution in Words: Righting Women, 1868-1871.*

Michael Real teaches in the Department of Telecommunications and Film, San Diego State University. He is author of *Mass-Mediated Cultural Realities* and *Super Media.*

Cedric J. Robinson teaches in the Political Science Department at the University of California, Santa Barbara. He is the author of *The Terms of Order* and *Black Marxism,* and he serves on the editorial board of *Race and Class.*

Mark Schulman teaches in the Communications Department at City College, City University of New York. He has been involved in developing WHCR-FM, a low-power broadcast facility on the CCNY campus that serves Harlem as a community radio station.

Annabelle Sreberny-Mohammadi teaches in the Department of Communication Arts and Sciences at Queens College, City University of New York. She is coauthor, with K. Nordenstreng, R. Stevenson, and F. Ugboajah, of *Foreign News in the Media: International Reporting in 29 Countries,* a UNESCO report.

Sari Thomas teaches in the School of Communications and Theater at Temple University, Philadelphia. She is currently editor of *Critical Studies in Mass Communication* and has edited the Ablex series *Studies in Communication.*

Brian Winston is Dean of the School of Communications, Pennsylvania State University, State College. He is author of *Misunderstanding Media,* and he led the research group at Glasgow University that produced *Bad News* and *More Bad News.*